KAROL WOJTYŁA

KAROL WOJTYŁA

*The Thought of the Man
Who Became Pope John Paul II*

Rocco Buttiglione

Translated by

Paolo Guietti and Francesca Murphy

WILLIAM B. EERDMANS PUBLISHING COMPANY
GRAND RAPIDS, MICHIGAN / CAMBRIDGE, U.K.

© 1997 Wm. B. Eerdmans Publishing Co.
255 Jefferson Ave. S.E., Grand Rapids, Michigan 49503 /
P.O. Box 163, Cambridge CB3 9PU U.K.

Printed in the United States of America

02 01 00 99 98 97   7 6 5 4 3 2 1

Library of Congress Cataloging-in-Publication Data

Buttiglione, Rocco, 1948-
    Karol Wojtyła: the thought of the man who became Pope John Paul II /
Rocco Buttiglione; translated by Paolo Guietti and Francesca Murphy.
        p.   cm.
    ISBN 0-8028-3848-0 (alk. paper)
    1. Catholic Church and philosophy.   2. Sociology, Christian (Catholic)
3. Catholic Church — Doctrines.   4. John Paul II, Pope, 1920-   .
I. Title.
BX1795.P47B87   1997
282′.092 — dc21
    [B]   97-23188
                                                        CIP

Contents

Foreword, *by Michael Novak*   vii

Preface   xiv

1. Judgment on Contemporary History   1

2. Biographical Notes about Karol Wojtyła   18

3. Karol Wojtyła's Philosophical Formation   44

4. Love and Responsibility   83

5. The Acting Person   117

6. Wojtyła and the Council   177

7. The Poetic Work of Karol Wojtyła   232

8. Conclusion: A Dialogue with Contemporary Philosophies   269

Translators' Afterword: Buttiglione on Wojtyła's Philosophy of Freedom and an Update on Fifteen Years of Studies of Wojtyła's Thought   307

Appendix: Introduction to the Second Polish Edition of *The Acting Person*   352

Index   381

Foreword

1. Meet Rocco Buttiglione

To meet Rocco Buttiglione is to like him. He is almost certain to greet you with a smile, a warm handshake, playful brown eyes, and a welcoming jest. He is likely to be carrying a pipe or a short Italian cigar. His English is excellent, but his German — the language in which he lectured at the International Academy of Philosophy in Liechtenstein for many years — and his French and Spanish (they say) are even better.

I suppose that Professor Buttiglione's Polish is pretty good, too, for it happens that as a young professor he went to Cracow to study certain aspects of the philosophical method, called phenomenology, that originated in the German-speaking world and that later gained an important center, especially in the fields of ethics and aesthetics, in Poland. (Many other important intellectual impulses of the early twentieth century — associated with philosophers such as Carnap, Wittgenstein, Popper, and Husserl and economists like Hayek and von Mises — originated in Austria and influenced Poland.) While in Cracow, Buttiglione came to know the new bishop, Karol Wojtyła. When the latter, quite suddenly, was elected Pope in 1978, Rocco was immediately among his close friends and counselors.

Rocco, who was born in Gallipoli in the "heel" of Italy, exactly four years to the day after D-Day, June 6, 1948, took up at the same time a professorship in Teramo, near Rome. So far as I know, Rocco Buttiglione is the only living philosopher from whom Pope John Paul II has ever directly quoted in a public address. I can testify from personal experience to the warm affection and filial regard the Pope has for him.

My own first meeting with Rocco occurred when I lectured at the Catholic University of Milan on Catholic social thought in the late 1970s. Rocco happened to be in the audience and, while my own memory is vague, Rocco remembers clearly arguing rather strenuously with me, partly (he says) because his interest was piqued, and partly because he wasn't yet convinced. Our friendship began in earnest in the winter of 1991, when we had dinner twice in Washington, and then later that summer, when he invited me to lecture at the International Academy of Philosophy in Liechtenstein. (Rocco was commuting to Liechtenstein weekly during the school year, even while keeping up his lectures at two different universities in Italy.) There we began planning an international seminar that would bring together several European and American thinkers to address problems of Catholic social thought in an international framework.

For two years, 1992 and 1993, we taught together (with Fr. Maciej Zieba, O.P., from Poland, Fr. Richard John Neuhaus, George Weigel, Fr. Robert Sirico, and Derek Cross) for the month of July. Meanwhile, Rocco again visited me in the United States, and I called on him when I went to Rome. For me, the highlight of our early friendship was in the early autumn of 1991, when the two of us were invited for a private dinner with the Pope and his two secretaries in the Vatican. This was one of the happiest and grandest evenings of my life.

Already in July of 1993, when the political crisis in Italy was reaching a boiling point, Rocco was torn by a call to compete for the leadership of the Christian Democratic Party of Italy. This would mean interrupting his teaching at the International Academy. By 1992, the "historic compromise" that democratic forces had forged in 1948 under the threat of Communist domination was falling apart. Great political scandals rocked the entire nation, and new standards of public integrity were demanded by strong majorities.

For a man as given to metaphysics and political philosophy as Rocco was, a student since his youth of the great Italian philosopher and social thinker Augusto Del Noce (1905-1989), a radical shift from philosophy to the political life entailed a great inner sacrifice, and he dreaded it. On the other hand, in the existing emergency, his love for Italy and for Catholic social thought inspired in Buttiglione the courage to welcome the sufferings it required with his customary good spirits, warmth, and humor.

In the ensuing breakup of the Christian Democratic Party, Rocco stuck to his principles and ended up founding a new small party, the Christian Democratic Union, the true heir (he argues) of the party of Don Luigi Sturzo and Alcide de Gasperi, founders of Christian Democracy. Rocco believes that the sociological foundations of the Italian economy are rapidly shifting. Whereas in earlier eras the reins of the economy were held by old aristocratic families who had become the owners of great businesses, it is now evident that new entrepreneurs in small and medium-sized businesses — more in the American model — are beginning to take over. About 1990, for the first time in history, the number of small enterprises in Italy exceeded the number in Britain, and by 1994, of the ten most economically dynamic regions in the entire European Union, four were in Italy.

Using the principles of Pope John Paul II's *Centesimus Annus* (1991), on which he lectured brilliantly and authoritatively in Liechtenstein, Buttiglione has tried to set forth a new social vision for Italy, by means of the small minority party of which he is now chairman. His hope was that the Christian Democratic Union would build the intellectual foundations of a new Italy. He hoped that it would come to have an influence on the other parties which exceeded the numbers of actual voters it represented.

Meanwhile, based on this and his other books, which include a study on the nature of the family, *L'uomo e la famiglia* (1991), an intellectual biography of his mentor, *Augusto Del Noce: Biografia di un pensiero* (1991), and a collection of essays on Catholic social thought, *Il problema politico dei cattolici* (1993), Professor Buttiglione has been called to lecture all over the world, on virtually every continent and in dozens of nations.

In the United States, Professor Buttiglione's essays have been published in various journals, including *Crisis* and *First Things*. In Italy, of course, his books and regular columns are extremely well known, and it is hard to open an Italian newspaper these days without finding stories in which his views have been quoted. For journalists, he is a master of the telling and good-humored phrase.

The Thought of Karol Wojtyła was first published in Italy in 1982, and continues to have worldwide influence. It sold very well in Italy and even better in its Spanish translation; the French edition is still in print, long after its first appearance. Buttiglione's early ties to Karol Wojtyła, and their shared philosophical interests, which continue to this day, have made the depth of his understanding of the social thinking of the Pope (and of the history of Catholic social thought) unequaled outside of Poland. Since so few persons in other nations have mastered Polish, and even fewer know the Polish intellectual scene firsthand, Rocco's insight into the formative stages of the Pope's mature thought offers a priceless gate of entry into the thinking of John Paul II.

2. Why Isn't the Bible Enough?
Why Do Catholics Spend So Much Time on Philosophy?

Catholic social thinking is entirely rooted in biblical sources. It begins with the affirmation "Jesus Christ is Lord!" and it sets forth Jesus as the image through whom and with whom and in whom the destiny of humankind is best revealed. For evangelical Christians who are not Roman Catholic, this would not be strange. In addition, however, the Catholic tradition encourages philosophical inquiry of a kind that makes many evangelicals uneasy. Such inquiry seems to Catholics a crucial defense against the philosophical pitfalls of each successive age. Not carefully attended to, conventional philosophical prejudices may easily, if unconsciously, undermine any authentic interpretation of the Scriptures.

Christians, for example, speak naturally of the Trinity as "three Persons in One." But in such locutions, what is the exact meaning of "person"? And what does it mean, for personal life as well as for social thought, to think of God as a "*communion* of Three Persons" rather than (as the Greeks, Muslims and even Jewish thinkers do) as a solitary "One"? Moreover, what does it mean to speak of Jesus Christ as a single "Person" with two "natures," divine and human? What, furthermore, do we mean by "liberty"? And which notions of "truth" are compatible with, and which are incompatible with, Christian revelation?

How are we to think of the difference between humans and other creatures? How do Christians explain the difference between "human rights" and "animal rights"? What, too, is the difference between "male" and "female," as when the Bible says, "Male and female he made them" (Gen. 1:27)? What does the injunction to build up "the kingdom of God" mean in concrete, institutional forms?

A clear philosophical understanding of such terms is a necessity today if Christians are to be faithful to the Word of God, for there are many possible understandings of these questions, many of which, history shows, lead down dangerous alleys. The Roman Catholic Church has lived through a host of such errors and partial historical understandings, and students of Church history have come to see that mistakes on such matters, even if embraced in good faith, can prove disastrous.

Furthermore, in reaching out to those of other religions and other philosophical traditions, Christians often find that if they attempt to state their faith in the terms of Scripture alone, their words are routinely misunderstood. They need to be able to diagnose what is going wrong in such attempts, and to find other ways to make the point. They need to cut through confusions, so that the Word of God can be grasped in its integrity. (In English, as in other languages, some translations from the original languages of the Scripture are far better than others.)

Not all Christians, of course, in meditating in their hearts on the Word of God, need or want philosophical reflection. We are not saved by philosophy, St. Augustine said. Indeed, much of the time we simply want to hear that saving Word in simple and direct ways. However, for those whose task is to worry about the culture as a whole — that culture in which Christ wishes to be incarnated, and to have His Word work as yeast in dough — the philosophical task is unavoidable. From the earliest days of the Church, the apostolic and postapostolic Fathers have undertaken it, in the idiom of their time.

For such reasons, the sustained attempt by the Catholic intellectual tradition to work out basic philosophical and empirical concepts quite clearly — and to do so anew in every generation — seems to have a utility of its own, a necessity for a correct hearing of the Word of God.

3. The Importance of Karol Wojtyła

Perhaps no thinker in the world today has attempted such a clear rethinking, in philosophical and theological terms separately and together, as Karol Wojtyła. Ravaged by two World Wars, the people of Poland came to understand the hard way the importance of fundamental ideas and a careful use of words. First under the assault of the nihilistic philosophies that became the fashion after World War I, then under the bombardment of Nazi propaganda, and finally under the systematic twisting of language by Communist rhetoric, Poles rediscovered what Pascal meant by the maxim: "The first moral obligation is to think clearly." Karol Wojtyła set out from his youth to clear away philosophical debris and to establish a philosophical realism in whose good soil the Word of God could take root.

Among evangelical thinkers, both Carl Henry and Francis Schaeffer have seen the need to undertake analogous philosophical and analytical tasks.

As for the importance of Pope John Paul II for the entire world as the third millennium opens, perhaps the words of Sir Michael Howard, Regius Professor of History at Oxford, best define it. There have been two great revolutions in the twentieth century, Professor Howard has said, the Marxist and — he admits to some surprise — the Roman Catholic. From having been a Church that was the pillar of the *ancien regime,* hostile to democracy under Popes Gregory XVI (1831-1846) and Pius IX (1846-1878), the Catholic Church under John Paul II (1978-) has become the world's single greatest voice for democracy and human rights.

As Professor Samuel Huntington of Harvard has also noted, the "third wave" of democratization around the world has become a largely Catholic movement. Moreover, Catholic social thought, slowly assimilated by and diffused through the world's more than one billion Roman Catholics, may be the single most solid and well-thought-out body of social thinking now operative on the planet.

4. My Favorite Passages

Although every writer wishes that readers would read his book through from the beginning, I can testify from my own experience that Rocco Buttiglione's book can be opened with profit at whichever chapter one chooses to enter it. Those who love poetry and drama may choose to start with Chapter 7, on the poetic work of Wojtyła. (When I was young, I too wanted to publish poetry and drama. Never having succeeded in these arts, I have learned a deep admiration for those who do, and marvel at Wojtyła's quiet success in them.) Another of my favorites is Chapter 6, concerning Wojtyła's role at the Second Vatican Council, as important as it has been unrecognized. Others may enjoy best the biographical chapters (2 and 3), or the two chapters (4 and 5) that go directly to two of Wojtyła's central philosophical and theological conceptions, human love and the human person (the acting person).

The William B. Eerdmans Publishing Company is to be congratulated for bringing this illuminating and important book to the English-speaking world, and for having sought out Francesca Murphy and Paolo Guietti as translators. It is a work of considerable ecumenical importance. Along with another recent Eerdmans publication, George Weigel's *Soul of the World,* which covers Wojtyła's social thought in the years following those Buttiglione covers here, this book provides the best available introduction to Wojtyła's thought in any language.

5. "A Pope Who Knows How to Pope"

Finally, am I mistaken in believing that even many evangelicals who are skeptical of the Petrine office in the Church have learned to see in Karol Wojtyła a brave and steadfast Christian pastor? In any case, I have heard evangelical friends observe that Wojtyła is one of those rare Christian leaders of our time who does not need to test the winds before preaching from the rooftops. This particular Bishop of Rome does not really care what the media say about him; theirs is not the judgment he fears.

Others have noted that, for his forthright orthodoxy, probably no other Christian leader of his time has borne (with good humor) as much criticism, hostility, and opposition, even attempted assassination. In that sense Wojtyła has been a rock.

A Baptist friend of mine, who is opposed to the papacy in general, recently said to some of us, "Boy! You have a pope who knows how to pope!" Wojtyła has given good Christian witness.

For the publication of this book, *Laudetur Jesus Christus!* runs the appropriate ancient exclamation: *May Jesus Christ be praised!*

Michael Novak
August 4, 1996

Preface

I must thank a number of people who have assisted, encouraged, and helped me during the three years in which I have been writing this book. For the initial idea and for crucial help with the difficulties which I faced at every step, I am indebted to Professor Fr. Luigi Giussani, who, during a long friendship, has introduced me to the problems of Christian thought. Those who know my earlier works will see the traces left by long companionship with the writings and the person of Prof. Augusto Del Noce, particularly in relation to questions regarding the philosophical interpretation of contemporary philosophy and the philosophical comprehension of history. My conversations with Professor Dino Pasini have germinated many seeds on the theme of human rights, which in diverse degrees have been planted in my arguments in the part of the book related to this matter.

To Mrs. Ludmila and Prof. Stanislaw Grygiel I have over the years contracted a particularly deep debt: their friendship, in addition to providing me with much detailed information about Poland, has introduced me to the ethos of its culture, and especially that of Cracow, which is the wider background behind the argument of this work. I also wish to remember Prof. Jozef Tischner and Fr. Francesco Ricci, with whom I discussed the main themes of this study during a conference in Latin America in October, 1981. Dr. Stanislaw Morawski of the Free International University of Social Sciences in Rome has assisted me greatly by lending me ideas and material difficult to obtain in Italy. Dr. Massimo Serretti and Dr. Pierluigi Pollini have helped by gathering material which has been used in the context of research about Polish philosophy in the School of Lublin/Cracow, financed by the Ministry of Public Education for the academic years 1980/1981 and 1981/1982. Together with Dr. Daniele Celli, Dr. Paolo Boni, and Dr. Marco Cangiotti, they also participated in a seminar which I held on the "Philosophical Formation of Karol Wojtyła and *The Acting Person*" during a course on Political Philosophy held in the Faculty of Education at the Free University at Urbino during the academic years 1979/1980 and 1980/1981. Dr. Marian and Dr. Barbara Szcztepanowicz showed me hospitality during my stay in Cracow in the summer of 1980. Many of the ideas and interpretations of the concluding parts of the book were discussed with Alberto Methol-Ferré and Hernan Alessandri and were enriched by these conversations. Finally, I must recall that the Centre for the Study of Eastern Europe in Bologna has helped me in various ways in the course of my work. My sincere thanks are offered to all of the persons and institutions which I have mentioned.

Special thanks are owed to the students in two seminars held at the House of Faith and Culture in São Paulo, Brazil. By enthusiastically following the development of difficult arguments, and by their questions and contributions, they have helped me to understand more deeply not only Karol Wojtyła's thought but also the life to which he has dedicated himself.

The question of how to use Wojtyła's major work, *Osoba i Czyn* [*The Acting Person*], posed a particular problem for me. The first edition of this work contains the latest developments in his thought; the American edition (which was more like a second edition than a translation) has been criticized by many on the ground that much of it is excessively "idiosyncratic." I like to quote the first Polish edition, but in some cases, where the American edition presents a novel emphasis, I have followed it. In these instances, it was helpful for me to to consult the work under way for the second Polish edition. For permission to cite the second Polish edition while it was in preparation, I cordially thank Dr. Stanislaw don Dzizisz. In these cases I have always indicated the passage in the first Polish edition, the page of the manuscript for the second edition, and the page of the American edition.

The purpose of this book is both very narrow and very broad. It attempts to be not so much an interpretation as an introduction and guide to Wojtyła's writings, by helping to place them in the complete horizon of his thought. This purpose will be achieved if readers read his philosophy for themselves and relate it to their own experience.

I have not added a bibliography to this book because there are numerous bibliographies of the works of Karl Wojtyła. The first, that of Alfons Schletz, dates back as far as 1967 and was published in *Nasza Przeslosc* 27

(Cracow, 1967) on the occasion of the Bishop of Cracow's becoming a Cardinal. A second bibliography, which included works written down to 1971, appeared in that year in *Logos i Ethos*, a publication celebrating the twenty-fifth anniversary of the ordination of Karl Wojtyła, under the supervision of Tadeusz Styczen. This was briefly preceded by a bibliography from the hands of Barbara Eychler in *Chrzescijanin w swiecie* 74 (1969). A selection of the main works of Karol Wojtyła is contained in an appendix to J. Piatek's *Persona ed amore nel pensiero filosofico di Karol Wojtyła* (Rome, 1968). After the election of Karol Wojtyła to the Papacy, a bibliography of his works was included in a special issue of the *Angelicum* dedicated to the illustrious alumni of the eponymous theology faculty. This bibliography, edited by Edward Kaczynski and Bruno Mazur, is found in *Angelicum* 56 (1979). Bibliographies such as those of Piatek and of Styczen are mainly theological and philosophical, omitting most of his homiletic and administrative works. The definitive bibliography, which is an indispensable tool for those who want to study these topics, is that prepared by Wiktor Gramatowski and Zofia Wilinska and entitled *Karol Wojtyła w swietle publikacji. Karol Wojtyła negli scritti* (Vatican City: Libreria Editrice Vaticana, 1980). A bilingual Italian-Polish edition provides brief but very useful introductions to "Karol Wojtyła poeta" (by Tadeusz Styczen), "Karol Wojtyła Teologo" (by Stanislaw Nagy), and "Karol Wojtyła pastore" (by Czeslaw Drazek). Finally, we must recall l'ISTRA (The Institute for Transition Studies) in Milan, in whose milieu most of this research was undertaken and completed.

16 ottobre 1978

O roku ow! Kto ciebie widzial w naszym kraju
Ciebie Lud dota zawie rokiem urodzaju.

A. Mickiewicz, *Pan Tadeusz*

1. Judgment on Contemporary History

Stanislaw Grygiel has been a friend and close collaborator of Karol Wojtyła since Wojtyła was a university professor and archbishop of Cracow. Grygiel has written a book called *Man Seen from the Vistula*.[1] It is perhaps not a very good title, but it has a profound meaning. Man actually does not seem the same when viewed from the extreme West of Europe as from the territories which extend along the Vistula, in the great plain delimited by the Oder, the Baltic Sea, and the Tatras Mountains, and which is bordered on the east by the Baltic Republics, Belarus, and the Ukraine. Grygiel once said to me that the river Vistula separates the East from the West and also, paradoxically, unites them.

Although we often think otherwise, Poland belongs to Western Europe: it chose, in the moment when its national identity was born, the Roman Catholic Church and the Latin liturgy, and it paid dearly for this choice, about which it has never wavered. On the other hand, it lies on the borders of the East and shares with it a Slavic ethnic and linguistic heritage. Because of this position the people of Poland are able to speak the language of two spiritual worlds and to link them together. Poland's very geography allows it a particular catholicity — an opening to universality to which it can remain faithful only by deepening, rather than denying, its Roman choice. If we look at it "from the Vistula," there arises for us an entirely different

1. Stanislaw Grygiel, *L'uomo visto dalla Vistola* (Bologna: CSEO, 1978).

idea of West and East, with their differences and their unity, their distinct meaning and their shared destiny.

There is a particular way of considering world history which derives from the specific experience of the Polish nation and culture, and which is deeply inscribed in the mind and thought of Karol Wojtyła. In his case, it is not a matter of a state of mind but, rather, of a judgment, sometimes stated explicitly but in any case accompanying, as an implicit premise, his approach to the most diverse ethical, religious, theological, and philosophical questions.[2]

One aspect of the distinctive character of his thinking may be seen in the view John Paul II has expressed several times, especially during his first trip to Poland, of the providential meaning of the election of a Polish pope on the eve of the conclusion of the second millennium of evangelization. In his homily for the Mass celebrated at Victory Square in Warsaw, he raised this issue with the greatest clarity:

> My pilgrimage to my motherland in the year in which the Church in Poland is celebrating the ninth centenary of the death of Saint Stanislaus is surely a special sign of the pilgrimage that we Poles are making down through the history of the Church, not only along the ways of our motherland but also along those of Europe and the world. Leaving myself aside at this point, I must nonetheless with all of you ask myself why, precisely in 1978, after so many centuries of a well-established tradition in this field, a son of the Polish nation, of the land of Poland, was called to the chair of Saint Peter. Christ demanded of Peter and of the other Apostles that they should be "his witnesses in Jerusalem and in all Judea and Samaria and to the end of the earth" (Acts 1:8). Have we not the right, with reference to these words of Christ, to think that Poland has become nowadays the land of a particularly responsible witness? The right to think that from here — from Warsaw, and also from Gniezno, from Jasna Gora, from

---

2. It is difficult to find an explicit philosophy of history in Wojtyła's properly philosophical works. One can, however, find traces of such a philosophy in all of his homiletic and literary writings. It flows into his work from the classical tradition of Polish literature, as we will see later. What influences him most, in this context, is not — as some believe — Polish romanticism, but rather Norwid's reaction against romanticism, which refounded the idea of the nation in what could be called an antiromantic sense. It would be interesting to make a comparative study of Norwid's idea of the nation and Rosmini's philosophical idea of "risorgimento." The two authors were ignorant of each other, but Norwid had, through Ballanche, close contact with Vico's philosophy of history, which, by different means, influenced Rosmini's thought.

Cracow and from the whole of this historic route that I have so often in my life traversed — it is our task to proclaim Christ with singular humility but also with conviction? The right to think that one must come to this very place, to this land, on this route, to read again the witness of his Cross and Resurrection? But if we accept all that I have dared to affirm in this moment, how many great duties and obligations arise? Are we capable of them?[3]

Forgive me for the length of this citation. It seems justified by its importance. John Paul II affirms that there is something which we all have to learn from the Polish Church and that this particular vision of man, which is conditioned by Polish history (and of course by a history of Poland read in the light of faith), is, in an eminent way, catholic. What, then, is the content of this vision of the human being? In the same homily which we have just cited, John Paul II sketches the essential traits:

To Poland the Church brought Christ, *the key to understanding that great and fundamental reality that is man.* . . . Christ cannot be kept out of the history of man in any part of the globe, at any longitude or latitude of geography. The exclusion of Christ from the history of man is an act against man . . . the history of each person unfolds in Jesus Christ. In him it becomes the history of salvation.[4]

These are affirmations to which one can relate and which are in fact related to everyone in the world; they are supremely catholic and thus universal affirmations. But what is particularly Polish in the Christian vision of man which they condense and proclaim? The key to answering this question is found again in the discourse in Victory Square. Let us listen to it:

The history of the nation deserves proper appreciation according to the contribution which it has brought *to the development of man and humanity,*

---

3. Pope's Homily in Victory Square in Warsaw, 2 June 1979. I cite the speech according to the translation in the *Osservatore Romano*, weekly English edition, 11 June 1979, pp. 4-5. But, since this translation sometimes departs from what was actually said, I have also used the text reported in *Jan Pawel II na Ziemi Polskiej*, published by Stanislaw Dziwisz, Josef Kowalczyk and Tadeusz Rakoczy (Vatican City: Libreria Editrice Vaticana, 1979). This work gives first the Italian translation and then, within parentheses, the Polish text. In the present case: John Paul II, "Omelia del 2 giugno 1979 in piazza della Vittoria a Varsavia," in CSEO-Documentazione 140-41, p. 256 (*Jan Pawel II na Ziemi Polskiej*, pp. 26-27).
4. "Omelia del 2 giugno 1979," p. 257 (*Jan Pawel II na Ziemi Polskiej*, p. 30).

3

to the intelligence, to the heart and to the conscience. This is the deepest current of culture. And it is its most solid support, its marrow and its force. Without Christ, it is not possible to understand and to appreciate the contribution of the Polish nation *to the development of man and of his humanity in the past, and his contribution also in our days.*[5]

With this, we reach the heart of the question which interests us. To appreciate its full scope, let us take G. W. F. Hegel's *Philosophy of History* as a point of reference. This book expresses the most sophisticated and the most coherent modern secular understanding of Western history, one to which the Marxist view of contemporary history is connected. Yet in this book, we find only a passing allusion to Poland and its history. For Hegel, the Slavic peoples live outside of history. The sole exception is Russia, which (according to Hegel, writing in the first half of the nineteenth century) was about to enter the theater of the history of European civilization. Hegel's judgment does not come from a preconceived hostility to Poland or to the Slavic peoples but is rather the necessary consequence of his understanding of history. It is indebted to an interpretation of human history which does not recognize, or misunderstands, the central position which it gives to Christ. It would be unjust to Hegel to say that he wishes to exclude Christ from human history. For the great dialectician of Stuttgart, Christianity marks the epochal turning point in the history of humanity, and he conceives his own philosophy as a rational development of Christian dogma. However, Hegel seeks to align the Christian principle of truth and of the Spirit with a different principle, always present in human history but which, in the course of these last centuries, has emerged with particular vigor: the principle of force and of power.

The Christian tradition does not deny the reality and the importance of power, but it seeks to subordinate it to its own axiom. St. Augustine, in one phase of his thought, creates an unnuanced opposition between the City of God and the City of the devil, without indicating any possibility of conciliation or mediation between them. But in *De Trinitate*, he distinguishes between *scientia* ("science"), which is the ability to manipulate the things of the world, and *sapientia* ("wisdom"), which is the knowledge of the truth of man: this truth indicates the purpose or "telos" to which the manipulation of things ought to be subordinated. Between *scientia* and *sapientia* there is no contradiction in principle, even if they can be opposed in fact, in the sense that *scientia* rebels against *sapientia* and denies its

5. Ibid.

4

prerogatives.[6] When this happens, man no longer masters nature in order better to realize the truth of his own person, but his domination becomes an end in itself, the unifying principle of all natural and social relations. To speak the language of a more recent philosophy, we could say that what then prevails and imposes itself is "instrumental reason." Along the same line as that indicated by *De Trinitate*, St. Thomas Aquinas stresses further the possibility of conciliation, in a hierarchical and harmonic order, between *scientia* and *sapientia*.

Hegel also wants to synthesize truth and force. But instead of subordinating force to truth, as the Christian thinkers had, he follows Spinoza in envisaging truth and force as following parallel roads. Consequently, the people who triumph in the struggles of history are also, necessarily, the bearers of increasingly elevated spiritual principles. Once truth is separated from force it no longer finds any point of support or defense. By radicalizing this perspective, Marx will then read history as the history of the modes of production, that is to say, of more and more efficacious forms by which the dominion of man over nature and over other men is achieved.

Is it possible to read the history of men and of nations in this way, as a history of force and not of truth? A Christian will say that this is not possible. Moreover, a Christian might ask, for example: "Apart from Christ, is it possible to understand and to judge the contribution of the German nation (or the American, or Russian, or French . . .) to the development of humanity?" On a cursory and superficial view, this does not seem impossible. These nations participate, nearly equally, in the play of force and of truth. One can attempt to understand the meaning of their history on the level of a materialist vision of human reality. Indeed, the nations themselves can be seduced by the temptation to understand and to judge their own history in this way. What, for example, is Nazism, if not a reading of the meaning of the history of Germany and of its mission in the world from the point of view of power and of force? The same observation could be made with respect to other, sometimes more subtle, forms of totalitarianism which persist in our time.

But *one cannot understand the history of the Polish nation in this way*. There we have to deal with a great spiritual culture which almost entirely lacks material force. Surrounded by neighbors more populous, more organized, and more powerful (Swedes, Germans, Austrians, and Russians), Poland has suffered harshly and has been for a long time deprived of

6. Augustine, *De Trinitate*, bk. 15, chs. 1, 15.

independence and of national unity. In the eyes of a Pole, the limitations of a Hegelian vision of history are immediately apparent: truth and force do not walk together at all.

The political-military history of Poland is a history of heroic defeats, of rebellions nourished by the desire to witness its own rights rather than any concrete possibility of victory. The last of these is the Warsaw uprising in 1944, on which John Paul II commented with these words:

> Without Christ, it is impossible to understand this nation, with a past so splendid and at the same time so terribly difficult. It is not possible to understand this city, Warsaw, the capital of Poland, which in 1944 committed itself to an unequal battle against the aggressor, a battle in which it was abandoned by the allied powers, a battle in which it was buried under its own rubble, if one does not recall that under this same rubble there was also Christ with his cross which can be found facing the church of Krakowskie Przedmiescie. It is impossible to understand the history of Poland from Stanislaw in Skalka to Maximilian Kolbe in Oswiecim, if one does not apply, to them also, that unique and fundamental criterion which bears the name of Jesus Christ.[7]

The meaning of Jasna Gora, the symbol of Polish national identity, is precisely the same. We know the history which gives this sanctuary its particular meaning. At the time of the great Swedish invasion which popular memory calls the "Swedish Deluge," when the king, the nobles, and the army were defeated and dispersed, the monks of Jasna Gora decided not to submit to the invaders' demands, but to resist. The Swedish army, at the time the best in Europe, failed to defeat a few monks defending an old monastery. The people's resistance was organized around the monks. They forced the Swedes to retreat.

Thousands of times defeated on the terrain of force, the nation is reborn each time thanks to the spiritual awareness of its own identity and of its own right, animated by Christian faith.

We can now attempt to express by a synthetic formula in which this particular vision of man which nourishes the Polish consciousness consists: it is the *cultural and existential certitude that Christ is the keystone for the understanding of man and of his history.* For a variety of reasons, this certitude is lost or considerably weakened at the western extremity of the continent. Blinded by the enormous potential for domination which the

---

7. "Omelia del 2 giugno 1979," p. 258 (*Jan Pawel II na Ziemi Polskiej*, p. 31).

industrial revolution offered them, these countries have made the measure of their dignity coincide with that of their power, and they have sought to construct on this basis their participation in world history. They have built great national states which have promptly sought to expand at their neighbor's expense and they have divided among them the defenseless people of all the regions of the earth. These states are opposed to the Church, which contested the reorganization of national life as a function of domination. Even the Church sometimes let herself be carried away by these developments, becoming an accomplice to this strategy or finding herself rejected, because of a rigid and blind resistance on the part of the more lively and dynamic currents of national life. That is the case, for example, in Italy. In the nineteenth century, the problem of Italian unification was on the agenda in Europe, just as Polish unification was.

Mazzini elaborated a concept of the nation as a cultural and spiritual unity precisely akin to that of the authors of Polish romanticism, with whom he was closely acquainted. Italy succeeded first in building a unitary state. This state, however, was born in the midst of a cycle of struggles in which religious and national consciousness were in conflict. The new state departed even from Mazzini's concept of the nation, conceiving itself as a simple expression of temporal power. Mazzini's followers, defeated on the ground of politics by the pragmatists of the "Piedmont party," could not even retreat and seek a rematch on the ground of the people's culture, because their anti-Catholicism prevented them from aligning themselves with ordinary people. The new state defined itself against both national and religious consciousness. It would have preferred to follow the example of Bismarck's Germany, but it did not have the means genuinely to be a state built on power and force. The circumstances of its birth have in large measure conditioned its later destiny.

Things developed differently in Poland. There the struggle for the construction of the national state was defeated. The two great rebellions of 1831 and 1863 did not succeed and were extinguished in blood. Once the Italian question and the German question were, in one way or another, resolved, Poland found itself alone in contesting the political reorganization of contemporary Europe, and it was forced to resign itself to its own destiny. Although the Polish revolutionaries were defeated on the ground of politics, they were able to retreat and to recover on the ground of culture. As they had never broken with the Church, they saw in the development of the Christian consciousness of the people the most solid foundation of the national idea, and of a national idea which could unite all the peoples of

7

the earth. While in Italy the constitution of the state prevents the formation of national spiritual identity, in Poland spiritual identity is constituted outside of the state and even in open struggle with the existing states, by setting the force of right of the individual and of the nation (which has its root and its defense in God) in utter opposition to the right of force exercised by the powerful ones of the world.[8]

History has preserved Poland somewhat from the influence of that *ethical immanentism* which has marked the rest of the continent. And Polish Christianity did not go to the other extreme of falling into that dualism which marked the Catholic experience of, say, Italy or France. In these cases, the rightful requirement that the ecclesiastical hierarchy respect the autonomy of the temporal sphere was turned into the claim that political activity on the part of Christians must be circumscribed by a secular interpretation of the past and the present of the nation, and by a criterion other than Jesus Christ. The breach between the national idea and the religious idea which was thus institutionalized and which has never truly healed, was elaborated in a general division of life between spheres which do not communicate with each other: one concerns man's earthly and social activity, and the other his movement toward eternal life.

What is here in question is not the necessity of determining precisely the difference between what is sacred and what is profane, but rather a spiritual attitude which precedes every theoretical awareness and which tends to obviate the unity of the person. For the person, even if he divides his activities between different domains, each of which is regulated by its own law, still remains indissolubly united, and the fundamental structure of human experience as such also persists as a unitary whole.[9]

8. On the social and spiritual history of the Polish nation see the interesting piece by Ewa Jablonska-Deptula called "The Family and the Nation in the Polish Century," presented at the congress on The Family at the Roots of Man, the Nation, and the Church (Rome, 5-8 December 1981). The acts of this congress are in the course of publication.

9. It would be interesting to write a parallel history of the influence of the thought of Jacques Maritain in Poland and in Italy. This influence was enormous in both cultural contexts, but I dare say that the effects and way in which he has been read have been completely different. I believe that it is incontestable that the Polish interpretation was much more comprehensive and less one-sided. In Italy, a similar type of reading found a certain resonance, but only during the 30s, in very restricted circles, and, lately, with the flourishing of studies stimulated by the celebration of the centenary of his birth. I hasten to add that Italy did not lack those who studied the thought of Maritain in a valuable way (Viotto, Pavan, etc.); the dominant interpretation, however, is a facile and secondhand political Maritainism.

The spontaneous trust in this unity has disappeared in the West for historical reasons to which I can only briefly allude. The blame is shared equally by the hubris of modern man and by Western Christianity's uncertainties, errors, and even prevarications.

This trust was maintained in Poland and was linked to the affirmation of the primacy of truth over force and to the appreciation of the courage of the one who was able to oppose truth to force. This is the teaching of the martyrs in whom the Polish Church recognizes herself, from Stanislas to Maximilian Kolbe.[10]

The basic framework of this particular vision of man, which is conditioned by the Polish spiritual experience considered in the light of Christian faith, is thus that it teaches the unity of the human person and the primacy, in the formation of this person, of the recognition of the truth over the capacity to impose one's own domination by way of force.

Thus, the apparent novelty of the witness to Christ which is made possible by Polish history and culture is actually entirely traditional. By its very existence, Poland witnesses to the error of ethical immanentism and of the philosophy of history which is linked to it. On this theme, which arises from the tradition and the development of several centuries, the events of recent history have thrown a particular light. I have already mentioned the specific characteristics which differentiate Poland's struggle to build a unified national state from the analogous struggles which took place in Italy and in Germany in the nineteenth century. But the way in which Poland faced the test of the Second World War and the witness of humanity and of faith which the Polish Church furnished on this occasion make the same point in an equally convincing way.

One can even recognize important symbolic meaning in the fact that the horrors of this war occurred on Polish soil, for it witnesses to the failure of the cultural perspective of ethical immanentism. In fact, the catastrophe inherent

---

10. Here are the roots of Wojtyła's particular conception of the relation between Christianity and culture: ". . . the confession of faith, that is to say the fact of bearing witness to Christ as an interior trait of the Christian, penetrates the works of culture created by the confessors. This penetration in the works is inevitable and is accomplished both with discretion and in a categorical way. . . . It is not a question of presence alone on the basis of material content, but of a presence much more important, in the sense of style, that is, of the formal content. It is a Christian measure of the creation itself, a measure which admits an enormous quantity of variations and of individualities, since the Christian culture of every Christian soul is, in a certain sense, different and entirely unique." Extract from "Chrzescijanin a kultura," in *Znak* 16 (1964), pp. 1153-57.

in such a vision of the world makes the truth contained in the history of Poland universally significant. What might appear as a mere footnote, a marginal notation in the history and culture of Europe, reveals itself to be the place where the truth of European civilization, its fundamental Christian character, is most clearly preserved. The *primary line* of that culture is evidently an "interrupted path," leading nowhere and even giving way before the awakening of irrational passions (which historicists created the illusion of transcending by assigning them to the primitive and barbaric stage of human history). The "secondary line" which is incarnated in the history of Poland appears as the only possible salvation for the European cultural heritage.

The concentration camp of Oswiecim, the Polish town which the Germans called Auschwitz, is both the most potent symbol of the horror of the war and, at the same time, the culmination of the immanentist culture. In a universe from which God has been expelled, any reason to respect man is forfeited. Man becomes simply an object, similar to other natural objects, on which other men exercise their will to power. Each, according to the project by which he constructs his own life, treats others instrumentally. Naturally each man becomes, himself, an object in the projects of other men, and social life becomes the stage of reciprocal instrumentalization, in which the Darwinian principle of the "survival of the fittest" (which Spencer applied to the human world) triumphs. The fact that the same error to which Auschwitz witnesses was reproduced in a radically different political milieu, shows how the great division which traverses contemporary history — that which truly opposes slaughterers and victims — influences the way we think of human beings. The antithesis is between the position of those who, although they seek their own interest, still respect a certain measure of truth and justice, and that of those who accept no limits in their race toward power.

The horror of Auschwitz is so immense that it must necessarily have a philosophical significance. It is not only a question of the number of victims and of the terrible way in which they were murdered. Auschwitz is the symbol of a humiliation of man which, under different (though no less emblematic) forms, does not cease to repeat itself in our time. It draws its force from a profound spiritual deviation, which one needs to understand at its root if one wishes to put an end to the barbarity.

No one has faced these questions more often and more deeply than Theodore Adorno.[11] He asks whether after Auschwitz it is still possible to

---

11. T. H. Adorno, *Negative Dialectics,* trans. E. B. Ashton (New York: Continuum, 1973, 1983).

write poetry or philosophy. For the world to which Auschwitz belongs is a world without soul, and the spiritual activities which remain only serve to furnish it with an appearance of legitimacy which flagrantly contradicts its reality. If the Second World War marks the catastrophe of ethical immanentism, it is precisely at Auschwitz that the fundamental dogma of that philosophy of history, the parallel march of justice and force, is contradicted in the most bloody way. Nor is the military victory of the Allies enough to overturn this judgment. One of the principal victors in the war maintained in its own country a Gulag system which would do justice to a Nazi camp commandant. Moreover, in order to achieve victory, the Allied forces delivered death to hundreds of thousands of innocents at Hiroshima and Nagasaki. Beyond a certain level it seems as if force is almost inevitably separated from justice.[12] Human history, once oriented toward indefinite progress, is faced with the menace of destruction. Even if this has not yet struck every city and destroyed human lives, it has already annihilated the values and the conscience which ought to animate those lives. The drama of modern man is that of having physically survived his own spiritual extinction.

Adorno applies this image to the Jewish survivor, but one can easily extend it to the "Aryans" and thus link the fate of the victims with that of the murderers.[13] When force is totally separated from justice, *homo sapiens* cannot claim to rise beyond the sphere of mere animality by reason of his capacity to accede to a superior order of values.

Adorno's question — whether it is still possible, after Auschwitz, to do philosophy, whether it is ultimately still possible to be human — has not found any response in contemporary culture. But it has nevertheless been taken up by John Paul II, first, implicitly, in his encyclical *Redemptor Hominis,* and second, explicitly, in the homily of the Mass celebrated on the square of Brzezinska, before the concentration camp of Oswiecim-Auschwitz.[14] This homily is centered on the figure of a Franciscan father, St. Maximilian M. Kolbe, a fascinating figure who enjoyed great prestige in Polish ecclesiastical and cultural life before the war. Fr. Kolbe, imprisoned

12. Simone Weil says (quoting Homer) that "justice flees from victors."

13. Adorno, *Negative Dialectics,* pp. 327-28.

14. Meditation on Auschwitz and its meaning has always been a fundamental theme of Wojtyła's preaching. Cf., for example, "Wymowa Osmiecimia," in *Notificationes e Curia Cracoviensi* 3 (1965), pp. 81ff. See also "Adam Stefan kardynał Sapieha, metropolita krakowski oraz duchowieństwo Archidiecezji w okresie ciemnej nocy okupacji," in *Notificationes e Curia Cracoviensi* 5, pp. 122ff.

11

in the extermination camp, was a continuous comfort and help to his companions, a living reminder of their human dignity, which was desecrated in that place. During a Nazi reprisal, Kolbe offered to substitute himself in the death chamber for another prisoner, a father of a large family, agreeing to be condemned to starve to death. Karol Wojtyła has always had a great devotion to St. Maximilian M. Kolbe.[15] He is, for John Paul II, the patron of our difficult century, not only for his spiritual stature, but also for the particular meaning which, in God's providence, his sacrifice has assumed. For this contains the answer to the fundamental philosophical question: whether, and how, it is possible to be human after the horror of the war. This answer is not the fruit of abstract reflection which comes after the events and seeks to cancel the memory of suffering, but is an answer whose witness is sealed in blood.

From the beginning, in his homily devoted to the figure of Fr. Kolbe, John Paul II welcomes Adorno's judgment on the meaning of Auschwitz for our epoch, but reverses it. He begins like this:

> This is the victory which has defeated the world: our faith (1 John 5:4). These words of the letter of St. John come to mind and penetrate my heart, when I find myself in this place where a singular victory for the faith was accomplished. For the faith which made known the love of God and of neighbor, the unique love, the supreme love which is "ready to give his life for his friends" (John 15:13; 10:11). A victory, therefore, for love, which faith has enlivened unto the extreme limit of the ultimate and definitive witness. . . . The victory by way of faith and love, that man (M. Kolbe) has carried back in this place which was constructed for the *negation of the faith* — of the faith in God and of the faith in man — *and to trample under foot radically* not only love, but all the signs of human dignity, of humanity. . . . In this place of the terrible massacre . . . Fr. Maximilian, by offering himself voluntarily to death in the bunker of

15. From the time of his teaching as archbishop of Crakow, reflection on the meaning of the martyrdom of Fr. Kolbe has been for Wojtyła the summit of his reflection on the meaning of the war and of Auschwitz. It is a theme which he often takes up; with St. Stanislas, Kolbe is perhaps the archetypal figure to whom Wojtyła most frequently refers. Among the numerous documents we cite, at random: "Przemowienie w Radio Watykanskim 5. Pazdziernika 1971 r." (for the imminent beatification of Fr. Kolbe), in *Notificationes e Curia Cracoviensi* 10, pp. 242ff.; "Znak naszej epoki," in *Tygodnik Powszechny* 25 (1971); several interventions in *W nurcie zaganien posoborowych. T. 6: Blogoslawiony Maksymilian wsrod nas*, ed. Bohdan Bejze (Warsaw, 1972).

hunger for one of his brothers, carried back a spiritual victory *similar to that of Christ himself.*[16]

Let us reflect for a moment upon these words. Auschwitz is a place constructed for the destruction of man, for the annihilation of his dignity. Power can certainly not kill all men: it has need of them as servants and instruments. To be sure of these instruments, it must, however, first annihilate their dignity, their self-respect. In the extermination camp, man is reduced to pure animality, and, by the programmed destruction of his spiritual personality it is scientifically demonstrated that he is not a bearer of any superior value but that he is merely a slightly more evolved animal than the others. He is like a trained monkey which can be domesticated, but which is always ready to return to the law of the jungle. From this point of view, humanity is not what is most profound in man, but what is most superficial. By looking at the brutalization of the victims (and that of the murderers), each is forced to remind himself of what he is in his deepest dimension, and what he could at any moment become if he offended the powers that be or if he did not show himself completely obedient to their orders. The ultimate purpose of the extermination camp is, in a certain sense, metaphysical: it shows that authentic human values in the name of which it would be right to defy power do not exist, because man is only matter, which can by material means be coerced to any end. If, therefore, there is neither truth nor justice in man, if these are only empty words, then in principle the root of all opposition to totalitarian power disappears. Any possible opposition would also have to place itself, if it could, on the terrain of force alone. Precisely for this reason, in virtue of this metaphysical depth which belongs to the horror of Auschwitz, the witness of Fr. Kolbe is not just a witness but a victory. For, by sacrificing his life, he makes the extermination camp useless; he spiritually annuls it by showing at the same time that humanity is what is most profound in man. It is more fundamental for him and belongs to him more intimately than the instinct for self-preservation and all the other natural tendencies that man has in common with other animals. In the place constructed for the annihilation of man, for the negation of his spiritual nature, Kolbe shows the essence of human greatness.

No success of the anti-Nazi alliance can annul what happened in

16. "Omelia del 7 giugno 1979 a Oświęcim-Brzezinska," in *CSEO Documentazione,* p. 305 (*Jan Pawel II na Ziemi Polskiej,* p. 204).

Auschwitz; no punishment inflicted on the murderers can balance the account of the innocent victims' pain. It is not possible to expunge Auschwitz and similar places of death from human history. But Fr. Kolbe has opened unexpected depths for the reading of their meaning. For these places are the cross of Christ on which contemporary man groans. The Christian knows that, lived in the spirit of Christ, as a participation in his suffering and his witness for man, they are the places of a fundamental victory of man and for man.

To grasp more exactly John Paul II's thought, we ought to take up for a moment the Polish text of his discourse because on one point the translation is not entirely faithful. When our translation says that "there is accomplished a particular victory for the faith," the exact Polish text pronounced by the Holy Father says: *"dokonalo sie szczegolne zwycietwo czlowieka przez wiare"* — literally, "is accomplished a particular victory of man through the faith." What conquers, through Kolbe, is not the Christian faith but man, man who through faith has arrived at the full possession of his own humanity. This possession coincides with the recognition that his own human truth is a gift which springs continually from the mercy of God. In the camp, man as such undergoes the trial of the cross, but it is the faith which allows him to overcome this trial, to regain fully and definitively, by means of the trial, his own truth and his human dignity.

The teaching of Dietrich Bonhoeffer, another victim of Nazism, comes immediately to mind. Bonhoeffer is often misunderstood because of certain points being lifted from the context of the whole of his work, which is both rich and problematic. According to the prevailing interpretation, in the face of the ease with which the Nazis triumphed over all ethical or religious resistance, Bonhoeffer develops the following thesis: man has henceforth arrived at his maturity, in which he must no longer live according to guidelines established by the divine law but according to his own autonomous political and ethical judgment.[17] In order to triumph over the enemy it is necessary to dirty one's hands, to accept the descent to the level of historical efficacy which is also the terrain of naked force. The teaching of Bonhoeffer is entirely understandable within the cultural tradition to which he belongs. The Protestant ethos has accentuated the opposition of the two

17. I am well aware of the fact that this vulgarization of Bonhoeffer does not represent the only possible reading of his thought and, probably, not even that which is today the most authoritative.

Cities, and has typically denied the resistance of the individual and of the people to an unjust power, thereby abandoning the world to the violence of the sword. By so doing, it exposes itself, when oppression becomes unbearable, to the possibility of a total reversal which ends up in a millenarianism wishing to establish perfect justice on earth by means of an unscrupulous use of power and even of terror.

By contrast, it would be wrong to make the figure of Kolbe into a symbol of surrender in the face of the oppressor, of a refusal to confront evil with worldly means. This position would be proper to the Protestant ethos but alien to the spirit of a people which remembers with veneration the casualties of so many bloody struggles for the independence of its fatherland, and which has had for a spiritual guide Cardinal Stefan Wyszynski, the chaplain of the insurgents of Warsaw.[18] When he was active in church and society, Fr. Kolbe's spirituality was marked with virility and a chivalrous spirit. It will suffice to recall the title of his journal, which reached a circulation of more than eight hundred thousand copies in Poland before the war: *Rycerz Niepokalanej*, The Knight of the Immaculata.

Kolbe's message is one of integrally catholic balance: the oppressed can and must fight for justice with worldly arms but the true victory is the spiritual victory, that which regains and rebuilds the truth in oneself and in others. Only by keeping one's eyes fixed on this victory is it possible to avoid crossing over inadvertently into injustice and losing sight of the human reasons which render the struggle worthy and noble. Kolbe has no part in the secularizing consequences which some have supposed they can draw from the thought of Bonhoeffer. His life demonstrates that in this tormented epoch of the history of man, the Christian faith is more than ever called to exercise all its capacity for humanization, so that the human heart does not surrender to barbarity.

Finally, let us attempt to sum up in a few words the judgment on contemporary history which emerges from what we have tried to expound: *the conflict which marks contemporary history is a conflict for or against the Christian image of the human.* Various forms of totalitarianism have sought to construct a city of man without God, in which (despite their occasional humanistic claims) man is inexorably reduced to being merely an instrument of power. In the face of this fundamental conflict, all the other struggles are, in a sense, secondary. Our intent is not to diminish the strife

---

18. Cf. Karol Wojtyła, "Znaczenie kardynała Stefana Wyszyńskiego dla współczenego Kościoła," in *Zeszyty Naukowe* (KUL) 14 (1971), pp. 19ff.

that divides classes or nations but to argue that such conflicts can be resolved in equitable, just, and humane conclusions only if they are oriented by a Christian vision of man: otherwise they end up by provoking an increase of injustice and ultimately the self-destruction of humanity.

It is easy to establish how this vision of contemporary history differs from that which is most widespread among us — the idea that the roots of the crisis of European civilization, which has brought about a terrible and continuing cycle of world wars, must be sought in the sphere of the economy, in the struggle between classes and between nations. What appears in the foreground and occupies most of our attention is the struggle between the different forms of modern totalitarianism. Indeed, the tumult of their competing interests makes us deaf to the quiet resistance of all those who refuse to renounce their human dignity and, instead of siding with one or another of the forms of totalitarianism competing for world domination, seek to build an alternative to them.

Poland has experienced the two most violent forms of modern totalitarianism and, in the face of them, has reaffirmed another vision of man by creating an essentially moral opposition. In September 1939, the physical resources of the Polish state immediately surrendered in the face of German military superiority. Nevertheless, the Nazis did not bring the moral resistance of the people to an end. They exterminated the intelligentsia and murdered a sixth of the priests with the intention of destroying the spiritual consciousness of the nation. The moral resistance reconstituted itself around the witness for man given by the Catholic Church and, through her, by some great men of faith. We have already spoken of Fr. Maximilian Kolbe. In this context, one must also mention Cardinal Sapieha, metropolitan archbishop of Cracow, a giant figure of a bishop and priest and symbol of the spiritual resistance, in whose sphere of influence the priestly vocation of the young Karol Wojtyła reached maturity.[19]

Guided by Stefan Cardinal Wyszynski, another great priest and bishop, the Polish church has also opposed Communist totalitarianism through her own moral resistance anchored in the vision of man as the "visible image of the invisible God." This witness stirred the conscience of the people. It signified the will to continue the struggle for truth and freedom, and at the same time it kept alive the awareness that what is more decisive

---

19. Cf. Karol Wojtyła, "Stulecie urodzin ksiecia kardynała Adama Stefana Sapiehy," in *Notificationes e Curia Cracoviensi* 5 (1967), pp. 94ff. This is a speech given on Vatican Radio on 12 May 1967 on the centenary of Cardinal Sapieha's birth.

than the political reform of the dominant regime is the reform of national consciousness — the rediscovery, by individuals and communities, of an essential steadfastness and persistent humanity in the face of the claims of power. The events of Danzig in 1979, the peaceful and firm protest of an entire people in the defense of truth and right, were a striking practical manifestation of this new spiritual disposition, to which Jozef Tischner, in *The Ethics of Solidarity*,[20] bears perhaps the most lucid written witness.

20. J. Tischner, *L'etica della solidazietà* (Bologna: CSEO, 1981).

2. Some Information about Karol Wojtyła

Karol Wojtyła was born in Wadowice on 18 May 1920. His mother, Emilia Kakorowska, died when he was just seven years old. His father never re-married. Instead, he dedicated himself completely to educating his sons. He was a low-ranking official. In Wadowice, Karol went to elementary school and then to Marcello Wadowita, the state gymnasium.

Wadowice is on Mount Tara, in the only mountainous region of Poland. The villagers have a strong sense of their unique identity — a great love for the countryside and the serenity of the land and for their own tradition and customs.

First Literary Influences

In the years in which Wojtyła went to the Marcello Wadowita gymnasium the local luminary was the poet Emil Zegadlowicz, whose journal *Czartak* opposed the cosmopolitanism which, through the influence of the Skamander circle, dominated the national stage. For young Wojtyła, however, the contemporary poet was less an influence than the great romantic writers of the nineteenth century: Adam Mickiewicz (1798-1855), Juliusz Słowacki (1803-1849), and Zygmunt Krasinski (1812-1859), as well as their followers and commentators, Cyprian Norwid (1821-1883) and Stanislaw Wyspianski (1869-1907). Well into his adulthood, Karol counted Norwid his favorite poet.

These five poets were the defenders of the national spirit during the hard years of partition, when revolt was often repressed with bloodshed, and when the Germans and Russians stubbornly tried to eradicate Polish culture and language altogether in order to assimilate each of the individual parts to themselves. After the final partition of 1863 the history of Poland is punctuated with a succession of revolts, each destined to defeat.

The key word of the moment was "organic work," signifying the defense of the language and of national culture and religion, against the invader. In the second phase the nation was organized outside the structure of the state, which remained under foreign domination; this created the conditions for the survival and the growth of spiritual self-consciousness despite the lack of a genuine national state. (Through this experience the Polish came to accentuate more than other European language the semantic difference between the word "nation" *(Naród)* and the word "state" *(Państwo)*. The idea of revolution was also charged with special meaning. Toward the end of the nineteenth century, the West came to understand the notion of revolution as implying a complete break with the past, whereas in Poland the idea of revolution continued to be understood as the resurrection of a forgotten value underlying the principles of the country's history. The central value is the vital community to which the nation had originally belonged. It was the fracture of the experience of mutual relationship that had allowed foreigners to dismember Poland; the resurrection of the spirit of national culture was at the same time the germ and the fruit of the awaited restoration of the national state.

The primacy of the problem of intellectual and moral reform explains the importance of the Catholic Church in this context, as the yeast of the moral attitudes which create the nation. On the other hand, according to the messianic interpretation of the Polish uprising [*risorgimento*], Poland has suffered for all the nations, and her rising up will show the way to restore a just national and social order to the whole world.

In assuming the form which we have briefly described, nineteenth-century Polish messianism had to face two crises. The first was military defeat. The response to this crisis, which we have called "organic work," is sketched in the legend of the foundation of the Order of Resurrectionists. The story goes that, after the failure of the revolt of 1831, some of the exiled leaders of the insurrection gathered in Paris. At a meeting on the day of Pentecost, 1836, after having repeatedly analyzed the situation and after having lost any hope of working it out politically, Mickiewicz concluded that what was needed was the foundation of a religious order, which would save the spirit of the nation. "We need a new order. There is no other salvation. But how could we found it? I am too proud."[1] It was at this point that the great poet pointed at Bogdan Janski, and he, together with Piotr Semenenko and Hieronim Kajsiewicz, founded the order of the Resurrectionists. There appears here the contrast, latent in the history of Poland, between a wild romanticism which would contest the existing order at any cost, and an attitude of responsibility for the life of the nation, whose first wish was to secure the conditions of its survival.

The great test for the survival of Polish culture came about when it was abandoned by Rome. The election of Pius IX awakened great hope in both Italy and Poland. It was believed that the Pope would lead the struggle for a new and more just international world order, correcting the respite given by Gregory XVI to the Russian repression of Poland in his encyclical *Cum Primum* of 9 June 1832. But in the end Pius IX also sided with the forces of reaction. Whereas the crisis of 1849 provoked in Italy an unhealed breach between Church and nation, in Poland this abandonment was experienced in a spiritual way, like the Father's abandonment of Christ on the cross, in order that He could make the deepest and most pure offering of his life for all men. The fact that this trial reinforced the hope of resurrection is expressed in the words of Juliusz Słowacki:

In the middle of the battle God will ring a vast bell.
For a Slavic Pope
He has also prepared a throne.
Listen, a Slavic Pope will come,
A brother of the people.[2]

---

1. Cf. Leonard M. Long, *Geneza I Rozwój Zgromadzenia Ksiezy Zmartwychwstańców* (Chicago: The Resurrectionists, 1942), pp. 12, 28; cited in G. H. Williams, *The Mind of John Paul II: Origins of His Thought and Action* (New York: Seabury Press, 1981).

2. Julius Słowacki, *Dzieła* (Ossoliński Wrocław, 1959), vol. 1, pp. 250-51. On the general theme of Polish messianism, see A. Walicki, "Polish Romantic Messianism in Comparative Perspective," in *Slavonic Studies* 22 (1978), pp. 1-15; Wiktor Weintraub, *Literature as Prophecy* (The Hague: Mouton, 1957). It is perhaps interesting to note that, immediately after his election to the papacy, the first thing which John Paul II is said to have done was to make a pilgrimage to the sanctuary of Mentorella, near Rome, which belonged to the Resurrectionist Fathers.

Kotlarczyk and the Rhapsodic Theater

During his gymnasium years in Wadowice Wojtyła met Mieczysław Kotlarczyk, professor of history in a local girls' school, but most notably a theater director and theorist of the theater of words. Kotlarczyk's theory of the Rhapsodic Theater was not to attain its complete formulation until the years of Resistance, when he had moved to Cracow. Nevertheless some of its features were probably already clearly delineated during his sojourn in Wadowice. He spoke especially of the evocative power of words, which not only communicate a meaning but also elicit an emotion, at once both entirely subjective and entirely objective; it is this power through which speech is lived. The value is in the profound intimacy of the speaker with those who listen: it is the actor who, through a unique personal ascesis, introduces us to that intimacy. The import of the performance, the plot, the communicative function in the usual sense are, of course, drastically reduced in this type of theater. What happens to consciousness is more emphasized than the events per se; the key thing is *the way in which* the objective reality is revealed in consciousness. This part of Wyjtyła's biography can perhaps help us to comprehend the unique and original way in which he lived and experienced many of the themes of phenomenology, especially the theme of consciousness. In a certain sense, his first initiation to phenomenology came about indirectly and outside of orthodox philosophy, through the theory of theater and, above all, the existential experience of being an actor under Kotlarczyk's direction.[3]

It is clearly not possible to pause for long over Kotlarczyk's thought, and we cannot even sketch a comparison with Stanislavsky's conception of the actor, or with the ideas of the theater found in Grotowsky or Eugenio Barba. The connection with medieval sacred representation, which in Po-

3. For an understanding of Kotlarczyk which supplements that given by Wojtyła, one should read Mieczysław Kotlarczyk, "Sztuka żwego słowa," *Gregorianum* (Rome, 1975), with an introduction by Cardinal Wojtyła. Kotlarczyk was a disciple of Juliusz Osterwa, the great Polish theoretician of the theater, and author of *Abecaddło wymowiste* (Cracow, 1941). Osterwa was married to Matylda Sapieżanka and thus acquired Cardinal Saphieha as an in-law. Another person who influenced Kotlarczyk was Rudolf Otto, with his conception of the sacred as a "mysterium tremendum et fascinans" which deepens the presence of the person to himself. On the relation between words and things, Kotlarczyk had read and meditated upon the works of the theosophical tradition (Helena Petrovna Blavatsky, J. Switowski, Ignacy Matuszewski . . .), phonetics and linguistics (Otto Jespersen), and the Jewish tradition (Ismar Elbogen); he made of all of these an entirely personal synthesis. See also footnote 4 below.

land has continued until the present at Kalwaria Zebrzydowska, is only theoretical, not direct. Another point of connection for the history of the theater and of dramatic theory would be Greek tragedy in its first phase, as it appears in Nietzsche's *The Birth of Tragedy out of the Spirit of Music,* and as viewed by Eliot and Claudel. A closer neighbor, in the common currency of Central Europe, is perhaps von Hofmannsthal and his play *Everyone.* In any case, it is certain that Kotlarczyk understood *the liturgical character of theatrical action,* the way in which it revives the presence of a universal value which renews mundane existence, judging its falsity but at the same time offering the possibility of entering into a new dimension and an unexpected authenticity. If one radicalized this perspective, there is little distance between the profession of the actor and that of the priest. Karol Wojtyła had probably already meditated upon that connection by the time he finished studying in high school and moved with his father to Cracow, to study Polish literature at the Jagellonian University. Initially, at least, this secret thought did not hold the young Karol back from attending his courses enthusiastically. And the War was already at hand.

On 1 September 1939 the German army invaded Poland; by the seventeenth day of the same month the Red army was also drawn up against the Polish troops. The whole of the country's interior was rapidly occupied. Wadowice was directly annexed by the Third Reich while Cracow remained under the general Government of Poland. On November 6,183 professors at the Jagellonian University were arrested and sent to the concentration camp at Oranienburg-Sachsenhausen. Many in that concentration camp were to lose their lives. At once, just a few kilometers away from Cracow, the notorious lager of Auschwitz began to be built.

During this period, Dr. Kotlarczyk moved from Wadowice to Cracow, where he made his living as a tram driver. The general Government of Poland had little time for intellectuals or professors or men of the theater. Hitler intended that Poland should disappear. Part of the population was to be assimilated; the rest were to be exploited to sustain the German forces and then eliminated. First among those to be persecuted, along with the Jews, were the intellectual custodians of Polish language and tradition, which had to be eradicated. For this reason, one of the main tasks of the Resistance, following in the tradition of "organic work," was the transmission of Polish language and culture. In this spirit, Mieczsław Kotlarcyzk organized clandestine meetings of the Rhapsodic Theater in Cracow. They met in private houses and staged the classics of the national tradition. If they were detected by the police, they could expect to be deported to concentration camps. One of the working groups of the Rhapsodic Theater was composed of Karol Wojtyła, Tadeusz Kwiatowski, and Danuta Michalowska. Together with Kristina Debowska, Halina Krolikiewicz, and Danuta Michalowska, Wojtyła also took part in directing the Rhapsodic Theater, under Kotlarczyk's supervision. He was also a member of Julius Kydrynsky's "Theatrical Confraternity," which, after the invasion, called itself Studio 39, and which, together with Kotlarczyk, worked on writing and printing the *Miesiecznik Literacki,* a *samizat* literary journal. Wojtyła secretly continued studying at the Jagellonian University, which had been reconstituted by the Resistance in May 1942.

After his father died of a heart attack in March 1941, Karol left their apartment at 10 Tyniecka Road in the region of Debnika, and moved to the nearby home of Julius Kydrinski. In the same area of Debnika lived Jan Tyranowski, who was to have a marked influence on young Karol's life. Wojtyła worked in a mine which belonged to the Solvay chemical company. His qualifications as a manual worker entitled him to a precious work card, which made him relatively secure against the German roundups and the threat of deportation.

During this period of theatrical activity Wojtyła performed in many of the classics of Polish literature, adapted for presentation in the Rhapsodic Theater. Among them were *Balladyna, Samuel Zborowski,* and *Krol-Duch* by Słowacki; Mickiewicz's *Pan Tadeusz;* the *Promethidion* and *Milosc czysta u Wod* of Norwid; *Wesele, Wyzwolenia,* and *Powrot Odysa* by Wyspianski; and Lubicz-Milosz's *Miguel Manara.* (During his Wadowice years, Wojtyła had performed in *Nie-Boska Komedia,* by Krasinski.)

Some Repertory Works of Wojtyła the Actor

It is perhaps useful, in drawing this sketch of the atmosphere in which the cultural and spiritual vocation of Wojtyła came to maturity, to lay out some elements of these leading literary works — especially *Nie-Boska Komedia, Promethedion,* and *Miguel Mañara.*

The *Nie-Boska Komedia* [4] is a fable about the end of the world, in which

---

4. Cf. Zymunt Krasiński, *Nie-Boska Komedia* (Warsaw 1981). G. K. Chesterton's introduction to the English translation, *The Undivine Comedy* (London/Warsaw: Harrap, 1936), is noteworthy. On Krasińksi, see Zygmunt Krasiński, *Romantic Universalist: An International Tribute,* ed. Wacław Lednicki (New York: Polish Institute of Arts and

the West is depicted as disintegrating in social upheaval and civil war. G. H. Williams, in *The Mind of John Paul II: The Origins of His Thought,* has rightly emphasized the importance of this work for Wojtyła's spiritual formation.[5] Williams clarified the social and political aspects of the process of dissolution which Krasinski describes, underscoring the conflict between Count Hendryk, defender of the spiritual values inherent in romantic tradition, and Pankracy, the leader of the rationalist and modernizing revolution. Pankracy conquers in politics, but he is nonetheless defeated spiritually by a vision of Christ — who looks at the abyss of civil war from the cross, with his head crowned with thorns. This vision seems to signify that the suffering and injustice accumulated in this process of social transformation can never be redeemed by the construction of any future society; and Christ knows the secret which can give meaning and value to these sufferings. For this reason the true lordship of history pertains not to the diverse victors of historical struggle but to Christ.

But there is more. The most vivid part of this work contains the key to its influence for Wojtyła's thought. Let us consider the first two acts, which show the internal genesis of the family and of the spirit of destruction which culminates in civil war. The central focus is Count Hendryk's family. The inside of the family is the real meeting place, in which the fundamental spiritual forces of civilization either collide, come together, or simply go their separate ways. It is only by analyzing the drama of Count Hendryk's family that one can comprehend his historical actions. Hendryk has committed a serious, indeed unforgivable sin: he has shown contempt for his wife, and this contempt has driven her to insanity. Hendryk is a romantic poet; his energy is entirely turned toward an ideal, the archetypal form of femininity which he identifies with the Virgin. Compared with this archetype, his real wife is infinitely inadequate. His crime is to demean and reproach his wife for falling short of his imagined standard. Hendryk says

Sciences in America, 1964) The title of this opera, performed by Wojtyła in the Rhapsodic Theater (the *Non-Divine Comedy*), carries an evident reference to Dante's *Divine Comedy.* My own interpretation of Krasiński is especially indebted to Prof. Rzyszard Przybylski, who gave a magnificent and illuminating paper at the Conference on "The Family at the Roots of Man, of the Nation and the Church" held in Rome on the 5-8 December 1981. Przybylski's paper, which was published with the acts of the Conference, was entitled "La Nazione e la famiglia alla luce della poesia." It contains a penetrating analysis of the *Nie-Boska Komedia,* considered as a synthetic expression of the contradictions which the romantic spirit introduced into the Polish family.

5. Williams, *The Mind of John Paul II,* pp. 58ff.

to his wife: "Woman of mud and clay, don't be envious, don't slander — don't blaspheme — behold (here he indicates the Virgin), this is the first thought of God as to how you should be, but you have followed the council of the serpent and become as you are."[6] A marital crisis ensues because Hendryk despises his wife: "O God," Hendryk says, "Is it you yourself who sanctified the union of two bodies. Is it You that declared that nothing can separate them, even when the souls reject each other, and each goes its own way, while the bodies remain close, like two corpses?"[7]

But marriage is a union not merely of souls, but of persons, each of whom has a soul *and* a body. Moreover, the Virgin, whom Christians venerate is not the archetypal feminine but herself a poor "woman of mud and clay," who had the wisdom to live in obedience to God within the human condition. For Hendryk the finite is an evil which must be despised if one is to rise into the ideal realm. His character echoes the heretical tendency of Andrej Towianski, even frankly identifying the Virgin of Jasna Gora with the Shekinah, the feminine aspect of God concealed within the world.[8]

In his quest for refuge in a purely spiritual realm, Hendryk thrusts the woman into the realm of pure materiality, dissolving the alliance of spirit with flesh which is contained in the sacrament of matrimony. It is this rift which is the root cause of all evil.

The struggle between Hendryk and Pankracy is thus a confrontation between apparent spiritual value deprived of earthiness and calculating earthiness which is blind to spiritual value.

This tension within the romantic spirit, which is also the fundamental to the Polish national spirit, was remorselessly criticized by Norwid. It is

6. *Nie-Boska Komedia*, p. 17.

7. Ibid., p. 13.

8. Andrej Towiański (1799-1871) maintained a particular version of Polish national mysticism, for which the idea of the nation has a true and authentic ontological consistency; he also developed a form of the doctrine of eternal return through the resurrection of the spirit of the nation and also those of individual men in diverse times and in different forms. We may detect the same position in Słowacki's *Król-Duch*. Jakub Frank was a Jewish messianist in 18th-century Poland who saw the advent of the Messiah as entailing liberation from the law and the legitimation of enjoyment in which the principle of interiority entirely overwhelms legal restrictions set up to defend objective values. The influence of Frank on Mickiewicz is particularly strong, according to the *Encyclopedia Judaica* (New York/Jerusalem: Macmillan, 1971), vol. 7, col. 71. Norwid's work will play an important role in countering heterodox nationalist mysticism with a more realistic vision of the nation, linked to Catholic mysticism.

for this reason that his *Promethidion* is worthy of our consideration.[9] Although Norwid criticized romantic mysticism it was he who most singularly identified the nation with Christ, as its supreme value. Christ is in fact a person, however, and not an abstract model. Following Christ means accepting one's own specific human vocation and its necessities and duties, thereby grasping the infinite within the finite. This reconciliation of the finite with the infinite is the genius of Catholicism and also, in a certain sense, the goal at which Norwid, as well the late Schelling, aimed.

The last work which I have chosen to recall from among those performed by Wojtyła is *Miguel Mañara.* Lubicz-Milosz is not normally considered among the great Polish authors, and although his origins were in Polish Lithuania, he wrote in French. There are, nonetheless, important parallels between his work and the *Nie-Boska Komedia,* which are worthy of our attention.

The title character of *Miguel Mañara* is a historical figure with a strong resemblance to Don Juan — the fascinating Spanish seducer whose story is recounted by Mozart (among others). But unlike his legendary counterpart, Miguel ended his days in a monastery, famous for his sanctity. Milosz attempts to unfold the stages of this conversion.

Miguel initially bears a strong resemblance not only to the notorious seducer of opera and drama but also to Count Hendryk in *Nie-Boska Komedia.* Miguel feels his life drifting away and wants to stop it, for he is drawn to an ideal of perfection and of beauty which no woman can incarnate. His libertinism is not the expression of an excess of carnality but rather of a rift between spirit and flesh. Miguel's salvation comes through his meeting with Geronima. Geronima has already rejected him; she does not pretend to occupy the infinite expanses of his spirit. At the same time,

9. There is probably a partial connection between the solution which Norwid proposed to the problem of the relation between the ideal and the real and Schelling's German Idealism. Norwid, perhaps through the mediation of Ballanche, who was also an important influence upon him, came into contact with Vico's thought. It would be interesting to go more deeply into the role which Vico's historicism had in allowing Norwid organically to rise above nationalist mysticism, without resorting to ahistoricism. In his *Essai de Palingénesie Sociale* (1830), Ballanche developed a Vichian theory of the Risorgimento of the nation in which he mentioned Prometheus, giving it not an atheist but a believing interpretation within which humanity is progressively created through culture and work. How profoundly these themes have, through Norwid, penetrated the thought of Wojtyła will be seen in the rest of this book. Norwid probably called his work *Promethidion* in connection with Ballanche's interpretation of Prometheus, and not that of Marx and other left-wing Hegelians.

she speaks to him about God and teaches him to pray. Within this ethos, this preoccupation with loyalty to God, Miguel becomes capable of experiencing lifelong human love.

Through learning respect, Miguel overcomes the contempt which isolates Count Hendryk. But Geronima is present in his life for only a short while. She soon dies. Miguel, realizing that what he is searching for is the invisible love of God, chooses to enter a monastery. At first he is shaken with a frenzy of mortification and penance, but his Superior restrains him: what he must learn is simply to obey, and to live every day to the full, appreciating the value of each moment. One must possess one's life in order to give it away. The pace of true love must be slow and constant if it is to achieve the fulfillment of its promise, the fulfillment of holiness.

The rift in the romantic spirit, and its recomposition in the sacraments — especially the sacrament of marriage — and in the family, and a Pascalian unity of finite and infinite, are all recurrent themes in Wojtyła's own poetry and philosophy. The influence of his experience with Kotlarczyk was to be profound and durable.

In these years, Wojtyła also composed a number of works himself: *David,* prepared for Christmas of 1939, *Job,* for Easter 1940, and a translation of Sophocles' *Oedipus.*[10] A little later, but still for the theater of words, he wrote *The Jeweller's Shop* and *The Radiation of Fatherhood.* Implicitly commenting on his earlier experience, Wojtyła observed in 1958: "This theater . . . defends the young actors against developing a destructive individualism, because it will not let them impose on the text anything of their own; it gives them inner discipline. A group of people, collectively, somehow unanimously, subordinated to the great poetic word, evoke ethical associations; this solidarity of people in the word reveals particularly strongly and accentuates the reverence that is the point of departure for the rhapsodists' word and the secret of their style."[11]

10. Translators note: *Job* is available in English in *Karol Wojtyła, The Collected Plays and Writings on Theater,* translated with introductions by Boleslaw Taborski (Berkeley: University of California Press, 1987).

11. Cf. A. Jawień [Karol Wojtyła], "Rapsody Tesiaclecia," in *Tygodnik Powschechny* 12; English translation in Taborski, *The Collected Plays,* "Rhapsodies of the Millennium," pp. 383-87, especially p. 386. See also Mieczysław Kotlarczyk (ed.), *XXV lat Teatru Rapsodycznego w Krakowie 1941-1966* (Cracow). Cf. *O "Boskiej komedii" w Teatrze Rapsodycznym,* pp. 142-43; Piotr Jasień, *O Teatrze słowo,* pp. 126-29. Both articles are reprinted in *Tygodnik Powszchny* i(1952), where another text by A. Jawień appears, a reprint of the one cited at the beginning of this note.

Toward the middle of 1942, Wojtyła's artistic career was brought to an unexpected halt. Wojtyła had decided to prepare for the priesthood by studying theology in an underground seminary in the diocese of Cracow. There enter at this point of our story two great figures who probably had a decisive influence upon this choice of life. One was a prince of the Church, Cardinal Adam Stephan Sapieha, and the other was a clothes-maker in Debniki, Jan Tyranowski.

The Influence of Tyranowski

Tyranowski[12] was a leading layman in the Salesian parish of the region of Debniki, dedicated to St. Stanislaw Kotska. Wojtyła met him in 1940, perhaps on the twentieth day of February. There was at this time a terrible scarcity of priests, since so many had been murdered or imprisoned by the Germans. Seven of the priests of the parish were in concentration camps. Father Jan Mazarski was responsible for the parish. Because of these circumstances he had to rely upon the laity more than was usual. Tyranowski was a particular help to him.

Father Mazarski held meetings for young people every Sunday. They discussed the reasonableness of Christian faith and the common objections to it, and argued about every theological question. Tyranowski was always the leader of these meetings and soon took formal charge of them. This tailor from Debniki, who had had no regular theological instruction, lived a profound and personal mysticism. Wojtyła remembers that his language was rather conventional; the striking thing about him was that the doctrinal truths expressed in the various manuals from which he drew were for him *the object of normal experience.*

Having verified for himself the truth of the faith, Tyranowski was not afraid to propose to the young people that they must meet to engage together in living this same faith. He was the leader of the "living rosary" in the parish — groups of fifteen young men (the same number as the

12. Wojtyła dedicated his first published writing to Tyranowski: "Apostoł," in *Tygodnik Powszchny* 5/35. This is a commemoration which also contains autobiographical information. An Italian translation of this article is found among Wojtyła's booklets: *I miei amici* (Bologna: CSEO, 1980), which contains other articles published by *Tygodnik*. On Tyranowski, see Williams, *The Mind of John Paul II*, pp. 77ff. In Cracow, where many people still remember Tyranowski, it is not difficult to find out a great deal about his life and his spirituality.

stations of the rosary) who committed themselves to a friendship directed toward Christian perfection. They covenanted to help each other in the diverse situations of life and above all to assume responsibility for walking together toward Christian perfection. Every group of fifteen constituted a "living crown" of the rosary. Tyranowski took responsibility for all of these meetings, and he built up the general character of the group.

Tyranowski had a great theoretical interest in psychology, and also, to judge from what his pupils say, a great practical aptitude for it. These are the two elements of his character which we find reflected in Wojtyła's works. Tyranowski's theological interests were directed to mysticism, especially its sources in the master of French spirituality, Adolphe Alfred Tanquerey, as well as the great Carmelite mystics, St. John of the Cross, St. Teresa of Avila, and St. Teresa of Lisieux.[13] It was probably through Tyranowski's influence that Wojtyła chose to do his doctorate in theology on St. John of the Cross; he would be enduringly influenced by Carmelite spirituality, so much so that, during an uncertain phase of his spiritual evolution, he considered entering Carmel.

And That of Sapieha

The other great figure whom Wojtyła encountered in this period was Adam Stephan Sapieha.[14] Archbishop Sapieha was descended from one of the most noble families of Polish princes. His grandfather, Prince Leone Sapieha, had taken part in the 1830 uprising against the Russians. His father, Adam Sapieha, participated in the revolt of 1863, after which he represented

13. Tyranowski also made use of some of Bernanos' works, and particularly the work of Piotr Semenenko, one of the three founders of the order of the Resurrectionists.

14. On Sapieha, see Williams, *The Mind of John Paul II,* pp. 81-92. See also Karol Wojtyła, "Adam Stefan Sapieha, metropolita krakowski oraz duchowieństwo Archidiecezji w okresie ciemnej nocy okupacji," *Notificationes e Curia Metropolitana Cracoviensi* 5-6 (1966), pp. 122-26; Stulecie urodzin ksie-cia kardynała Adama Stefana Sapiehy. Discourses given on Vatican Radio on 12 May 1967 and then published in *Notificationes e Curia Metropolitana Cracoviensi* 5-6 (1968), pp. 94-96; Dwudziestopieciolecie śmierci śp. ksiedzacia kardynała Adama Saphiehy, metropolity krakowskiego. Przemówienie wygłoszone podczas odsłoniecia pomnika przy Bazylice OO. Franciszkanów w Krakowie dnia 8 maja 1976 r. *Notificationes e Curia Metropolitana Cracoviensi* 1 (1976), pp. 187-88; W zwiazku z.25-ta rocznica śmierci kardynał Stefana Sapiehy metropolity krakowskiego, *Notificationes e Curia Metropolitana Cracoviensi* 1 (1976), pp. 40-41.

the provisional Government in Paris and in London and defended the autonomy of Galizia, working in the High Chamber in the Parliament of Vienna.[15] Adam Stephan Sapieha was a man of extraordinary energy and personal courage. During Pilsudski's dictatorship he did not hesitate to oppose the dictator, and he became a national hero by defending against Latinization the Uniate minorities who used the Greek-Orthodox rite; Latinization was being forced on them for political reasons. After the Nazi invasion, despite the strict German control of his official communications, Sapieha attempted twice to warn the Vatican about Nazi plans to exterminate Polish nationals and the Jewish minority. In 1940 he asked Prof. Bochenski, a professor of philosophy at the Catholic University of Fribourg and a Swiss citizen, to memorize a message full of the atrocious details of the crimes committed by the occupying army. A second attempt was made through an Italian chaplain in February of 1942, but nothing came of it. The Vatican did not recognize the importance of the message or, perhaps, was powerless to intervene.

In the meantime, Sapieha was the leader of the moral resistance of the nation against the Nazis, and committed all of the diocesan resources in addition to his personal resources to assist the persecuted and to support both the armed struggle[16] and, more importantly, the cultural resistance, which was sustained by "organic work." Within the cultural sphere, the preparation of a new generation of priests seemed to Sapieha to be of greatest importance for the future of Poland. For this reason, despite his many commitments, he preoccupied himself centrally with the underground seminary. In the decisive days when the Germans during their effort to abandon Cracow, were seizing every able-bodied man, he brought together the seminarians in the archbishop's house to protect them against

15. Cracow, an autonomous city from 1815 until 1846 when it was occupied by the Austrians, has a special place in Polish history in the 19th century. The Austrians, alone among those who have occupied Poland, were Catholic, and did not persecute the Church. The Hapsburg Empire, moreover, was a pluri-national Empire and was relatively tolerant of the diverse cultures which lived together within it. Cracow became a point of refuge for Polish national culture and gave birth to the utopian dream of a constitutional transformation of the Austro-Hungarian Empire into a Triple Monarchy: Austrian, Hungarian, and Slavo-Polish. This cultural atmosphere explains good relations between the great patriotic families such as the Sapiehas and Austria-Hungary.

16. The most effective thing the Cardinal did was to authorize the issue of baptism certificates for some Jews who would otherwise have perished in the massacre. The young seminarian Wojtyła naturally took part in the various forms of assistance given to those who were persecuted.

being called up. It was in this way that, after two years of theological instruction, undertaken in free time from exhausting labor in the workshops, Wojtyła was able to begin a normal course of theological study. The Rector of the underground seminary was the Reverend Jan Piwowarczyk. But Wojtyła was entrusted to the care of Reverend Kazimierz Klosaka, a student of natural philosophy. Klosaka had him read his first work of metaphysics, *Ontologja czyli Metafizyka*, a treatise by Kazimierz Wais. This book, which reflects the influence of transcendental Thomism, the school of Louvain which attempted to reconcile Kant and St. Thomas, is still famous among Polish students, largely for its nearly insuperable difficulty.

After the Communists came to power, Sapieha realized immediately that culture would be the decisive battleground between them. This feature of Polish Catholicism distinguishes its choices from those of other national Churches. From the beginning, the Polish bishops decided not to petition on their own behalf against the regime which violated their ancient rights, guaranteed by tradition and confirmed in the Concordat of 1925. They chose instead to take a position in support of fundamental human and national rights, *renouncing any particular reclamation* which would have indicated that they made a distinction, not to say a contradistinction, between human rights and religious rights, between the inspiration of the nation and that of the Church. This program, which was initially criticized as minimalist, would in the course of time prove its own justice.

The Post-war Intellectual Movement

In March 1945 Sapieha created a new weekly journal, *Tygodnik Powszechny*. He entrusted its direction to Jerzy Turowicz, who eventually became emblematic as a leader of free Polish culture. The year after the war saw the birth of a monthly journal, *Znak*, also produced in Cracow and initiated by Sapieha. The organizers behind it were Irena Slawinska, Stefan Swiezawski, and Czeslaw Zgorzelski. There came about informally within the two journals an important intellectual movement in which Wojtyła soon took part. He had one particular function which went beyond his assiduous collaboration in the two magazines. It would therefore be worthwhile to pause for a moment over the group.

Turowicz came from the *Odrodzenie* movement, which in pre-war Poland was the more European and less nationalist wing of Polish Catholicism. *Odrodzenie* was naturally affiliated to the great national tradition, but it most of all desired to learn from the more culturally advanced experience of French Catholicism; it was orientated toward Paris and profoundly shared the aspirations of that culture. After the war especially, this group is represented by familiar names such as Mounier, Maritain, Marcel, Bernanos, and Péguy. French was the foreign language which the editors of *Znak* knew best. *Znak* may in fact have modelled itself after *Espirit*. Wyszynski belonged to *Odrodzenie*. It seems that, after the Russian invasion, the Polish Church rapidly decided to allow itself to be steered in the future by its more progressive wing. Yet there is a great difference between the outcomes of Polish progressivism and European and especially French progressivism. It is reasonable to ask about the source of the difference between them.

In an article which appeared in the first number of *Tygodnik Powszechny* and entitled "Ku Katolickiej Polsche," Jan Piwowarczyk indicated one of its important features.[17] Piwowarczyk underlined the fact that Christians had no reason to wish to reconstruct the economic structure of old Poland. What was needed was not reconstruction but fundamental restructuring. Catholics had a culture capable of change and of assessing clearly how such restructuring could be brought about. Catholics do not rely on Marxist analysis for criteria by which to comprehend reality. In an article published shortly afterward in *Znak*, Stanislaw Stomma contrasted the sterility of the social initiatives found in French Catholicism with the robust social presence of Catholicism in Poland.[18] For all its greatness, French Catholic culture had not brought the masses with it, whereas Polish Catholicism had retained its connection with the people. It is also significant that *Znak* and *Tygodnik Powszechny* were held back from engaging in a more intimate and potentially destructive dialogue with Marxism by the fact that a group of Catholics who came from the extreme right and fascist O.N.R annexed that ground with decisive and aggressive demagogy. Boleslaw Piasecki, who had been the editor of the O.N.R journal *Falanga,* suddenly after the end of the war began to assemble the Catholic collaborationists who belonged to the Pax movement within a new newspaper, *Dzis i jutro.*

Beyond all of these factors, however, one must not underestimate the overarching authority of Wyszynski or the intellectual guidance exerted

---

17. *Tygodnik Powszechny* 1 (3 March 1945).
18. "Maksymalne i minimalne tendencjé społeczne w Polsce," *Znak* 1. Stanisław Stomma is the president of the Primate's Social Council.

by Wojtyła. The result was a unique form of religious and cultural identity which is difficult for those who have no close contact with Polish Catholicism to understand. Polish culture expresses in large part the position of the progressivists in the 1950s and 60s, but without their Integrist involutions, and without the typical tendencies toward secularist and quasi-Marxist or even markedly dualistic positions which defined much of Western progressivism.

In a sense the fundamental cultural hypothesis which directed cultural progressivism was that of the superiority of religious existentialism to atheism and within that a general understanding of the history of contemporary culture which made existentialism the point beyond which it could not go. The progressive culture had a coherent philosophy of existence which began from an unbiased analysis of the questions and of the evidence present in human life. On this basis, it posited that it is necessarily superior to have a religion than to be an atheist. Existentialism would be ultimately forced to choose between religion, which gives a stable meaning to the world, and despair. Since the latter is unlivable, it would follow that the existentialist crisis leads back to the affirmation of a religious culture.

In the West this development was blocked by the confluence of existentialism and Marxism. Jean-Paul Sartre's writings are an exemplary case of this trajectory. The addition of Marxism to existentialism gave it an historical concreteness which it had lacked and, at the same time, restored to Marxism an extraordinary vitality and cultural fascination. This perspective, which flourished in the West in the late 1960s and 1970s, began to draw progressive Catholics beyond the limits of their faith. In attempting to initiate with Marxism the same dialogue into which it had entered with atheist existentialism, Western Catholicism risked losing its sense of identity. Because it deconstructs human beings into the social structures which constitute them, Marxism has a peculiar philosophical point of departure: it thinks that the responsibilities toward human beings and the basic humanisms which were the main feature of both atheist and religious existentialism are naive. The dialogue therefore starts off on the wrong foot and the conversation ends before it can begin.

Things took a different turn in Poland. There the confrontation of atheistic existentialism and religious existentialism was won by religious existentialism, and Marxism, which had come to the field of anthropology with Kolakowski and Schaff, was caught up in this defeat. It was in this context that Wojtyła's philosophy began to develop. But these same circumstances became the crucible for his mature philosophy, which, reflecting upon the essential theme of action, has struck at the root of the notion that a Marxist philosophy of praxis is something higher than a philosophy of conscience. Here, too, the original inspiration of the Second Vatican Council was able to develop with greater freedom and to achieve a special pertinence at the global level when the crisis of Marxism brought glaringly to light the dead end into which Western Catholic progressivism had driven.[19]

Wojtyła at the Angelicum and in France

Wojtyła was ordained priest by Cardinal Sapieha on 1 November 1946, and celebrated his first Mass on November 3 in the parochial church of St. Stanislaw Kotska in Debniki. Immediately afterward he was registered at the Angelicum, the Dominican faculty of Theology in Rome, in order to prepare for the doctorate in theology. He was to gain this doctorate in June 1948 with a thesis on the question of faith in the thought of St. John of the Cross.[20] Among those teaching at the Angelicum were Massimiliano de Furstenberg, Mario Ciappi, and Pierre-Paul Philippe,[21] with whom the young Wojtyła developed his thesis. The great personage who dominated the faculty was Father Reginald Garrigou-Lagrange, incontrovertible authority on both philosophical and theological Thomism as well as an attentive student of St. John of the Cross. Wojtyła received from Garrigou-Lagrange rigorous training in the most traditional form of Thomism. But a careful reading of his doctoral thesis indicates that, from the time he began to study philosophy, he had an affinity for a variety of different interpretations of Thomism. At the Catholic University of Louvain in Belgium, for example, there was an effort to bring about reconciliation between Thomism and modern thought (particularly that of Kant). In France, Maritain and Gilson were giving Thomism an existential dimen-

19. On the dialogue between Catholicism and Marxism and also on the more recent history of philosophy in Poland, cf. J. Tischner, *La svolta storica* (Bologna: CSEO, 1981).

20. The thesis was only published in 1979: Karol Wojtyła, *La fede secondo San Giovanni della Croce*, Pontifical University of St. Thomas (Rome: Herder, 1979). Published in English as *Faith According to St. John of the Cross*, trans. Jordan Aumann, O.P. (San Francisco: Ignatius Press, 1981).

21. They all later became Cardinals.

sion by maintaining that Thomas's principal philosophical contributions were the distinction between essence and existence and his legitimation of a certain eidetic intuition in the interpretation of the process of abstraction.[22] These latter perceptions would be reinforced when, shortly after completing his doctorate, Wojtyła was sent to France to study the life and the pastoral methods of Jeunnesse Ouvrier Catholique. It is likely that he also came into closer contact with existential Thomism in these years, for we find many traces of it in his thought. The influence of Garrigou-Lagrange, however, remained paramount. One might observe that Wojtyła's works do not, in fact, take a direct position on the intellectual controversies which run through Catholic thought; he limits himself to indications and suggestions within an authentically personal exploration which will eventually flow into an original construction.

In an article in which he speaks of his experience in France,[23] Wojtyła has given us precious documentation of his spiritual situation at the beginning of his priestly mission and also of his intellectual creativity. Like all Poles, he had an immense admiration for the intellectual products of French Catholicism. Precisely for this reason, he was all the more shaken by the discovery that France was only nominally Catholic. How was this possible, and what could be done? What was most needful, Wojtyła reasoned, was for the riches of faith to become an attitude of life, shaping the fundamental disposition toward existence. The rock upon which the French Church risked shipwreck was the unity between culture and life. A new style of priestly and laical presence in the world would therefore be necessary. In Poland such a presence would keep the masses from apostasy; in France it would have to bring the people back to the faith.

It would be hazardous to suggest that in these notes Wojtyła had already formulated the fundamental concepts which he would lay out in his interpretation of the Council: as, for example, the concept of the self-realization of the Church or the concept of the enrichment of the faith. Nonetheless it is certain that his experience in France contributed to the reflections which would ultimately lead to such conclusions.

---

22. It is interesting to note that the main objection which Father Garrigou-Lagrange made to Wojtyła's work concerned the fact that he refused to use the term Object in relation to God. Garrigou-Lagrange followed the thesis as a correlator, and made many other observations which are set out in the appendix to the Italian edition.

23. Karol Wojtyła, "Mission de France," *Tygodnik Powschechny* 5/9.

KAROL WOJTYŁA

The Cultural Ambience of the Universities of Cracow and of Lublin

For some time after his return to Cracow Wojtyła was assigned to pastoral work in St. Floriano, but Cardinal Sapieha soon decided that he should prepare for an academic vocation by taking a second doctorate. Despite the young priest's expressed preference for pastoral work, the Cardinal was adamant, and Wojtyła began to work toward a doctorate in philosophy. It was concerned with the possibility of grounding a Christian ethics upon Max Scheler's philosophical system. Wojtyła's answer to this question would be negative, but this study stimulated the enterprise of a reform of phenomenology which was to form the basis of all his later philosophical work.[24] His critical approach to the philosophy of existence did not renounce Thomism but rather made it an essential key to the interpretation of phenomenology. This would be a principal factor distinguishing Wojtyła's position from the usual direction of religious existentialism, conferring upon it a certain speculative robustness. Wojtyła's thesis was approved by a committee which comprised Professors Swiezawski, Wicher, and Ingarden.

Swiezawski was one of the major proponents of an existential Thomism in Poland and had also translated into Polish the treatise "On Man" from the *Summa Theologica*. Rather later, Swiezawski, having developed a great estimation and friendship for his one-time pupil, participated as a *peritus* at the Second Vatican Council. At the end of the Council Swiezawski attempted to set out an account of the problems and emerging tasks of philosophy in *La Philosophie a l'heure du Concile*,[25] written in collaboration with Jerzy Kalinowski. It was to Kalinowski and Swiezawski that Maritain directed his famous *Lettera sulla filosofia nell'ora del Concilio,* in which he strongly underlined the role of intuitive experience in philosophy, as against a philosophy simply understood as a catena of compelling logical deductions. "The misfortune of ordinary scholastic teaching," Maritain wrote in that letter, "and above all that of the manuals, is in practice to neglect this essential intuitive element and

24. *Ocena możliwości zbudowania etyki chrześcijańskiej przy założeniach systemu Maksa Schelera* (Lublin, 1959). The work did not gain an enthusiastic reception, but was greeted critically. Cf. Józef Keller, "Zwodnicze rozwiazanie źle postawionego problemu." The Italian translation, entitled *Max Scheler,* was published in 1980, in a Logos edition, with an interesting introduction by Cardinal Palazzini.
25. Société d'Éditions Internationales (Paris, 1965).

to replace it with a pseudo-dialectic of concepts and formulas. There is nothing doing so long as the intellect does not see, so long as the philosopher or student philosopher do not have an intellectual intuition of essence."[26] This is perhaps the closest approach which Maritain makes toward a phenomenological position which recognizes the indispensability of a preliminary eidetic intuition for the construction of philosophical knowledge. It is possible that Karol Wojtyła meditated on this observation, written to an old teacher of his,[27] during the years in which he was preparing his own major work, *The Acting Person;* in any case it was appropriate to the climate of research into new philosophical tasks at the time of the Council.

Another of the examiners on his second doctoral thesis was destined to have a great influence on Wojtyła's future development. This was Roman Ingarden. One of Husserl's earliest students, Ingarden always refused to follow his teacher in the idealistic direction of phenomenology. His monumental *Streit um die Existenz der Welt* ("The Controversy about the Existence of the World") upholds a realistic interpretation of phenomenology. Moreover, Ingarden manifested a particular interest in the intuition of value in ethical and aesthetic life; his way of interpreting phenomenology was thus very close to Scheler's. His phenomenology was not only a detached preparation of the material of intellectual intuition but also a passionate engagement in the life-world, a heroic attempt to encounter the truth and to live in accordance with it. His pupils remember the prolonged discussions which took place in his seminars, when he proposed a definition of the thing itself and the phenomenal reality which is given to eidetic intuition, practicing phenomenology in a thoroughly Socratic manner. Over time, Wojtyła and Ingarden established an important intellectual alliance; many disciples of the one would be disciples of the other. The diffusion of Wojtyła's thought over the international philosophical scene came about largely through the work of an old friend of Ingarden, Anna-Teresa Tymieniecka.

In 1954 Wojtyła began to teach in the Faculty of Philosophy in the Catholic University of Lublin. After two years he was given the professorial

26. Cf. Jacques Maritain, *Approaches sans entraves.*

27. It is interesting to observe that Swiezawski was a student of Adjukiewicz and, above all, of Twardowski. Twardowski, in turn, was a disciple of Brentano, and moved in a circle of philosophical interests which have many close points of connection with the problems of phenomenology.

chair of Ethics. Wojtyła will always remain deeply tied to this university. Only after his election as Supreme Pontiff did he agree to give up teaching. He was replaced by one of his most brilliant students, Professor Tadeusz Styczeń.

When the young Wojtyła entered it, two main types of philosophy were prevalent at the Catholic University of Lublin: traditional Thomism, represented by the Professor of Metaphysics, Stanislaw Adamczyk, and existential Thomism with an opening to phenomenology, represented by Prof. Swiezawski, whom we have already met, and who was teaching the history of mediaeval philosophy. Quite soon a different variety of Thomism would be affirmed here, a Polish version of the transcendental Thomism of Louvain, and elaborated by Mieszysław A. Krapiec, mainly after publication in 1959 of his book, *Teoria analogii bytu.*[28] Among the professors who worked in close contact with Wojtyła several are worthwhile of special mention: Jerzy Kalinowski, a philosopher of law who moved later to Lyons; Marian Kurdziałek, a historian of ancient philosophy; Feliks Bednarski, a student of ethics (who was later transferred to Rome); and Stanisław Kamiński, professor of epistemology. Among all of these divergent methodologies, each of which contributed to a vibrant intellectual interchange, the Lublin philosophy school was united in these years in a fundamental commitment to the defense of human rights against all theories which would dissolve the unique dignity of human beings in the infinite currents of history, and also in the decision to exhibit the profound alliance between human reason and Christian faith. There was thus a fundamentally personalistic philosophy, Thomistic in inspiration (in a more rigid sense in Krapiec's case and a more open one in Wojtyła's) but welcoming dialogue with any thought which took seriously the problem of being human.

Pastoral Engagement

After 1958 a new commitment fell on the shoulders of the young Wojtyła, one which would remove him from his studies and his apostolate among students which he was able to conjoin with innate suitability to his University position.

In July 1958 Wojtyła learned that he had been named auxiliary bishop

28. Lublin: KUL, 1959.

of Cracow, and shortly afterward he was consecrated. The Primate's summons came while he was on holiday with a group of young men in Mazuria, in the Lake district. After accepting the nomination, Wojtyła asked to be able to stay for a little longer with his friends, so that they could finish their summer's camping. In June of 1962, after the death of Msgr. Baziak, Wojtyła became the chief administrator of the diocese of Cracow and later Archbishop and Cardinal. Finally, on 16 October, 1978, Karol Wojtyła was elected Pope and took the name of John Paul II.

First, however, it is important to say a word about the method and the particular quality of his pastoral work with young people. In essence it was based upon the intuition which he had during his journey through France: faith must become life. This can happen only through a fellowship which shares with young people all the events of their lives, and which contains a fundamental concern for their truth and human authenticity. Within a fellowship which is orientated toward the deepest human destiny, it would be possible to teach that the more that one learns from the other, from the miracle of life, the more God will become present in oneself. Through such a fellowship which awakens the human in man, one is led to the awareness of the greatness of his own vocation and to engage both creativity and patient generosity, progressively extending the presence of a youthful ambience in the Church.

Wojtyła began his pastoral work (although it would be better to speak of friendship for life than of pastoral work) with some, and gradually this friendship/pastoral work embraced the entire nation.[29] The young men called him "Uncle," which makes one think of a parental spirituality which is very discreet but also demanding. In a special way Wojtyła was intent upon accompanying the young men at the moment of their passage into adulthood, at their encounter with work, and the creation of a family.

---

29. A particularly pregnant and moving example of Wojtyła's manner of sharing a common destiny with his friends is given in his commemoration of Jerzy Ciesielski. Cf. "Wspomnienie o Jerzym Ciesielskim," in *Tygodnik Powszechny* 24.

A Way through the Principal Works

It was this experience of life with young people which brought his first original work of philosophy, *Love and Responsibility*, to birth. Using a phenomenological method and the light of Christian ethics, it describes the decisive experience of love and of falling in love in order to demonstrate that the Christian conception of value fully appreciates the human value of sensuality. The demonstration springs from a profound analysis of human experience and calls for existential verification.

Love and Responsibility appeared in 1960.[30] The experience of the Second Vatican Council immediately followed. Afterward, Wojtyła wrote his principal philosophical work, *The Acting Person*,[31] which is the fullest formulation of his philosophy. This work appeared in 1969, and shortly afterward, on 16-17 October 1970, the book was discussed by the entire teaching faculty in a special conference at the Catholic University of Lublin.[32] Wojtyła, then Cardinal, in his introduction to the work, invited all participants to express themselves with complete frankness and not to say anything just to please him. With great tact and also with absolute intellectual honesty the more orthodox Thomists among the faculty, especially Krapiec, expressed their reservations concerning what they perceived to be a disrespectful mixture of Thomism and phenomenology; they argued the necessity of achieving the same objective of founding a more adequate personalism by purifying St. Thomas's thought from successive interpretations which had reduced it to Aristotelianism.[33] Among the

30. *Miłość i Odpowiedzialność* (Cracow: Znak, 1960).

31. *Osobo i Czyn* (Cracow: Polskie Towarzystwo Teologiczne, 1969). The work was actually produced over time, and parts of it had already been published. These are "Osoba i Czyn w aspekcie świadomości in the anthology *Pastori et Magistro;* "Praca zbiorowa wydana dla uczczenia jubileuszu 50-lecia kapłaństwa Jego Ekscelencji Ksiedza Biskupa Doktora Piotra Kałwy, Profesora i Wielkiego Kanclerza" (Lublin: KUL, 1966); "Osoba i Czyn. Refleksyjne funkcjonowanie świadomości i jej emocjonalizacja," *Studia Theologica Varsaviensia,* 6, pp. 101-119; "Osoba i Czyn na tle dynamizmu człowieka," in Bohdan Bejze (ed.), *O Bogu i o człowieku. Problemy filozoficzne* (Warsaw, 1968), pp. 204-26.

32. The result of the discussions was published by *Analecta Cracoviensia* (1973/1974), with the title "Dyskusia nad dziełem kardynała Karola Wojtyła 'Osoba i Czyn', Z zagadnień filozoficznyk."

33. This precaution against modernizing interpretations of St. Thomas can be seen as the inherited influence of Garrigou-Lagrange. In Wojtyła perhaps the diffidence about a modernizing interpretation is accompanied by an explicit conviction that it is necessary to integrate St. Thomas and to develop in an original way those facets of the Christian philosophy which he did not examine.

younger professors, or at least some of them, the book provoked great interest and enthusiastic support. Noteworthy in this category are Stanislaw Grygiel, Jozef Tischner, Marian Jaworski, and Tadeusz Styczen.[34]

Three years later, Wojtyła's book about the Council, *Sources of Renewal,*[35] was published. It was to serve as a fundamental text for the Synod of Cracow, which would, in turn, prove decisive in the actualization of the Council in Poland. Between 1970 and 1978, drawing on the many critical observations which others had offered, Wojtyła tried to clarify his terminology and to explain himself more precisely in a series of lectures at international conferences and, above all, through his collaboration with the *Analecta Husserliana.* In some ways, he softened the elements which had attempted to reconcile Thomism and phenomenology, and highlighted instead what is perhaps its most original thinking, its character as a new philosophy which draws upon some of the main elements of Thomism and of phenomenology.[36] This brings us to the new American edition of *The Acting Person,* which appeared in 1979, under the supervision of Anna Teresa Tymieniecka. This publication gave Wojtyła's thought worldwide diffusion, although the English translation

34. Cf. Stanisław Grygiel, "Hermeneutyka czynu oraz nowy model świadomości," *Analecta Cracoviensia* (1973/1974), pp. 139-51; Tadeusz Styczen, "Metoda antopologii filozoficznej w "Osobie i Czynie" kard. Karola Wojtyła," ibid., pp. 107-15; Josef Tischner, "Metodologiczna strona dzieła *Osoba i Czyn,*" ibid., pp. 85-89; Marian Jaworski, "Koncepcja antropologii filozoficnej w ujeciu kard. Karola Wojtyly (Prába odczytanu w oparciu o studium *Osoba i Czyn*)," ibid., pp. 91-106.

35. *U Podstaw Odnowy. Studium o realizacji Vaticanum II* (Cracow: Polski Towarzystwo Teologiczne, 1972); English translation by P. S. Falla, *Sources of Renewal: The Implementation of the Vatican Council* (Collins, 1980).

36. Cf. "The Personal Structure of Self-Determination in Tommaso d'Aquino nel suo VII Centenario" (Acts of the International Congress in Rome/Naples, 17-24 April 1974), pp. 379-90; "La struttra generale dell'autodecisione," *Asprenas,* 4, pp. 337-46; "The Intentional Act and the Human Act that is Act and Experience," in *The Crisis of Culture, Analecta Husserliana,* vol. 5 (Dordrecht, 1975), pp. 269-80; "Osoba: podmiot i wspólnota," in *Roczniki Filozoficzne,* vol. 24, fasc. 2, pp. 5-39; "Das Problem der Erfahrung in der Ethik," in *W 700-lecie śmierci św. Tomasza z Akwinu. Próba uwspółcześnienia jego filozofi,* ed. Stanisław Kamiński (Lublin), pp. 265-88; "Teoria e Prassi nella filosofia della persona umana," *Sapienza,* 29/4, pp. 377-84; "Participation or alienation?" in *The Self and the Other, Analecta Husserliana,* vol. 6 (Dordrecht, 1977), pp. 61-73; "Il problema del costituirsi della cultura attraverso la "praxis" umana," in *Rivista di filosofia neoscolastica,* 69, fasc. 3, pp. 513-24; "Subjectivity and the Irreducible in Man in The Human Being in Action," *Analecta Husserliana,* vol. 7 (Dordrecht, 1978), pp. 107-114.

has been criticized as excessively interpretative and unfaithful to the original.[37]

In March 1976 Wojtyła was called to preach the spiritual exercises in the Vatican under the reigning Pope, Paul VI. This experience gave rise to his booklet *The Sign of Contradiction,* which summarized his spiritual vision.[38]

It is not possible to conclude this chapter without calling attention at least briefly to Wojtyła's extensive writing and publications, especially for the monthlies *Znak* and *Tygodnik Powszechny.* Through his many articles and contributions to discussion, Wojtyła rapidly became a leader within the group of intellectuals associated with these journals, a group which had a leading voice in Polish Catholic culture. At a key turning point, their influence was significant in turning back the attraction in Eastern Europe to supine imitation of the theology and culture of the West, and in convincing many of the possibility that they might be able to create an original critique of the European way of life.[39]

It remains finally to say a word about Wojtyła's poetry. The first known document appeared in 1946 in a Carmelite journal in Cracow, published as an anonymous collection of verses called *Song to a Healing God.*[40] There would follow, under the pseudonyms of Andrzej Jawien and Stanislaw Andrzej Grudi, numerous other poetic compositions, the *Canticles on the Splendor of the Sea* and *The Mother,* which were finished in 1950, and *Reflecting on the Homeland,* published in *Znak* in 1979.[41]

Wojtyła's many-sided personality encompasses a philosopher, a mystic, a theologian, and, above all, a pastor and man of action. There is a profound

37. In particular, Tymieniecka's edition is criticized for having disregarded "subjectum" and "the upokeimenon," i.e., the exact philosophical terminology, in the Aristotelian-Thomistic tradition. This is an important point for Wojtyła's philosophy, as we will see.

38. Milan: Vita e Pensiero, 1977. The Polish edition appeared in 1976, *Znak,* Któremu sprzeciwiać sie beda. Rekolekcje w Watykanie, Rzym-Watykan Rzym Stolica Apostolska 5-12/III/1976 (Poznań, 1976). See also the recension of Stanisław Grygiel, "Doświadczenie i świadectwo," in *Tygodnik Powszechny* 31.

39. These articles were published by Wojtyła in *Znak* and *Tygognik Powszechny;* there are collected in a single volume, *Aby Chrystus sie nami posługiwal* (Cracow: Znak, 1979).

40. "Głos Karmelu" (Marzo, 1946). It is Williams who attributes these anonymous pieces to Wojtyła: see *The Mind of John Paul II,* p. 109. I have not found definitive evidence.

41. Andrzej Jawień, "Pieśń o blasku wody," in *Tygodnik Powszechny* 6 (1950); Andrzej Jawień, "Matka," in *Tygodnik Powszechny* 6 (1950); Stanisław Andrzej Gruda, "Myślac Ojczyzna . . . ," in *Znak* 31 (1979), pp. 1-2.

unity of soul in this many-sidedness. This unity is not imposed by the force of will intent on enclosing the many dimensions of life within a single predetermined scheme but, rather, derives from ardent faithfulness to the gift of God — a God who is in himself wonderfully coherent and who asks nothing but to be mirrored with fidelity by human consciousness.

3. Karol Wojtyła's Philosophical Formation

The years between the end of the War and 1960 (when *Love and Responsibility* was published) became for Karol Wojtyła a sort of philosophical apprenticeship. During this time he went first to the Theology Faculty of the Angelicum in Rome, which was particularly shaped by the figure of Father Reginald Garrigou-Lagrange, and then to the faculty of the Jagellonian University in Cracow, whose most respected member was Roman Ingarden, friend of Husserl and the father of Polish phenomenology. Garrigou-Lagrange introduced Wojtyła to St. Thomas and to St. John of the Cross, and Ingarden (and the other Cracow phenomenologists) made him aware of Scheler and of modern philosophy, especially that of Kant. In this chapter we will follow the progressive formation of Wojtyła's original philosophical position, through his dialogue with St. John of the Cross, with Scheler, and with Kant. We will give a section to each of these philosophers and their relation to Wojtyła, concluding with his eventual return to Thomas, which followed each of his meetings with modern philosophy. This return, upon which he meditated critically, was the means by which Wojtyła created an original philosophical construction.

Wojtyła and St. John of the Cross

The doctoral thesis which Wojtyła submitted for examination at the Angelicum Theology Faculty was his first theoretical work. It was called *The
Doctrine of Faith According to St. John of the Cross*.[1] His choice of theme
developed partly because his human and priestly vocation came to maturity
under Jan Tyranowski's influence, and Tyranowski's masters, the two saints
who had enabled him to understand his own mystical experience, were St.
John of the Cross and St. Teresa of Avila. Perhaps it was from Tyranowski
that Wojtyła derived a natural tendency to read in St. John of the Cross a
kind of phenomenology of mystical experience.

Garrigou-Lagrange evidently influenced this choice of theme as well,
for he too was a student of St. John of the Cross.[2] Indeed, during this period
he was attempting to apply his knowledge of the Spanish mystic in defining
a new priestly spirituality which would fit the questions and the problems
of a world left devastated by the War. He continually and urgently sought
the presence of the absolute within everyday life, that is to say, *a presence
of mystical contemplation in the world*.[3] This is a little-known side of Garrigou-Lagrange. Garrigou-Lagrange is usually remembered as a defender
of a rather rigid and plodding Thomistic orthodoxy, but, from this vantage
point, he shows an outstanding modernity.

Wojtyła's doctoral work on the literature of the problem of faith in St.
John of the Cross had two main intellectual touchstones (apart from the
work of Garrigou-Lagrange). The first was represented by an article written
by Labourdette, *La foi théologale et la connaissance mystique d'après S. Jean
de la Crois;*[4] the other by Baruzi's book *Jean de la Croix et le problème de*

---

1. *Doctrina de fide apud S. Joannen a Cruce*, trans. into English by Jordan Aumann,
O.P., as *Faith According to St. John of the Cross* (San Francisco: Ignatius Press, 1981).
2. Among numerous articles and minor pieces see, for example, Réginald Garrigou-
Lagrange, *Les trois âges de la vie intérieure, prélude de celle du ciel*, 2 vols. (Paris: Cerf,
1938), and *Perfection chrétienne et contemplation selon St. Thomas d'Auin et St. Jean de
la Croix*, 2 vols. (Saint Maximin, 1923). See also *Les trois conversions et les trois voies*
(Paris: Cerf, 1933).
3. *De sanctificatione sacerdotium secundum exigentias temporis nostri* (Turin, 1947)
and *De unione sacerdotis cum Christo Sacerdote* (Turin, 1948). Wojtyła will make the
theme of priestly holiness his own. Cf., among other pieces, "Służebność kapłaństwa,"
in *Duszpasterz Polski Zagranica* 26 (1975), pp. 389ff.; La sainteté comme carte d'identité,"
Seminarium 30, pp. 167ff.
4. In *Revue Thomiste* 42 (1936-37), pp. 16ff. On Labourdette see also "Le développe-
ment vital de la foi théologale," in *Revue Thomiste* 43 (1937), pp. 101ff.

l'experience mystique.[5] The problem which both of these works attempted to confront was the relation between dogmatic and mystical faith. Baruzi tended to oppose them, and, consequently, he also tended to oppose St. John's mystical conception of faith to that found in St. Thomas. On the other hand, Labourdette, a disciple of Garrigou-Lagrange, tried to reconcile St. Thomas and St. John of the Cross.

This was also Wojtyła's intention. He strongly emphasized the personal character of the encounter between God and man which engenders faith. Declarations of faith are orientated toward the proper object of faith, which transcends them. Mystical experience is a God-given experience in which creaturely boundaries transcend themselves toward God. Faith in a dogmatic sense and faith in a mystical sense are two aspects of a unitary process by which creaturely limits are transcended; in a certain sense, they represent a single faculty of theological transcendence.[6]

For St. John of the Cross faith is a proportionate means which makes the human encounter with God possible. At this point one encounters a difficulty for Thomistic interpretation: according to St. Thomas, faith is a virtue of the intellect which does not involve the will, whereas for St. John, the faith which establishes a *"proporcion de semejanza"* between God and the human being is an obscure faith in which the intellect knows that, in the "night of faith," it has to give up attempting to know. It is possible to interpret these positions as reflecting an opposition between an intellectual and a vitalistic view of faith: a conception of the faith which anchors it to the truth that man can know, and which begins from meditation upon finite things versus a conception of faith which makes it a capacity for the infinite unbounded by the limits of the intellect (a little like the Hegelian 'Vernunft').

Wojtyła observes quite rightly that unitive faith, a faith enriched by the gift of the Spirit, and in particular by a gift of the intellect, and by being an organic part of the intentional tendency of the person toward God, involves all his faculties and virtues. This is living faith. Moreover, the obscurity of faith does not contradict the engagement of the intellect. In fact, the intellect, in the obscurity of the night of faith, recognizes the non-objectivizability of its proper object, which is God himself. It realizes that the highest wisdom one can achieve about God is knowing that one

5. Paris: Félix Alcan, 1924.
6. Cf. *The Mind of John Paul II*, pp. 106ff.; K. Wojtyła, *Faith According to St. John of the Cross*, pp. 245, 264.

cannot objectivize one's knowledge of Him. It recognizes that God does not come to be known as an object is known, but as a person is. As a person, he can be known only in a reciprocal relation of self-giving. In this way a human being dwells within God's personal interior and God within him, without the two being merged and without the difference between God and the human person being obscured. It is in this sense that we must interpret the intense affirmation of St. John of the Cross according to which the goal of every human being is to become *"Dios por participación."*

Although Wojtyła's exposition is largely faithful to Garrigou-Lagrange, one can see evident traces of personal thinking which go beyond that of his teacher. From the notes which were appended to the thesis it is clear that Garrigou-Lagrange was aware of these differences.

The first note states: "Instead of the expressions, which are frequently used, 'divine form received in an intentional mode' and 'the form which is at the intentional level unlimited' one should simply say 'divine object'. To speak of a 'form' is to risk being understood erroneously, as the 'intentional species,' whereas we know that in the beatific vision the divine Essence is immediately seen, and this excludes every mediation of intentional species; it is the same Essence which functions as the *species,* both *species impressa* and *species expressa,* and which replaces both."[7]

In fact, the thesis has an evident tendency not to translate the experiential language, which comes from the subject of St. John of the Cross, into a metaphysical language which relates to the object. The young Wojtyła's main preoccupation was to read the writings of St. John of the Cross as a phenomenology of mystical experience. In this perspective, one can understand why Garrigou-Lagrange chose to criticize these expressions; Wojtyła was more concerned with danger of equivocity in the expression which qualifies God as an Object rather than the expression of "divine form perceived in an intentional mode."

It would perhaps be wrong to think in terms of an opposition between the doctrines of Garrigou-Lagrange and those of Wojtyła. Rather, we can see that the latter as a matter of principle tended to develop the subjective side of the problem, while seeing it not as autonomous but as tightly bound to the objective side. St. John of the Cross has a particular importance here. From one side he shows the way in which faith is subjectivized by becoming experience. Simultaneously, from the other side, this subjectivization is

---

7. Wojtyła, *La fede secondo S. Giovanni della Croce,* p. 316. Garrigou-Lagrange's notes do not appear in the English *Faith According to St. John of the Cross.*

shown to be, so to speak, absolutely objective. Absolute value, God himself, comes — in mystical experience — to be perceived in a bare way, without any emotional content. In this manner we perceive in the most limpid way a relation with truth as it is constituted in the same subjective experience. This is a lesson which Wojtyła was not to forget but which would accompany him in all of his intense and fruitful encounters with Scheler's thought. Scheler offered a phenomenology of emotion which was completely different from, and at the same time complementary to, this aspect of St. John of the Cross. Wojtyła's point of reference in his engagement with Scheler would always be St. Thomas Aquinas, yet Thomas understood through St. John of the Cross; St. Thomas was thus given an experiential and existential dimension which made it easier to link his thought with phenomenology. St. John's phenomenology of mystical experience takes man towards the irreducible core of the person, and shows the necessity of transcending this core toward that truth who is God himself, by responding to the initiative of God toward human beings.[8] This divine initiative, which traverses natural human structures, illuminates and, in a certain sense, makes the irreducible core of the human person experienceable; this core is normally left out of phenomenological description.

If, on the other hand, faith is the key to the comprehension of human beings, because it permits an experience deeper than the human truth, mysticism is the experience which faith brings to the most acute level of subjective perception. For this reason, if one wants to understand the human condition, one has to begin from mystical experience.[9]

This approach is foreign to much Catholic thinking and provocative to secular philosophy. Both disciplines are accustomed to dividing philosophy and theology neatly between themselves and to tucking mysticism away within one of the more abstruse compartments of theology — an especially unsightly one in the eyes of modern secular thought. Things were different for the great philosophers of the past. Their work inevitably reached into the domain of mysticism as they tried to take seriously and realistically the depths and the heights of the mystery of the human being,

---

8. It seems to me that this particular experience in which phenomenological analysis encounters its own limits and sees that it needs to be supplemented by metaphysics is crucial to Wojtyła's approach to phenomenology. This latter accepts that mystical experience can include the experience of shame (which can be developed into a metaphysics of sexuality) and of duty (which unfolds into a metaphysics of the person).

9. In this sense one can say that faith gives not so much a particular doctrine as, primarily, a particular human experience, which illuminates each universal value.

who finds himself set between the finite and the infinite. While such mysticism is not resigned to conceiving man as merely a finite being, it also cautions that he cannot reach infinity.

This theme of the relation between finite and infinite is the heart of Hegelian dialectic and, in its wake, of all of modern high culture. The modern project has been to secularize the great Christian affirmation of the meeting of the finite and the infinite in Christ, presenting this reconciliation as having been brought about by the autonomous forces of nature, history, and humanity — not as the gratuitous presence of God through grace. This idealistic position was attacked most combatively by some positivistic Catholics who opposed to it a literal division between finite and infinite. In the thinking of such Catholics, the consolidation of this divide between nature and supranature has led to the displacement of the unity of finite and infinite, the relation of which is the real solution to the human problem, beyond history and beyond the world. It has also led to the philosophical defense of the position of a man who is satisfied with finitude and to the philosophical attack upon the innate human tendency to transcendence, frequently denounced as hubris.

If we pursue this line of thought much further we will bring to the surface the identity between the two opposed positions which have for a long time monopolized cultural debate. On the one side, we find the revolutionary thesis, which is posited on the Marxist development of the Hegelian dialectic and which maintains the reconciliation of finite and infinite in history through revolutionary action. Insofar as revolutionary action is not actually able to effect an ontological change in the human condition, the revolutionary position is forced to attack individuals who are exposed as unfit for the design of history; the revoluntaries have to take recourse to terror and ultimately relapse into a state of general hypocrisy and demoralization in which they are left only with the selfishness of individuals and the arrogance of the dominant caste.

The reactionary argument goes to the other extreme. Those who hold it believe that we cannot live in this world in relation with the infinite; they wish, if possible, to extirpate from the human heart the nostalgia for the infinite, since this perpetual restlessness endangers the balance of temporal interests. In its extreme form the reactionary position is resolutely atheistic (as in the case of Charles Maurras) and uses the promise of a world beyond to exorcise the human desire for the infinite within this life. In its moderate form the reactionary stance can sit alongside a sincere faith, but it will be in some way devitalized and, above all, prevent one from seeing how far the revolutionary position is true, in human and in Christian terms.[10]

From a Catholic viewpoint, the reactionary position is too close to that of the Enlightenment. All of the heterodox mysticism of modernity is a response to the expulsion of the genuine mystical moment from social and individual life. Only a revival of orthodox mysticism can respond to heterodox mysticism. In the sixteenth century, St. John of the Cross proposed just such a revival in the face of the naturalism of the *"alumbrados"* of his own time.[11] It is for this reason that his thinking contains, in germ, the response to the fundamental problem of modernity.

Historically, as Ernst Bloch has shown in his *Avicenna und die aristotelische Linke*,[12] there is a subterranean but substantial link between all the forms of heretical mystical-gnosis, which derive from Averroës and Avicenna, from there into Paduan Aristotelianism and the thought of Giordano Bruno, and finally from there to Hegel and Marx. Bloch probably did not know the *"alumbrados"* who were the adversaries of St. John of the Cross, but if he had he certainly would not have hesitated to include them in his catalogue of precursors of modern dialectical thinking. In confronting them, St. John reaffirmed a Catholic equilibrium and rapport between the finite and the infinite; he did this not with a metaphysical treatise but with a phenomenology of mystical experience, with an articulate description of its manifestation. As St. John describes his experience, it is, on its most profound level, completely lacking in any emotional content.

The night in which all human sentiment is silent is also the experience of the absolute distance of God, the incomprehensibility of God, that which exceeds the entire measure of finite intelligence and, together with that his real presence, his drawing near within faith. No positive knowledge of God is possible, he argues; in this, the Spanish mystic is in accord with St.

---

10. I am using "revolutionary" and "reactionary" to refer to philosophical rather than political positions. But it can happen that a reactionary philosophy presents itself, for contingent reasons, as politically revolutionary.

11. The argument against the alumbrados is central to St. John of the Cross's vindication of the connection between grace and contemplation. Contemplation, the unification of the finite and the infinite, is a gift of God and not a human achievement. That is, this gift is brought into history by the presence of God in the world, which is mediated by the Church. On this theme, the fundamental article is by Arintero: "Inanidad de la contemplación adquirida," in *La Ciencia Tomista* 87 (1924), pp. 331ff.; see also 88, pp. 5ff. This article had a decisive influence on Garrigou-Lagrange.

12. Frankfurt a. Main: Suhrkamp Verlag, 1963 (first edition, Berlin, 1952).

Thomas. Nonetheless, human faith truly encounters God, and God himself becomes the form of the human intellect. This happens not because the human person comprehends God, but because he welcomes God into himself and is welcomed by Him. For St. John, one knows God through a personal relation with Him, which is one of reciprocal giving. In this relation the night of the intellect becomes light, man understands that God, by not giving himself as an object of the intellect, wants to dwell as a person in the soul. What emerges from St. John's mysticism is, at one and the same time, both the ineffability and the personality of God. In this, it directly opposes heterodox mysticism, which typically makes the contrary affirmation of the impersonality of God and of the possibility of constructing an esoteric science of the divine which allows man to master God. God comes to be considered as just one part of the possible contents of the human mind, which can be thought about and taken possession of in order to make Him the subject of a science of the absolute.

Wojtyła draws three important conclusions from his analysis of St. John. First, human beings cannot know God as an object. The furthest that the exploration of natural reason can reach is to say that God exists; it cannot comprehend what God is. Second, faith is not given an intellectual grasp of what God is, for that would turn it into an absolute, God-like knowledge which knows the world and all that is within it. Faith is given a personal encounter with God which is real but, in this life, always remains in an obscurity ("the night of faith"). The nonobjectivizability of God for faith is different from the nonobjectivizability of God which is appropriate to natural reason. It is in the light of faith that this nonobjectivizability is seen to be an aspect of the personality of God, part of the essence of his person and through which he enters into a personal relation with us. The nonobjectivizability is thus the personal form of the relationship with God, and God initiates it. This is more important than may be captured in an emphasis on his absolute transcendence in respect of all relations which human beings attempt to set up with Him. Thirdly, understood in its purest form, the personal encounter with God in mystical experience occurs in an absence of emotion. All of the emotional aspects which are commonly thought to constitute the mystical experience as such are rather, in its essence, absolutely foreign to it.

We must turn at this point to the fundamental affirmation that, as Genesis says, the key to the understanding of man is his resemblance to God. It is necessary to say, at this point, that the mystery of the human being is rooted in the yet greater mystery of God. For if we have no positive knowledge of God, then we have no positive knowledge of the human being, inasmuch as he or she is an image of God. It would certainly be possible to have some knowledge of human beings insofar as they belong to the animal kingdom and are thus objects with a physical structure and a psychology (because the psyche, up to a certain level, appears as part of the order of nature in the phenomenological sense). But we would not have any knowledge at a more profound level, the level which is constitutive of humanity, of what makes one human.

This lack of knowledge is not, perhaps, an absolute ignorance.[13] We know that God and human beings resemble one another in being essentially persons, and precisely for this reason they are nonobjects, irreducible to instrumental reason. Persons cannot be spoken of as if they were things, nor are they reducible to a volatile and provisional state of emotion. Mystical experience comes to us like the perception of the value which another person, that is, God himself, gives us. Together with that perception, we experience the higher value of this person, attained in a complete emotional void. The most profound experience of a person touches his ontological nucleus through conscience. It is not entirely accurate to say that St. John of the Cross provides a phenomenological analysis of the ontological nucleus of the person. The phenomenological method can not attain the ontological level. But the phenomenological analysis of mystical experience certainly moves toward and lightly touches the ontological nucleus of the person, thus furnishing in experiential terms the proof from which the analysis of conscience can commence.

Rather than a positive anthropology, reading the deep resemblance to God in this way grounds a negative anthropology like the one which Adorno thought necessary, but for which he was not to give a foundation.[14] Our analysis of the thought of St. John of the Cross and Wojtyła's interpretation of it can be directly connected with a personalistic norm, which can be formulated as a prohibition against violating in oneself and in others the mystery of the person. This prohibition also concerns the transformation of the person into an object. A negative anthropology so understood is not

13. One may say that Wojtyła is carried by his interpretation of St. John of the Cross toward a recovery of many of Pascal's themes. Thomas and Pascal do not clash, in Wojtyła's thought, but complement one another. Among others, the Pascalian theme of "Deus absconditus" is important.

14. T. H. Adorno, *Negative Dialectics*, trans. E. B. Ashton (New York: Continuum, 1973, 1983). Grygiel also speaks about negative anthropology in *L'uomo visto dalla Vistola*, pp. 51-52.

at all an anthropology without any content but, rather, an anthropology which creates its own content from the person and then, by developing itself, gives life to an ethics founded on the personalistic norm.

How is it possible that the affirmation of the nonobjectivizability and, in a way, of the unknowability of human beings gives rise to positive norms? It is necessary to consider the fact that the first affirmation which derives from the thesis of human resemblance to God is that the human mystery is in itself a high value which has to be taken into account. On the other hand, insofar as a person is also a natural and embodied being and engages in a set of relationships to the world which have his body as their center, it is necessary that the treatment and use of the body take place within an human ethos. An anthropology which proceeded in this way would not want to circumscribe the statement of the essence of humanity, nor would it want to possess an absolute knowledge of that essence. Even less would it want to become a technique for the manipulation of human beings. Rather, by flowing into an ethics, such an anthropology dictates rules for the respect of human freedom and safeguarding human dignity — rules which allow it to face with more serenity and truthfulness the unforeseeable and surprising adventure which is human life.[15]

The engagement with St. John of the Cross strengthened Wojtyła in the conviction of the eminently personal character of Christian certainty. This was not born from a omnicomprehensive theory but by penetrating the heart of the person. It is because it is bound to the liberty of the person that it defends the person against objectivization and exploitation. But this does not imply the renunciation of a more solid anthropology which would elevate and give value to the person, and not humiliate and abandon him. In this way it will overcome the lack of ethical content which weakens certain nonmetaphysical "negative anthropologies," causing them to descend into a bottomless scepticism.[16]

---

15. The knowledge of the nonobjectivizable dignity of man, of the transcendence of the person, is in this perspective the basis of the integration of the diverse objective sciences of man which provide the internal and external observations upon which the human sciences are based. This is a fundamental principle of Wojtyła's anthropology, which is given its definitive systematization in *Love and Responsibility* and in *The Acting Person*.

16. For Wojtyła on St. John of the Cross, see also "Quaestio de Fide apud S. Joannem a Cruce," in *Collectanea Theologica* 21 (1950), pp. 418-68; "Zagadnienie wiary w dziełach św. Jana od Krzyża," in *Ateneum Kapłskie* 42 (1950), pp. 24ff., 103ff.; "O humaniźmnie św. Jana od Krzyża," in *Znak* 6, pp. 6ff. On Wojtyła as an interpreter of

KAROL WOJTYŁA

Wojtyła and Max Scheler

In a comprehensive assessment of Wojtyła's theoretical interests, the figure of Max Scheler stands near St. John of the Cross. Wojtyła dedicated his *Habilitationsschrift* to the German philosopher, calling it *An Evaluation of the Possibility of Constructing a Christian Ethics on the Basis of the System of Max Scheler;*[17] he wrote numerous other essays about him, some of which are collected as *Person and Community: Selected Essays.*[18] It is difficult to say exactly how Wojtyła came by his interest in Scheler. One can conjecture that his interest in St. John of the Cross and in Carmelite spirituality led to his discovery of the philosophical work of S. Benedicta of the Cross, more commonly known as Edith Stein. Edith Stein, who was Husserl's friend and assistant, came through philosophical study within the phenomenological method to a recognition of the truth of Catholicism and, after her conversion, entered the Carmelite Order. She died in Auschwitz, sharing in this way the fate of the chosen people to whom she belonged in the flesh.[19] Whatever it was that provoked Wojtyła's interest in phenomenology, the decisive factor which consolidated it was certainly his encounter with Roman Ingarden, one of the greatest and most original of Husserl's disciples and a dominant figure in the cultural milieu of Cracow.

Stein and Ingarden were disciples of Husserl rather than of Scheler. Nonetheless, both had a marked interest in anthropology and in ethics and in using phenomenology ethically rather than eidetically or cognitively, that is, using it, not to perceive the pure form of a phenomenon, but to grasp the value which is implicated in it. Ingarden was above all a student of the early Husserl, the author of the *Logical Investigations.* Husserl's later turn

---

St. John of the Cross see A. Huerga, "Karol Wojtyła, comentador de San Juan de la Cruz," in *Angelicum* 56 (1979), pp. 348ff. This issue of *Angelicum,* which is called "Studia in honorem Caroli Wojtyła" ['Studies in Honor of Karol Wojtyła'], is an indepensable source for an introduction to the study of Wojtyła. On Wojtyła and St. John of the Cross, see also Raimondo Sorgia, "Approccio con l'opera prima di K. Wojtyła," in *Angelicum* 57 (1980), pp. 401ff.

17. *Ocena możliwości zbudowania etyki chrześijańskiej przy założeniach systemu Maksa Schelera* (Lublin: Towarzystwo Naukowe KUL, 1959). The thesis was presented in 1953. There is an Italian translation by Sandro Bucciarelli with a preface by Cardinal Pietro Palazzini (Rome: Logos, 1980) entitled *Max Scheler.*

18. Trans. and ed. Teresa Sandok (New York: Peter Lang, 1993).

19. Sister Benedicta of the Cross is recollected along with Father Kolbe in the discourse on Oswiecim-Brzezinka: "Omelia del 7 giugno 1979 a Oswiecim-Brzezinka" (CSEO Documentation) 140-41, p. 305.

to Idealism, which came about in the '20s, precipitated a break with not only with Ingarden himself, but with Max Scheler, Martin Heidegger, Nikolai Hartmann, Oskar Becker, and Hedwig Conrad-Martius.

For Ingarden, phenomenology is not a philosophical system but a method of philosophical inquiry which can be applied in diverse ways and which can work together with the most diverse philosophies. Ingarden himself maintained a fundamentally realistic direction, and a marked interested in the problems of ethical life.[20] This was exactly Scheler's path, the path which led him away from Husserl.

For Scheler, the experience of reality is always charged with affectivity. That is, it is never neutral. The experience of an object, which is something in itself, is always connected with an affective charge, with an attraction or with a repulsion. In short, it is connected with a value and a disvalue. Phenomenology allows us to isolate the values connected with experience; it is, for Scheler, a method of analyzing experience which permits one to grasp values. Ethics is shown to be a fundamental dimension of experience in general. One can thus create an ethical system which is objective and which, in one aspect, stands in antithesis to Kant's preeminently subjective speculative system.[21] For Scheler, the subject recognizes value in the experience of objects. What we have here is a material ethics of values.

From a Catholic point of view, which cannot accept the absolute formalism of Kantian ethics, Scheler's ethical objectivism represents a powerful ally. And besides its merely theoretical aspect, the novel way in which Scheler developed the phenomenological method gave it a very good pastoral and apostolic application. For it allows us to return to values through the analysis of common experience and to go on from there. It takes from ethics the rigidity inherent in a system of absolute commands which have not been engendered by subjective experience and makes, instead, the individuality of values the essential point of reference of personal experience. Further, Scheler identified and suggestively described the role of "following" in the process in apprehending values. It is by appropriating

20. On Ingarden see, for example, A. T. Tymieniecka, "Beyond Ingarden's Idealism/Realism Controversy with Husserl — The New Contextual Phase of Phenomenology," in *Analecta Husserliana*, vol. 4 (Dordrecht, 1976).

21. See especially Scheler's main work, *Der Formalismus in der Ethik und die materiale Wertethik. Mit besonderer Berucksichtigung der Ethik I. Kants,* first published in the *Jahrbuch für Philosophie und phänomenologische Forschung* 1, 2 (Max Niemeyer Hall, 1913, 1916). This thesis was republished by Francke Verlag, edited by Maria Scheler (Bern and Munich, 1966 [5th ed.]), as vol. 2 of the *Collected Works.*

KAROL WOJTYŁA

another man's ethos that one can identify with the values and qualities to which his life testifies. These are not transmitted by intellectual teaching. This principle of "following," which offers a great and decisive pedagogical lesson, at the same time recalls the fundamental Christian idea of "following Christ."[22]

Closely linked to the concepts of value and of following is Scheler's concept of the person. If value is objective in itself, it is not a product of subjectivity; nonetheless, it is only in the person that it manifests itself. The person is the place in which value is experienced. On the other hand, the main experience of value which one can have is that of the value of the person, which takes place in personal relationships. It is in mutuality and in becoming conscious of the value of the other that the person becomes aware of his own value; things themselves receive a value by being part of a personal relationship.

One perceives reality in general as the carrier of the experience of value before one identifies with the unique emotional center which is the person; the latter comes about in time (it is only slowly that the child is able to identify with its own emotional reasoning, as distinct from the world around it) and through specific structures.

In fact, the person identifies the authentic perception of value within a more complex affective state, one which gives a unique tonality to the human ambience, and makes it distinct from that of the other people with whom one enters into relation. In the same way the person grasps the other's experience as the experience of another, and in a certain way he makes it his own even if he recognizes that it belongs to the other. Scheler's identification of the faculty of empathy and of sympathy (also studied by Edith Stein) breaks with a rooted tradition in modern thought which imprisons the person in a subjectivity, making him a monad separated from living communication with other subjects.[23]

22. Cf. Max Scheler, "Vorbilde und Fuhrer," in *Schriften aus dem Nachlass* (Bern: Francke Verlag, 1956), vol. 10 of the *Collected Works*.

23. Max Scheler, *Wesen und Formen der Sympathie* (Bern and Munich: Francke Verlag, 1973), vol. 7 of the *Collected Works*. The first edition, which was called *Zur Phenomenologie und Theorie der Sympathiegefuhle und von Liebe und Hass. Mit einem Anhang über den Grund zur Annhme der Existenz des fremden Ich*, first appeared in 1913 (Max Niemeyer, Hall). The second edition, with significant modifications which stabilized the central thesis, was published in 1923 (Bonn: Verlag Friedrich Cohen, 1923). It was printed in English as *The Nature of Sympathy*, trans. Peter Heath (London: Routledge and Kegan Paul, 1954).

Scheler made a unique attempt to break away from the prison of solipsism which, in diverse ways, weighs down the whole of modern philosophy. This does not consist so much in the negation of extramental reality external to the subject as in the denial that reality in general can be reached in a form different from its interpretation by a subject from within his sensations and his interiority.[24] The idea that the interpretation and comprehension of the other is an obstacle to be scaled only by virtue of a resemblance to his actual mental state is the rock upon which all of modern philosophy has run aground. Scheler's marked virtue is that he retrieved the possibility of knowing the other *as the other,* the possibility of sharing the experience of the other as other, and the possibility of receiving, through this intersubjectivity, an objective reality which is implied in the relationship between subjects. (Also, as Wojtyła emphasizes, the experience of the person always remains ultimately incommunicable.) In this way the abstract problematic of the subject gives way to the concrete problem of the person. This person is precisely the human "I" — when one does not abstract from its concrete cognitive and emotional contents — and it is that which characterizes its unrepeatable individuality, an individuality which is nonetheless open to reality, through sympathy.

All of these elements are certainly enough to explain the enthusiasm with which Wojtyła appropriated the phenomenological method; he especially valued the unique construction which Scheler accomplished through this method.

His appropriation is, nonetheless, a critical one. It is accompanied by a careful evaluation of Scheler's philosophy and a reform of the phenomenological method itself. In order to understand Wojtyła's criticism of Scheler, we shall begin with three questions. First, what type of perception of value is this philosophy trying to describe? Second, what is the "following" of which Scheler speaks and upon what does his proposal for character formation turn? Third, what does the person consist of, in Scheler's perspective?[25]

In considering the first point, one must note that phenomenology makes only emotional values evident. The person's emotions are struck by phenomena which allow them to resonate in the sounding box of his interior conscience; the conscience does not judge what flows from it. As a

24. One superficial Catholic definition of modernity defines it solely in terms of the negation of the reality of the extramental objects. This is too extreme and is untrue of some directions of modern philosophy such as positivism, empiricism, materialism, and sensualism.

25. Cf. Wojtyła, *Max Scheler,* pp. 231ff.

result value never appears as the goal of a conscious action directed toward its realization. Moreover, the value is simply ascertained, not elaborated by conscience. It is true that when values are ascertained, they are said to be joined together in something like a hierarchy, but it is not possible to establish an objective order among them, through which one could develop and build an ethics of the person. For Scheler, the highest value is always that which the subject responds to most intensely, because of his own intrinsic excellence. But is it possible for us to say that in every case the value which receives the most intense response is also that which the person must choose in order to realize his own moral perfection?

From Scheler's point of view, this question cannot be asked. In accordance with his emotionalist presuppositions, Scheler denies that the good of the person can be the end of action. For him, moral value can never be the purpose of an action. Rather, it is manifested *on the occasion of an action.*

There is, then, a breach in Scheler's system which can be exposed when a pure phenomenological method is used. Prior to phenomenological analysis, among other phenomena of ethical life, there is the action of the moral conscience which judges and prescribes the choice of values which the person must realize through his actions. While he does not deny the existence of a moral conscience, Scheler tries in every way to depreciate it, claiming that it has no positive function. In his legitimate concern to counter a moralism which would not accept the effective assistance the manifestation of value in experience can give to the development of the moral life, he becomes excessively polemical and ultimately creates an obstacle to the construction of a coherent ethical system. He also, by this means, contradicts the moral experience of the person as it is revealed by unprejudiced phenomenological analysis. If it is an emotional perception which motivates the person, this perception must undergo a judgment which recognizes and clarifies the truth, before the value, which the emotional experience presents, can be accepted as authentic. Scheler's argument tends rather to set aside and to obscure the problem of the truthfulness of values and of how to assess it, although its manifest evidence is obvious to a phenomenological analysis of moral conscience.[26]

---

26. At the root of this defective ethics must be a flawed metaphysics. For Scheler, the subject has no access to knowledge which does not go through an emotionalized consciousness. It is against this that Wojtyła describes the structure of the person through the interaction of two structures: that of consciousness which subjectivizes and that of knowledge which reflects the object. This argument is found in *The Acting Person.*

In relation to the second point (concerning the "following" of which he speaks), Scheler projects an aesthetic image of following, but this is arbitrary, because he gives no rational grounds for it. The value, in the name of which one follows a master, is actually the value immanent to the master's ethical experience. This belongs to the master's ethos, but is not (necessarily) the value which reveals itself to the subject himself.[27] Scheler's idea of following is very close to the Augustinian idea of the master, but differs from it on one crucial point. Augustine speaks of an *interior* master. The interior master speaks to the heart of each man and forms his ethos from within. The disciple has an external master in other men, but he listens to and obeys an interior master. What is decisive is not the emotional impact which the discourse and the example make, but the correspondence between the proposed values and the objective ethical exigencies of the person, accessible to his own rational self-understanding. In Christian "following," the disciple tries to repeat in himself the moral perfection of the master through an ethical work which entails a personalization of value; for Scheler the miracle of the ethical universe which the master reveals and the person's emotional identification with his world are not a prelude to the ascent to the world of values through their verification and personalization. For this reason he risks confusing Christian following with a different and debatable concept of following: that of barbarism. It would certainly be superficial to identify the *"Gefolgschaft"* of which Scheler speaks with the Nazis; nonetheless, there are parallels between them which the Christian idea of "following" completely excludes.

We finally reach the third question, to which the first two lead: What does the person consist of? The person, for Scheler, is the place in which values are made manifest. It is not, however, the center of a judgment and of actions which turn toward the realization of value. One could put it like this: one does not become more good or more evil, better or worse, according to whether one's action concludes in a positive or negative value. In Scheler's system, the judgment of value is understood in relation to a single act, and not to the person as a whole, who is a subject of actions which unite and cohere with the actions which follow them. Such a person ultimately lacks ontological consistency.

This defect shows the way in which Scheler's philosophy can be under-

---

27. Cf. Wojtyła, "Ewangeliczna zasada naśladowania. Nauka źródeł Objawienia a system filozoficzny Maxa Schelera," in *Ateneum Kapłanskie* 49 (1957), pp. 57ff.

stood in an irrationalistic sense, as distorting both the meaning of "follow-ing" and the affirmation of value and subtracting critical rationality from both. In fact, a rational critique can be brought about only by an ordering of ends within the person, by a unitary comprehension of them as a means to the unique end, which encompasses all the other ends, that is, the moral realization of the person himself.

If one is to explain the person and values in this way, it becomes necessary to pass from the level of pure phenomenology to that of an ontology of the person. The phenomenological analysis of moral conscience actually shows the necessity of investigating the objective makeup of that ontological support of the person; in a purely phenomenological inquiry this is always partly concealed. A phenomenology which was freed from Scheler's emotionalist biases would guide us toward an ontology of the person but still could not constitute or replace it. Scheler, however, not only did not carry out the passage from pure phenomenology to an ontology of the person but, because of his position on the problem of moral con-science, actually prohibits phenomenology from becoming conscious of its own insufficiency, and of its need to be integrated with ontology.[28]

In the conclusion to his *Evaluation of the Possibility of Constructing a Christian Ethics on the Basis of Max Scheler's System,* Wojtyła formulated two theses which are significant here because they form the basis of his own writing in the years to come. The first thesis states that "The ethical system constructed by Max Scheler is not at all suitable as a means of formulating a scientific Christian ethics."[29] Since we have already provided a succinct explanation of the reasons for this assessment, it requires no further illustration. This first thesis does not necessarily imply a deprecation of the phenomenological method per se. A first limitation of the negative judgment made upon phenomenology is found in the explanation, which Wojtyła provides, of the first thesis: "Scheler in his system has decisively cancelled the normative character of ethical acts, and this is an understand-

---

28. In his criticisms of Scheler Wojtyła takes particular account of the objections formulated from a phenomenological point of view by Dietrich von Hildebrand in *Zeitliches im Lichte des Ewigen* (Regensburg, 1932). For the engagement with Christian ethics, especially as formulated by St. Thomas Aquinas, the most relevant source is perhaps Anton M. Rohner, "Thomas von Aquin oder Max Scheler. Das Ebenbild Gottes" and "Thomas von Aquin oder Max Scheler. Ethik der Vorbilder," in *Divus Thomas* I (Freiburg, 1923), pp. 329-55 and 250-74. See also by Rohner "Die Wertethik und die Seinsphilosophie," in *Divus Thomas* II (Freiburg, 1924), pp. 55-83 and 257-76.

29. Wojtyła, *Max Scheler,* p. 232.

able consequence of his distancing of values from the acting person. This is all the more surprising inasmuch as the same conscience is the experience of the person and the object of phenomenological experience. If Scheler's phenomenology analyzes acts of consciousness without converging upon a living relation to the person in respect of ethical values, this is for reasons which lie outside his phenomenology. The reason is the 'emotionalist' premises from which he begins."[30] Phenomenology is not to blame for the defects of Scheler's ethical system. Certain criticisms need to be drawn into the phenomenological method, but this does not exclude in principle the utility of a suitably reformed phenomenology for an adequate formulation of Christian moral theology.[31]

The second thesis confirms the partial acceptance of phenomenology which Wojtyła expresses in the first thesis: Although the ethical system which Max Scheler created is fundamentally unsuited to the interpretation of Christian ethics, it may still be collaterally helpful in a scientific work about Christian ethics. It can assist in the analysis of ethical facts within a project of "experimental" phenomenology.[32]

At this point, phenomenology can be understood as a method of inquiry to be applied to the analysis of ethical facts. If it remains there, it confronts a double limitation. On one side, the foundation of ethics needs more ontological profundity than even a reformed *phenomenology* can supply; it is not able to replace the questioning of being, which can only be achieved in metaphysics. There remains, nonetheless, the possibility of a route into ontology starting from the phenomenology of the person which could actually enhance the ontological enterprise. This will involve a placing in question of being which begins from man. Such a route was seen intuitively by Pascal. As Wojtyła delineates it, it becomes a critical appropriation of the fundamental postulate of modern thought: *the starting point is man.* This means starting from the concrete reality of the person, not from the hypostatization of the notion of the subject.

---

30. Cf. "Problem oderwania przeżcia od aktu w etyce na tle pogladów Kanta I Schelera" (Studies), all by Wojtyła, in *Roczniki Filozoficzne* 5 (1955-1957), pp. 113ff. The Italian translation is in *I fondamenti dell ordine etico,* with the title, "Il problema del distacco dell'esperienza dall'atto nell'etica nel contesto del pensiero di Kant e Scheler," pp. 69ff.

31. This indicates the outlines of Wojtyła's moral theology, as expressed in "Czym powinna być teologia moralna?" in *Ateneum Kapłanskie* 51 (1959), with the title, "Che cosa dovrebbe essere la teologia morale?"

32. Wojtyła, *Max Scheler,* p. 240.

The other apparent limitation upon the use of phenomenological method devolves upon the choice of object to which this type of method can be applied. It is not as if any phenomenological analysis whatsoever is equally useful in helping to complete the construction of a Christian ethics.

> When . . . with the help of phenomenological experience, we select a value and examine it, we are making an experimental study of a moral experience. It is possible to apply this method of experimental examination to Christian ethics. Given that our choice of moral experience as an object of examination derives from the belief in the ethical principles supplied by Christian revelation, then the examination allows us to penetrate into Christian ethical values, to uncover the essence of the experience and to verify its uniqueness and specificity in comparison with non-Christian ethical values, and also the borders at which they touch one another.[33]

If one is to use the phenomenological method fruitfully in the construction of a Christian ethics, one must begin from Christian experience. Christian ethics, as scientifically elaborated, is no more than what one sees when Christian moral experience is laid out in an orderly conceptual system. At the same time, Christian ethical experience is really a human ethical experience; it is also the most deeply rooted of all human ethical experience and therefore throws light upon human ethical experience as such. The elaboration of a philosophical human ethics cannot retreat from an encounter with the particular experience of human ethics which is Christian experience.

Kant and Scheler

Wojtyła's engagement with Max Scheler's writing is indirectly a dialogue with the whole of modern philosophy, seen especially through its Kantian roots. The lines of the engagement have two aspects: from one side, there are indications of an appropriation of the elements of truth which it is possible to retrieve from the modern approach to the problem of thought and of man, while from another angle there is a critical refutation of the inadequacies of this way of thinking, which become evident in its own aporia. To assume Schelerian phenomenology as a point of departure is to

33. Ibid., p. 241.

accept the process of self-criticism within philosophy which modern thinkers have developed. In fact, as can be seen even from the most superficial examination of Scheler's thought, the deepest motive which inspired him was opposition to Kantian formalism, and it is only by thinking about the grounds of his criticism of Kant that it is possible to enter into Scheler's problematic.

On the other hand, it is not necessary to assume that the continuation of a Schelerian critique of modern thought distances Wojtyła from Kant's philosophy. On the contrary, as we have seen, because he did not have the courage to call into question Kant's original division of ethics into a logic and a psychology, Scheler ends by completely losing the positive elements in Kant's position. Consider the title of Scheler's principal work: *Formalism in Ethics and Non-Formal Ethics of Values*. It opposes the material content of ethics to the form of ethics, developed a priori by Kant, with the intention of being indifferent to any determinate content. The material content of ethics, to which the value is per se immanent, has the character of being ethical for Scheler. If in Kant's philosophy, therefore, the sole object of ethics is the abstract form of duty and of responsibility, then Scheler reacts by excluding the legitimate aspect of this from the sphere of ethics. In this way he mislays not only formalism but also the very foundation of ethics, its ground and beginning in the subject's activity and responsibility. In his desire to emphasize a different aspect — one opposed to that upon which Kant dwelt — Scheler himself fell victim to the abstract division between intellect and will, between reason and sensibility, which constitutes the horizon and the a priori to which Kant was wedded. His philosophy opposes an ethic of pure duty to an ethic of pure value. This opposition does not bring to light the unity in the person which enables one to consider the equilibrium between the moment of duty and the active responsibility of the person and, on the other hand, the receptiveness of conscience to value.

The confrontation between the ethics of Kant and of Scheler allows Wojtyła therefore to go to the root of the detachment of modern thought from the totality of human experience, and its inability to grasp this totality.

Wojtyła touches upon this confrontation, upon which we have commented, in numerous essays and articles, but the theme is treated most carefully perhaps in the essay "The problem of the detachment of experience from act in ethics in the context of the thought of Kant and Scheler."[34]

34. Cf. "Problem oderwania przeżcia od aktu w etyce na tle poglądów Kanta I Schelera" (Studies).

Wojtyła begins by remarking upon the paradoxical character of ethics, which is simultaneously an empirical and a normative science.

"The consciousness of performing a determinate act, of which one is the author, carries with it the sense of responsibility for the moral value of this act. Therefore I am the object of my life, my own person, as the efficient cause of the good or the evil of my own person."[35] Thus, in ethical experience, the person appears simultaneously as the subject and the object of the action. From the subjective point of view, he brings the action into being, while from an objective point of view he registers in himself the effect of the act. Because this registering in oneself is the experienced fact of its positive or negative value, it then orients one's own volition. In the ethical thought of Aristotle and St. Thomas this fundamental structure of the ethical act is grasped and respected. It is made comprehensible through the paired concepts of potentiality and actuality. Reality contains in itself the possibility of a determined level of perfection which can be realized only through a conscious human action. Through the same action, from a subjective point of view, there is realized a more or less complete perfection of the human being himself. A human act, therefore, simultaneously improves or degrades both external reality and the person who performs it.[36] By making use of the concepts of potentiality and actuality, which represent the heart of their respective philosophical systems, Aristotle and St. Thomas are able to supply a realistic account of actual ethical experience. With Kant, the fundamental orientation represented in ethics by the theory of potentiality and actuality is lost. In this way traditional metaphysics and the ethics founded upon it collapse together.

"Kant's intervention," Wojtyła says, "is above all related to the scientific character of metaphysics:

> Kant's critical stance has its greatest consequences in his conception of ethical action. Any attempt to perform ethics in the manner of an exact science which adopts the empirical-inductive method will not be able to bring about the decomposition of the conception of an ethical action as long as it does not cast doubt upon the same theory of potentiality and actuality, upon which such a conception is based, and, even more important, so long as it does not contest the relationship with experience which

---

35. Ibid., p. 69.
36. Cf. Wojtyła, "Wposzukiwaniu podstaw perfekcjoryzmu w etyce," in *Roczniki Filozoficzne* 5 (1957), pp. 303ff.

is the ground of the conception of ethical action for the whole of the Aristotelian-Thomistic philosophy of being.[37]

The separation of the subject and the object, and their opposition, marks the development of modern scientific thought; it was precisely this which Kant carried to its conclusion and extended to the sphere of ethics. Through the empirical-inductive method, the human being stands before the world of objects as one who would investigate their specific causal connections. While Aristotelian physics understood the real through the cognitive model of human acts and their real combination of both a subjective and an objective aspect, the empirical-inductive method will from now on recognize the specific autonomy which governs the series of causes which effects the world of nature. There is in this, without doubt, a great cognitive gain. In this new vision of the physical universe, the concept of potentiality and actuality loses part of its significance. All of this, however, is no obstacle to an accurate definition of the problems of ethics so long as it does not throw into question the place of the theory of potentiality and actuality within ethics, thereby negating the unique feature of human experience. At this point the "humanizing" of nature, which somewhat characterizes medieval physics, has been replaced by a naturalization and "thingifying" of human subjectivity. The empirical aspect of ethical experience is absolutized and, on the opposite side, its normative aspect is lost. There is also a profound contradiction here, inasmuch as ethical experience itself, considered without prejudice and as a whole (from a phenomenological point of view and not only phenomenally), attests unequivocally to its having a normative element.

Kant found himself entangled in this contradiction and expended much energy upon retrieving the normativity of ethics. But because of the characteristic presuppositions of his metaphysics, he had to speak about a normativity which had been completely separated from the empirical experience of value. He was also compelled to expel the empirical experience of value from the sphere which is proper to ethics. For Kant, ethics, like metaphysics, makes use of concepts which protrude beyond the limit of all possible experience and which are not verifiable through the analysis of the phenomenal realm. Thus, in the case of ethics, the "phenomenal" man provides no validation of the freedom of the will,

---

37. "Il problema della separazione dell'esperienz dall'atto nel contesto del pensiero di Kant e di Scheler," in *I fondamenti dell'ordine etico*, p. 71.

and the freedom of the will is the most important basis of any possible ethics. This is not to say that Kant denies the freedom of the will. But freedom of the will is reached only by the "noumenal" man, who is in some way accessible to the awareness of the experience of moral conscience. Man creates both the experience of the world and the experience of himself. But interiority is not directly knowable. It is always exhibited to some extent through exteriority. The connection between the phenomenal man and the noumenal man is perhaps guaranteed by those a priori categories of moral experience which condition human existence and allow one to think about it. One of these a priori categories is precisely the freedom of the will, for without it the particular type of experience which is moral experience would be unintelligible. Kant thus tries to save both elements which we have seen to be present within the Aristotelian-Thomistic conception of ethical action. But they now lack any connection to one another. If one wants to understand ethical action, one needs the entire phenomenal realm.

When human beings allow their choices or actions to be influenced by considerations which come from the sensible world, then they have abdicated genuine liberty. Thus practical reason enjoys a certain immanence of freedom to the extent to which the very moral law, that is, the a priori legislative form of practical reason, constitutes the genuine and true ethics of the human person. This is the *formalism* of Kantian ethics: man must detach himself from any particular (phenomenal) content if he is to be turned toward pure duty; it is in this that freedom consists. Kant expels from the sphere of ethics, in its true sense, everything which for Aristotle and St. Thomas had constituted the essence of ethical action (the person's conscious direction toward a good). An ethical action is solely a pure willing of the law, which gives to a particular willing the universal form of the law. Because every concrete human act is always turned toward a particular good, it is doubtful whether this conception of an ethical act can have an empirical example — that is, if we can still speak about an ethical action within Kant's system. Nonetheless, this objection would not move Kant at all, but only reinforce his conviction. In fact, his conception, which is not based in experience (or at least human experience considered in its indissoluble unity), does not ask experience to confirm it. Moreover, for Kant it is clear from the outset that ethical action does not belong in the phenomenal realm but rather in the noumenal. If we take into consideration the categorical imperative — "Act in such a way that the maxim of your will can always be willed as a universal legislative principle" — we see it as being (at least for Kant) totally within the sphere of practical reason and lacking any possible connection with experience.

Naturally, this detachment from the realm of sensible experience cannot be complete. It has, as a minimum necessity, a point which human beings can use as a lever to elevate themselves into the realm of pure duty. To be this it must have an empirical-sensible side while through another aspect it is able wholly to respect the chosen connection which almost identifies practical reason and will. This negation of the sensible realm within the same sensible realm is furnished by a sentiment of respect for the law: "Insofar as man nourishes a similar sentiment, that much more profoundly he lives his duty, which is nothing else than the subordination of the will to the law, and to the law insofar as it is law."[38]

If we recall for a moment the comments made earlier about St. John of the Cross, we will see that there is at this point an important similarity between the thought of the Spanish mystic and that of the German philosopher. Both recognize that beyond the phenomenal realm there is a realm which adheres to supreme value and which is devoid of any emotion. The mystical element, it is as well to note, is not in fact alien to Kant's pietistic education. This point, at which Kant's thought draws near to that of St. John of the Cross, has a decisive importance for the construction of ethics. It blocks the way to any empiricist reduction of ethical experience to the realm of pure sentiment which would deny the presence of a normative moment and, together with this, the causality and the responsibility of the person for his actions.

But this analogy cannot be taken any further. If it is possible approximately to condense into a single formula the distinction between St. John of the Cross and Kant, I think one would possibly say that in St. John of the Cross the sphere of sensible experience is simultaneously judged and transcended, while at the same time mystical experience is above all passive. In it, the person opens up to the presence of God, manifested most purely in the "night of faith," which is the same presence which is at the ground of any particular experience. For Kant, sensible experience is disregarded rather than transcended, and the experience of duty entirely lacks the passivity and availability to the presence of value which St. John emphasizes. The reason for this is that St. John's approach is, quite unconsciously, phenomenological and so drawn from the totality of experience as it presents itself, while Kant's approach is phenomenalist. So, when he develops

38. Ibid., p. 78.

the themes of liberty and of the ethical action of the person, he cannot begin from experience. The same idea of experience immediately undergoes an initial reduction which crucially impoverishes it.

Scheler criticizes this aspect of Kant's thought. Despite the nominal similarity, Scheler's phenomenology stands at the extreme opposite of Kant's phenomenalism. It represents a road toward the classical, Aristotelian and Thomistic, conception of knowledge. There is, in fact, for phenomenology no Kantian distinction between phenomena and noumena. Instead, knowledge is a whole given from experience. and only through a successive process of abstraction within it is one able to distinguish one of its sides as being cognitive, and another side as affective and emotional. This unity of experience is the great discovery of phenomenology and, at the same time, the unifying element among all those who practice it. The often very profound divisions begin when phenomenologists qualify this whole which one reaches through phenomenological "reduction."

The application of this method to ethics allows one to reconstruct, albeit partially, a relation to experience. "Scheler's presuppositions guarantee that he will be able to examine the ethical experience of the human person as lived experience, because he is a phenomenologist and has gone from a position of a-priorism and subjectivism, toward an objectivist position . . . It thus confronts instead the empirical makeup of the ethical experience of man and immediately affirms that this experience has the character of a personal act."[39] Intelligence and will appear then as faculties of the person, and as engaged in his acts.

If this appears to bring us back toward the Aristotelian and Thomistic position, this impression is nonetheless true only within clear limits. Scheler does not push to its conclusion an integral recovery of the fundamental metaphysical principles of potentiality and actuality. As described by him, the acts of the person coincide only terminologically with those acts as described within the Thomistic tradition. The act of which Scheler speaks is an intentional act. The notion of an intentional act which he upholds is that which Brentano developed against Kant: if it is true that a psychical act is also a subjective act, it is also true that it is directed toward an object which transcends the subject. The act which is directed toward an object (whether ideal or real, abstract or concrete) remains outside its object. In this way the act is qualified as intentional, from the etymological meaning

39. Ibid., pp. 80-81.

of the Latin verb *intendere*. Experience contains this reaching out toward objects and thus the creation of a polarity between subject and object which in some way makes it possible for the object to be grasped in its complexity, within experience. Experience, it is true, requires the intervention of a process of abstraction, but experience is the preliminary condition of this process. In a certain sense the abstraction is directed against experience and impoverishes it in order to organize it. This tendency must not be pushed to the point of negating the moment of experience, if one does not wish to cut at the root of the possibility of knowledge. Scheler applies the model of intentional act to the analysis of ethical acts. He is thus able to observe that the whole of ethical experience is an (intentional) reaching toward values. In the realm of ethics the object intended is value.

A question which perhaps remains outside Scheler's perspective is this: What happens to the person when he is intentionally directed toward value? And, given that the person himself is a value, what is the relation between the person as the subject of the action and the person as value? Since Scheler lacks the notion of potentiality and actuality, it is impossible for him to grasp that the person directed toward a value which is external to himself is simultaneously realizing a potential value which is internal to himself, and which is making the person intrinsically better or worse. Scheler's desire to oppose Kant was so strong that he could not be content with correcting Kant's one-sidedness; he had to leap into a different form of one-sidedness.

"Scheler," Wojtyła writes, "could not bear to think that duty could constitute the objective content of an experience, and his system does not even allow for the idea that it can be born of value itself. . . . Obviously, it is not a question only of a sentiment of respect for law, a psychological factor distinct from the lived ethical experience. It is a question instead of the moment of duty within the set of ethical experiences of the human person."[40]

This negation of duty goes together with a certain irrationalism. Values are, in fact, experienced through an emotion which has a cognitive value but which is not primarily cognitive. The emotional intuition not only admits the emotional experience of value, but also leans toward the ordering of values which is given in emotional perception. Every man has his own world of values (an ethos) which is articulated in the loves and hates which make up his personal life. This world of values is not entirely subjective, for value is objective and the subject's emotional experience brings

40. Ibid., pp. 81-82.

him into contact with this reality. This contact with value is perhaps not under the control of practical reason, and is not subjected to any rational organizing activity.[41]

Scheler obviously does not ignore the fact that in ethical life one not only *feels* value but also aspires to value. Nonetheless, he does not make this point clear. The decisive experience remains for Scheler that of the sentiment of directing oneself toward the highest values. The experience of the good is connected with this orientation toward the highest values; on the other hand, the good itself cannot be an object of volition. The experience of good is always manifested on the occasion *(auf dem Rücken)* of a realization of the highest value from among those which present themselves. Love and hate are the two a priori emotional categories which govern human life: one of them coincides with the experience of the enlargement of the emotional universe while the other coincides with its restriction and impoverishment. Man's reaching out toward the highest values proves to be an enrichment and an intensification of his life; when the opposite happens, he has allowed himself to be seduced by the lowest values.

For Scheler "the good, as also the evil, is bound inseparably to an emotional experience, and it is in a certain sense so implicated in the emotion that the person who acts cannot detach himself from it and realize it in a completely objective and detached way."[42] From this it follows that the act itself will be the punishment or the reward of the person who brings it about, because of its emotional effects upon him.

There is certainly a positive implication of good or evil, and thus of value, in the act itself. In this way ethics can retrieve the human dimension which Kantian formalism divested of it. Nonetheless, as Wojtyła observes, the essence of ethical experience does not consist in emotion, no matter how large is the role which is justly attributed to emotion. Its essence is, rather, in willing: "Scheler has not noticed the most elemental and fundamental thing, he has not seen that what we call ethical value is solely that value which has as its efficient cause a person's action."[43]

In other words, the person is not limited to registering and following the emotion, by moving his own will according to it. The person judges the

41. This is the central problem to which Wojtyła turns in "Zagadnienie woli w analizie aktu etycznego," in *Roczniki filozoficzne* (1957), pp. 111ff.
42. "Il problema della separazione dell'esperienza dal'atto nel contesto del pensiero di Kant e di Scheler," in *I fondamenti dell'ordine etico*, p. 84.
43. Ibid., pp. 85-86.

emotion and acts upon the basis of that judgment, and the importance of the emotional perception cannot be sufficiently emphasized; nonetheless, it is not a purely emotive act but an act of the whole person which involves his intellect and his freedom.

This limitation is thrown into relief even by phenomenology. Wojtyła makes references to the school of phenomenological psychology which was led by Ache and by Michotte and which was also developed in an interesting and original way in Poland in the studies made by Abramowski, Dybowski, Mielczarska, and Reutt, among others.[44] Scheler's philosophical preoccupation with opposing Kant prevented him from developing the phenomenological method in all of its wealth. The experience of bringing about a genuine action through an authentic volition is the fundamental experience of ethical life and the ground of every possible theory of responsibility.

At the base of the defects in Scheler's work there stands, we repeat again, an inadequate theory of ethical action. Such action is purely intentional: it is turned toward an object which it neither modifies nor makes real; and this relation to an object is an authentic potentiality of the subject as such. What is lacking is an idea of the perfecting of the person through moral action. What is also lacking is the possibility of defining a strategy to reach that perfection and a strategy for explaining it rationally.[45]

Kant divides ethical life methodologically into two parts. One part provides the categorical imperative, which is wholly internal to the person's subjectivity and to his practical reason. This is not derived from experience, but is an a priori logical category of moral action. For this side ethics may be resolved into a logic of pure moral thought. The other part is on the

---

44. Wojtla relies above all on the work of J. Lindworsky, *Der Wille. Seine Erscheinung und seine Beherrschung* (Leipzig, 1923); of M. Dybowski, *Działanie Woli na tle badan eksperymentalnych* (Poznan, 1946); of W. Miecczarska, *Przeżycie oporu I jego stosunek do woli* (Poznan, 1948); of J. Reutt, *Przedstawienie celu a postepowanie* (Poznan, 1947), and *Badania psychologiczne nad wahaniem* (Poznan, 1949). I have never found any references to Kepinski in Wojtyła's writings, but I have reason to believe that he has had a particularly incisive influence on this aspect of Wojtyła's thought. On Kepiński, cf. J. Tischner, *Il pensiero ed i valori* (Bologna: CSEO, 1980), especially the chapter called "Gli uomini nei nascondigli (Annotazioni in margine al pensiero etico del prof. Antoni Kepinski)."

45. On this theme, cf. "O kierowniczej lub służebnej roli rozumu w etyce. Na tle poglądów Tomasza z Akwinu, Hume'a I Kanta," in *Roczniki Filozoficzne* 5 (1958), pp. 13ff. Italian translation in *I fondamenti dell'ordine etico*, as "Il ruolo dirigente o ausiliario della ragione nell'etica nel contesto del pensiero di Tommaso d'Aquino, Hume, e Kant," pp. 91ff.

same side as emotional experience, whose quality can only be dealt with from a psychological point of view (the phenomenal man lacks the element of freedom). Despite his opposition to Kant, Scheler does not really escape from this dualism. Within this dualism, Kant placed all of his interest in the development of the logic of moral thought, whereas Scheler emphasizes and absolutizes the importance of a psychology of moral phenomena.

The solution to the problem of ethics requires the reestablishment of the unity of the ethical act, and especially an understanding of the real relation of its emotive and cognitive aspects. Phenomenology provides an access to this authentic unity because it begins from a unified experience which is there before abstraction. It is this which allows it to see that an emotional and empirical aspect is always the basis upon which the activities of the mind and will are exercised: "There is contained within ethical experience not only value as an objective content, but also the normative moment in which values are reorganized and given as a task to be realized."[46]

In comparing Scheler and Kant we have seen that each of them developed only one side of moral experience in isolation. We have also seen how Wojtyła elaborated this comparison by placing these authors within the horizon of the Aristotelian and Thomistic conception of ethical action, anchored in the notion of potentiality and actuality.

These metaphysical notions are the focus of Kant's destructive critique. But without them it is impossible to restore an adequate approach to ethical experience. It is therefore legitimate to ask whether and on what terms one can return to Thomas's vision of ethical action.

Scheler and St. Thomas

Wojtyła's reading of St. Thomas takes his ethics and anthropology as a point of departure. This choice naturally derives in part from his own overarching ethical concern. But it also seems to reflect more than simply a rigorous attention to his own discipline. As we have seen, even if Wojtyła begins from St. Thomas's ethics, he nonetheless continually refers to his metaphysics. It is, after all, impossible to understand and to participate in Thomas's ethics if one does not grasp and accept his fundamental ontology. But it is

46. "Il problema del distacco dell'esperienza dall'atto nell'etica nel contesto del pensiero di Kant e di Scheler," in *I Fondamenti dell'ordine etico*, p. 89.

necessary to say that an interpretation of St. Thomas which bases itself on his ethics as furnishing a complete vision of his philosophy is certainly original, and represents a decisive innovation in relation to other current interpretations. Thomas's philosophy is usually considered as a variant of a more general philosophy of being. From Wojtyła's perspective, this philosophy is, rather, qualified as a philosophy of the good. From a Thomistic point of view this operation is wholly legitimate: for *ens et bonum convertuntur* (being and good are convertible). The affirmation that God is the summit and the source of the order of the good and of that of being is the heart not only of Thomism but of all Christian philosophy. What is more: the Thomistic investigation of being is wholly animated by a movement which leads to a personal encounter with God. It is because this is what most profoundly drives its search for truth that the *Summa Theologiae* is in its own way an *Itinerarium mentis in Deum*.[47]

From a methodological point of view, perhaps, it is not quite the same thing to begin from being, as the most general concept proposed to intellectual reflection, as to begin from personal experience.[48]

Metaphysical reflection always comes after a preliminary investigation which deals with some object in the world, or some determinate domain of experience. Some have advanced the idea that philosophy always enters into scientific knowledge so as to resolve its aporias or to pose the ultimate questions which it implies. If we follow this intuition, we must notice that in Aristotle's philosophy metaphysics appears to come after physics, not only in the order of the Stagirite's writings, but also in the explicative pedagogy of his thought. The collapse of his physics brought about the collapse of the metaphysics which had been made dependent upon it; when the rise of modern physics made them obsolete, the fundamental categories of Aristotelian physics could no longer support the metaphysics.

In the light of this, it becomes clear how important it is to ask whether

---

47. It is especially Josef Seifert who has pointed out the presence of a Bonaventurian element in Wojtyła's thought. What seems to me more unarguable than a strict philological dependence is that he came upon this in the course of his own autonomous research. However, Wojtyła's interpretation of St. Thomas is on more than one occasion close to the great Franciscan saint. Cf. J. Seifert, "Karol Cardinal Wojtyła (Pope John Paul II) as Philosopher and the Cracow/Lublin School of Philosophy," in *Aletheia*, vol. 2 (1981), p. 164.

48. Seifert also says: "The difference *within* substance between persons and non-persons is more decisive for the understanding of being than any differentiation between all categories of being as such." Ibid., p. 198.

the fundamental categories of Thomistic metaphysics can be regained on the basis of a reflection upon the moral experience of the person, as conducted with the phenomenological method. If that were possible, one would regain the anthropological and philosophical Christian position, by freeing it from all of those elements which placed it in opposition to modern science, and so supplying a definitive solution to the "Galileo affair" which has profoundly disturbed the Catholic conscience in modern times. By the same maneuver, moreover, one would be to some extent poised to assimilate what is most authentic and legitimate in the will of modern thought "to start from man." Within Wojtyła's enterprise, one can go as far as follows: only the Christian conception of man is able to save the great intuition of modern thought by not allowing man, who is the point of departure of this philosophical perspective, to be lowered into the abstract notion of the subject which is understood purely intellectually, and from which the richness and the drama of the moral life are excluded.[49]

The starting point in St. Thomas' ethics and anthropology also permits us to reappropriate for Thomism the greatest intuition which Catholic thought has achieved in modern times — that of Pascal. In this way one may draw a relation of continuity and of reciprocal illumination between Pascal's phenomenology of the human condition and the Thomistic anthropology. To begin from the phenomenology of moral experience and to graft metaphysical reflection into the matters and the problems which phenomenology emphasizes (but because of its own internal dynamics must leave unresolved), permits one to arrive at the question of being from the question of man, through the question of the good.[50] This, for the rest, repeats the dynamism of the human research which can no longer pose the problem of man without at the same time posing the question of being in general, because in man the question of being rises to awareness. In this journey Thomism itself will be purified and amplified. It will be purified, first, of those contingent elements which flowed into it from the atmosphere

---

49. From Descartes onward, modern philosophy creates a radical division in human beings between intellectual subjectivity and emotional subjectivity. Ever since, philosophy no longer succeeds in creating a balanced relation between the two, and ends with alternately preferring a passion unmeasured by reason (as with Scheler) or a reason deprived of all human content (as with the rationalists).

50. It may be possible to show that the whole of Pascal's thought converges on the conviction that the truth of being is revealed only in that man who is interiorly inclined toward the good. On this point see the fundamental essay on Pascal by Augusto del Noce, in *Il problema dell'ateismo*, 2nd ed. (Bologna: Il Mulino, 1970).

of his time. And it will be amplified in the sense that "existentialist" Thomism, which has always accompanied the "essentialist" Thomism of tradition (but which the Thomistic tradition has failed to develop) can now be understood as foundational to St. Thomas's system. Returning to the sources and being faithful to tradition are the guides for the discovery and appreciation of the novelty which the spiritual temper of our times demands. This manifests the eminently creative character of this enterprise.

We will, on the basis of Wojtyła's other works, seek to emphasize the way in which he proceeds to reformulate St. Thomas's thought, and to outline the other consequences which follow from this interpretation of St. Thomas.

The general vision of St. Thomas's philosophy which Wojtyła provides is close to that of Gilson. It is probable that in one way or another Gilson is one of Wojtyła's direct sources. The thought of St. Thomas is thus not schematically opposed to that of Augustine. On the contrary it appears from this perspective as a synthesis between the Aristotelian elements and the Platonic-Augustinian elements, within which the Platonic and Augustinian idea of participation is central.[51] "Given that the good is really identified with being, this relation is accompanied by another relation, which is accidental being — which possesses being by participation *('ens per participationem')* — and the determinate being — which is an autonomous entity *('ens subsistens')*."[52] The notion of existence is thus drawn into the Aristotelian conception. Existence is the participation of *"ens"* in being. This occurs *secundum speciem, modum, et ordinem.*

Not everything that is "in being" participates in being in the same way: there is in being a hierarchy which articulates itself in the diverse species of being, and in an order which regulates the relation between the "entities" of the diverse species and their relation within the same species. This metaphysical order is at the same time an ethical order, because participation in being is inseparable from participation in value. With this we come

---

51. Perhaps we should not forget the decisive influence of Garrigou-Lagrange, which made Gilson's research turn toward a new interpretation of the text of St. Thomas, which is developed by Wojtyła by way of a creative integration of Thomism with elements of phenomenology.

52. "O metafizycznej I fenomenologicznej podstawie normy moralnej (W oparciu o koncepcje św Tomaza z Akwinu oraz Maksa Schelera," in *Roczniki Teologiczno-Kanoniczne* 6, pp. 99ff. Italian translation in *I fondamenti dell'ordine etico,* in the chapter called "Il fondamento metafisico e fenomenologico della norma morale sulla base delle concezioni di Tommaso d'Aquino e di Max Scheler." The citation is on p. 108.

upon an element which is enormously important for the structure of ethics: "We must see in the order of existence the ground of the real perfection of being in the mode which is appropriate to it, while the good becomes an object of knowledge only from the side of the essence, that is to say, the essence alone becomes a notion."[53] It is therefore not possible to reduce ethics to the eternal contemplation of an order of ideal essences. It regards, rather, the realization of values within existence. The fundamentally practical nature of ethics is thus recognized, as it was by Aristotle. If we connect this principle with the further principle that the nature which belongs to man is personal, we can see that the object of ethics is properly the person's coming to maturity through his freedom and not simply his fitting himself in with a given order. God is the Highest Good, and he has the fullness of existence. He is the superior and transcendent measure of beings. The "end" of every perfect being is a more perfect being, and all have their "end" in God, who is absolute perfection. On the other hand, God recapitulates in himself the perfection of all beings while always infinitely transcending them: he communicates being and goodness to everything which exists. "From this follows the resemblance to God of all creatures in being; this resemblance has its own gradation. Both the resemblance as such and its gradations are gathered together and known in the mind of God as exemplars: the Creator sees in Himself the highest exemplar out of which beings are created and knows them in His image, that is to say, inasmuch as they imitate His essence, which is the first object of his knowledge. It is here that we find the nucleus of the normative order."[54]

Every being, therefore, has its truth in God and it approaches Him by imitating the divine perfection. The metaphysical measure of being is bound to the divine exemplarity and to its imitation by particular beings.

In every experience of a particular good human reason recognizes a relation with the good. This is not because — in Platonic mode — it continually fixes its eyes upon the idea of the Good in itself but rather because it meets

---

53. Ibid., p. 110. Seifert (who is perhaps unaware of this text which clearly supports his own thesis) observes: ". . . I think that his [Wojtyła's] position constitutes a genuine breakthrough and criticism of the Aristotelian position insofar as it recognizes that moral goodness is of higher value than intellectual cognition as such." In "Karol Cardinal Wojtyła (Paul John II) and the Cracow/Lublin School of Philosophy," p. 196. But it remains to be seen whether this breakthrough does not bring to light what is implicit in St. Thomas's own Augustinianism.

54. "Il fondamento metafisico e fenomenologica dell norma morale sulla base delle concezioni di Tommaso d'Aquino e di Max Scheler," pp. 111-12.

the good in and through things, through a process of abstraction, reflection, and generalization *upon the essence of the good.* In this way St. Thomas avoids the two pitfalls which lie in wait for ethical reflection: to uphold a notion of the good which is completely cut off from experience; and to begin from an experience deprived in advance of that element of good which alone qualifies it as ethical. Instead, for Thomas, the good is immanent in a particular experience, and if we are to understand this particular experience in its fullest bearing, we must place it within the immanent horizon of absolute Good, that is, of God Himself. By arranging single goods in this horizon reason places them in a just and definitive hierarchy which links one to another. This hierarchy has both an objective aspect and a subjective aspect, which takes priority because the good is accomplished in concrete existence. The construction of the subjective order of values begins from the question: Which value will achieve at this moment in this situation the concrete perfection of the person which I am? To pray is usually a higher value than to eat, but my concrete existential situation may require that I put eating before praying if I want to realize the concrete perfection which is appropriate to me. The exemplarity of God is the basis of the entire normative order. It is therefore not abstract but personal.

This entirely dissolves the accusation of moralism which Scheler raised against the possibility of a normative order which imposes itself externally as a rule by which the subject is measured. The normative order which is based in divine exemplarity is, rather, the internal rule of goodness within any being, and it is objective for him because it contains at the same time the ultimate truth of his subjectivity. Reason, through which man becomes conscious of this order, therefore, has to speak about the ethical life and not just wrap itself up in simple emotionalism.

Another question is, rather, whether the objective ethical order can become part of a person's awareness and realized in it. It is clear, for the existential presupposition which we have described, that this will come about only through the free consent of the person, which, one hopes, will reorganize his affective perception of reality in the light of objective truth. Objectivity without the person's free consent cannot realize the ethical good because the human moral good comes about only through the act of a person. And yet, the objective ethical order does not lose its genuine objectivity if it is not recognized. If an objective value cannot be an existentially concrete good without being freely chosen, how much less can an objective disvalue be qualified as good, even if it is chosen in good faith by subjective conscience.

Wojtyła never dealt explicitly with the question of Thomas's proofs of the existence of God, but the way in which he deals with the problems of ethics takes us back through the idea of participation to what is, on this problem, most in common between Augustine and St. Thomas. If we examine the *Summa Theologiae* I, q.2 a.3, we see that St. Thomas indicates five ways through which it is possible to demonstrate that God exists. The first two have their roots in Aristotelian physics and refer to Aristotle's conception of motion and of the order of efficient causes. Since modern physics has criticized and invalidated these aspects of Aristotelian physics, the assault upon the rationality of affirming the existence of God has always focused most of its force upon the refutation of the first two arguments. I would not wish to deny the possibility of reinterpreting these arguments and giving them a new foundation, nor would I argue that Thomas intended them in a strictly "Aristotelian" sense. But I shall limit myself to saying that the most obvious interpretation of these arguments indicates that they must be linked to Aristotle's physics, and this is what most of the commentators have done. In this way one goes from the physical order of being to God.

The other three ways which Thomas sets out are different. St. Thomas's third way moves from the realization of the contingency of being and affirms that one could not rationally understand contingent being without the horizon of necessary Being. The fourth way *"sumitur ex gradibus qui in rebus inveniuntur"* ["is taken from the gradations to be found in things"]. In this, the Good and the True (and we may add the Beautiful) appear as the single horizon within which it is possible to know the truth, goodness, and beauty of beings, and which is also unarguably witnessed to by experience. The fifth way moves from the teleology which is observable within nature.

The third and the fourth ways, which may also have a somewhat Aristotelian resonance, draw their essential features from St. Augustine and St. Anselm, and have as their point of reference the ethical and ontic experience of the person. The metaphysical depth of Wojtyła's ethics is built upon these ways. The phenomenology of the moral life shows the centrality of the moment of judgment, of the free choice of the will illuminated by reason. Phenomenology yields to metaphysics, which formulates the only reasonable explicative hypothesis of this particular structure of the moral life. This explicative hypothesis must refer to the divine exemplarity as the origin of the normative order.

In this perspective, all of the positive features of Scheler's thought, which we have many times recalled, are accepted and esteemed and carried to a greater level of profundity. This is possible by beginning from the recognition of the ontological consistency of the Divine and the human person. The recognition that human persons effect ethical action compels one to recognize their ontological consistency. The personality of God, on the other hand, is the only horizon within which the ontological consistency of the human person can be thought. Considered through the concept of participation and posed as the ultimate root of the ethical order, God's exemplarity radicalizes Scheler's recognition of the centrality of "following" in the ethical life and at the same time divests his explanation of its irrationalism. That which one follows is ultimately the perfection of God, which must be reproduced in the person. Norm and value, therefore, have the same root, and it is thus possible to recognize a normative order without falling into the hypocrisy which condemns life in the name of an abstract precept. Wherever that which is lived with the utmost emotional intensity is sacrificed to that which is lived without emotional intensity, but is acknowledged as true, there the fascination of the more perfect good is actually made real and paradoxically coincides with the truth about the less perfect one. Man is made for the truth, and no values can be lived out which are not illuminated by truth. Analogously, this perspective takes Scheler's idea of God to a level of greater purity, and of infinitely greater profundity. As interpreted in relation to ethical questions, Thomas's metaphysics, at the same time, can show different aspects from those which the customary interpretation brings out, and can be seen in a way which is both more modern and more traditional.

Wojtyła's reading of St. Thomas begins from the *Commentary on the Ethics,* and especially from the treatises "On Man" and "On Beatitude" of the *Summa Theologiae,*[55] although we must not forget that Thomas's ethics continually draws upon his metaphysics. This approach, even if it is not very conventional, has the advantage of regaining St. Thomas's concept of experience. A major difficulty which a genuine grasp of St. Thomas's thought has to encounter is the alteration which the meaning of "experience" has undergone in the language of modern times since the dissemination of modern methods of scientific observation. Experience, as we generally understand it,

---

55. But the fundamental conception of the person may be traced in the treatise on the Trinity. This conception, which is the key to the revelation about God (who is a person and who lives in the reciprocal self-giving of the persons of the Holy Trinity) is also the key to the study of man in himself.

is the product of abstraction, which as objectivized by stripping away the affectivity which is immediately immanent to it is the datum of experience. The word "experience" has become almost synonymous with sensation, and it thus coincides with the objectifiable side of experience. Phenomenology, by allowing us to recapture the original and founding dimension of experience,[56] rediscovers the co-implication of ethics and metaphysics. Moral knowledge is a knowledge which introduces us to the truth of being. And what is more, there is no divided form of knowledge, in which the ethical aspect has been excluded in advance, which can introduce us to the truth of being. The reciprocal implications of ethics, anthropology, and metaphysics have their heart in the Thomistic notion of "persona."

Thomas assumes Boethius's definition of the person: *"rationalis naturae individua substantia."* That which has access to an immaterial knowledge cannot be defined as an object within the order of material nature. Rather, it is defined by a relation with the truth, and has a personal character. On the other hand it is only in a personal relation that the truth can be posed and affirmed as such.

"The rational nature does not have a genuine autonomous existence as nature; it subsists as a person. The person, therefore, is an autonomous subject of existence and of action, which otherwise could not be attributed to the rational nature. Note well: this is why God must be a personal being."[57]

St. Thomas especially applies this notion of the person in his treatise *On the Trinity*, which considers the personal being of God. Thus, God is not, as in Aristotle's naturalistic interpretation, a kind of place of ideas considered from an objective point of view. God is, rather, a person, and as such is a subjective agent who puts ideas into being through his creative work. The affirmation of God as Creator is directly connected with that of the personality of God; it is here that St. Thomas's philosophical and metaphysical innovation in relation to Aristotle can be seen most clearly.

On the other hand, personality, or being a person, is also the mark which man shares with God, in the sense of their original resemblance of which the Scriptures speak. Although the affirmation of the Trinity belongs only to the sphere of Revelation, the idea of God as a person is also typical

---

56. In which the knowledge of the thing is always accompanied by the discovery of value.

57. Wojtyła, "Personalizm tomistyczny. Dyskusja," in *Znak* 3 (1961), pp. 644ff. Italian translation "Il Personalismo Tomista," in *I fondamenti dell'ordine etico*, pp. 141ff. The text cited is on p. 143.

of contemporary philosophical reflection and is the source of a radical and new understanding of being. We have claimed that it is the heart of the whole corpus of St. Thomas's metaphysics and this heart is perfectly accessible upon the basis of ethical and anthropological reflection.

If we compare the Thomistic conception of the person, in God and in man, with the modern conception, we will see that from Descartes onward the idea of the person has been impoverished. The *suppositum* (substrate) which makes the person an intelligent and freely responsible being disappears. Rational nature is considered without any reference to an *individua substantia* (individual substance). As a result God becomes the place of true ideas, and deprived of an authentic freedom of creation. At the same time man is divided into extended substance and thinking substance, through the process of abstraction which we have already described, which bars access to the experience of the whole and to the causality of the person in relation to his own actions. We are left, therefore, with the person, as an empty consciousness which endlessly mirrors itself, and to which not even Hegel, despite the prodigious and the nearly infinite fertility of his philosophical genius, has been able to restore the pathos and the ethos of living existence.

In this chapter we have sought to illustrate the way in which Wojtyła's thought presents the necessity of *turning to the founding principles of the anthropology and the ethics of St. Thomas.* But in philosophy, as in history, one can never go backward. That is possible only as an archaeological and scholarly operation. In every time, philosophy must explain once again the genuine road to truth, beginning from the experience which is fitting to its own historical moment. So if it is necessary to return to the central foundations of the anthropology and the ethics of St. Thomas, this return cannot be simply entail the acquisition and repetition of his principles, but must involve the construction on their basis of a new philosophy able to provide a way into the truth of being which is adequate to the people of our times. The return to St. Thomas must be creative, as Leo XIII argued in the encyclical *Aeterni Patris.*

At what points is it necessary to innovate in relation to St. Thomas? Or, it may be better to ask, how does having lived through the adventure of modernity (and signally through Scheler's thought) allow us to deepen the same Christian wisdom *(sapientia christiana)* which St. Thomas summed up for his own times?

In accordance with the profoundly realistic genius of his philosophy, St. Thomas provided fundamental principles which allow us adequately to understand the human person and thus his personal relation with himself, with other human persons, with things, and with God. Nonetheless, having taken Aristotle and his philosophy as his special interlocutor, St. Thomas was driven to develop these principles in an way which is above all objectivist. He did not adequately develop the subjective side of the life of the person. Thus, although we find in St. Thomas the essential note of the freedom and the intelligence of the person, and his moral perfectibility and his causality in respect of his own actions, which are his responsibility, the dynamic interaction between these categories is not developed. Perhaps it is not by chance that, although the personal being of man is not placed in doubt, the questions of the *Summa* which are explicitly dedicated to man do not take the person as the fulcrum of the development of its inquiry. We find that the dynamics of the life of the person are developed, rather, and here extraordinarily by the Doctor Communis, when he speaks of angels and of God Himself.

In sum, St. Thomas provides an objective personalism, a set of objective features which are necessary to work out an authentic philosophy of the person. But the side of subjectivity lacks adequate development, as founded in human experience. "At this point we can observe," Wojtyła notes in one of his essays, "how far the conception of the person which we find in St. Thomas is objectivist. He appears not to analyze conscience and self-consciousness as genuine and specific symptoms of the subject-person. . . . St. Thomas shows the single faculty, both spiritual and sensitive, thanks to which the entire conscience and self-consciousness of man is formed, the personality in a psychological-moral sense, but in practice he ends there. Therefore in St. Thomas we can see very well the person in his objective existence and action, but it is difficult to catch sight of the living experience of the person."[58] This is the importance which Scheler has for philosophy in our times, despite his limitations. Scheler's phenomenology (amended in the sense which Wojtyła indicates) allows us to develop on the basis of personal experience a reflection which concludes in the confirmation of the Thomistic ontology of the person. This is the task which Wojtyła carried out in his main works. These are attempts to philosophize from experience, with a phenomenological method and the light of St. Thomas Aquinas.[59]

58. "Il personalismo Tomista," pp. 146-47.
59. There is also an experimental synthesis in the form of a short elementary manual of ethics, published in installments in *Tygodnik Powszechny,* in a kind of ethics column with the title "Elementarz etyczny," which appeared between 1957 and 1959. This is an exposition of the fundamental positions of Catholic ethics in existential language. We do not examine this text because its fundamental theoretical structure is based on the academic article which we discussed, or in some cases because it anticipates the solutions which will be given in the major works.

4. Love and Responsibility

The Method

Love and Responsibility contains Wojtyła's first positive attempt to build an ethic which could create an organic synthesis of ontology and phenomenology. It is worth carefully analyzing its structure, methodological framework, and contents.[1] The book analyzes sexual ethics in the context of interpersonal life. However, the chapters entitled "First Meaning of the Word 'using'" and "General Analysis of Love" make a claim about the principles of personalistic ethics which goes far beyond the particular question which the book addresses; the structure of the work provides a model of the integration of phenomenological analysis with an ontological per-

---

1. *Miłość i Odpowiedzialnosc. Studium etyczne* (Lublin: KUL, 1960). A small part of this, with the same title, appeared in *Znak* 12, pp. 561-614. A second Polish edition (this was unprecedented for a Catholic book) appeared in 1962, published by the editors of *Znak* in Cracow. In 1965 there appeared a third Polish edition, printed in London, and a French translation with a preface by Henri de Lubac. In 1969 a Spanish edition came out (Madrid: Razón I Fe), and the Italian edition: *Amore e Responsabilità. Studio di morale sessuale,* translated by Amrbetta Berti Milanoli, with a preface by Cardinal Giovanni Colombo (Tourin: Marietti). The third Italian edition contains a useful critical apparatus edited by Tadeusz Styczen, Adam Rodziński, Jerzy Gałkowski, and Andrzej Szostek. This edition contains improvements to the translation (for example, the translation of the word "uzjwac," which is rightly altered in the first chapter, from "godere to "usare" [from "to enjoy" to "to use"]. The translators, in this instance, have used the revised English translation by J. J. Willetts (London: Fount/San Francisco: Harper-Collins, 1981, 1982): *Love and Responsibility.*

spective. This element is present from the first page of the book, which summarizes the results of the critique of Scheler and of the dialogue with St. Thomas, which Wojtyła accomplished in the earlier phases of his thought, working toward the positive task of a new interpretation of the moral life.

"The world in which we live," writes Wojtyła, "is made of many objects." He goes on to observe that "the word 'object' here means more or less the same as 'entity' ":

> This is not the proper meaning of the word, since an "object," strictly speaking, is something related to a "subject." A "subject" is also an "entity" — an entity which exists and acts in a certain way. It is then possible to say that the world in which we live is composed of many subjects. It would indeed be proper to speak of "subjects" before "objects." If the order has been reversed here, the intention was to put the emphasis right at the beginning of the book on its objectivism, its realism. For if we begin with a "subject," especially when that subject is man, it is easy to treat everything which is outside the subject, i.e. the world of objects, in a purely subjective way, to deal with it only as it enters into the consciousness of a subject, establishes itself and dwells in that consciousness. We must, then, be clear right from the start that every subject also exists as an object, an objective "something" or "somebody."[2]

The affirmation that the world is made of many objects immediately calls to mind a series of alternative notions which have been present to the history of human thought in its effort to comprehend what the world is and what constitutes its "worldness." In order to understand the exact nature of the position which we are examining, it is worth briefly recalling some of these positions in order to understand where they concur with and where they diverge from that proposed by Wojtyła.

For Wittgenstein, the world is a set of facts. The facts impose themselves on the subjective spirit and because of that they are indubitably objective. A fact, however, is not precisely the same thing as an object. The fact is the self-giving of the object to the senses of the observer. In its turn, the protocol proposition which fixes and describes the facts cannot transcend the senses of the one who registers it, although the regulative ideal of the kind of knowledge to which Wittgenstein refers almost completely excludes the subjectivity of knowledge. The objectivity toward which this path leads is

2. Wojtyła, *Love and Responsibility*, p. 21.

an objectivity or a universal intersubjectivity of sensation, without ascending toward the Socratic or Platonic concept which alone allows the founding of a real universality. There are no means by which a knowledge whose only reference point is sensation can achieve objectivity and universality. The notion of an object is, on the other hand, more objective than that of a fact. The object is understood as existing in itself independent of the senses of the observer who registers it: its objectivity is not at the level of sensation, no matter how scientifically refined and controlled, but at that of the concept. Men can abstract the universal concept from sensible knowledge; only this is authentically objective. On the other hand, and from another point of view, the object considered by Wojtyła is even more subjective than Wittgenstein's "fact." Within the category of objects we find the subject himself, that is, the person. In Wittgenstein's perspective the person as such can never be present. We can go as far as considering the psychic acts in which he composes his existence, but the real support of these acts, the ontological substance of the person, is found nowhere in the horizon of the *Tractatus Logico-Philosophicus*. For this reason Wittgenstein must conclude that "that of which one cannot speak one must be silent" even if that about which we must be silent is actually the only thing worth speaking about — the personal being which, in his real depth and his living totality, is not the object of scientific research.

On the first page of *Das Kapital*, Marx remarks that the world appears to us in an unmediated way as a vast agglomerate of commodities. The idea of commodity contains the links between subjectivity and objectivity. The commodity is actually a thing which has been the object of human work, through which it incorporates human subjectivity. But the relationship between subjectivity and objectivity appears inverted.

Wojtyła calls attention to the fact that the subject, instead of appearing as the main and substantial element, is reduced to a mere appendage of the thing; man's human essence is thereby expropriated. Moreover, the subject does not appear as an "objective being" with his own given structure, which regulates his relations with other objects. The category of subjectivity is, rather, a general one, never sufficiently deepened. It is interpreted in two opposite ways by Marxists. For left-wing Hegelians, the subjectivity which is contained in the commodity should be understood as a Promethean self-consciousness which continuously objectifies itself in order to reappropriate itself in the revolutionary process of history. For others, subjectivity is, on one hand, an after-effect of the dynamics of social relations and, on the other, a product of the psychological and physiological dynamic of the

diverse basic compulsions which the human sciences study. In the first case
the idea of subjectivity is left in an idealistic fog. In the second it does not
transcend sensism. Marx's idea of dialectical materialism is constructed to
synthesize these two positions, but this attempted synthesis is not success-
fully achieved. The two positions are therefore once more divided, reviving
the old controversy between Marxist materialism and idealism (a dispute
which generally pits interpretations favoring the young Marx and his relationship with Hegel on one side and those favoring the mature Marx on
the other).

The traditional Aristotelian and Thomistic approach comes to mind
as one considers Wojtyła's critique. In this more traditional perspective, the
beginning of philosophical reflection is a consideration of being and the
wonder provoked by the being of being. This is, of course, the element of
the philosophical tradition which is the closest to Wojtyła's thought. In the
face of modern thought, which has attempted to take subjectivity as its
point of departure, Thomism always claims the primacy of being and
Wojtyła fully concurs. He does, however, immediately feel the need to
qualify this primacy of being by explaining how it differs from the mere
primacy of objects. The concept of object contraposes itself to that of the
subject. Object refers to a something, as opposed to a someone. The concept
of being also includes personal being. The subject is also a being. Thomism's
true point of departure, therefore, *does not imply a primacy of objects more
than a primacy of subjects,* because the notion of being embraces both the
subject and the object equally. The typical polemic against the modern
philosophies of subjectivity inclines to an excessive emphasis on the objective moment. But Thomistic philosophy must be saved from this tendency
if one wants to practice philosophy in the contemporary world. It would
be more appropriate to say that in order deeply to understand the world
of beings, one should begin from the subject rather than the object. In fact,
every thing is a presence and a participation of *being.* Being is that which
is. The being of things is always a limited and particular being. Every thing
is an utterly imperfect and an entirely inadequate likeness of the absolute
Being, God himself. But there is a hierarchy among beings. Some of them
contain in themselves a greater degree of being, a greater perfection, and
therefore a particular likeness to God. Of all created beings the person is
that being which most perfectly possesses this similitude to God. In the
person the being of beings becomes the object of wonder and therefore a
problem; and the person is the only being which is set the problem of
responding to the gift of being which comes from God. The person is

therefore that being in which the problem of the intelligibility and morality of one's own particular existence and of being in general arises and finds, in a certain sense, a solution.

For these reasons it would be better to begin by saying that the world is composed of a great quantity of subjects. The internal dialectic of Thomistic thought leads therefore to the fundamental requirement of modern sensibility which wants to begin from man rather than from dead objectivity.[3]

However, a methodological cautiousness restrains Wojtyła from explicitly beginning with the subject rather than the object. Despite certain similarities and despite his openness to the legitimate anthropological claim of modern thinking, there is an insurmountable difference between his approach and the main direction of modern thought, which goes from Descartes to Spinoza and Hegel. It is not the same to say that philosophy's point of departure is the subject (or subjects, taken in their plurality) as it is to say that its point of departure is that being which is the subject. In the modern sense beginning with the subject implies a fundamental forgetfulness both of the fact that there are other beings besides personal being and the fact that the subject is himself a being who as such *receives* the gift of being and by no means constitutes an absolute point of departure. Consequently in the modern perspective, even in those directions which are not defined in a idealistic way, the object is reduced to that which enters the subject's consciousness and, therefore, exists in and through the subject. Moreover, forgetfulness of the category of being leads one to make a beginning not from the concrete human being, but from abstract subjectivity by hypostatizing the activity of thinking as the essential characteristic of subjectivity and by neglecting and by trying to obviate the concrete substance, that Aristotelian "hypokeimenon" in which that activity inheres. The intelligence and freedom of the person are also understood outside their concrete incarnation, through the creation of a ghostlike meta-humanity, in the face of which real humanity, in its limits and grandeur, appears to be contemptible.

3. Josef Seifert was right to say: "Wojtyła is one of the contemporary philosophers who has emphasized that metaphysics, insofar as it is the science of being qua being not only in a universal general sense but in a sense of 'that which possesses being in the most authentic sense,' cannot culminate in a philosophy of substance as such. In fact, a completely new and deeper sense of being is encountered in the person." "Karol Cardinal Wojtyła as Philosopher and the Cracow/Lublin School of Philosophy," in *Aletheia* (1988), p. 198.

To keep faith with the legitimate claim of modern thought, which wants to begin with man, one needs to specify from the first that that man from which one begins is a being, that is to say a creature, and thus to set the anthropological problem within the philosophy of being.

Thus we arrive at the central concept of Thomistic anthropology, understood in Boethius's classical definition: *"rationalis naturae individua substantia."* The *"individua substantia"* is the "hypokeimenon," the real substrate in which the rational nature inheres.[4] Being connected with reality through the concept of person, it is not free to transform itself, as happens in Hegel, into a hypostatized idea of which the empirical subject is a mere carrier or exemplification. The likeness to God which belongs to rational nature is always and only the likeness to God of a really distinct individual being, which is distinct from God through its own "hypokeimenon."

Moreover, as Wojtyła explains, "The term *persona* has been coined to signify that a man cannot be wholly contained within the concept 'individual member of the species' but that there is something more to him, a particular richness and perfection in the manner of his being, which can only be brought out by the use of the word 'person.' "[5] The emphasis on the fact that the person is a being and on the identification of the person with the concept of being among other objects which are in this way infinitely different from God should not prompt one to forget the greatness of the difference between that very particular being which is the person and all other beings which are merely things. The other things participate in the perfection of the world only through their realization of their species' being, and the individual existence which comes to be and passes away in time acquires a degree of permanence through the endurance of the species. The species represents a higher level of perfection than the individual, and the individual achieves its perfection in the world by being a member of the species. Things are different for human life, for it achieves a particular participation of being through its intelligent and free adherence to the good. The human being can know and love the truth, and as a person he can turn to the person of God Himself and enter into a personal relationship with Him.[6] The act of freedom which recognizes the true and the good and

4. Colletti has recently rediscovered the importance of the hypokeimenon; within Italian philosophy, this has represented an important stage in the process of Colletti's departure from Marxism. See Colletti, *Tramonto dell'ideologia* (Bari: Laterza, 1980), esp. pp. 104ff.

5. *Love and Responsibility*, p. 22.

6. Wojtyła, "Człowiek jest osoba," *Tygodnik Powszechny* 18 (1964).

conforms itself to it is an individual act. For that reason, from a certain point of view, the individual has an eminent dignity superior to that of the human species, because he achieves a perfection of being, a likeness to God, higher than that which is given to the species. Consequently, the concrete person can neither be reduced to the activity of thinking, as Hegel wanted to do, nor to the species, nor to practical activity, as Feuerbach and Marx did (they were anticipated in this by Aristotle).

The human being has the capacity to know the truth and to want the good. Being endowed with reason, he questions his own being and considers his beginning and end. His search is oriented by two fundamental questions: "What is the first cause of everything?" and "How can I be good, and how can I reach the fullness of good?" The entire theoretical and practical ethical activity of human beings is referred to these two questions.

Of course, insofar as man has a body he is an animal; he belongs to the general order of his own species and of nature. He has consciousness, and is able to transcend the species order, but that does not mean he should ignore or prescind from that order. But his belonging to nature comes about through the mediation of his intelligence and his freedom. Engagement with the world of objects and of exteriority, including his body and his faculties, comes about through interiority. The "person" is indeed "that objective entity which, as a defined subject, has the closest contacts with the whole (external) world and is most intimately involved with it precisely because of its inwardness, its interior life."[7] The person can neither achieve nor know himself, nor can he develop his own potential to be good except through his own engagement with the reality which surrounds him. This structure of human being entails that the person can be responsible and the co-author of its own destiny. This is the reason why the person is *"alteri incommunicabilis."* No human being can be a substitute for another in his own free decision. And the objective good of the species, which is given to animals by instinct, must be perceived by reason and approved by will in man, in such a way as to be incorporated in the fundamental orientation of the person which, insofar as he is an intelligent and free being, tends to the truth and the good. Recalling St. Thomas's fundamental thesis on the natural desire to see God, which is closely linked to the fact that the human desire for happiness is not fully met by any created thing, one might say that the relationship with objects should always be such as to respect that

---

7. Wojtyła, *Love and Responsibility*, p. 23.

inclination to the Good which is God Himself, and which constitutes the fundamental axis of the ethical life.[8]

A problem arises here. How, if we wish to respect the dignity of the person, should we think about mutual relationships among human beings and in general about the relation of subjects with the world of objects? To this question Wojtyła responds with a profound analysis of the Polish word *"uzjwac."*[9] Man has the right to use the objects which are in the world. Moreover, the fact that his interiority is radically implicated in the world of things implies that he can only realize himself through the reasonable use of the objects of the world. "Reasonable use" implies that they should be used according to their intrinsic character, and without useless devastations and cruelties. But what of the fact that among these "objects" are included also one's own body and those of other human beings? The case in which the person is the object of one's actions is more complex.

Wojtyła explains that "Nobody can use a person as a means toward an end — no human being, not even God the Creator. On the part of God, indeed, it is totally out of the question, since, by giving man an intelligent and free nature, He has thereby ordained that each man alone will decide for himself the ends of his activity."[10] Reworking and integrating the Kantian formulation of the categorical imperative, Wojtyła formulates the personalistic norm which constitutes the fundamental axis of his ethical thought in the following way: ". . . whenever a person is the object of your activity, remember that you must not treat that person as only the means to an end, as an instrument, but must allow for the fact that he or she, too, has, or at least should have, distinct personal ends."[11] Wojtyła continues in this way: "This principle, thus formulated, lies at the basis of all the human freedoms, properly understood, and especially freedom of conscience."[12] Whereas the objectivistic view, holding as it does to the idea of the primacy

---

8. Cf. Thomas Aquinas, *Summa Theologiae*, I-II, qq.1-5.

9. This is also the opinion of the Italian translator of *Love and Responsibility (Amore e Responsabilità)*, who, in the third edition, has corrected the translation in the same direction.

10. *Love and Responsibility*, p. 27. Cf. also Wojtyła's "O znaczeniu miłości oblubieńczej (Na marginesie dyskusji)," in *Roczniki Filozoficzne* 22 (1974), pp. 162-74.

11. Wojtyła, *Love and Responsibility*, p. 28. God Himself prescribes some ends of the person, which must be achieved through the use of his freedom. This principle stands at the basis of all of Wojtyła's writings about the person and grounds his interpretation of the Second Vatican Council and its philosophical importance.

12. Ibid.

of objective truth, can go so far as wanting to impose it on those who do not recognize it, the personalistic view, which is rooted in a genuine philosophy of being, maintains that while the person indeed has the moral duty to adhere to the truth, he cannot be made to do so by overriding the choice of his freedom and his conscience.

How is it therefore possible to take the person as the object of one's act without undermining the personalistic norm? Only when two freedoms meet each other in the pursuit of a common good can the person be the object of reciprocal action conforming to the personalistic norm. In this case, the end of the act is a good toward which the will of the agent and the will of the one who is acted upon are both directed. The meeting of the wills which are oriented toward the good is the ethical substance of love.[13] In *Love and Responsibility*, of course, the analysis of love is oriented toward that particular form of love pertaining to conjugal union. The general indications which he gives have a wider application: love is really the only adequate attitude which one can take in the face of a person when that person is in any way the object of our acts. Of course the tonality and the affective quality of this love will change radically in different cases. But its ontological substance remains unchanged: one should want the good of the person and should orient one's own acts toward a good which is common both to oneself and to the person who is the object of the action and, by doing so, also respect that person's freedom.

The fact that love is not considered primarily as a feeling does not eliminate the fact that it is normally formed through and lives in a rich affective substance, which qualifies the different kinds of love. In any case, love implies the freedom of the other and turns toward his good, through the discovery of an agreement or even an identity between *the other's good* and *one's own good*. In this way loving is the opposite of using. In an act oriented by love the agent does not use the other for his own ends, but both are involved together in a movement toward a common objective good.

It is evident how much this approach owes to St. Thomas, from whom all of the fundamental categories of this discourse are taken. It is equally evident how much Wojtyła owes to Scheler and to all of modern thought.

---

13. In love the incommunicability of persons is preserved but also superseded and transcended. It is in this that Wojtyła's view is opposed to atheist existentialism (like that of Sartre); there the idea of the incommunicability of the person relates to one's thrownness into the world and one's insuperable loneliness.

The fundamental orientation is toward an ontology of the interior order, at the center of which is the person. The manifestation of the person and of the particular character of personal existence, within which values reveal themselves, is Scheler's great discovery. It manifests some important philosophical weaknesses, but keeps its force intact when one is trying to found a phenomenological psychology directed toward the uncovering of the values which structure psychic life. A similar psychology has a peculiar importance for the elucidation of the links between the sphere of experience and that of being.

The same personalistic norm, finally, is the keystone of Wotjyla's ethical conception, which is not fully comprehensible without reference to the work of Scheler and his view of the person as the place where values are manifested. Allied to this is the view that, although they exist independently, values are never realized or manifested in the absence of persons.

The personalistic norm depends equally upon the Kantian categorical imperative. Wojtyła gives a more comprehensive and wider interpretation of it. His criticisms of utilitarianism are entirely drawn from the parallel Kantian critique. Utilitarianism reduces the moral life to a simple calculation of advantages and disadvantages deriving from a specific action. Its point of departure is a limited and purely subjective view of the good of the individual, which is identified with pleasurable or painful feelings. Altruism, in this perspective, can only be founded on the pleasure which the good or the happiness of the other gives to me. The duty of wanting the good of the other depends on the measure in which such a good provokes a positive emotional reaction in the subject of the action. Utilitarianism misses the fact that man experiences a good which is not merely subjective, but objective, and insofar as that objectivity is also universal, such that in it the good of an individual joins together and meets the good of all other human beings, and the good of all the created universe. Kant was able to rise to this conception. The true good of the person coincides for him with the experience of that particular dignity which puts it beyond every created being. Hence the Kantian formulation: "Act in such a way that one never treats the other person merely as a means, but always as an end of your action." But this perception of the value of the person remains abstract for Kant, because it is consciously distinguished from every experience of pleasure and pain which accompanies a concrete action. The feeling arising from duty for duty's sake is the only feeling which has ethical relevance. But the objective good perceived in the person is absent from the world; in the world it is impossible to fix upon any binding order of values. As we have already seen, this is the point from which Scheler's criticism of Kant proceeds, although it falls into the extremes of emotionalism.

Return to a more comprehensive ethical principle, and to an Aristotelian and Thomistic realism, appears to Wojtyła not as a way of making cultural warfare against the modern world but as a necessity imposed by the wish to create a synthesis out of the antithetical principles which modern ethical philosophy is able to enunciate but cannot reconcile harmoniously, because of the weakness of the ontological presuppositions which it employs.

The Structure of the Work

In the first part of this chapter we have developed some fundamental methodological concepts which form the skeleton of *Love and Responsibility* and which form the first example of the synthesis which Wojtyła makes through the engagement with Kant and with Scheler, elaborated through a constant reference to the general principles of Aristotelian and Thomistic ethics and ontology. We intend now to provide a summary of the central contents of the work and of its articulations. The exposition will follow the philosophical structure of the work itself. The element of theology, especially moral theology, which we will occasionally introduce will support our comprehension of the philosophy of human sexuality developed by Wojtyła. It would be possible, of course, to take another approach, examining this book from the point of view of moral theology.[14] But we will forgo this option, since it seems to us that Wojtyła's true originality is in producing a view of man which arises from faith, the foundation of a renewed and deeper comprehension of the human reality, gained through an essentially rational method. Faith illuminates the intelligence without violating the natural way in which it proceeds.

Wojtyła first analyzes the relationship between the person and sexual

14. On Wojtyła as a theologian, see Stanisław Nagy, "Karol Wojtyła teologo/Karol Wojtyła teolog," in Wiktor Gramatowski-Zofia Wilińska, *Karol Wojtyła w świetle publikacij/Karol Wojtyła negli scritti* (Vatican City: Liberia Editrice Vaticana, 1980). This contains a bibliography which is an indispensable instrument for anyone working on the thought of Wojtyła. It also provides a series of introductions to the diverse aspects of our author's work, by Zygmunt Kubiak, Tadeusz Stycen, Stanisław Nagy, and Czesław Drazek.

instinct. The sensible and affective impression in which sexuality manifests itself takes place in the person. The person is inseparably body and soul. The end of sexual morality is to raise the sexual instinct to the level of the person, by transforming sexuality from something which simply happens in the person into a set of conscious and willed acts through which the person consciously realizes himself, in conformity to his dignity, in the sexual sphere. Sexual acts, which always have another person as their object, are only right and worthy when they happen within the sphere of love. Indeed, love is the only attitude worthy of the person, for it does not reduce the person to an object of enjoyment but respects the autonomy of its own end.

In the second section of the book, Wojtyła proceeds to an analysis of love, both in its psychological and its moral aspects, and he concludes that it is only in the moral judgment that one finds the key to an integral truth of love. Love is more than simple sexual attraction, more even than affective dedication. It implies a value judgment which has as its subject the person and his own good. Only a love which is founded on this value judgment and on the responsible decision of those who are engaged in it can have real stability and fecundity.

In the third section, entitled "The Person and Chastity," the author develops the moral virtue of the person, which masters the sexual instinct by channeling it into the order of love. This section addresses issues of chastity, shame, and continence.

The fourth and last section of the book, devoted to "Justice toward the Creator," deals with the experience of conjugal love and how it is part of a more universal order of existence within which alone it can manifest its entire meaning. Love is the welcoming of the person by a person. This welcoming, in its purity and definitiveness, can come only from God. Equally, the one who loves wants for the beloved a greater good than his love is capable of giving — that perfect happiness which is God himself. The concept and the notion of marriage and of vocation are inscribed in human love and in the sexual instinct which is at the basis of human love in the complete order of being. Finally, in an appendix, there are some particular questions about the relationship between sexuality and morality.

The Person and Sexual Instinct

In an animal sex is an instinct which can be fully understood by an external comprehension of its existence, such as that afforded by the behavioral sciences or biology. Human sexuality should, on the other hand, be defined as a tendency because a material instinct is drawn up into reason and liberty and therefore elevated into the sphere of the person. Considered from a personalistic point of view, sexual activity is charged with symbolic and cultural meanings. This is why it is necessary to bring it within a moral horizon.

The sexual tendency reveals to man his natural dependency: in order to complete himself he needs another human being of the opposite sex. To achieve his own destiny he needs to meet the freedom of another person and to depend on it. The demands of the flesh, which are expressed in the sexual tendency, are strictly linked to a more general, ontological, demand to be welcomed by another person. Moreover, sexuality is the most realistic school through which man learns the law of dependency which is at the same time the law of love. We have to deal with a dependency which is not imposed on the person from outside but arises from his own interiority and is the fullest expression of his liberty which recognizes self as made for the other. "If man would look deeply enough into his own nature through the prism of that need it might help him to understand his own limitation and inadequacy, and even, indirectly, what philosophy calls the contingency of existence (*contingentia*)."[15] This discovery of dependency has its definitive and organic expression in the recognition of man's dependence on God. It is God who is the sufficient object of that desire for happiness which draws a man toward a woman and one person toward another. This recognition happens through an education and a history; the sexual tendency is one of its essential levels so long as it is not reduced to its biological dimension. The object of sexual acts (understood in a wider sense) is never simply the body but the person of the other and because of this man is morally responsible for such acts: they must be worthy of the person. Of course sexual acts also have a biological meaning. They enter into the proper dynamism of that particular animal species which is *homo sapiens* and take part in the preservation and propagation of the species. But it is necessary to integrate the value of those biological acts into an existential and personal value. The two aspects illuminate one another: from the biological perspective we see sexuality as being linked with procreation, that is, with the coming into being of man himself. The new human being conceived through sexual acts is also a person. The meaning of sexuality is therefore completely existential. It enters in a decisive way into the research which

15. Wojtyła, *Love and Responsibility*, p. 48.

human beings conduct into the meaning and value of their existence. By generating another human being the person goes back in a certain way into the original place of his existence.

It is unavoidable that sexual behavior reflects one's self-esteem and one's own destiny; conversely, the development of sexual life strongly influences the person's self-understanding and his own fundamental attitude before being and in the face of life.

> The problem of the sexual urge is one of the crucial problems in ethics. In Catholic teaching it has a profoundly religious meaning. . . . The world is made out of creatures, or in other words entities, which have no existence of and by themselves since they do not themselves contain the final cause or source of existence. This source, and so the final cause of the existence of all creatures, is always and invariably to be found in God. Nonetheless these creatures participate in the general order of existence not only in that they themselves exist, but also because some of them at least help to transmit existence to new beings. So it is with human beings, with the man and the woman who use the sexual urge in sexual intercourse and enter as it were into the cosmic stream by which existence is transmitted. The distinctive characteristic of their situation is that they themselves both consciously direct their own actions and also foresee the possible results, the fruits of those actions.[16]

The preceding remarks have a peculiar importance when set in relation to the concept of "nature." In modern theology there is a tendency to say that the order of nature is the same as the set of results of the single science which deals with nature and man. With regard to sexuality the natural order would then coincide with the biological order. The personalistic principle which makes us enter into human interiority tells us that a complete account of human nature cannot be given by an external observation of bodily mechanisms. Thomas Aquinas himself said that natural law "is a participation of the eternal law in the rational creature."[17] What is natural for man is only what his reason judges to be right because it is in agreement with the original inclination of his being toward the truth and the good.

The behavior of a person is moral when it takes in a free and rational way the inclinations inherent in the sexual tendency by contextualizing them in the complete order of one's own personal life and by subordinating

16. Ibid., p. 54.
17. Thomas Aquinas, *Summa Theologiae*, I-II, q.91, a.2.

them to the law of love. Emotional and sexual pleasure which is connected to a sexual relationship finds its right place in this context. It is in itself a good thing and it is also a powerful stimulus to the development of love between persons. But it cannot be taken as an autonomous end, because the goal of the relationship between the two sexes cannot be the search for pleasure but must involve a deep and personal relationship in which the other is welcomed and respected. Sexual pleasure enters into the experience of love which must necessarily be subordinated to the complete dynamic of the person.

In the light of these principles, Wojtyła takes a stand against both rigorism and sexual permissiveness. In spite of their apparent polarity both rigorism and permissivism agree in the following: both presuppose that it is possible to separate the enjoyment and the biological end of sexuality, love, and procreation. Both systematically ignore the integration of both of these elements in personal action. Rigorism justifies sexuality only insofar as it is oriented to procreation; through the sexual instinct the human body appears as a mere instrument used by God or by nature to assure the survival of the species. The only moral position then becomes the human consent to an instrumental use of one's body, and the more empty of physical and emotional enjoyment the consent is, the better. Thus separated, physical pleasure becomes an independent end in itself; and this follows necessarily from the rigorist's negative attitude to it. In the correct personalist perspective, man freely collaborates with God and with another human person in procreation. All of the elements of sexuality are raised together toward the level of the person, and in this is also found the fullest realization of the components of enjoyment and play which are inseparable from sexual life which is both existentially authentic and morally good.

> The problem for ethics is how to use sex without treating the person as an object for use. Rigorism, which is so one-sidedly intent on overcoming the element of *uti* in sex, unavoidably leads to precisely that, at least in the sphere of intention. The only way to surmount the element of *uti* is to embrace simultaneously the alternative, fundamentally different, defined by St. Augustine as *frui*. There exists a joy which is consonant both with the nature of the sexual urge and with the dignity of human persons, a joy which results from collaboration, from mutual understanding and the harmonious realization of jointly chosen aims, in the broad field of action which is love between man and woman. This joy, this fruit, may be bestowed either by the great variety of pleasures connected with differences of sex, or by the sexual enjoyment which conjugal relations can bring. The

creator has designed this joy, and linked it with love between man and woman insofar as that love develops on the basis of the sexual urge . . . in a manner worthy of human persons.[18]

It goes without saying that from an existential point of view rigorism is incapable of ensuring a balanced esteem for sexuality. It separates pleasure from the objective procreative finality of the sexual instinct. When the tendency toward pleasure is not understood positively it is shoved back into the unconscious instead of being integrated in a personal and authentic love. Paradoxically, rigorism leads to an inevitable reaction of permissivism. Permissivism is the other side of the same coin. It considers the subjective side of the sexual tendency as the true end of sexuality and regards pro-creation as an accidental element. Sexual life, instead of being elevated to a personal level, is separated from interiority. Moreover, given the great importance which sexual life has for the person's moral existence, one can say that the whole sphere of interiority, which entails a value judgment on sexual instincts, is denied. The person limits himself to registering what happens within him, in a subjectivism deprived of any authentic interiority, and conforms his behavior to instincts without exercising discernment and responsible decision. The mechanism of sublimation, through which sexual instincts are channeled to collaborate with the development of affectivity and the cultural value of the person, is undermined at its own foundations. The unitive nature of the experience of love is minimized in this perspective, just as it is in utilitarianism.

In love the person transcends himself, is dislocated from himself and moves into the other, orienting himself toward an emotional and affective center which he shares with the beloved. Because of this, conjugal love and care for offspring, which are strictly tied, are among the fundamental social instincts through which human community is formed. Permissivism, however, makes individual pleasure the center of sexual experience; it impedes the development of a stable relationship of reciprocal dedication between two persons; it blocks the channels which link procreation and the genesis of the family. Permissivism introduces the utilitarian principle into the sexual sphere and prevents the harnessing of one of the fundamental human energies in the construction of the person's full moral maturity. This "must, clearly, affect the whole spiritual position of man. After all the human spirit here on earth forms a unity of substance with the body, so that spiritual life

18. Wojtyła, *Love and Responsibility*, pp. 60-61.

cannot develop correctly if the elementary lines of human existence are hopelessly tangled in contexts where the body is immediately involved."[19]

The personalistic perspective, finally, imposes upon us a reconsideration and a deepening of the traditional doctrine of the ends of marriage. These are, traditionally, "procreation of children," "mutual help," and the "remedy against concupiscence."

From a personalistic point of view, these three ends do not, in themselves, legitimate the union of man with woman. The norm which regulates this union is love, insofar as it is the only valid attitude of one person toward another. The ends are the concrete determination of that which love implies in the sexual sphere: the collaboration in the destiny of the other, which is achieved through bodily and spiritual fecundity, that is, through paternity and maternity; reciprocal assistance and the right orientation of desire. It is therefore false and reductive to try to translate *mutuum adiutorium* into the modern idiom by calling it "love." Love is not one of the ends of marriages but the fundamental norm which regulates it, and it is only within it that the ends achieve a full moral value. The correct estimation of the love of man and woman which is the foundation of the institution of marriage, therefore, does not come from an alteration of the traditional doctrine (as would happen if one were surreptitiously to introduce love among the ends of marriage); rather, it should come from a deepening of that doctrine in the light of Christian morals.

The Person and Love

It may be that both Wojtyła's debt to Scheler and the degree to which he has corrected Scheler's methodology are most evident in this section of the book.

At the beginning of love there is the experience of attraction, and this attraction includes an implicit recognition of value. A human being never feels a pure sensual attraction which is not accompanied by the recognition of value. The fact that one is pleased by a body implies the judgment that it is a good and contains a good in itself. The faculty of grasping attraction and affectivity is in itself a positive human quality. It allows one to perceive

19. Ibid., p. 66. In his critique of sexual permissivism and libertinism, Wojtyła is particularly critical of Freud. In some ways, his criticisms recapitulate those of Scheler in the *Nature of Sympathy*. It is necessary to say that in the final phase of his thought Freud partially corrected his position, perhaps in response to Scheler's criticisms.

reality as charged with nuances, interesting particularities, and variegated tonalities. The more an individual's affectivity is enriched, the more he will be in full and satisfying contact with the reality around him and the more this reality will seem to worth loving and living. In affectivity, the values of reality reveal themselves and are lived with immediacy and transport. Values reveal in their manifestation a certain hierarchy which has a special correspondence with the temper of the individual. Not everyone is charmed by the same values and to the same extent. The hierarchy in which values present themselves in affectivity is not necessarily the same as that which they have if they are considered in an objective and non-emotional way. In affectivity attention is focused upon the feeling which one experiences, in its intensity and its authenticity. However, the force through which value is grasped does not necessarily correspond at all to its objective worth. Thus, in the case of sexual love, affectivity is concentrated on the state of consciousness which the presence of the beloved provokes in us, ignoring its correspondence with the object which produces it. The object of love appears to us idealized and overcharged with every virtue; this perception can obstruct an objective attitude to them.

Affectivity has an extraordinary importance for the moral life: only a moral life can make us discover values in a concrete way as living experiences. Without affectivity the moral life is thin and gray, and it inevitably turns into moralism. However, affectivity alone is not sufficient. It needs the standard of an objective judgment. Affectivity concentrates our attention on the values which the other provokes in us rather than on those values which the other really possesses. And this is a weak base for love between persons. Personal love gains its maturity only when it turns itself away from what the other makes me feel, and toward what the other is in himself or herself, considering not this or that particular characteristic of the beloved which exercises a special charm upon us, but the person as such. Sexual attraction, the charm of femininity or masculinity, therefore becomes a path which leads to the emotional perception of the value of the person. Only the value of the person can sustain a stable relationship. The other values of sexuality are wasted away by time and are exposed to the danger of disillusion. But this is not the case for the value of the person, which is of a different ontological quality, one which is stable and in some way infinite. When love develops and reaches the person, then it is forever.[20]

20. Scheler's attitude toward love in *The Nature of Sympathy* is similar in some respects and very different in others from that of Wojtyła.

This is why the conjugal covenant is indissoluble; it is a covenant of reciprocal giving founded on the recognition of the value of the person.

In order to accomplish this it is first necessary to go from simple attraction (which the medievals called "love of desire"), which is already love but only in an inchoate and germinal way, to the true and proper love ("love of goodwill").

In simple attraction or "love of desire," the other is recognized as a good for me, as someone of whom I feel a lack, and who makes my existence fuller. The other is loved not as an object to satisfy mere passion but desired, nonetheless, as a good for me, as an answer to a privation or a lack in my own being. Yet this is a precarious state into which concupiscence can easily enter and prevail. Concupiscence itself is not sin, that is, a breaking of love, but it is the occasion of sin, a temptation to make the other person a mere tool of one's own sensual and intellectual satisfaction. In order to avoid such an abuse of love it is necessary that the attraction mature into a profound goodwill.

The specific feature of the "love of goodwill" is that one seeks first the true good of the other:

> Goodwill is quite free of self-interest, the traces of which are conspicuous in love as desire. *Goodwill is the same as selflessness in love:* not "I long for you as a good" but "I long for your good," "I long for that which is good for you". . . . Love as goodwill, *amor benevolentiae,* is, therefore, love in a more unconditional sense than love of desire. It is the purest form of love. Goodwill brings us as close to the "pure essence" of love as it is possible to get. Such love does more than any other to perfect the person who experiences it, bringing both the subject and the object of that love the greatest fulfillment.[21]

The love of goodwill introduces something new in the relation between man and woman. The desire for the other as an answer to one's own ontological insufficiency and as the completion and the company of one's own person no longer comes first. Something else comes first: the wonder aroused by the other's beauty and the will that that interior beauty of the person which is perceived in the lover's glance should realize itself. The love of desire is not cancelled out, for the lover still desires the beloved for himself, but only on the condition that this is the path through which the beloved can attain her own destiny.

21. Wojtyła, *Love and Responsibility,* pp. 83-84.

After the development of such love in the interiority of the person the fundamental problem of the integration of love arises. It is not enough that one person loves in such a way, nor is it even enough that two persons love one another in such a way. It is necessary that their subjective loves meet one another and integrate one another and by so doing constitute a love between them, a relationship which objectively influences and characterizes a concrete human space of existence. The integration of love is the integration of the personalities of those who love one another. The desire which is at the basis of the attraction is simultaneously achieved and transcended, so that one is protected from the danger of treating the other as an instrument. What the lover desires is now that the beloved participate in the realization of that personal truth which is the common love, that is, the expansion and the integration of their persons in their reciprocal relationship. The sexual tendency and desire are redirected within this personal polarity. For this reason there can be in love a true reciprocity which would not arise without goodwill; a lesser reciprocity, founded only on sensuality or affectivity, would depend upon reciprocal "enjoyment" and would only be secure "as long as things work out."

Man usually experiences many sexual stimuli and many emotional inducements which continuously offer equally or more seductive possibilities of new sexual relationships. Hence the argument that human beings are "naturally polygamous." If the beloved is only an instrument through which something, say, sensual pleasure or affective sensations, happens in oneself, then he or she can easily be replaced in such a function, a fact which casts a permanent shadow of doubt over the relationship. The case is different when through goodwill love reaches the person and bases itself on it. Then the other is loved not for the quality that he has (and which one can lose or which others could have in a higher degree) but for the mystery which is the destiny and the fullness of being toward which a man and a woman are drawn together. Only then is their living together something more than the joining of two selfish individuals, and capable of achieving a real personal unity.

Spousal love is properly the gift of oneself to the other as well as the welcoming of the gift of the other to oneself; in such love, the will toward and the realization of a reciprocal belonging are founded on the acknowledgment that in such a way the greater good is accomplished and with it one's own destiny and the destiny of the beloved. In love, freedom finds a sufficient object to whom it can give itself in order fully to realize itself in dependence on the other and in obedience to a common destiny. The person, who essentially belongs to himself, can belong to another only through the free gift of one's own love. But such a gift cannot imply a one-sided dependency, a concession of the right to be used as an instrument by the other. It requires the reciprocity and the engagement of the other in the construction of an objective as well as common love.[22]

Wojtyła's fundamental concern in the summary analysis which we set out is to give due weight both to the subjective and to the objective aspects of the experience. Both are important: what happens in the human being matters, especially the sexual and affective reactions which are the building blocks of spousal love, but the truth of things matters more. If the subjective passion does not correspond to the truth, if one attributes to the other a set of qualities which he does not really have, if one erroneously identifies what is truly good for the other and what is good for oneself, it is not possible to create a proper love, no matter how sincere the subjective feelings are. Of course the true judgment must also reflect one's own subjective state of mind, which is also in its own way an objective given for which one must account. The true judgment is always a judgment about the person, and not about a dead objectivity, with which one can deal without concern for what happens in the conscience and for the way in which the person experiences the situation. The true judgment is in a certain sense a synthesis of subjectivity and objectivity: an objective judgment on a situation which also exists in the subject. However, what man wants is ultimately decisive, that is, the assent of the will to the feelings matured within the person through the spontaneous attraction for the other's value, after reasonable reflection and the guidance of reason which has its point of reference in the truth. The pivotal role is played here by the fundamental Thomistic distinction between the "act of man" and the "human act." This distinction is one of the leitmotifs of Wojtyła's ethical thought; at the same time, it is the critical point at which he introduces Scheler's phenomenology into an Aristotelian and Thomistic framework.

The act of man is what happens in man without the cooperation of his will or the judgment of reason. It implies merely instinctive reactions. But the human act is what is achieved by man insofar as he is a man, that is, through the engagement of intelligence and reason. Sexual attraction is

22. It is evident that if one concedes to the other the right to use one's person, one is not helping him to follow his own true good. The requirement of reciprocity is not only called for in order to defend one of the pair who participate in a common love, but also to defend the love as such.

an act of man, because it *happens* in man. Falling in love, inasmuch as it is above all an emotional phenomenon, also *happens* to a person, and the person merely registers that in-loveness arising in himself. Love is, by contrast, a human act, an act in which the person engages all of his faculties. Sexual attraction and falling in love draw the will toward a decision, by making it appear desirable. However, reason should always decide whether it is right to engage the will in the way in which what is happening directs. Only in such a way is love drawn up into the sphere of the person, and only in such a way can it direct itself not toward those particular qualities which arouse sexual and emotional reactions but toward the value of the other person, which manifests itself through its femininity or masculinity.

One can well understand in this perspective the reason for Wojtyła's opposition to situation ethics. Situation ethics supposes that the ultimate criterion of judgment is in the authenticity of subjective experience. Life is always concrete and existential and cannot be judged on the basis of general and abstract norms. One needs to let oneself be led by what happens in existence and by the values which manifest themselves in this existence without trying to coerce them. Such a position is certainly comprehensible and even beyond criticism if we prescind from the constitutive links which lie between reason and freedom. Freedom, however, cannot engage in the situation if it does not let reason guide it, that is to say, if it is not guided by the true and objective knowledge of the values at stake. Here we encounter the problem of obligation. Knowledge of objective value, understood in an ontological sense, obligates the conscience. The conscience puts at stake its own freedom, both in the face of value and in the face of the norm, which follows a true knowledge and which judges the perceived values according to the truth. Freedom is always a choice between either adhering to that fullness of being and goodness which reason acknowledges or allowing oneself to be seduced by the fascination of a minor truth and the lesser fullness of being which is found in the attractiveness of the immediate, sensible, and emotional presence. If one suppresses the norm[23] which is the standard of measure of freedom, as atheist existentialism and situation ethics both prompt one to do, then one deprives oneself of the indispensable conditions by which one can understand the drama of freedom. Then freedom loses its ontological content, the fact that it is a choice

---

23. The influence of the Thomistic conception of the norm as *regula et mensura humanorum actuum* [rule and measure of the human act] is evident in Wojtyła's writings (cf. *Summa Theologiae*, I-II, q.90, a.1).

between life and death. Paradoxically, by the overemphasis upon the tragedy of the human condition, existentialism ends by completely emptying it. If the choice is not between good and evil, all choices are ultimately the same and choice no longer exists, only self-abandonment to multiple and transitory seductions.

Wojtyła emphasizes that it is through choice that human beings rise to the moral level and lift their love to that level. The emotional and sensual elements are by no means eliminated; on the contrary they are the condition of the exercise of judgment. Reason cannot orient the person's choice except on the basis of the concreteness of lived experience and of the emotional states which make it up. But in moral choice these emotional states are transcended; it is through them that the ethical substance of the person is engaged. If one follows out the logic of this, one must say that love is a virtue which is formed by esteeming and mastering sexuality and affectivity.

Sexual relationships between persons are the expression of their union, of an ec-stasis in which each of them sets the center of his moral life outside himself, in the other, on the basis of a mature judgment which identifies this self-giving as a way to fulfill one's personal destiny. If one takes this affirmation to its deepest level one understands why any true love is, properly speaking, in God. God is indeed the ultimate destiny of the person, and to love another is always to will this destiny for the other, and to offer oneself as a partner in this process. Of course, one does not have to be aware that one is going toward God in order to experience love; rather, it is in the dimension of love that one really learns (much better than through any abstract proposition) the meaning of tending toward God, that is, toward love.

This tending toward God of every true love is the reason why the Church elevates marriage to a sacrament and makes it the most engaging and concrete way in which man learns how to love. That is, he learns what is the right attitude to the person, and that attitude will be mirrored in different ways in every human relationship.[24] The sexual tendency leads men and women toward the hardest and most efficacious school in which they learn in patience, in dedication, and also in suffering what life is and how the fundamental law of life, that is, self-giving, concretely shapes itself.

---

24. Cf. Wojtyła, "Instynkt, miłość małżeństwo," *Tygodnik Powszechny* 8 (1952); "Myśli o małżeństwie," in *Znak* 9 (1957), pp. 595ff.; "Propedeutyka Sakramentu Małżeństwa," in *Rola kobiety w Kościele* (Lublin, 1958), pp. 87-92.

Of course it will be impossible to require that this complete awareness be present from the beginning of every marriage. It grows through conjugal life — through the generation and the education of children, through the engagement of characters, temperaments, and obligations in common experience, through the test of suffering which is an ineliminable element of complete human experience. It takes a long span of time to learn that the only way truly to possess the other is to respect her irreducible destiny, by accepting that one must lose the beloved in order to find her again in the shared path toward God.[25] To begin a marriage (that is, to begin a proper sexual life together) it is sufficient to be open to living the experience of human love without reserve and limitation; this, according to its internal dynamic, will lead to such an outcome.

The Person and Chastity

The virtue of love, which is Wojtyła's key for understanding sex, and even more for understanding ethical life in general, requires a deeper elucidation of the traditional moral doctrine of chastity.

According to St. Thomas there are two principal types of "passion of the soul": the concupiscible appetite and the irascible appetite.[26] Temperance is a virtue which moderates and restrains the concupiscible appetite and chastity is the virtue which moderates and restrains the concupiscible appetite insofar as it directs itself to sexual objects.[27] The dominant concern in the virtue of chastity is therefore directed toward the integrity of the person.

If one accedes to a superficial interpretation of chastity it is easy to see it as an obstacle to love. According to this common perception, chastity keeps man constantly within himself while love takes him out of himself; in losing himself in an ecstatic situation, in a certain way, he loses self-control. Chastity, on such a view, would be the virtue which attempts to keep the person locked within a mediocre life, a life which is emptied of vitality and ultimately selfish.

Without denying the connection between chastity and temperance,

---

25. The depiction of this truth is at the heart of Wojtyła's *The Jeweller's Shop*, which will be discussed later in this book.

26. Thomas Aquinas, *Summa Theologiae,* I-II, q.23, a.1.

27. Ibid., II-III, q.143, a.1.

Wojtyła overturns this perspective by bringing the end which chastity serves to the foreground. The fundamental point of reference of chastity is not the integrity of the person. Rather, it is the integrity of the love toward which the person orients himself, as toward his fulfillment. Chastity has the function of making love possible as love of the person.

We can speak of love as ec-stasy, as going out of oneself, in two ways. First, it is that in which the person lets himself be overcome by what happens to him, surrendering to his impulses. Second, it is that in which the person consciously puts the center of his emotional life and in a certain way his own ontological consistency in the other. In this case the passion is confirmed by a mature and free judgment which recognizes in it a sign and a path toward the fulfillment of the destiny of the person and consigns all of its energies to it. Chastity aims to preserve the possibility of this latter kind of ec-stasy, which is the only authentic one, whereas the former kind is only a feeble imitation.

Chastity is therefore opposed to love only if one makes love synonymous with what happens in sensuality and affectivity. If one places the essence of love in freedom and in will, chastity is the indispensable condition of love. In love, in any case, the freedom and the will lose themselves because love is a greater value than freedom. However it is an essentially different thing to be carried away by passion and to engage oneself by recognizing in the value of the other something which merits true dedication. In the latter case freedom is superseded, but in a deeper sense it is also maintained and achieves its maximum realization.

If we strictly connect chastity with love we see how mistaken is the belief that chastity consists in a negation of the value of sex and of the body or that it is a negative attitude, such as an obligation to abstain. On the contrary, chastity engages one in a correct appreciation of the value of the body and of sex, which are perceived in their truth only insofar as they are related to the person. These values are esteemed and loved as the quality of the person, and they are treated according to the dynamic which is peculiar to the interpersonal relationship. Moreover, chastity does not require a merely negative attitude. It consists of a fundamental assent to the value of love, from which follows a series of denials, directed to protecting the possibility of a full development of this love.[28] Consecrated chastity has its center in a loving personal relationship with God in Christ, and not in

28. Cf. Wojtyła, "Miłość i Odpowiedzialnosc," in *Ateneum Kapłańskie* 51 (1959), pp. 163ff.; "Wychowanie miłośći," in *Tygodnik Powszechny* 14 (1960).

the belief in the generic superiority of spiritual values over the values of the body and of sex.[29] Rather, chastity reminds us that the key of true human happiness or even sexual happiness is not in the body, one-sidedly considered. This key is rather in the totality of the person and the dynamic which is proper to it.

This interpretation of chastity brings the experience of sexual shame into the foreground. The identification of love as the fundamental virtue of the sexual life stands between the traditional view of chastity and Scheler's phenomenological analysis of shame.[30] When the traditional picture of chastity is referred to love of the person it gains phenomenological concreteness, while in Scheler's position it receives a metaphysical consistency which is not part of its original makeup. Scheler had already noticed that shame is not necessarily linked to the embarrassment about an evil or about a value which is considered as negative or inferior. Shame can also be linked to a good, which belongs to the interiority of the person and to the fact that he could be wounded if he is exposed to everyone's regard. Sexual shame is bound to the fact that sexual love is one of the most fundamental as well as most delicate experiences of the life of the person. Shame functions to prevent appreciation for the sexual values of the body, becoming an obstacle to (rather than leading toward) the proper value of the person. It protects the person from the sexual reaction which his body arouses in others as well as from the sexual reactions of his own body, and in so doing it defends the possibility of love. Its link with chastity is therefore obvious. "We see then that the proper understanding of sexual shame gives us certain guidelines for sexual morality in general. A mere description of the phenomenon, even if it is as perceptive as that of the phenomenologists, is not sufficient here — a metaphysical interpretation is also necessary. Sexual ethics may find an experimental point of departure in the feeling of shame. . . ."[31]

In shame one can see in a certain way the respect for the mystery of the person who through his acts simultaneously uncovers and conceals himself. The person in his spiritual substance never presents himself except with his natural reactions and in concomitance with them. Because of this,

29. Ibid.; see also K. Wojtyła, "Religijne przeżywanie czystosci," in *Tygodnik Powszechny* 9 (1953).

30. Cf. Max Scheler, "Shame and Feelings of Modesty," in Max Scheler, *Person and Self-Value: Three Essays,* with an introduction, edited and partially translated by M. S. Frings (Dordrecht: Martinus Nijhoff, 1987).

31. Wojtyła, *Love and Responsibility,* p. 178.

the spiritual substance of the soul is never available to phenomenological description. However, the analysis of some specific human situations reveals in a more evident way how the behavior and the processes of the state of mind which phenomenology describes are, so to speak, determined from above by a higher power. By virtue of its action, it orders and sets in being those situations which can be the object of description. The person therefore is not only the place where values come about, but the real subject in which they inhere. The phenomenological analysis of shame indicates in the person the "hypokeimenon" which supports the universe of sexual values both in a passive and in an active sense. The former functions as its support; the latter promotes it with one's own action. To indicate is not the same as to explain. The explanation of these elements, to the extent to which it is possible, is the task of metaphysical interpretation which, for the particular relationship with this phenomenological point of departure, we could also call "transphenomenological."[32] In shame we see an instinctive recognition of the subordination of instinct to a superior power, which is rational and more intimately personal.

Metaphysical analysis brings us, therefore, once again to the recognition of the moral virtue of chastity as the ultimate implication of the phenomenon of shame, which is profoundly rooted in the person.

Chastity is also, in the moral order, strictly bound up with the virtue of continence. Continence is the custom of mastering bodily concupiscence, a custom which allows a chaste use of the sexual powers of the person. A clear awareness of the value of the person is at stake in sexual experience. It is the consideration of objective values which leads one to avoid false values by fostering a correct use of every energy and all of the potentiality of the person. This happens especially through dialectical sublimation. The restraint of concupiscence transforms it by a moral

---

32. The feeling of shame has an analogous role to that of the feeling of duty in the thematic organization of Wojtyła's thought. A sentiment which is the object of phenomenological description, it is nevertheless not completely summed up in that description. This marks a limiting point beyond which phenomenology must give way to metaphysics. For its own part, such a metaphysics must *pass through* phenomenology. "We use the word 'metaphysics' to mean not something which is 'independent from phenomena' but something which is 'transphenomenological,' and thus not 'beside' or 'above' phenomena; rather, in and through the manifested form, which shows in the experience of the entire human being as an affective and subsistent agent; we must see the subject of this being and this action." "Person: Subjekt und Gemeinschaft," in AA.VV., *Der Streit um den Menschen. Personaler Anspruch des Sittlichen,* "Kevalaer" (1979), p. 19. Originally in *Rocziki Filozoficzne* 24/2 (1976), pp. 5-39.

action into an authentic value. To the degree that the person allows himself to be penetrated by the fascination of objective value, the energy of affectivity and even of sexuality turns toward it. Sublimation is precisely the process through which energy which was initially bound to an inferior value turns toward superior values. A correct process of sublimation gives an invaluable aid both to the affective life and to the moral life. Of course, the process of sublimation presupposes the subject's acceptance of his or her own sexuality together with the will to elevate it into the sphere of the person and a patient openness to ascesis:

> We can speak of objectivization only when the will is confronted by a value which fully explains the necessity for containing impulses aroused by carnal desire and sensuality. Only as this value gradually takes possession of the mind and will does the will become calm and free itself from a characteristic sense of loss. For it is a fact which we all know from our own inner life that the practice of self-control and of virtue is accompanied, especially in the early stages, by a feeling of loss, of having renounced a value. This feeling is a natural phenomenon, it tells us how powerfully the reflex of carnal desire acts upon the conscious mind and will. As true love of the person develops, this reflex will grow weaker, and values will return to their proper places.[33]

Phenomenology alone is unable to understand and justify the renunciation of a value which is evident and charming for the sake of a higher value which moral conscience perceives but is not able to present with sufficient experiential evidence. The metaphysical analysis of values, on the contrary, justifies this choice which is confirmed by the enrichment of moral as well as affective experience, which usually comes afterward.

Of course the dialectic of sublimation is concerned above all with affectivity. It constitutes in itself a first transcendence of sensuality which makes it malleable and relatively docile as well as open to being integrated in a relation and to being oriented to personalistic values. This view, which draws upon the contributions of both Scheler and Aquinas, is clearly differentiated from Kant's view, which excludes the empirical, sensible element as part of the moral act. Here the empirical is not only admitted but furnishes the material to which the intelligence and freedom of the person give the right moral form. The experience of tenderness, which emerges from the integration of the emotional aspects into the personal whole, presupposes continence and

---

33. Wojtyła, *Love and Responsibility*, pp. 198-99.

initiates the fully human way to live one's sexuality; the emotional and sensual dynamics of relationship are contextualized within the respect and the reciprocal welcoming of man and woman as well as the requirement of recognizing and respecting the other as a person and not as a mere object of one's enjoyment within the sexual act.

The particular need for tenderness which seems to distinguish feminine sexuality needs to be understood in connection with the danger of being treated as a mere object of enjoyment. For biological and social reasons, the woman is particularly exposed to this specific danger. The fact that a woman carries in herself the product of conception makes it more difficult for her to forget the existential implications of the sexual act.

Justice toward the Creator

The right personalistic attitude toward sexuality can neither be understood nor achieved if it is not placed within a more general understanding of what the person is and of the fundamental dynamic which governs his life. We have spoken briefly about that fundamental lack which constitutes the most intimate kernel of the person, in which the experience "of not being self-made" (and therefore also of depending on the other as the very source of one's own being) presents itself in the most obvious way. But this lack and this dependence, which are strictly connected, make man a being who is innately driven to search for his own fulfillment and for the adequate and authentic form of his own existence. The encounter with the other person is a fundamental step in the human pilgrimage in search of objective truth and subjective authenticity.

In this encounter persons finally experience a welcoming which permits them to feel at home in the world and to see their own existence as legitimated and charged with meaning. Because this encounter relocates the human center outside or beyond the self, one now sees that the world around one is charged with emotional values, which flow out of the person and into the world. For the person lives in a world of things, which are used by the person, or simply present to him.[34] This happens at the beginning of life: the child is introduced to the world through his relationship

---

34. Cf. Wojtyła, "Rodzina jako 'communio personarum'. Próba interpretacij teologicznej," in *Ateneum Kapłanskie* 83 (1974), pp. 347ff.; "Rodzicielstwo a 'communio personarum,'" in *Ateneum Kapłanskie,* 84, pp. 17ff.

with its mother, and reality will always have the liveliness and the affective tonality which the woman was able to communicate to the child in its first encounter with the world.

Of course not all relationships with persons have the same degree of intensity and of engagement. Most of them touch only the surface of our existence without really leaving a mark. Man easily forgets and loses himself in manifold distractions whose only purpose is to avoid the central questions of existence; Pascal called these *"divertissements."* But there are some relationships between persons which are endowed with a peculiar emotional intensity and which for this reason have a particular educational function. By living through them man is forced to understand his own self and that of others, the dynamic of relationship, and the right attitude toward the person. People who live these intimate relationships with depth and authenticity are wide open to extending this truth to all of their relationships.

Among these special relationships are those which have the family as their center: relationship with one's parents, with one's spouse, with one's children, and with those who exercise a particular spiritual fatherhood. All of these involve the fundamental mystery of the origin of life as well as with its meaning and its articulation in the family. The family exists through these relationships and becomes the human environment which both guards the mystery of birth and begins to reveal its significance.

But no human relationship can sufficiently express the meaning of the encounter with the person. The person of the other is experienced always in a partial and provisional way, and therefore the mystery of being and of the meaning of life are never manifested in their fullness.

Every personal relationship among human beings is necessarily exposed to the experience of limitation, whether such limitation is experienced as a mistake or as destiny or, even more profoundly, as sin. The value of the person, which is intuited especially through the relationship between the man and the woman and with the children, does not coincide with these relationships and does not entirely dwell within them. These relationships, rather, lead toward another relationship which includes and justifies them — that is, the relationship with God, the absolute person. Just as relationship with God is unique in giving adequate value to the person, so also in God relationship between people finds its fullness of value. Only if one places marriage in this context does one fully understand its essence. If marriage takes its meaning from the reciprocal self-giving of persons, this gift cannot realize itself outside the fundamental dynamic of their existence as persons. If loving the other means to will his happiness, this implies willing the fulfillment of his destiny in God. Man and woman cannot belong to each other if God himself does not freely give one to the other and if the acknowledgment of this act of God does not underlie their decision. This happened at the beginning, as Genesis says, for the first man and the first woman. And the same continues to happen at the beginning of every coming together of a human couple.

This gift implies some rules, which are immanent in a personalistic understanding of sex. By virtue of that mutual gift which is marriage, man and woman take the dynamic of the sexual life into their own interiority. In so doing they demonstrate respect for it and its ultimate character, and they are responsible for that finality of procreation which is naturally proper to sexuality.[35]

We should, perhaps, consider the complex question of the relation between the natural and the biological order. From a biological point of view, not every sexual act is turned toward procreation. There are different ways of intervening in the physiological mechanism so as to avoid procreation. The very idea of a biological order, however, is created by denuding sexuality of every emotional and affective charge, that is, by treating it as a science of pure objects and, it goes without saying, a science of pure bodies — which limits itself to the objective relationship between things. Biology cannot establish what corresponds to human nature and what is right and appropriate for nature.

On the one hand, it is necessary to consider God's purpose in creating sexual difference and the function which this difference has in the general taxonomy of nature. On the other hand, it is necessary to consider the symbolic order through which the subject charges reality and defines his relationship with it. From both points of view we can see that sex implies an openness to the possibility of maternity and paternity. That does not mean that the sexual acts of man and woman must primarily intend to generate offspring. This element is absorbed by the fuller purpose of manifesting mutual love.

Because of this, in their reciprocal self-giving, paternity and maternity are inseparably implied, and cannot be divorced from the will to realize one's own fullness of being together with that of the other.

On the basis of this metaphysical analysis of love, Wojtyła founds the

---

35. Cf. Wojtyła, "Zagadnienie katolickiej etyki seksualnej. Refleksje I postulaty," in *Roczniki Filozoficzne* 13, pp. 5ff., esp. p. 14.

natural and universal human character of all the essential aspects of marriage as they have been defined by Christian thought.

Marriage is monogamous and indissoluble, first of all, because it is founded on the acknowledgment of the value of the person rather than on an agreement based only on emotional and sensual values. Moreover, the stable union of father and mother gives the human being his first safe point of orientation for a balanced and authentic development of his personal existence. No wonder that when Christ revealed the whole of human nature to us he radicalized and intensified the ethical substance of marriage.

On the basis of the same principles, Wojtyła explains the attitude of the Catholic Church toward the problem of the control of fertility.[36] This attitude by no means implies either making sex a sin or taking a closed-minded approach, rejecting the notion that in the exercise of sexuality human beings have the task of mastering nature through reason. To understand the Catholic position as Wojtyła does, one needs to remind oneself that the reference to nature is not to biological but to personal nature. Human beings can, and must, subsume the biological order into their purposes, but in agreement with the moral norm. At this level Wojtyła affirms that "acceptance of the possibility of procreation in the marital relationship safeguards love and is an indispensable condition of a truly personal union."[37] By doing so, Wojtyła moves the center of the problem from the means used to prevent conception to the fundamental attitude toward sexual life. Marriage implies offspring; the judgment concerning the means of regulating fertility depends on whether or not the connection between sexuality and procreation is respected. (Of course, this relationship must be experienced rationally; every couple must try not to bring into the world more children than they can realistically afford to raise and to educate.) In preventing pregnancy one should act in such a way that the fundamental symbolic order which links the sexual acts to the possibility of procreation remains intact. The safest way of doing so seems to be the natural method, which uses the woman's periods of infertility, and so avoids conception without directly entering the mechanics of the act and therefore without altering the symbolic and moral values which have a more or less

36. Wojtyła's book was written before the encyclical "Humanae Vitae," but concurs perfectly well with its teaching. On the theme of the encyclical, Wojtyła elsewhere expresses himself many times, with clarity. Cf. "La visione antropologica della 'Humanae Vitae,'" in *Lateranum* 44 (1978), pp. 124-25; "Prawda Encykliki Humanae Vitae," in *Nasza Rodzina* (1975), pp. 8-20.

37. Wojtyła, *Love and Responsibility*, p. 230.

direct relationship with it. The choice of natural methods implies an effort of self-mastery and of integration of sexuality into the fullness of sexual life. Such a choice appears disproportionate to anyone who is implicitly or explicitly a utilitarian, that is, to anyone for whom happiness consists in the greatest possible amount of pleasure. But it is a very reasonable choice for any ethic which sees man as primarily engaged in the search for objective truth and the fullness of the good. Wojtyła quotes Gandhi on this issue:

> In my view, to say that the sexual act is an instinctive activity, like sleep, or the appeasement of anger, is the height of ignorance. The existence of the world depends on the reproductive act, and since the world is God's domain, and a reflection of his power, this act must be subjected to controls, the purpose of which is the continuation of life on earth. The man who understands this will strive at all costs to master his senses, arm himself with the knowledge that it is necessary to the physical and spiritual welfare of his posterity, and transmit this knowledge to the future for his benefit.[38]

Marriage, as we have already seen, is not the definitive and ultimate answer to the search for the welcome to one's own value and for the meaning of one's own existence. The impulse which moves man toward woman is only one aspect, the most immediately sensible aspect, of the more general dependency of man, of his lack of possession of his own origins and therefore of his turning toward that essential completion of his person.

The human tendency toward the Other and toward the Good is appeased by God alone. But in the order of nature it is possible to live one's journey toward God only by passing through sexuality and the family. We might add that, besides marriage, there is another way to live one's relationship with the family and experience one's own sexual identity — that is, in a spousal relation to God, of reciprocal self-giving. This relation is possible because God is a person and remains present in Christ and human history. Man recognizes that he owes to God everything that he has and everything that he is. He recognizes that justice in the relationship with

---

38. At the basis of this attitude, as with all of Wojtyła's thinking, stands the conviction that the person is a subsistent subject (who does not only exist as a relation to an other), which, however, becomes aware of itself only in the relationship with another, and this relation is what binds man to God, whether directly, as in consecrated virginity, or indirectly, through marriage.

God is not possible, because even if he could give Him everything that he has, he would remain indebted for the very fact of his existence. In the order of exchange, justice between God and man is not possible. But it is possible in the order of love. In love each one gives everything that he has and everything that he is and does not ask for anything, except that the other does the same. In the logic of giving the one who is rich is no different from the one who is poor because what is at stake is the most intimate kernel of the person. Consecrated virginity is a this-worldly anticipation of the spousal relationship between man and God in a form which is symbolic and visible to all. The experience of marriage tends to the same conclusion even if it travels by a different road. Consecrated virginity makes present the eschatological sense, the ultimate and definitive meaning.

5. *The Acting Person*

Structure of the Work

The Acting Person is clearly Karol Wojtyła's major work, the homecoming of his philosophical journey. In *Love and Responsibility,* the new approach gained through the critical assimilation of Scheler and of phenomenology is empirically tested against one aspect of human life. In *The Acting Person,*[1] the new

1. *Osoba i Czyn* (Crakow: Polskie Towarzystwo Teologiczne, 1969). The American translation, amply corrected and revised, of 1979 is edited by Anna-Teresa Tymieniecka (Dordrecht/Boston/London: Reidel) and bears the title *The Acting Person.* The work appeared also as volume 10 of the *Analecta Husserliana* in a translation by Andrzej Potoki. A second Polish edition of *Osoba i Czyn* was prepared for this translation, and it was from this text that the American translation was then made. An important discussion about this occurred. Some (including Alfred Bloch, Andrzej Poltawski, and, at least indirectly, also Andrew N. Woznicki) have criticized Anna-Teresa Tymienicka for an interpretive revision of the book, which, by carefully avoiding the technical terms which Wojtyła uses, excessively phenomenologized both his language and his ideas. The effect of this was to reduce the importance of the *hypokeimenon* or of the *suppositum,* which is the metaphysical subject to which all attributions regarding the person refer. This debate makes the position of the scholar who wants to use Wojtyła's main work particularly difficult. The first edition is outdated, but the new American translation is unreliable, or at least overshadowed by doubts. Such doubts have been heightened by Anna-Teresa Tymieniecka herself, who in "A page of History, or from 'Osoba i Czyn' to 'The Acting Person'" (*Phenomenology Information Bulletin* 3 [October, 1979], pp. 3-52) has spoken of collaboration of two authors in the translation and practically raised herself to the rank of co-author of the book. By so doing she has legitimated suspicions about the fidelity of the translation. I have been relieved of embarrassment through the courtesy of Stanislaw

foundation is expounded in itself and is, so to speak, set free from the patient work of philological reconstruction and of theoretical comparison through which it was obtained. At this point, it is mature enough to propose itself as an interpretation of the being of man in the world and of the meaning of his being-person. This interpretation certainly depends on continuing dialogue with the classics of philosophy, but in a sense it leaves the debate itself behind. It proposes a hermeneutic of human existence which requires confirmation through the experience of each reader. Each reader is, in fact, asked to compare the results at which the book arrives with those which emerge from his or her own being in the world as well as his or her own personal reflection. In this way philosophy gains its proper status as reflection upon an experience.

The author's resolution and mental attitude are reflected with precision in the Preface to the American edition of the book. Wojtyła first acknowledges his own philosophical debt both to Thomism and to phenomenology. Granted the author's acquaintance with traditional Aristotelian thought, it is, however, the work of Max Scheler that has been the major influence upon his reflection: "In my overall conception of the person envisaged through the mechanisms of his operative systems and their variations . . . may indeed be seen the Schelerian foundation studied in my previous work."[2] Of course, the Schelerian foundation which is assumed is the one which emerges from the consistent critique of Scheler's thought contained in those works. The philosophical background is therefore one which partially accepts Kant (especially the Kant of the *Metaphysics of Morals*) as a correction to the Schelerian perspective, which cannot, by itself, understand the relationship between person and act or the ontological consistency of the person as such.

If we skim through the *Analecta Husserliana,* we see how the recent reflection of phenomenology on itself and on its development has acknowledged the centrality of the questions set by Wojtyła since the 1950s. Anna-Teresa Tymieniecka remarks that phenomenological research has come more and more to focus on the theme of the phenomenology of man and of the human condition and in this way it has developed around that "irreducible element in man."[3] But this irreducible element, which to some

---

Dziwisz, who has consented to my use of the typescript of the second Polish edition in preparation, which will be made from the improved text which was used for the American translation.

2. *The Acting Person*, p. viii.

3. Cf. Anna-Teresa Tymieniecka's "Editorial Introduction" to *The Acting Person,* p. xix.

extent escapes phenomenological analysis, is necessarily its center because everything which the phenomenological reduction provides as description derives from this irreducible element and flows back to it. Moreover, the Husserlian principle "back to the things themselves" also induces one to keep faith in the moral realm.

Volume 7 of *Analecta Husserliana* is devoted to human action: it is called *The Human Being in Action*.[4] The action of human beings escapes the comprehension and description which traditional methods of phenomenology attempt: ". . . neither transcendental genetic analysis, which focuses upon the genesis of human consciousness constitutive of the life-world, nor eidetic analysis of the structures of objectivity as such, has approached human agency directly. Human activity, which carries the first and enacts the second, escapes the immediacy of the inspection practiced by both."[5] A certain kind of metaphenomenology, which goes beyond the limits which phenomenology has set for itself, thus becomes necessary. This metaphenomenology is situated in the deepening of that relationship with Aristotle, mediated through Brentano, which is certainly the crux of every self-understanding which phenomenology attempts. Without betraying the phenomenological method, it is necessary to recognize that, rather than being itself a self-sufficient philosophy, it furnishes the presuppositions of a new and better philosophy. As Eugen Fink had remarked, the descriptive analysis which phenomenology gives must be the premise of a philosophical reconstruction which adequately articulates the understanding of that which has been described. The two volumes of *Analecta Husserliana* devoted to *The Phenomenological Realism of the Possible Worlds* (1974) and to *Ingardiana* (1976) exhibit an attention to the realistic aspect of phenomenology which starts to set the philosophical horizon within which Wojtyła's contribution is received. This development culminates with the American translation of *The Acting Person* (1979), representing one of the most significant avenues of phenomenological research in our time.

Wojtyła sees in the Thomistic conception of the *actus humanus*[6] ("human act"), the act which engages the intelligence and the freedom of the person, the answer to the search for the irreducible element of man. It is a question of the person who engages in the act and who, through his own engagement, confers on it his peculiar human characteristics. Because

4. Dordrecht: D. Reidel, 1978.
5. "Editorial Introduction," p. xx.
6. Thomas Aquinas, *Summa Theologica,* I-II, qq. 6ff.

of this element the *actus humanus* is distinct from the *actus hominis* ("act of man"), an action which, even if accomplished by a man, does not engage his humanity. But how is it possible for the question about the *actus humanus* to pass through a phenomenological investigation? The assumption underlying this question comes from a metaphysical investigation which, of itself, contains very little of the descriptive richness made possible by the phenomenological method. This is precisely the question upon which *The Acting Person* is built: "What is the relationship between action as interpreted by the traditional ethic as *actus humanus*, and action as an experience?"[7] The conception of the action as *actus humanus* and the ontological concreteness of the person which it presupposes cannot be demonstrated by starting from the data which phenomenology obtains from its analysis of experience.

If one starts from phenomenology, it is impossible ontologically to found the person. But the data of the phenomenological description make it possible to find the ontological consistency of the person and to show how these data can be integrated into a whole. By working in this way Wojtyła gains a new position within philosophy which in a certain way can be compared only to that of Marx. "Since Descartes," Wojtyła explains, "knowledge about man and his world has been identified with the cognitive function. . . . And yet, in reality, does man reveal himself in thinking or, rather, in the actual enacting of his existence — in observing, interpreting, speculating, or reasoning . . . or in the confrontation itself when he has to take an active stand upon issues requiring vital decisions and having vital consequences and repercussions? In fact, it is in reversing the post-Cartesian attitude toward man that we undertake our study: by approaching him through action."[8]

The concrete man — not an abstract subject but a subject which is at the same time a created being, and therefore an object, and who manifests his complexity in action — is Wojtyła's point of departure. He begins, thus, from a place beyond the controversy between subjectivism and objectivism. Philosophy of being and philosophy of consciousness appear to us as two unilateral emphases and, in a way, as a result of the split of the integral philosophical point of departure which is man himself. Modern subjectiv-

7. "Author's Preface to the English-American Edition," *The Acting Person*, pp. xiii-xiv.

8. "Preface" to *The Acting Person*, p. vii. Like Marx, Scheler was an adversary of the idealistic-intellectual reduction of experience.

ism is defeated not so much by demonstrating its limits but by gaining a point of view which is more comprehensive and more faithful to what it means to be human.

As I have said, in the history of modern philosophy, the only parallel with this position is found in Marx. The rejection of idealism and the return of the concrete man seen in action are elements which link the thought of Wojtyła and that of Marx. But the fundamental gulf that separates them lies between the implications and development of the Wojtyłian concept of "action" and the Marxian concept of "praxis." We will come back to give a more adequate and deeper treatment of this topic in a different part of this work. But it is important to anticipate that the notion of action is more comprehensive than the notion of praxis. While praxis consists above all in human behavior directed to the material reproduction of existence, which abstracts from the intentions and motivations of individuals, action comprehends human activity *as a whole*. Wojtyła's main effort is directed to establishing the right relationship between the objective aspect and the subjective aspect of action. In other words, between praxis and action there exists the same difference which we have already noted between the biological order and the natural order, which is here referred to as the world of human acting. Praxis is what remains of the action if one abstracts from it its moral side and its personalistic meaning. Such a procedure can be useful for some limited ends (e.g., building a purely objective science of behavior), but it becomes destructive if its outcome is taken to be an integral knowledge of man.

Assuming man in his acting as his own point of departure provides Wojtyła's philosophy with a distinctive character and method. The philosophies of subjectivity, which do not have a criterion by which to recognize the ontological consistency of the person, culminate in the dissolution of the person into a succession of psychic representations which occupy his interior space, and are ultimately compelled to place their own criterion of truth in the history of culture and philosophy. Philosophy is the most abstract representation of the idea which human beings have of themselves. The history of philosophy is therefore the recapitulation of the development of human self-consciousness. But historicism no longer has the popularity which it used to enjoy even though it lives on, on account of fatigue and lack of alternatives, often by being reduced to a sterile show of erudition. One interprets the thought of past philosophers without being able any longer to pass from that interpretation to an investigation of how things are in themselves.

The only alternative seems to be an equally arid positivism or neo-positivism which reduces philosophy to pure logic, to a pure articulation of conceptual instruments which one is not allowed to apply in a rigorous and coherent way to the comprehension of human life. All that remains is abstract and complacent thought which deals with its own restricted confines.

By choosing the experience of the person as a point of departure, Wojtyła is able to work out a philosophy which is a reflection on experience and which finds its criterion of truth in the recognition and in the confirmation which it brings to the experience of the other, of the reader as of every human being. It is, therefore, neither a reflection on the history of philosophy (no matter how erudite) nor the attempt to force assent through abstract argumentation (no matter how logically rigorous) but, rather, an articulated discourse on the fundamental structure of the experience of life which solicits every person to reflect on his own self to confirm and to enrich the author's reflection. The philosopher limits himself to interpreting, to bringing to a higher degree of consciousness, what happens in common experience.

"First of all," Wojtyła explains, "daring though it may seem in the present day — in which philosophical thinking is not only nourished by, and based upon, history, but in which to 'philosophize' often means to reflect upon theories about theories — the present work cannot be seen other than as a personal effort by the author to disentangle the intricacies of a crucial state of affairs and to clarify the basic elements of the problems involved." He goes on to define further his own territory: "I have, indeed, tried to face the major issues themselves concerning life, nature, and the existence of the human being — with its limitations as well as with its privileges — directly as they present themselves to man in his struggle to survive while maintaining the dignity of the human being: man, who sets himself goals and strives to accomplish them, and who is torn apart between his all too limited condition and his highest aspirations to set himself free."[9]

The complexity and the extension of this program of inquiry into the problems of human praxis — such as they present themselves in the theory of a struggle for survival which underlies both positivism and of Hegelian Marxism — is evident. But, while including the theme of human dignity, for which narrower conceptions of praxis cannot make room, it subordinates the Hegelian-Marxist dialectic to a Pascalian dialectic which sees in

9. Ibid.

the human being the intersection of the tension between finite and infinite: it finds in the human person the place in which the meaning of the whole creation is revealed.

After an introduction which explains the concept of experience, *The Acting Person* is set out in four parts. The first deals with the consciousness and efficient causality of the person. Wojtyła analyzes here the reflexive role of consciousness and *the fundamental experience of being the cause of his own actions* which forces us to admit that the person is not only a place of psychic happenings, in which sensation and experience of value follow one another, but is properly the subject of action.

The second part deals with *the transcendence of the person in the action.* Through the analysis of the personal structure of self-determination it shows that the person is the efficient cause of the action because he is self-determining; he does not simply reflect internal and external conditioning but can decide by conforming his choice to the truth which he knows about the good. This is how the person realizes himself.

The third part deals with the integration of the person in the action. The person realizes his own self-mastery not by suppressing but by orienting the natural dynamisms of the body and of the psyche, integrating them in action which is expressed in the unity of the person. The person not only moves beyond the body and the psyche by transcending them but also integrates them in action. Action is the factor which belongs neither to one's transcendent spiritual faculties nor to one's psychic or bodily dynamisms but to the personal unity which integrates all these aspects.[10]

The fourth part is devoted to participation, that is, the acting of man together with other men which is, along with transcendence and integration, one of the fundamental dimensions of the person.

The argument of *The Acting Person* is central to the present book. We will therefore discuss it at some length, giving a section to the introduction and to each of its four parts.

Experience

The Acting Person begins from the experience that man has of himself, which has an essentially unitary character despite the many-sidedness of its artic-

---

10. The reference to the Thomistic doctrine of the soul is evident, if not explicit.

ulation.[11] In experience man encounters reality and reality comes to dwell
with him. This reality is made out of things but is made also and above all
of other people. This is the basis of the experience of man. This expression
has a characteristic ambiguity. It indicates the experience of which man is
the subject and also that of which man is the object. Each of us has an
experience of humanity as it is manifested in his own "I" and an experience
of himself which derives from the reflection on his own being and acting
among other men. Each one, then, has also an experience of the other man.
The experience of the other man is differentiated further into experiences of
his own interior reaction communicated through language and experiences
of those external actions which we are able to notice directly. There exists,
therefore, in oneself and in others, a sphere of internal experience and a
sphere of external experience; finally, there also exists through language a
relative communicability of the experience of the other. The experience of
the other can be an object of a cognitive act of mine or an emotional act
of mine, without which I can never properly live the experience of the other
man.

All of this can seem complicated but it actually deals simply with the
source of human experience, the aspects in which it presents itself. Human
experience is profoundly unitary because the different acts of experience
converge in that object which is man and they nourish the knowledge of
man. The external experience enlightens the internal experience and is
enlightened by it. So also the experience which I have of the other man
clarifies that which I have of myself and is also illuminated by it.

The epistemology which Wojtyła presupposes is neither empiricist nor
Kantian. A human being does not receive a pure set of sensations from the
external world which are then ordered in his intellect. Experience is a structured, organic whole, not only in the sense that it has to do with the very object
of knowing and not with isolated sensations, but also in the sense that different
acts of experience compose themselves in an organic whole which is *human
experience*. The language which Wojtyła uses is that of phenomenology, but
what he intends also has to do with Thomistic metaphysical knowledge. The
stabilization of the object of experience which is proper to man happens

11. The concept of experience is taken in its phenomenological version, which,
however, does not contradict the Thomist version. Experience is the self-giving of the
intelligible object in the cognitive act whatever the species of the object or the type of
its intelligibility. In this way phenomenology opposes itself directly to empiricism, which,
of all the possible forms of experience, knows only the sensible.

through the induction which produces a universal concept. Induction allows one to grasp the unity of meaning in diverse experiences and to build them into a progressive unveiling of the meaning of the intelligible object. In contrast to the usual way of understanding the Aristotelian-Thomistic induction, there is here a strong accentuation of the fact that the abstraction, through which the universal concept is constructed, does not imply oblivion to the richness and multiplicity of the particular experience but rather constitutes its appropriate articulation. In the idea of beauty, for instance, different beautiful things are not forgotten or denied but contained and comprehended as elements and moments of the manifestation of that plenitude. Such a conception of the universal was not unknown in the Aristotelian-Thomistic conceptual universe, but was attributed to the angels. Wojtyła, without denying the difference of principle between human knowledge and angelic knowledge (which, evidently, does not proceed by induction) sees the manifestation of the universal value in human experience as an opening to the inductive search for the harmony and value-structure which permeates the universe.

It is possible to arrive at the same result which Wojtyła achieves through this concept of induction, through a firmly *realistic* interpretation of phenomenology. In this case the character of organic and structured totality with which the intellectual experience presents itself to phenomenological observation is assumed as an index of the self-giving of the object in the subject. Moreover, the phenomenological component is very much present and could even be seen to predominate.

The Acting Person is neither an attempt to demonstrate that man is a person nor an attempt to classify human acts from the point of view of their personalistic value. It is a question, rather, of understanding how a human being is a person, in which way *the person reveals himself in action,* and how the action can serve to interpret the person who dynamically manifests himself only in his acting.

It is evident that we are close to the focal point of the tremendous crisis of modernism which is shaking the Catholic Church. This crisis arises from dissatisfaction with an objectivistic way of thinking which is not able to understand the subjective side of existence and the dynamic of moral experience. The title of Blondel's famous book *L'Action* emphasizes the need to understand action. Wojtyła deals here with the same problem, even if with a different method and with different results. Wojtyła wants to see how the person realizes himself in action.[12] The phenomenological method

12. *Osoba i Czyn,* pp. 13ff.

which enables one to inquire how man is a person here encounters Thomism. This does not confuse the issue but rather helps one to develop that consideration of the subjective side of experience which traditional Thomism lacked:

> . . . An action presupposes a person. This has been the standard approach in different fields of learning that have as their object man's acting, and is especially true of ethics, which treats of action that presupposes a person, that is, presupposes man as a person. In our study, on the other hand, the aim is to reverse this relation. . . . For us, action reveals the person, and we look at the person through his action.[13]

The very term "action," even if it has a Blondelian resonance which Williams, among others, has noticed,[14] is solidly anchored in the Thomistic conception of "*actus humanus.*" For St. Thomas, the act in which the human being is involved as a person, with his intelligence and freedom, is *actus humanus.* Over and against the *actus humanus* is the *actus hominis,* the act which does not imply either intelligence or freedom and, therefore, even if it is accomplished by a man, does not involve his moral responsibility. The fact of having moral value is therefore characteristic of the type of human action with which Wojtyła is concerned. His attention in *The Acting Person* is focused on anthropology more than on ethics; but in his conception no anthropological discourse is possible in which space is not given to the fact that human beings are, constitutively, moral beings and the value of their actions is primarily moral value.

As we have seen, the stabilization of the object of experience is obtained through induction. It is this which, in general, gives us the connection person/action or, better, gives us the person as subject of the action. This connection, however (and here lies the difference from traditional Thomism), needs to be further unveiled if we want to grasp the person in his dynamic essence. The Aristotelian-Thomist induction must be followed by a reduction (which is not exactly the same as the usual phenomenological reduction) if we want to do adequate justice to the existential depth of the person. "We already noted that in ethics the person is simply presupposed, while here our chief task is to examine and interpret the person. This is

13. *The Acting Person,* p. 11.
14. Williams, *The Mind of John Paul II,* pp. 147-48 gives extensive and accurate information on the genesis of Wojtyła's thought, but its philosophical judgments are not always reliable.

why in this study the argument is based on reduction. . . . The aim of interpretation is to produce an intentional image of the object, an image that is adequate and coincident with the object itself."[15] The reduction proceeds by giving the most adequate description of the object possible, but not with a demonstrative method. To demonstrate something is very different from describing it. The force of the conviction of reduction does not lie in the logical strength which compels assent but in the exactness of the description of the fundamental structures of experience which give rise, in anyone who has lived it, to the recognition that the thing is exactly as it is described. The assent arises in this case from the recognition that one's own experience of life is adequately expressed by the phenomenological description, and in such a way as to be at the same time judged and corrected.[16] This, of course, presupposes the concept of experience which we indicated at the beginning — an experience which is not incommunicable because it is oriented in every human being toward universal concepts and values. An adequate phenomenological description of human experience judges all the inadequate conceptions which arise from the emphasis given to one or another of its particular aspects and at the same time it saves their positive contribution. This approach starts from the totality of experience without privileging either its subjective side or its objective side. Philosophy of being (at least in its usual forms, which should really be called philosophy of entity) and philosophy of consciousness privilege external experience (the extramental reality of the world of things) or internal experience (the act of consciousness) without being able to integrate the two aspects with each other. Rather, they can be adequately understood only in their mutual relationship because experience is fundamentally unitary and while the knowledge of external reality happens within man, the

---

15. *The Acting Person,* p. 17. Induction allows us to understand that the person is *cause.* The reduction helps us to understand *the way in which the person is cause.* Phenomenology denies the role of induction. Moreover, where, as in Ingarden, phenomenology is realistic, its central task is the a priori intuition of essences which does not draw on an induction which could check the exactness of the intuition itself. Cf. Roman Ingarden, *Z badán nad filozofia współczesna* (Varsavia: PWN, 1965), p. 318. On Ingarden's realism, cf. Anna-Teresa Tymieniecka, "Beyond Ingarden's Idealism-Realism Controversy with Husserl: The New Contextual Phase of Phenomenology," in vol. 4 of *Analecta Husserliana,* "Ingardiana" (Dordrecht, 1976), pp. 241-418.

16. From the pedagogical point of view it is important to notice that the assent which is given to the truth on the basis of this recognition is an assent which engages the emotional energies of the person, while the purely intellectual assent does not have an equal capacity to affect existence by transforming it.

subject knows himself by placing himself in the world and by understanding himself as man, that is, as that particular being in the world which is man. It is forgetfulness of this fact which has impeded post-Cartesian philosophy from knowing the complete human being as he is given in the totality of his experience: this implies his being an entity in the world. Moreover, philosophy of being, at least insofar as it has forgotten that being is first of all the act of being and that this culminates in the action of the person, makes itself one-dimensional by becoming a mere philosophy of entity:

> Perhaps we have the right to assume that the divergence of the two great currents in philosophical thought, separating the objective from the sub-jective and the philosophy of being from the philosophy of consciousness, has at its root the experience of man and that cleavage of its inner aspect from outerness which is characteristic of this experience. . . . Much more important than any attempt to attribute absolute significance to either aspect of human experience is the need to acknowledge their mutual relativeness. . . . We owe the understanding of man precisely to the inter-relation of these two aspects of experience, and this interrelation serves as the basis for us to build on the ground of the experience of man . . . our conception of person and action.[17]

It seems that the intention of the author in writing *The Acting Person* must be linked to the issue which, in his opinion, defines the fundamental historical meaning of Vatican II, in which he took part as a bishop. Provoked by modern subjectivism, the Council elaborates a discourse on the person, on consciousness, and on freedom which had remained implicit in the traditional formulation of her doctrine. This novelty is, however, carefully incorporated in the traditional edifice of the philosophy of being. In this perspective the true fundamental content of the Council is the recognition of freedom of conscience, based on the eminent dignity of the person and on the respect for the path which is proper to the person on his or her way to the truth.

The whole of *The Acting Person* is a reflection on this conciliar devel-opment in the understanding of the relation between consciousness and truth. One of the goals of the Council was to unify the cause of truth with the cause of human freedom. If this is to be achieved, however, it will be necessary to correct all of the interpretations of the Council which see it as submitting to the modern world and to philosophies of consciousness

17. *The Acting Person*, p. 19.

which contain an implicit moral relativism. This correction happens in *The Acting Person* by the positive development of the anthropology which results from the conciliar enunciation in its precise balance — in its great novelty as well as in its stalwart maintenance of tradition. In the fulfillment of this task Wojtyła uses phenomenology but also recovers, through it, the decisive contribution which the Augustinian current of tradition brings to the philosophy of man. Although he is not quoted a great deal, Augustine is very much present as a dialogue partner on Wojtyła's philosophical enterprise. He is at least as much present as St. Thomas, and is often encountered when the attempt to "go to the things themselves" finds its mark.

Conscience and the Efficient Causality of the Person

The traditional Aristotelian and Thomistic doctrine of the human act implies a metaphysical conception of potency and act. From the metaphysical point of view, to say that there is a specifically human act means that there is a specific potency which corresponds to it, which the act realizes. This potency is the precise core of the human. It is the human ontological substance which is realized in the act. Besides this ontological aspect the classical conception says that the human also has a psychological aspect. The human act is voluntary and conscious. In it the human being is the source of action.

All of the contents of the Thomistic anthropology are taken into Wojtyła's conception, but aligned with a different methodology. Whereas the scholastic analysis of the human act simply presupposes the metaphysical concepts of potency and act, and the philosophical point of departure is the concept of being in general, Wojtyła attempts to grasp man in action and to approach his ontological structure through action. Action is considered insofar as it is given immediately in experience and in conscience, and the person is seen not only as the subject of the action, which carries the responsibility for it, but as the conscious subject of the action who becomes actual and knows that he is doing it.

In the scholastic conception the idea that conscience is a constitutive element of the human act is established, but only sporadic attention is paid to the fact that human beings not only act consciously (that is, engage their own intelligence and freedom in action), but are also conscious of acting, that is, capable of self-reflection on their own acting, which takes place in their consciousness. "For the scholastics, this was an implicit and hidden

129

side of rationality, and on the other hand, was entailed in the will. . . . The task that we set ourselves in this work is to go beyond it and to explain it as an intrinsic and constitutive aspect of the dynamic structure of the person who acts."[18]

This suggests giving a great importance to consciousness and self-consciousness without recognizing the conscience as the true subject of knowledge and action. The structure of Wojtyła's theory of knowledge is Thomistic, and on this point he is not afraid to correct Husserl: "In opposition to classical phenomenology we propose that the cognitive reason for the existence of consciousness and of the acts proper to it does not consist in the penetrative apprehension of the constitutive elements of the object, in its objectivization leading to the constitution of the object."[19] The object is constituted *in* consciousness but not *by* it. This is always present in the cognitive process, which Wojtyła understands in an eminently realistic way as reflection. But consciousness allows interiorization in the way that is proper to it, that is, by reflection.

Consciousness is therefore connected with the cognitive faculties but is not identified with them. Knowing something is not the same as being aware of something. Being aware implies further reflection on something which has already been worked out in the cognitive faculties. Wojtyła gives a particular importance to the relation between consciousness and self-knowledge, since self-knowledge is strictly linked with the "I," as is the conscience. But this link should not lead us to forget that self-knowledge is always a cognitive act and therefore objectivizes man, in making his own consciousness an object of knowledge. Consciousness itself is the object of self-knowledge in the sense that in the cognitive act in which man knows himself, he knows himself as a conscious subject. However, there is a difference between knowing oneself as a conscious subject (in this case consciousness itself is, as it were, objectivized) and being aware of oneself. Self-knowledges gives the "I" the cognitive material which is reflected in one's consciousness of one's self. All the constitutive elements of human conscious action are objectivized by this self-knowledge so that man can know his own actions and judge them. Self-knowledge, moreover, has to do with the "I" and is therefore not a knowledge of the universal kind. On the one hand, the "I"'s self-knowledge goes together with everything that the subject knows about man in general; on the other hand, self-knowledge

18. Ibid., p. 35.
19. Ibid., p. 32.

gives essential material for knowledge about man. Despite this, self-knowledge is strictly linked to the "I," and does not go beyond its border. For Aristotelian philosophy, it can seem strange that this knowledge is not knowledge of the universal but of the particular. However, we must remember that we are dealing with that particular which is the "I," that is, a microcosm in which the totality of the world is somehow reflected.

The purpose of this discussion, and of the distinctions which it makes, is to find the appropriate place for consciousness, and to avoid the danger into which idealism falls: consciousness subsumes the whole of man and the whole of the process of knowledge. Here consciousness reflects self-knowledge which is founded on real data external to consciousness. It enters into self-knowledge as one of the objects which can be known. A function of consciousness is that of interiorizing and subjectivizing the "I." In so doing one uproots the error of idealism, the idea that consciousness indefinitely reflects itself and its own acting so that the real object of knowledge is eliminated. But far from constituting the object of its own process of reflection, consciousness reflects self-knowledge, which in its turn has as its content the "I" considered as an object.

At this point consciousness appears to be the duplication of self-knowledge turned toward the subject's interior. One could ask what the difference is between the cognitive reflection of the "I" on itself, which takes place in self-knowledge, and consciousness. It is important to remind ourselves what has been said about the character of consciousness, that is, that it is turned toward the interior of the "I." It is not limited to mirroring what the "I" does and what the "I" is, but it allows us to experience the action insofar as it is an action which personally belongs to us. It is through consciousness that we experience reality. Things are charged with affectivity for us to the extent to which they are reflected in consciousness and become personal experience. This is why the reflexivity of consciousness is a different thing from the reflection with which human intellect seizes upon some particular content (be it even the "I" itself) in order to know it better. "The consequence of the reflexive movement of consciousness is that this object — because it is, from the ontological point of view, the subject — simultaneously has the experience of its own 'I' and of itself as a subject."[20]

We need to distinguish three different things: being the subject of an action; knowing oneself (objectively) as the subject of an action; and being

20. Ibid., p. 44.

aware of oneself as the subject of an action. This threefold distinction should not make us forget the connection between these three moments.

It is because I am a subject that I can know and experience myself as such. The primacy of being, from this point of view, cannot be put in doubt. However, it is equally true that the particular being which I am is endowed with consciousness. Without the reflective function of consciousness we would not be able adequately to know the intimate structure of the human act and we would have only an external knowledge of human beings. Our knowledge of the human would lack the essential contribution of the interior of our conscious subjectivity. On the other hand, a man deprived of the reflexive faculty of consciousness would not be like us. Experiential subjectivity and ontic subjectivity can be fully understood only in their reciprocal relation.

But the point of departure remains the being of man as reflected in consciousness. It is by beginning from this reflexive function that the function of subjectivization is placed in the right light; this is a different way of proceeding from those philosophies of consciousness which begin from the subjectivity of consciousness and arrive at an enfeebled objectivity which is considered only as a function of internal experience. "The consciousness in intimate union with being and ontologically founded action of the concrete man-person does not put his dynamic reality in the shadow of his being, but to the contrary opens it 'toward the interior' and in such a way it reveals and covers a specific distinction and unique concreteness."[21]

In consciousness man experiences his own spirituality and experiences the values which constitute it, even if the ontological root of his being a person does not directly appear in experience but can only be inferred from it. The moral value of action is reflected not only in intellectual experience but also in emotional experience. It is through action that man experiences good and evil and at the same time experiences his own being as the subject of good or evil action. He not only knows it but experiences it, and the action becomes part of the objective reality of his being a person. It is not a question of a pure reflection in consciousness of an action whose moral and personalistic value is already entirely constituted in itself. On the contrary, if the action is a moral one, consciousness takes part in its constitution. What is objectively good or evil is experienced in human conscience as good or evil, and without this becoming personal it would not be possible to understand the structure of human acts.

21. Ibid., p. 48.

Wojtyła shows through these reflections the place where Scheler's analysis of emotional consciousness should be incorporated into St. Thomas's objective personalism. Consciousness is founded on being but does not simply mirror it: it is a particular subjectivization and personalization which calls for an autonomous and accurate inquiry. Unity is given by a view of consciousness which, making abundant use of Scheler's lessons, differentiates it through an essential feature: in consciousness the experience of value happens in concordance with the act, but the person experiences simultaneously the person as the cause of the act. This allows one to link the objective evaluation of the act (whose cause is the person) which is furnished by self-consciousness with the subjective experience which takes place in consciousness.

All human and psychological events are reflected in consciousness; it reflects sensible as well as emotional experience. On one side consciousness is linked to self-consciousness; on the other it receives sensible and emotional impressions. Through self-knowledge, which also has emotion as its object, consciousness is able not only to reflect emotion in itself but to subjectivize the judgment that comes to it through self-knowledge.

Human beings not only experience what happens in them but also experience the judgment which self-consciousness makes when that occurs. When this complex process takes place sufficiently, consciousness not only reflects emotion but it is also able to integrate it into the complete human experience. But it can happen that because of the strength of the emotion or because of the weakness of the cognitive faculty, the balance breaks down and consciousness becomes overly emotional. Then it limits itself to reflecting emotion but cannot judge it objectively; that is, it cannot subjectivize the psychic material which self-knowledge has already objectivized. Consciousness is then reflective but not capable of personalizing. In this case passion happens in man but is not a real experience of man; the person does not act and does not experience anything but is merely acted on by what is happening in him. Scheler's great mistake is omitting the distinction between this pathological emotionalization of conscience and its normal function. Scheler is right to negate the moment of efficacy and causality in relation to behavior directed toward values. But he did not understand that conscience reflects not only emotional value but also the rational judgment which comes from self-consciousness. It is his elucidation of the function of self-knowledge that distinguishes Wojtyła's analysis of subjectivity from any form of subjectivism. Subjectivism separates experience from action, and eliminates the experience of one's own responsibility and one's own causality in relationship to the action. Therefore, it considers that values automatically create themselves in the conscience when the action takes place: values are not derived from an objective reality. Generally speaking, for subjectivism, reality is what happens in consciousness; it has no criterion which allows one objectively to discriminate between the events of consciousness.

This being said, Wojtyła's position is not the same as traditional objectivism. He gives the subjective side of human experience a rigorous foundation, and this sympathetic attention creates a genuine realistic philosophy of consciousness. Such a philosophy is realistic because in it consciousness does not found being but reflects it. But consciousness also reflects the person and the efficient cause of the action.

This realistic foundation has as its presupposition the distinction between consciousness and self-knowledge. Man reflects himself in consciousness as a cause of the action inasmuch as it is through self-knowledge that he grasps that he himself is the cause. It is, therefore, necessary to consider further such a distinction and to examine it from the point of view of the following affirmation: the person is the efficient cause of the action.

First of all, we should note that consciousness does not reflect the whole of the objective dynamism of man. For example, the vegetative function takes place largely outside of the sphere of consciousness. On the other hand, one cannot say that only the aspects which belong to the human as such are reflected in consciousness.

We have seen that not only man's act but also what happens in man is reflected in consciousness. For these reasons the act of man cannot be analyzed only from the point of view of consciousness: it must be situated within the full human dynamism. Knowledge of such a full dynamism supposes not only the internal experience of man but also his external experience and his knowledge of the whole of reality. It is at this level that the study of the human being forces us to ask about the more general problem of being. On the other hand, knowledge about being is reflected in self-knowledge and through it in consciousness and thus contributes to its orientation. Wojtyła understands the proper dynamism of man by analogy with the more general dynamism of being as it is expressed by the Aristotelian and Thomistic category of potency and act. Potentiality is a mode of being which proceeds toward a fulfillment it does not yet possess. Thus a child is a man in potency and a seed is a tree in potency. An act is the fulfilled realization of a potency. In the actualization (sometimes called by itself "act") the passage from potency to act is achieved, as is the dynamic transformation of the potency in act.

If we apply this structure to the comprehension of the proper dynamism of man we see that the term "act," understood as actualization of a potency, has a wider application than the "human act," which is proper to man insofar as he is man. *Both* the structures which we have earlier analyzed are actualizations of a potency: the one which shows that man acts and the one which shows that something happens in man. Even if the first shows the activity of a person while the second shows a certain passivity, it is certain that in both of them there is a passage from potency to act, and therefore an act, although, as is clear, not every act of man is also a human act.

The experience which the subject has of being the author and the efficient cause of the act creates the difference between the human act and the act of man. The act of man also implies an actualization of the potentiality which is proper to the human being. But this actualization does not happen through the active intervention of man. The attention goes to that which happens in man and departs from his subjectivity, which, in its deepest dimension, is not engaged in the action. Here a phenomenological element (the experience of being an efficient cause of one's action) is indispensable for a deeper penetration of man's ontological structure.[22]

By experiencing his own being as the efficient cause of action, man discovers that he is completely immanent in action and simultaneously transcends it. The subject is completely immanent in the action because it is his action and he identifies himself with its end and assumes responsibility for it. Nonetheless, man is also transcendent in relation to the action. He sets it into being, he chooses it, and he thereby identifies himself as the agent-subject of the action; he is not one of the many elements of the action, elements which are subordinated to the intrinsic dynamism of the action. On the contrary, it is the subject which gives the action its own subjective dynamism. The human act is therefore that act through which man actualizes those potentialities which are proper to him insofar as he is a person, and this is the way in which he builds his personality. Through his acts man to some extent creates himself, his own interiority and moral personality.

---

22. It is interesting to notice a point which confirms the impossibility of entirely separating phenomenological analysis from metaphysics: the experience of man as the efficient cause of his own action is the model upon which Aristotle built his entire theory of efficient causality.

We see how in the understanding of the human act phenomenology encounters metaphysics. Phenomenology describes a human experience which, to be understood and adequately explained, needs an insight which goes beyond simple description. To a pure phenomenological analysis the subject appears to be composed of two sides and of two different structures. On one side consciousness reflects on what happens in man and on the other consciousness gives the experience of being the efficient cause of the action. These two structures can be developed autonomously but must then be brought together again. In a certain way, a phenomenology which avoids Scheler's emotionalist deviation is able to develop both of these structures of consciousness. By doing so phenomenology risks giving a divided and contradictory representation of man. The opposition between the one-sidedness of Kant and the one-sidedness of Scheler derives from this division, which comes about not only in phenomenology but in the whole of modern philosophy. Scheler escapes dualism by choosing the reflexive side of consciousness and devaluing the experience of being the cause of action. Kant follows the opposite path and does not recognize the aspect of passivity as being innate to man; this makes man an object of actualization which does not depend on practical reason.

It is possible, finally, to develop both these aspects at once without being able to bring them to a satisfying synthesis.

The problem can only be worked out in an analysis which goes to the ontological kernel of the person. By so doing it discovers the origin of both dynamisms and underlines the fact that the experience of causality accompanies but does not eliminate the fact of something happening in man. The human act is in fact also an act of man and the causality of the person in relation to the act is achieved by using the bodily and emotional dynamisms, not by eliminating them.

If one goes to the ontological kernel of the person one must realize that, even before it acts at all, the subject exists. The act through which it comes to be and remains in being fully establishes its further dynamism. But even prior to being a subject in which the dynamisms which we have described take place, man is also a being, even if he is a completely peculiar being, essentially endowed with the characteristic of being a subject.[23]

---

23. Generally speaking, Wojtyła's Thomism resembles that of the Roman School of Garrigou-Lagrange, under whom he took his doctorate. It is characteristic of this school to speak of an Aristotelian-Thomistic philosophy, and not to mention the philosophical originality of Thomas in relation to Aristotle. Nevertheless, on this decisive

This process is possible to the extent that we allow that our knowledge of man arises not just out of consciousness but by using the set of data which comes from our cognitive faculties. This is to say that both the knowledge which man has of the world and also his metaphysical understanding of being contribute to self-knowledge. The idea of being in general helps us to understand the being of man even if we should not forget the specificity of this being in comparison with all other beings. Man is a being who is someone and opposes himself as such to all beings which are only *something*. There exists, therefore, an essential proportion between the structure of this being and that of any other being, and an equally essential disproportion. Both proportion and disproportion are reflected in all of the proper actualizations of this being. Both simply to exist and to exist as a person are inscribed in the ontological structure of man. It is because of this that he is the subject of the actualization of the potentiality which is peculiar and personal inasmuch as he realizes it as a person. Those structures of action which on the phenomenological level appeared as mutually irreducible therefore rediscover their unity on the metaphysical level. On the other hand, since this happens at the metaphysical level, this unification by no means reduces the manifold richness of human existence as it manifests itself at the two levels of phenomenological analysis. A metaphysically oriented phenomenology provides the basis for the appropriate integration.

The identification of an irreducible ontological kernel is not enough to give a complete picture of the person and his action. It is, rather, the foundation on which we can build the integration, also at the phenomenological level, between the efficacy and subjectivity of the person.[24] Our study leads us to the ancient question about the nature of man. From a

---

point of the conception of the act of being he draws on the more modern interpretation of Thomas's thought, as in Gilson and Fabro, or, especially, J. De Finance. Fabro's attempted to develop the existential aspect of Thomism by bringing it into relation with Kierkegaard's philosophy is comparable to Wojtyła's dialogue with phenomenology. Wojtyła's direct source is probably De Finance's book, *Etre et Agir dans la philosophie de Saint-Thomas* (Paris: Beauchesne, 1943). Existential Thomism also influenced the Lublin philosophy department, which is described by M. A. Krapiec, *Ja-człowiek: Zarys antropologii filozoficznej* (Towarzystwo Naukowe Polskiego, Catholic University of Lublin, 1974). An abridged version of this book has been published in English as *I-Man: An Outline of Philosophical Anthropology,* translated by Francis J. Lescoe and Roger B. Duncan (New Britain, CT: Mariel Publications, 1985).

24. The word "subjectivity" is used here is the sense of the scholastic "subjectum" and not the modern "subject." It means the capacity to be the object of an action.

certain point of view, nature is the stable basis of man's acting, the source of the dynamisms which happen and realize themselves independently of his will. In this perspective, nature certainly means what happens in man and the dynamisms which operate in him by the simple fact of being born as a member of the human species (nature comes from the Latin *nascor*). Nature has nothing to do with the experience of freedom which is expressed in being the cause of the action. Such a view can take us as far as the naturalistic determinism which denies human responsibility. Or, in a slightly different version, it can lead to a moral objectivism, which imposes a natural obligation on man, disregarding the personal character of authentic moral obligation. But experience shows us that there is an integration of nature and person, of innate dynamisms and freedom. In this integration the human person realizes himself in his ontological specificity or subsistent spiritual nature, existing in and through a physical body.

From a metaphysical point of view, it is more proper to use the word nature to indicate the essence of being (and not the proper dynamism of being as existing being). In this sense nature is the foundation of every action and passion of being. These two meanings of nature show themselves to be distinct when we take into consideration the being who is *human*. Man's proper dynamisms as an object in the world by no means constitute either the whole of man's acting or even its most important aspect. In fact, being a person belongs to human nature, correctly understood in a metaphysical sense: it is an ability to actualize and finalize oneself which is entrusted to one's freedom. In man nature is integrated in the person and has a real existence only in the person. The human individual is not just an example of the species, an individualization of the universal human essence, but a fully personal existence. His dignity comes not from his being an exemplar of the species but an unrepeatable personal existence.

This explains why it is not sufficient for man to rely on the good of the species by responding to the natural passions given to this end, but it is necessary that he realizes the good in a personal way. Personal and free existence is founded in human nature. That is, it is founded in the set of dynamisms which constitute the concrete context within which one can develop the initiative of freedom. Here we find the Thomistic view, for which the human soul is from one side spiritual substance and on the other side the form of a physical body. Through it man is immanent to the material reality of his body but again he transcends it by impressing a personal orientation upon the dynamism of the body.

According to the classical Aristotelian and Thomistic conception, the soul, in addition to having a spiritual dimension, also possesses a vegetative and an animal dimension, insofar as it is the form of a body which has vegetative and animal functions. Wojtyła's phenomenological analysis confirms this point of view but attains it through a consideration proper to the dynamisms of man's acting. What, from an ontological point of view, is a potency is, from a phenomenological point of view, a dynamism. Potency and dynamism refer to the same reality in different ways: dynamism speaks of the structure of the acting and the happening, potentiality of the underlying reality of such a structure.

Wojtyła's intention is to reach the immediate proximity of potentiality through analysis of the dynamisms and to show how the reference to the ontological level of the question simplifies the phenomenological investigation.

We can mark off three dynamisms which contain all of the events which take place in human beings.

In the first place, there is a vegetative dynamism, which deals with the function of the body and to which corresponds an infinite situation of particular events and a collaboration with all of the events which take place in man. Secondly, we have a psychic and emotional dynamism, in which all of the human emotions and passions take place. Finally, there is a third dynamism, proper to the free personality, which is expressed in being the efficient cause of one's own actions.

These dynamisms are constantly related to each other, and concrete human acting results from their interconnection. Moreover, they are reflected differently in consciousness. Most of the events which take place in the body happen without our being aware of them. Many bodily dynamisms come to awareness only when a bodily disfunction makes us painfully aware of it; for instance, we realize that we have a liver only when it is in bad health. What happens in the emotional sphere reflects itself more vividly in consciousness. In general, the events of the somatic sphere enter into consciousness through some emotional mediation. Even psychologically, not everything which happens in human beings is reflected in consciousness. There are psychological dynamisms which constantly push forward toward the sphere of consciousness without ever being able to reach it, as explained, for instance, by Freud with reference to the category of the unconscious, but as noted also by the philosophical tradition from Leibniz to Schopenhauer. The elements excluded from awareness by the superior faculties of the subject do not evaporate: they are shoved into the subconscious and are nourished there by the different instinctual mechanisms according to their own dynamisms. This explains the fact that the subconscious is not a mere random aggregation of materials rejected by consciousness, but has a precise structure.

On the other hand, whereas the vegetative dynamism often remains completely inaccessible to consciousness, there is a relatively permeable line of division between the psychic subconscious and consciousness. What is contained in the subconscious struggles to rise to awareness. This fact reveals that the hierarchical structure of human potentialities culminates in consciousness. For consciousness is the sphere in which man experiences himself in the fullest way as man and assimilates to himself the different materials of his psyche. It is the task of a moral education to bring to the surface of awareness the contents of the subconscious in order to allow their objectivization and integration into experience. Psychological energy needs to be disciplined and sublimated but not repressed if one does not want to block off one of the primary sources of the general human dynamism.

Each of the different dynamisms which we have examined realizes a certain becoming of the person and contributes to his realization. Man transforms himself through them into something or someone by realizing the potentiality originally entailed in his act of being. Each of them, moreover, has a peculiar relationship with the person's efficient causality and with his consciousness. The vegetative potency of man is almost completely autonomous. The subject can at most determine the external condition of these events. Things are different in the psycho-emotional sphere. Here man himself furnishes the material for his development and for his direction. This happens because at the apex of the psychological and emotional dynamism is the experience of the subject's causality toward his own action, an experience which is accompanied by his own responsibility for it. "I can, but I am not forced to do it": this is a fundamental experience in which the choice and the free act of man roots itself. The spiritual nature of man manifests itself here. In experience, this spiritual nature is not another sphere in relation to the psychic and the emotional one, but rather a particular capacity for self-mastery which makes man responsible for his actions and therefore morally good or evil. On the other hand, being good or evil in a moral sense means being good or evil insofar as one is human.

This dynamism of freedom corresponds to that potency of the person which is, in Aristotelian and Thomistic metaphysics, the will. In other words, the transcendence of the subject in relation to the action is based on freedom. It is not only the fact that the subject cannot be reduced to his actions and has an ontological subsistence which precedes it but also from the fact that man is free in the face of his action. The transcendence of the person in relation to his action is therefore dynamic and enables persons to guide the action by making it an expression of personality. This distinguishes the human act from any other kind of act which happens in nature and which tends to the simple development of the potentiality proper to a certain kind of being.

This transcendence of the person is realized through the act of the will. In this first part of the work Wojtyła builds up to a comparison with, and a reformulation of, the structure of the Cartesian *cogito,* which is at the foundation of modern philosophy. In the *cogito,* the consciousness of thinking founds the consciousness of being. Being and thought are founded together in the act of consciousness. Consciousness is thus uprooted from the external world and the place of reality is taken by the succession of states of consciousness.

By distinguishing clearly between consciousness and self-knowledge, Wojtyła welcomes the great modern discovery of subjective consciousness, the fact that nothing is fully real for man if it does not pass through his consciousness. But he does not derive from this acknowledgment a denial of being and of the objectivity of the world in which man finds himself. The subject's awareness reflects the objective knowledge which the subject has of the world and of himself. This knowledge must be subjectivized in order to reveal its proper human meaning. Neither a pure knowledge which prescinds from the act of consciousness, nor a consciousness which does not reflect the cognitive element of reality and of man, can lead to a full understanding of human acting. The relation of consciousness to self-knowledge indicates the point of reciprocal insertion of the problematic of being and that of consciousness.

The experience of the "I can but I am not forced to do it" marks the emergence, within consciousness, of something beyond the state of consciousness. This "beyond" is the subject of the states and is also the subject of the action. This shows the transcendence of the subject in relation to consciousness. This transcendence, from the metaphysical point of view, appears to be realized in the will: the will is the ontological potentiality which underlies the dynamism of "I can but I am not forced to do it."

The transcendence of the subject in relation to the state of consciousness, which shows in its capacity of being the subject of the action, leads us beyond any kind of idealism and *allows us to set the coordinates for a decisive debate between action and praxis.*

KAROL WOJTYŁA

The Transcendence of the Person in Action

The preceding analysis helps us to understand how the person is the efficient cause of his action. It is through the decision of his will that the person becomes a cause of his action. For this reason we cannot consider the will simply as an experience which happens in man. It must be understood, rather, as one of the essential constitutive elements of the person, one of the faculties through which the person realizes itself. Without this particular connection with the most intimate kernel of man, the will would not be able to engage the person in action. Will, therefore, is a revealing moment of the person's interior structure, which possesses itself and governs itself. Upon this structure the particular dignity of the person and his freedom is based: the act of will through which the person actualizes his proper dynamic and realizes himself cannot be delegated. The choice of one's freedom adds to the world a perfection which no one else can add.[25] It is this which differentiates the person from every nonpersonal being.

The concept of self-determination is essential to the understanding of the way in which the objectivization of the person happens alongside one's proper subjectivation. Self-determination presupposes that the person is at the same time the subject of the action and also the object of the action. Through the self-determined action the person really modifies himself and influences the process of his own becoming and his own self-realization. This relationship with the "I" as the first object of the act of the will should not be confused with the relationship with the object of the will which takes place in every act of volition when the subject tends toward an object or a given value. The will can have this kind of relationship with the person, but it does not have to. What is necessary is that the turning toward the person — not as an intentional object but as the content of the very structure of the self-possession and the self-governing — is the presupposition of every act of self-determination. This distinction elucidates how it is possible that the person turns toward himself and wants his own perfection without any narcissism or Pharisaism, because the act of the will in this intimate structure cannot be reduced to an intentional inclination toward a value, as Scheler imagines.[26]

25. When it realizes itself the person realizes an infinite value. The foregoing argument has renewed the affirmation that, in his free act, the single human being has a higher dignity than the whole human species, considered from a purely naturalistic point of view.

26. Scheler confuses "the evaluation of the good itself, the perfection of the person itself," with "the evaluation having the experience of a rewarding emotional connection

The experience of "I want" contains the intentional moment but cannot be reduced to the intentional element alone. But we can also have the experience of an intentional inclination toward an object or a value which does not imply a real act of will. It can happen that a man is attracted by an object or a value without volitionally consenting to it. One can also be aware of needing something without wanting it, without one's will yielding to the inclination. Volitions which happen in man are thus distinguished from the acts of his will. The act of the will involves the entire structure of the person and manifests its transcendence in action. A large part of the philosophical tradition has correctly linked the will to the object, because willing is always willing something. However, this fact should not lead us to forget that the first object toward which an act of will turns is the subject itself, and that it is only by passing through the subject that it is able to reach the object. This contradicts Scheler's view, for he does not want to consider the person as an object; especially in the case of moral action he assumes the subject to be completely disinterested, so that the improvement and perfection of the subject who acts never appears as an object of the action.

But Wojtyła's view is also different from some traditional Thomistic conceptions, because what is at stake is not simply the actualization of an individual substance of a rational nature but the living self-determination and self-realization of a unique, unrepeatable person whose objective becoming is a lived experience, because it is subjectively mirrored in consciousness.[27] In a certain way the person must want the good outside of itself by willing its own good. The person can neither truly wish an external value except in union with the realization of its own value as a person nor really wish its own realization as a person outside of an encounter with an objective value which is external to it. One of the metaphysical presuppositions of Aristotelian and Thomist thought is the double effect of action, according to which the action has a transitive effect which passes into the object and an intransitive one which remains in the subject itself. This doctrine is seen in the light of existential philosophy.

These remarks throw further light on the relationship between subjec-

---

with the experience of one's own perfection." This second attitude is pharisaical, but the first is the fulfillment of the necessity of collaborating with the fullness of the good according to its own possibilities. Wojtyła had learned from St. John of the Cross that one can move toward one's perfection within an emotional desert.

27. Wojtyła, "The Intentional Act and the Human Act, that is, Act and Experience," in *Analecta Husserliana,* vol. 5, "The Crisis of Culture" (Dordrecht: Reidel, 1976), pp. 269-80.

tivity and the efficient causality of the person. In self-determination, efficient causality turns toward the interior of the person and is thereby objectivized before the act of the will. This is possible by virtue of the subject's self-knowledge and his knowledge of external reality. On the other hand, the entire process is reflected in consciousness and we have therefore a simultaneous and continuing deepening of the subjectivization and objectivization of the "I" which are reciprocally illuminative. In this process metaphysical subjectivity is the basis on which the phenomenological experience of one's own subjectivity is built; the guiding role does not belong to the consciousness which reflects and objectivizes but to self-knowledge.[28]

In self-determination, all the dynamisms and events of man converge and integrate in the person. In nature the mechanical result of different forces is instinct, which does not coincide with the simple animal urge, but is already a beginning of integration, although at the level which is individual but not personal. But in man the integration of different dynamisms happens at the personal level. That means that the "I" is the fundamental element which integrates all the different events. The "I" is self-determining. Freedom is not abstract and devoid of conditions: it is only in relation to different events that happen in him that man exercises his own freedom by deciding the place and the level of their integration in his personal acting. This concept of freedom — which has everything to do with the empirical and concretely existing human being — is utterly distinct from the form of Idealism which permits the discussion of freedom and the analysis of the ontological structure of the person but culminates in an abstract hypostatization of freedom (and of consciousness).

Freedom affirms itself both by transcending natural determinisms which takes place in the person and through providing the basis for their integration.[29]

This transcending of the person toward his own interior, toward his irreducible kernel, must be distinguished from the common use of the word

28. The processes of subjectivization and of objectivization show the reason for the distinction, evident to one philosophical tradition, between the immanent action (which remains within the person) and transcendent action (which goes outside of the person toward exteriority). In the perspective which we have developed, the action is considered both immanent and transcendent, because it is always subjectivized and objectivized and also because it does not matter whether it is externally perceptible.

29. Aristotle also speaks in the *Politics* (1.3) and in the *Nichomachean Ethics* of the nature of politics and of diplomacy, and he does not absolutize the dominance of the intellect or the emotions.

"transcendence" in phenomenological language, even if it contains something in common with it. In phenomenology "transcendence" is usually used in an horizontal sense, to indicate that the individual intentionally transcends himself, with the cognitive or voluntary act, toward the object which is external to him. But in this case, the person turns toward the interior, toward his intelligent and free essence which lies beyond emotional dynamisms. This intentional turn toward the interior of the self implies a different kind of transcendence: not horizontal but vertical, moving toward the ultimate depths of the person in which, by knowing and by wanting truth, it meets the highest values.

This transcendence allows us to affirm that the person is not only, as Scheler thinks, the place in which value manifests itself, but is also an autonomous subjectivity which is at the source of the action and makes free decisions by orienting the different events which take place in it and by giving or denying his own assent to them. To say that man is free therefore implies the affirmation that he empowers his own subject.

Of course, the will always turns toward an object, but the object is not a sufficient cause of willing. The will is always a will to something, but it is not necessarily the case that what attracts me or what I need is what I want.[30] The experience of "I want something" must be understood primarily from the willing subject rather than from the willed object. The root of freedom is found in its self-determination rather than in its indetermination toward external objects. Free will, understood as self-determination, is the properly human form of determinism. The will is the ontological correlate of the process of self-determination. On the other hand, a will has as its own condition an understanding and a rational choice, and therefore it can only belong to a rational nature, that is, to a person.[31] Free will is nothing other than the *person's* capacity to be free. This freedom is gained by overcoming conditioning, as well as by orienting it. Freedom and rationality are the properly human instinct, which belong to man as such.[32]

---

30. Thomas Aquinas, *Summa Theologiae*, I, q.83, a.1.

31. Wojtyła often repeats Boethius's definition, which St. Thomas used: "persona est rationalis naturae individua substantia" ["the person is an individual substance with a rational nature"]. One should observe that in Wojtyła's conception the "rationality" has its significance above all as an element which, together with the will, necessarily enters into the constitution of the act of the person.

32. This expression, precise in itself, could become dangerous to the extent that it risks not fully comprehending the extent of the difference between the natural person of man, which is founded in self-determination, and the dynamisms which are proper to the whole of the rest of nature.

Of course, this analysis acknowledges and appreciates what Scheler noticed about the horizontal transcendence of the act of the will — that it turns toward an object or a real value. But it also calls attention to vertical transcendence. By vertical transcendence we mean the subject's transcendence of his act. From a phenomenological point of view, this element distinguishes the will from cognitive process. When it knows, the subject intentionally tends toward the object, but this intentional tending remains within it. But when the *will* is concerned with an object, the person moves toward it, moving out of his interiority. The experience of decision is linked to this outgoing.[33] Choice and decision exclude every mechanism and every determinism in the relationship between the subject and the object, or the subject and the value. Of course the motive of the action remains, but the will rationally verifies it before giving its consent to the action and, therefore, in the process of the decision, the rational verification and the judgment of the person enter together with the value.

The readiness to turn toward the good is the element which underlies every decision and makes it nonarbitrary. This original innate spontaneity of the will means that one may eliminate any intellectualistic view of it, which claims that human decisions are made without reference to the appealingness of reality. The will is not indifferent to the attraction of reality, but it observes those attractions in a rational and conscious way.[34]

Of course, this relationship of the will to the object comes to the best light in the experience of choice. Sometimes a value attracts our attention and we turn toward it immediately, choosing it for ourselves. But sometimes we are divided between the contrasting attractions of diverse values. Our inclinations are opposed and we cannot follow them immediately: we must choose. At this point will appears to be separated, at least methodologically, from the object. I know that I will, but I do not yet know exactly what I

33. By moving the person toward the object and making it act on objects, the will produces a modification of the object. This is also important for the issue of cognition because praxis is the best verification of the adequacy of cognition. There is here both a resemblance to and a difference from the Marxist doctrine of connection between theory and practice, which we have already noted and to which we shall return.

34. The immediate fascination which the object exercises on consciousness is a judgment of the objective knowing which is proper to consciousness and self-consciousness. The knowledge of the fascination which the object exercises on consciousness also naturally enters into the judgment of self-consciousness, by way of the force of the emotional perception of its value.

want. What I must want is precisely the object of decision.[35] Here we can see how the self-determination of will does not presuppose an indetermination or an exercise of the will in a vacuum. Freedom is not freedom from objects or from values, but freedom for objects and for values. This freedom to choose is undermined both by the absence of the object and by any imposition of a specific object over another. The act of will is the person's answer to the appeal of the values, in the light of the person's self-discipline.

For traditional philosophy, from the scholastics to Leibniz, will is a rational appetite. This expression makes us aware of a constitutive relationship between reason and will. If the individual does not immediately follow his impulse, or that dynamic synthesis of his impulses which we call instinct, what is the specific element which can judge the instinctual appetites? It is only through reason that man can know the meaning of his being in the world and orient his actions according to that meaning. The reference to truth is therefore constitutive of the act of the will. I not only recognize what I want in what I want, but I also judge the presence of a value which should be realized through my action. The acknowledgment of the value implies a cognitive act. Although in itself it is not an act of knowledge, the act of the will depends internally on the acknowledgment of the truth about the object. For this reason the subject verifies the motivations and does not just allow itself to be determined by them. The independence of the will from the emotional sphere is explained by its dependence on the truth. The person is in control of his own decisions, whose constitutive elements become objective in the process of self-knowledge. This dynamic is based on the fact that every human act is faithful or unfaithful, good or evil, from the point of view of its reference to the truth and the good. The opposition between good and evil, which is the fundamental criterion of any judgment on the action, would be incomprehensible if willing the object did not imply the acknowledgment of the measure of good contained in the object which would justify the action toward it.

Knowledge is therefore the condition of will. It is impossible to turn toward values without knowing them. Knowledge of the truth about the object toward which the will is oriented is a fundamental part of the experience of value. The will's intentionality goes toward the object, but it is only to the extent that a judgment of the truth of the object is made that this intentional tending becomes a real intention, an act of the will.

---

35. For Freudian psychoanalysis also, the drive does not transcend the interior sphere in action without the consent of the "I" which controls access to mobility and which initiates action.

Of course, the cognitive act is an act of the person, in which all of his dynamisms are reflected.[36] Thinking is different from knowing. It implies, first, a certain passivity of the person which sees the succession of representations happening in itself. From this point of view, thinking itself has a certain passivity which makes it akin to something which happens in man. In judgment, by contrast, man experiences his own subjectivity in reference to the act of thinking. The judgment links the subject and the predicate to one another, and so constitutes an affirmation about the state of affairs. Here the subject assumes his responsibility toward the truth. As long as thought abstains from judgment, it remains essentially different from the will. Willing turns toward an object outside of the subject, whereas knowledge intentionally tends toward the object without going out of itself and by cognitively reconstructing the object within the subject. In judgment, an affirmation about the truth comes into play by which thought engages itself in reality. This is why thinking culminates in judgment and judgment in action, or, in a certain sense, judgment itself is an action. For this reason the structure of judgment is similar to that of decision, and decision and judgment are usually strictly connected, even if it remains true that while decision is an act of the will judgment is an act of the intellect. By affirming the truth about the object, judgment takes it intentionally into the subject and creates a "fit" between interiority and exteriority. Truth is a condition of judgment and decision; it is also the basis of conceptual/experimental knowledge and of the person's transcendence in his action. In a value judgment the apodictic aspect of judgment is the attribution of value to an object. The order of knowledge and the order of will are never as close as they are in this judgment. Every act of will presupposes a value judgment. This does not put in doubt the creative role of intuition in the perception of value. In a way, the intuition of value can happen passively and can impose itself through its own force rather than being the result of discursive research. But if we analyze this intuition of value, generally speaking we understand that it is either achieved at the end of research or it sets off a discursive research during which the initial intuition is verified. There is a kind of cognitive experience in which the cognitive element immanent in

36. Wojtyła takes care to emphasize that the cognitive experience of truth of which he speaks is meant in a purely assiological sense; he distinguishes carefully between logical or ontological truth and practical truth. It is possible to ask whether, in Wojtyła's conception, it is not this assiological truth which provides human access to truth in general and supplies the basis upon which one may investigate every other kind of truth.

every experience is presented, so to speak, as already explained, because of the particular circumstances in which the experience takes place. That the cognitive process usually happens intuitively or discursively is unimportant, however. What really matters is the orientation toward objective truth and its verification in praxis.[37]

The conception which we have explained seems necessarily to demand the verification of praxis. The entire process of thought culminates in judgment, which is linked to decision and fulfilled by action. Action is, in a way, the test of the entire process. The criterion of truth, which is external to pure thought, is that reality with which man comes into most intimate contact through his acting. It is not an exaggeration to say that the analysis which we have given leads toward a genuine philosophy of praxis. This is reached through the realistic rethinking of the Cartesian cogito. However this philosophy of praxis is essentially different from that of Marx.

At this point we must focus our attention on one element which we have already noted, but whose implications we now have fully to develop: *in completing an action the person simultaneously realizes himself.*

We have said that the person is also the object of the action. The efficacy of the person in the action, on the one hand, reaches external reality: by acting man brings about a change in his environment. On the other hand, by acting man changes himself. While the action reaches external reality, its intransitive aspect remains in the agent, modifying it. Every agent makes himself through his actions. Action, which can be good or evil, makes the human being who accomplishes it good or evil, because the moral value remains immanent to his person. Anthropology, therefore, contains the foundation of ethics, for it conceives of human beings as responsible subjects of their actions, which are realized through themselves. The realization

---

37. The whole of Wojtyła's analysis of the cognitive experience of value and of the regulation of the will is heavily dependent on St. Thomas Aquinas, *Summa Theologiae,* I, 83, and also upon the psychological and psychiatric research which has made descriptively evident the experience of being the voluntary cause of action, contradicting Scheler on his own ground. On this theme, Wojtyła was able to use N. Ach, *Ueber den Willensakt und das Temperament* (Leipzig, 1910), and N. Prümm, "Le choix volontaire et ses antécédents immediats," in *Arch. de Psych.* 10 (1910). In Poland the same theme was developed between the two World Wars by M. Dybowski. One must not forget two other fundamental works, D. von Hildebrand's *Ethik,* in *Gesammelte Werke,* vol. 2 (Stuttgart: Hebbel-Kohlhammer, 1974), and N. Hartmann, *Ethik,* 4th edition (Berlin: De Gruyter, 1962). This work, which he came upon during the time that he was working on Scheler, is essential to Wojtyła's philosophical culture.

of the person is linked to the acknowledgment of the truth concerning the good and to his realization in the action, whereas its nonrealization is linked to the theoretical and practical disregard of the truth. By conforming himself to the good which he acknowledges, the person can transcend his determinisms and, therefore, can properly realize himself as a person. The correctness of the reference to the good (that is, that one identifies as good what is really good) is reflected in the intransitive effect of the action, in the way in which the ontological kernel of the person is modified by it. Now it is even more clear why, also from a phenomenological point of view, it is both necessary and fitting to admit an irreducible kernel of the human being. The dynamisms of action can not be sufficiently explained on the basis of a conception of interiority and of the person which identifies in them only a flux of conscious data and is unable to frame them into a picture of the becoming of the person.[38] Moreover, only this perspective can strike a proper balance between human freedom and the sense of duty which is the experiential manifestion of the fact that the person's self-realization depends on the truth.[39]

The dependence of action on the transcendentals — that is, on the true, on the beautiful, and on the good — through the feeling of duty, appears to us as an *internal* criterion for evaluating experience, required by the faithfulness which the person owes to his self-realization, rather than an *external* obedience given to natural law which is not also the law of his self-conscious personality (and which would be able to enter into contra-

38. Wojtyła's thesis is opposed not only to Scheler but also to Husserl. According to the founder of phenomenology, in fact, the "I" is not an object of phenomenological research because it does not have an eidetic aspect and it is inherently indescribable. In the *Cartesian Meditations* and the *Ideas* I, Husserl discusses the existential foundation of being human and of the life-world through the analysis of the fluid structure of the consciousness-act-"I" pole of the "I." This indicates an internal foundation with an intentional pole, but not a real essence. The realistic conception of intentionality, which has generally led toward the affirmation of the reality of the object toward which the subject intentionally reaches out, is taken in this case toward an affirmation of the reality of the "I." Josef Seifert, perhaps the most radical of the phenomenologists who have followed this path, also admits a direct perception of the soul in the phenomenological analysis of experience. In this perspective, the neat distinction between phenomenological and metaphysical argument tends to be blurred or overturned.

39. Cf. Josef Seifert, *Das Leib-Seele-Problem in der gegenwärtigen philosophischen Diskussion. Eine kritische Analyse* (Darmstadt, 1979). See also Seifert's *Leib und Seele. Ein Beitrag zur philosophischen Anthropologie* (Salzburg, 1973) and "Karol Cardinal Wojtyła (Pope John Paul II) As Philosopher and the Cracow/Lublin School of Philosophy," in *Aletheia*, vol. 2 (1981), pp. 130-99.

diction with this self-realization in certain conditions). Consciousness is not restricted to reflecting the action, but in the moment in which it subjectivizes it, it introduces it into the person through a value judgment which is extended to the person himself. The person as such experiences in the action his own self-realization or failure. Through the value judgments interiorized by consciousness, ethics becomes a constitutive dimension of the person.[40] As moral consciousness, conscience is directly interested in the process through which man intends the truth. All other values are perceived in relationship to the truth, and this creates the person's transcendence. Loyalty toward the truth has a logical and speculative character and even an aesthetic element, but it is predominantly ethical. Loyalty toward the truth is at the same time human loyalty toward self-realization through action.

The norm which obligates man toward the truth and makes loyalty to the truth the keystone of his personal realization is the center of the entire normative system. Contemporary analytic philosophy, especially when it is applied to moral philosophy and philosophy of law, has often claimed that it is not possible to derive an "is" from an "ought," a moral from a descriptive judgment. Weber expressed the impossibility of deducing a value judgment from a factual one, and vice versa. The order of facts and the order of values are separated and there is no bridge between them. What we have been saying so far shows that a bridge can be built if one takes as a point of departure the analysis of the structure of the person and of the action which would bring to light the general obligation toward the truth and the good which constitutes the kernel of human freedom. From the affirmation "this is truly good" it follows that "this must be done." There is a human obligation to bring the good into reality; this constitutes the human person since his self-realization as man is at stake. It is the connection between truth and freedom which enables one to found a normative order. Generally speaking, the foundation of all duties is therefore the duty of the person toward himself and toward his own self-realization. From this fundamental duty there follow all other duties that a person can have toward other people and toward normative impersonal orders. The root of duty is freedom, which constitutes the person as responsible for his own action. In this construction the moment of objectivity is made immanent to the subject:

40. It is right to give in full the genuine anti-Kantian polemic at the end of the evaluation of the sentiment of duty, one of whose elements is twisted in an emotionalist sense in Scheler's philosophy.

the acknowledgment of the just norm enters into his process of self-realization. The contrary is also true: the objectively right norm must be realized as such in the conscience of the subject, and must be lived as an indication of his own good to realize his own moral value. The good of the subject consists in living in truth, in which the true value of the object is the genuine experience of life.[41]

The fundamental good which the person must realize is his fulfillment as a person. This cannot happen without the full participation of his acts of conscience and of subjective interiority. Of course, conscience does not legislate for itself. But being in truth is linked to experiencing truth in one's own life and not simply to conforming one's behavior to the norm. The norm ought to be obeyed in a personal way; that is to say, it must be accepted by the conscience as true. It becomes individuated by entering into the process of self-realization of this unique and unrepeatable person. This is the *rationabile obsequium* (reasonable obedience) of which St. Paul spoke. Normative objective order and individual conscience meet in the truth which founds and justifies both. When value is acknowledged by conscience, and becomes in this way an experience of the subject, obligation arises. Many obligations take the form of prohibitions. But the primary form of obligation is positive. This is the attraction exercised by value, acknowledged as true by conscience. But the simple attractiveness of value does not found obligation without the judgment of its truth, which conscience formulates. The concept of vocation or calling is linked to the concept of obligation. The obligations which are negative in form also derive their force from putting themselves on the trajectory in which the call which comes to everyone to be a person is realized. The rational foundation of every norm is its justice, that is, its truth referred to the realization of the person. We find here again the scholastic axiom "there is no law that

41. In the theme of "living in truth" Wojtyła's thought encounters that of Solzhenitsyn and of Jan Patocka. For Havel, see "The Power of the Powerless," in *Living in Truth*, ed. Jan Vladislav (Faber & Faber, 1991); on Jan Patocka, *Saggi eretici sulla filosofia della storia* (Bologna: CSEO, 1981), with an important introduction by Vaclav Belorahdsky. The argument developed in the preceding pages presupposes that, as Scheler claimed, the existence of value is an objective matter of fact, but nonetheless value is known through experience. From this point of view, the opposition between "is statements" and "ought statements" appears as a more refined formulation of Weber's position; this is compatible with Scheler's thesis on the nature of the experience of value. Such compatibility ceases, however (here is the difference between Scheler and Wojtyła), once one admits that the perception of value creates in a person, as a subject of action, an obligation toward that value.

has not been just" *("nulla videtur esse lex qui justa non fuerit")*, against every theory which founds the normative order on ethical voluntarism or legal arbitrarism. Values and obligations are the scene in which the drama of the lives of persons is played out. The realization of the person cannot be one-sidedly linked either to knowledge of values or to the intentional acts through which these are perceived. A person realizes himself and shows his transcendence through the particular modification of intentionality and self-determination which is the taking up of obligations which belong to him according to the truth.

Obligation introduces us to the theme of responsibility[42] in a more complete way than the simple consideration of the causality of the person in the action. One is responsible not so much for what one does, but rather for the fidelity or infidelity to what one has the obligation to do. The root of the word responsibility is *"respondeo,"* "I answer." The meaning of this root can be developed in two directions, both of which belong to the structure of responsibility. One is a matter of responding to values, that is, of being open to the attraction of value. The other concerns the correspondence of the action to the truth. It is necessary that one answers to the value and tends toward it, conforming to its truth and to that of the person. Responsibility enters into the constitution of the obligation (I am bound because I am responsible), and is founded on it (I am responsible because I acknowledge the truth of the value and my obligation toward it). The person is responsible for the realization of values and at the same time for the realization of himself as a value. These two sides are closely connected because in order to realize any value it is necessary to bring it about in the person and, by so doing, to perfect the value of the person. Moreover, the person is responsible to himself for the realization of his own value. But responsibility toward the objective moral order and toward God is not cancelled out by the transcendence of the person. Rather, it is founded upon it. The transcendence of ethics as an objective order of values is closely linked with the transcendence of the person. There exists a responsibility toward others, but this is founded on the person's responsibility toward himself. In sum, the person is the subject which is responsible but is also the object of responsibility and is the subject toward which one is responsible.

The realization of the person in action brings happiness to him. It consists in the realization of freedom through the truth. This means that

---

42. This show the contingency and the freedom of man, whose full realization as human depends on his own action.

happiness comes about not only through the person's relation to himself but also through his relation to other persons and toward God. But, as we shall see below, this happens because the relationship with others enters into the process of self-realization. The connection of happiness with truth and with freedom implies that happiness has a strictly personal structure. One can only speak about happiness in relation to the person.

At the conceptual level we must carefully distinguish between happiness and pleasure. It is not only a question, as Scheler thought, of a difference of degree but, rather, of the fact that pleasure is something that happens in the person, while happiness follows an act of man. Of course it is not easy to trace a clear borderline between pleasure and happiness: on one side man can consciously turn his activity toward pleasure; on the other hand, some form of pleasure accompanies most types of happiness. In any case, however, happiness is a modification of the irreducible kernel of man (and so is its contrary, despair), and therefore it has nothing directly to do with the sum of pleasures and pains which happen in him. The concept of transcendence has an enormous importance in all of this discussion. We need to summarize here the different meanings attendant upon it in this discussion.

From a phenomenological point of view, transcendence is the direction of intentionality beyond the limits of subjectivity. From a metaphysical point of view, those objects which cannot be defined in the usual way "through a proximate genus and a specific difference" are called transcendent because they transcend all genera and species. The vertical transcendence of the person which is the keystone of all Wojtyła's thought moves beyond subjectivity, toward the interior, rather than toward the exterior. It moves toward the irreducible kernel of man who is also transcendent in the metaphysical sense. In action man reveals himself to be "someone" through the capacity for self-government and self-possession, which in turn enables him to experience himself as a free being. This experience of freedom leads us to admit the efficient causality of man toward action and therefore his responsibility for it. Freedom rests on the person's relationship with the truth, enabling him not to be determined by circumstances. The relationship of freedom to truth is finally the decisive element of the transcendence of the person in his action.

Wojtyła develops this line of thought with the phenomenological method. It seems, therefore, that phenomenological analysis can go as far as showing to us the essential spirituality of man. By the word "spirit" we indicate the transcendence of the person witnessed by freedom, responsibility, and loyalty toward the truth. We discover spirit as really immanent to being/man. Phenomenological transcendence of the person in the act takes us to the threshold of the transcendence of the person understood in a metaphysical sense.

One might ask at this point: "Was it worth going through such a speculative effort to get to a truth which has been known since time immemorial to classical metaphysics?"

The answer is positive. We have made an important cognitive gain over classical metaphysics because now we know how human spirituality descriptively manifests itself. The analysis of experience led us to the threshold of the ontological affirmation. Our point of departure is the fact that man is a person. We have seen the transcendence of the person in action, and from it we infer the spirituality of the person. In fact, the spiritual nature of man is nothing but the person and can only be thought in connection with personal being. Among other things, this analysis raises our awareness of the fact that if one is to apply it to the person, the concept of nature must be profoundly modified. If the spiritual nature of man is being a person, then from his nature one must infer essentially and above all the requirement of his freedom. "Personal freedom rejects the necessity which is proper to nature."[43]

43. On this theme Wojtyła's thought is quite close to that of Ingarden, in his essay "Ueber die Verantwortung (Ihre ontischen Fundamente)" (Reclam Universal-Bibliothek, 1979). This essay was reprinted in a collection of Ingarden's essays in English as *Man and Value* (Philosophia Verlag/Catholic University of America). This aspect of Wojtyła's thought is marked by Tadeusz Styczen in "O metodzie antropologii filosoficznei. Na marginesie Osoby I czynu K. Wojtyła oraz ksiazecki o czfowieku R. Ingardena," in *Roczniki Filozoficzne*.

The basic thesis of "Ueber die Verantwortung" was read by Ingarden in one of the weekly gatherings which Wojtyła held, a meal with the intellectuals of his diocese a short while before the paper was officially presented to a philosophical congress in Vienna on 2-9 September 1968. At that date, according to Styczen and Anna-Teresa Tymieniecka ("A Page of History, or from *Osoba I Czyn* to *The Acting Person*," p. 106), *Osoba I czyn* had already been completed. Wojtyła had composed the three papers which contain his major theses before his encounter with Ingarden: "Osoba I Czyn w aspekcie świado-mości" (in *Pastori et Magistro. Praca zbiorowa wydana dla uczczenia jubileuszu 50-lecia Kapłaństwa Jego Ekscelencji Ksiedza Biskupa Doktora Piotra Kałwy Profesora I Wielkiego Kanclerza*, ed. A. Krupa [Lublin: KUL, 1966]); "Osoba I Czyn na tle dynamizmu człowieka," in *O Bogu I o człowieku. Problemy filozoficzne*, ed. Bohdan Bejze (Varsavia, 1968), and finally "Osoba I Czyn. Refleksywne funksjonowanie świadomości I jej emoc-jonalizacja," in *Studia Theologica Varsaviensia* 6/1 (1968). Much more relevant and surprising is the encounter between his fundamental theses of responsibility and the fundamental structure of the person, and Ingarden's themes. Ingarden's main work is *Die Streit um die Existenz der Welt* (Tübingen: Niemeyer, 1965), in which he argues for his own realistic conception of phenomenology.

Phenomenological analysis has shown both the person's complexity and his profound unity. It has discovered a set of symptoms which must have a common origin, and this origin produces and integrates the complexity of the person which is the spiritual element of man. "So the transcendence of the person in action, understood in a phenomenological sense, leads us toward an ontological conception of man in which the unity of his being is determined by the spirit."[44]

It is possible to infer a spiritual potentiality or virtuality from the presence of spiritual dynamisms in man, brought to light by phenomenological analysis. These are the dynamic reference to the moral truth, the cognitive function, and freedom in dynamic dependency on truth. At the foundation of these powers it is easy to hypothesize intellect and will as correspondent metaphysical faculties. In particular, this necessity of a metaphysical supplement to the phenomenological analysis is evident in the case of the soul. Only a metaphysical analysis can fully develop a discourse on the soul, but the rich material provided by phenomenological description will be of great utility in enlivening it, by making the metaphysical analysis existentially comprehensible.

The discovery of the transcendence of the person as the subject of action in relation to the conscience leads Wojtyła toward the philosophy of praxis. We come to see this philosophy of praxis developing through a patient and punctilious analysis of the mechanism of action. What contradistinguishes it is the reference to truth and responsibility toward the truth as elements immanent in praxis. The responsibility toward the truth is also a responsibility toward the value of the person. In contrast to Marxist praxis, which is essentially a praxis which transforms nature, Wojtyła's praxis is one which transforms nature in its transitive aspect and transforms the person in its intransitive aspect. Here ethics is at the core of praxis. And this analysis of action is at the heart of that distinction between objective work and subjective work which John Paul II later developed in *Laborem Exercens*. There is a clear opposition to the absorption of ethics into politics and to the primacy of economy which are distinctive elements in any Marxist philosophy of praxis. We will come back to this in the last part of this book.

44. *Osoba i Czyn*, p. 192; *The Acting Person*, p. 184.

The Integration of the Person in Action: Integration and the Body

We have seen how, through self-government and self-possession, the person transcends the dynamisms which simply happen in man. It is not possible to understand that dynamic totality which is the person and his action if one disregards the transcendence of the person. But one cannot stop, either, at the affirmation of the transcendence of the person. It is necessary to explore the dynamisms which happen in him, and the way in which they integrate themselves in the dynamic totality of the person and his action. This is the moment of the integration of the person, which complements his transcendence. Without integration, transcendence remains without support in concrete existence. Self-government presupposes both an active moment in which the person is the subject who governs, and a passive moment in which the person submits himself to government. Through the integration of the person in action the passive side of the person is submitted to the active side. The word "integration" does not mean here a simple assemblage of diverse constitutive components of the person, but rather their unity, which has as its basis a complexity of structures and faculties.

From an experiential point of view the most direct approach to the integration of the person is given negatively from the experience of personal disintegration. This is ostensibly studied by the psychological and psychiatric disciplines which are concerned with the pathology of the person.[45] The disintegration of personality is always due to an unraveling of the mechanism of self-government and self-possession of the person. Beyond the diverse classifications of the psychiatric diseases, they always bring to light an "I" without self-government and self-possession. The diverse dynamisms which dwell in the person remain without unity and therefore the person is not integrated.

This, of course, sets a limit to the transcendence of the person, which cannot govern and orient a rebel "I." Transcendence and integration are only two sides of the dynamic totality person/action; it can only be realized in a reciprocal relationship, even if for purposes of analysis we can study them separately, as Wojtyła does.

The integration of person and action gives us the key to understanding the psychosomatic unity of man. The defect of the usual way of conceiving such a unity is that it is just a result of adding up the diverse and discrete

---

45. *Osoba i Czyn*, p. 193; *The Acting Person*, p. 192.

elements, each of which is treated by one of the empirical human sciences. These elements can only gain their full meaning by being united in an organic whole as interpreted by the phenomenological analysis of the experience of human action. Only in the light of the unity person/action can one see in the mutual relationships of these elements the psychosomatic complexity of man. Man's action is a dynamism of a superior kind; it is governed by its own proper logic, which transcends the single partial dynamism furnishing the matter of his development even while it respects it. At this level the image of man is created, and it is oriented toward the comprehension of its psychosomatic complexity. The integration of the person is nothing but the psychosomatic complexity considered in its constitutive relationship with the transcendence of the person. The individual physical and psychical dynamisms considered by the empirical sciences are events which happen in the person. The person integrates them into the process through which the person realizes himself, by way of intellect and will.

This approach cannot disregard the result of the individual sciences; nor can it oppose itself to them. But it provides the basis for their integration, which is the reference to the person. Outside these personalistic contexts, the data of the individual sciences lose a large part of their meaning, and can at worst turn against man himself.[46]

In the analysis of the dynamisms which are integrated in the person, the most important problem with which we must concern ourselves is that of the independence of the psyche from the soma.

The human body is endowed with a particular interiority and exteriority. The exteriority is immediately perceptible in the shape of the body, in the harmony of the members, in the fluidity of the moments. The

---

46. It seems to me that we find here a close analogy with the need, expressed by the critical theorists, for the critical self-reflection of the individual sciences. Such a need is affirmed in relation to the science of man but it is easily generalizable. Wojtyła emphasizes more energetically than the Frankfurt school (apart from the late Horkheimer) that this critical self-reflection can come about only in relation to a philosophy of man. It is not too much to say that the crisis and the dissolution of the Frankfurt school occurred because it had not sufficiently comprehended this. This connection enables us to understand and to thematize the thought of Horkheimer and also Adorno, who did not have enough energy to restate the entire edifice of critical theory on a new basis. For a formulation of Max Horkheimer's program of critical theory, see his "Bemerkungen über Wissenschaft und Krise," in *Zeitschrift für Sozialforschung,* 1 (1932). For a study of this way of explaining the evolution of Horkheimer's thought, permit me to recommend Rocco Buttiglione, *Dialettica e Nostalgia* (Milan: Jaca Books, 1978).

interiority of the body is the set of the functions of these organs which are often outside the field of awareness but which deeply condition all of the organism's activities. The psyche depends on the body; psyche is understood here not in a metaphysical sense but in a physical and empirical sense — as a manifestation of human activity which, although it depends on the body, is not just material. On the other hand, there also exists a kind of conditioning which goes in the other direction, from the psyche to the body.[47]

The person expresses himself through his body. One's personality permeates one's visible shape and interacts with the internal dynamisms of one's bodily organism. This interaction was recognized by Aristotle in his classification of the diverse human temperaments, which was subsequently taken up by anthropologists, who have constructed various psychophysical typologies. In order adequately to frame the participation of the body in action, we must use the concept of objectivization, which we have already explained. The body enters the person as the object of his self-government; its availability or reluctance to submit to such self-government influences in a decisive way the entire process of objectivization and self-control. It is through dominion over the body that the freedom of the person is realized and comes into contact with the external world.

The body, as it appears to us, is endowed with two interiorities. On one side it is submitted to the interiority of the person, which commands it in the process of self-government; on the other hand, it has a merely bodily interiority, which is that of the organism. Organism has its own dynamism, which belongs to the order of nature and which has an essentially reactive character. The internal dynamism of the human organism reacts to external circumstances with physiological events. These belong essentially to the vegetative process which builds, keeps alive, and reproduces the human organism. In these events, which are directed to self-preservation and reproduction and which react to external and internal stimuli, the body manifests a marked autonomy.

There is, therefore, an efficacy and an efficient causality which is proper to the body, which happens in the person without being caused by it and which belongs to it on the basis of the ontic unity of man. Inside the personal structure of man and intrinsic to it is a bodily structure which is

---

47. Cf. Wanda Połtawska, "Koncepcja samoposiadania podstawa psychoterapii obiektywizujacej (w świetle ksiażki kardinażła Karola Wojtyła)," in *Analecta Cracoviensia*, 5-6, pp. 223-41.

empowered according to the laws of nature and not by those of the personalistic order. The integration of the person is realized when the somatic subjectivity and the transcendent subjectivity of the person meet and cooperate. The person expresses the efficient causality which belongs to him by using the bodily dynamisms; for instance, if I go somewhere, my action is accomplished through bodily events which really put my body in movement toward my intended destination. The synthesis of the two forms of subjectivity presupposes the integrity of the body and its openness to direction by the transcendent subjectivity through the structures of the person's self-government. The habitual integration of the person is a virtue. Once this habit solidifies, the perception of the efficient causality of the person can attenuate until it almost disappears, because the body spontaneously moves according to an indication of the will, almost anticipating it. The virtue can become a second nature. In this relative concealment the transcendence of the person affirms itself in its utmost force.

A milestone in the integration of the person is represented by the control of motility, which is linked to the external manifestation of the person. The struggle for the control of motility is a decisive part of the struggle for the self-government of the person (a point with which Freud concurs).

Of course, with the breakdown of the integrity of the body, the manifestation of the personality can be blocked without diminishing the moral value of the person (unless the person himself is accountable for the disintegration of the body).

Bodily dynamisms have their first synthesis in instincts. Wojtyła distinguishes between instinctivity and instinctuality. Every bodily event has an instinctive character, but not every reaction has an instinctual character. Instinct does not indicate any single event which happens on a natural basis, but rather the accumulation of a series of events on their way to a natural end. When we feel ill the various functions of the organism which protect it are activated and reestablish a condition of health.

The instinct of self-preservation is different: it implies a dynamic integration of different events in order to attain an end. This dynamic integration happens only at the level of the body but is nonetheless an element of the existence and the complex experience of the person. From one point of view, the major human instincts introduce us to the main metaphysical truths which are inscribed in the dynamic of being. The instinct of self-preservation implies the affirmation that it is better to be than not to be and that it would be evil to lose one's own existence. It introduces man to the comprehension of the value of being, of the fact that to be is a good, and, moreover, that the Good is Being. The sexual instinct also reveals a fundamental metaphysical truth about the structure of the person, that "it is not good that he is alone" because he experiences and discovers his own value in the encounter with the other person, by dwelling with the other, and by being enriched by the relationship with the other. Moreover, the major vital instincts forcefully engage human affective life and influence its emotional dynamisms. They cannot be integrated and pull these conflicting aspects together without elevating themselves beyond the pure somatic level.

The body defeats virus attacks (but even here the curative activity of the person consciously intervenes). But one does not ward off a criminal's attack just with one's body. Here the choice of the means to use to defeat aggression involves the whole person and engages him in an ethical choice which can by no means be reduced to bodily dynamisms. This truth is even more evident in the area of sexuality. In contrast to animals, man does not achieve his proper good through events which happen in him and in which the order of nature is achieved. The proper human dynamism requires that the meaning of instinct be subjectively lived, freely recognized and realized. It is necessary at this point to extend our analysis of the integration of the psyche in the person, in order to understand this process.

Personal Integration and the Psyche

Wojtyła develops the analysis of the psyche and of its contribution to the integration of the person at the phenomenological level. Psyche is not here understood as synonymous with the soul in a metaphysical sense. It is, rather, the set of the elements of the integral being of the person — as it is manifested to internal and external observation — which cannot be reduced to the body. This notion of psyche must also be accurately distinguished from the interiority of the body, that is, from the set of vegetative processes inside the organism. The difference is that psychic activity is reflected in consciousness.

Defined in this way, the psyche has emotion as its main dynamic manifestation. Just as bodily dynamism is essentially reactive, so psychic dynamism is essentially emotive. The emotive dynamism is founded on the reactive dynamism and conditions it so often that one speaks of "psychological reactions." Since the psychophysical complex expresses a substantial

161

unity, this way of speaking has its own legitimacy. On the other hand, the dynamism of the psyche is strictly linked to that of the person, even if it remains conceptually distinct. Action always moves toward a value through a conscious choice; the emotion makes the subject aware and in a certain sense compenetrated by an experience of value and in this way provides the "prime matter" upon which the judgment of intelligence and the act of the will exercise themselves. Emotion allows one to feel value in a spontaneous and intuitive way. Through the analysis of emotions it is possible to reach a better understanding of the transcendence of the person in the action which is affirmed by transcending and integrating emotions. This in its turn always remains in touch with sensibility and connects the bodily element with the spiritual. On one side, the emotional dynamism is profoundly sensitive to the great spiritual value of beauty, truth, and good and gives to them a suggestive personal resonance by mobilizing the energy which allows one to orient one's action toward them. At the opposite extreme, emotion and reactivity share a "frontier": there are stimuli to which one responds first of all simply with an emotional change, with a feeling. In feeling, which is not a bodily impulse, the body is objectivized by the psyche and is reflected in consciousness. This sensible and cognitive reflection of the body belongs to the psyche, just as in general the fundamental feeling which each one of us has of his body does. The diverse sensations reach unity in a single feeling about oneself (the one which is present in the expressions "I feel good" or "I feel bad") which has as its object the somatic "I" considered as a whole and in its intrinsic belonging to the person. This feeling that we have about our body allows us to establish an affective contact with it and reveals the subjectivity of the body to consciousness. But consciousness is also the object of a psychological feeling in the sense that we feel emotionally our own consciousness. This is the most delicate point of the structure of personal self-mastery, because it presupposes that feelings in general, and in particular those feelings which deal with one's own body, do not prevail on consciousness, despite the fact that they are reflected in consciousness, allowing us to feel and to live our body as something which belongs to us and which can and must be integrated into the person as such.

Man has the feeling of his own body, the feeling of his own "I" and the feeling of being there in the world. These feelings are unified in the experience of being in the world. We have feelings which reflect our main spiritual values. This capacity to feel does not simply correspond to sensibility understood in the traditional sense. It includes an experience of value which is meta-empirical. However, its relationship with values is not rational and is not founded on the decisions of the person: feelings just happen in it, over and above its will. While sensitivity intentionally reaches out toward an object, it also has an inclination toward value. For this reason an experience of value can easily crystallize around a feeling. But, in order to have an authentic experience of value, it is necessary that the sensitivity be turned toward true values, that is, that it be integrated into the truthfulness of the value. The subjective authenticity of the feeling is not enough; the object toward which the feeling is turned is also necessary. It is necessary, in other words, that the person or the thing toward which one is intentionally directed really possesses the perfection which it appears to have. This can be given only by a rational judgment. Scheler's error is in thinking that loyalty toward values which are felt through experience precludes their rational evaluation. On the contrary, only that value which is objectively true is a solid basis for personal realization, and the person sometimes should realize it even at the cost of sacrificing his own subjective feeling.

But the value is present in the cognitive faculty only in its abstract generality. Only emotional intuition allows one to live the value as an adequate answer to the person's intentional reaching toward being and the good, and interiorly to feel it as belonging to personal self-realization. In sum, the experience of value always requires the agreement of the objective and the subjective element, of the judgment of the experience and of decision. In the case of a conflict, however, it is necessary to do what is objectively right even if this means to go against all of one's subjective feelings. But this is not the ideal ethical and anthropological situation; rather, the right balance of emotion and cognition permits one emotionally to engage in reality by attributing the right value to every thing.

St. Thomas underlines the necessity that the action be directed toward the good which is objectively proportioned to it. For him the senses provide the knowledge of the objective reality which is then elaborated by the intellect. In the same way irascible and concupiscible appetites provide the will with the raw material upon which its capacity to decide, guided by the intellect, is exercised. But when St. Thomas turns his attention to the emotional dynamisms of the person, he develops not a psychological typology but an axiological one. This is founded upon the concept of desire, which characterizes the passions which are directed toward a positive value, and irascibility, which characterizes the passions which are directed toward a negative value. The Thomistic position has the advantage of underlining the directive role of reason in ethics, but, on the other hand, it does not provide a description of emotional dynamisms which would explain what can and must support reason in exercising this directive role. For this reason, Wojtyła puts St. Thomas's axiological typology side by side with a different typology founded on the distinction between excitement and deep feeling. We find excitement at the lower level of the psychic dynamism. It does not have a cognitive content and it is not even directed toward a determinate object, but is just a subjective condition of the psyche.[48] The excitement always induces a certain bodily reaction, even if it must not be confused with it.[49]

Excitability, that is, the capacity to be excited, is the explosive core of human emotion. Excitability must be distinguished from affectivity, because in it the blind side of emotion, the irrational awakening of the passions, prevails.[50]

Excitement differs from the hereditary dynamic of the most profound emotions which bring to light otherwise inaccessible psychical dimensions. These emotions are less linked to sensuality than excitability is, and have more to do with human spiritual life. They plumb deeper levels of the person and are directed toward the true, the beautiful, and the good. The great human emotions spring from this source, and they make important values emotively perceptible in a particularly sensible way. Emotions are generally unstable; they come and go easily. Sometimes, however, especially if they are approved and consolidated by the will, they can become a state of mind.

This depiction of the structure of the emotions departs from a large part of the philosophical tradition in not attributing irrationality to emotions. This reevaluation of emotion depends on the distinction between

48. The phenomenological analysis can be developed in parallel with the Aristotelian/Thomistic theory of the soul. This is the form of the body, comprehensible only in its relation with a being as the vital synthesis of an organism (the "first form of a physical body with potential life"). There exists in the human soul an element which is metaphysically — and not only phenomenologically — spiritual, responsible for the higher functions of the person, the exercise of thought and of liberty. In Wojtyła's analysis, this appears as the irreducible core of the person, to which he attributes the person's self-transcendence.

49. Bodily excitement has the general feature of being irascible or concupiscible because of its entirely subjective character, which makes it ill-adapted to an assiological classification.

50. Although this excitement always has a bodily effect, its source is not necessarily bodily but can also reside in a spiritual value. In this case Wojtyła prefers to use the word "elation."

deep emotion and excitement, a distinction which avoids the reduction of emotion to sensuality. Even if, at the beginning of every emotional process, excitement is likely to be present, the emotional energy is nonetheless susceptible of being transformed from a superficial to a more profound level, on which it establishes a strict reference to values. Freud seems to speak of this same process in his theory of sublimation. Within the psychological structure which we are describing, excitement aroused by bodily stimulus at least partially gives its energy to a deeper emotion which tends to integrate itself with the efficacy of the person as such. This is the process of the integration of the person, which presupposes the overcoming of the resistance of the sensible, of the reason and emotion, in order that the person can master himself.

The unrepeatable uniqueness of the person's personality, and his particular path toward truth and good, depends on the way in which he realizes this task. We have seen how the emotions can crystallize in a state of mind and in interior habits. When these are determined by the will, the whole psychic energy of the person, through a system of sublimations, is under the control of the will. But when these crystallizations are either outside the will or subordinate it to themselves, the whole of consciousness is emotionalized and the subjectivism of emotion prevails. Between emotion and reason there is, therefore, neither a preestablished harmony nor a fixed opposition. There is between these two areas of the person an objective correspondence which is the basis of integration: the directive role of reason makes the integration possible. The efficacy of the emotion, like that of the person, has its source in values, and this is what makes an integration objectively possible. The stimuli of the body and its instincts also refer ultimately to fundamental metaphysical values, even if they do so unconsciously.

The fact that (whether or not they do so consciously) the will, the emotions, and the bodily dynamisms are oriented toward the same values provides the objective basis for the integration of the person. Will does not have the task of tyrannizing over the body and the emotions in order to pursue an aim which is antithetical to theirs. Rather, it ought to lead the whole person toward this unified end by orienting both the bodily mechanisms and the emotions. The fact that the will and the reason have a directive and not merely repressive role in ethical action is founded upon the fact that everything in man is directed toward the good. Difficulties in this field for the will especially come from the sphere of emotions. The emotions make a value present but cannot move either the intellect or the will toward it. But by influencing the cognitive faculty, they can give rise to a state of mind or to an emotional reflex. The experience of the value given by emotion has a spontaneous character which makes the subject entirely absorbed and satisfied in himself and arouses the desire for an absolute proximity to the object which causes the emotion. This is the reason for the fascination exercised by emotional experience. But in this state of mind one runs the risk that the fascination with the emotional value becomes an obstacle to a reasonable judgment on its truth and therefore value comes to be willed and lived outside the truth. Hence the task of education and in particular of ascesis and the moral virtue which realizes the submission of the emotion to the intellect in defining its object, thereby allowing a full integration of the person. By fostering the conversion of excitement into profound emotion and the formation of a fitting emotional crystallization of states of mind, the will can lead one toward the true good by using the spontaneous attraction or repulsion which is present in the emotions, illuminating and correcting them. In the moral sphere, integration is a task which ends only with death; in a certain sense, it is the lifelong task through whose accomplishment the person generates or creates himself. While the integration of the body presupposes a mastery of the bodily functions which one acquires in the first years of life, that of the psyche, which coincides with the generation of the human psychic and moral personality, concludes only with the end of life.

This analysis shows that underneath the complex dynamisms which we find in human acting, and which cooperate with it, lies a simplicity and a fundamental unity. But this does not amount to a claim that one is able to clarify the mind-body problem. The soul and its relationship with the body is outside of experience and beyond phenomenality. The experience of the transcendence of the person in action is not an experience of the soul. Only the reflection on the unity of human experience as real being in the world gives a basis to the metaphysical analysis of the soul. But the phenomenological analysis brings us in a certain way to the threshold of the relationship between body and soul, allowing us to grasp the congruity of the metaphysical doctrine of the soul with the data of experience. We have seen that whereas the body is the source of the physical dynamisms and indirectly also of the emotional ones, the integration of these two dimensions can be understood only on the basis of the transcendence of the person. It must share a foundation with it. Can we infer that the soul is the principle both of integration and of transcendence? The hypothesis is not demonstrable in phenomenological terms, but it would seem to be confirmed by the structure of the experience of the acting person.[51]

Wojtyła's thoughts about the integration of the person, besides clarifying the complex mechanisms of the action, also have great methodological import, about which we should say a few words. The diverse dynamisms which take place in the person are the object of different human sciences so that, for instance, the diverse branches of medicine deal with the mechanism of the human body and the diverse specializations of psychology study emotional dynamisms. Other human sciences study particular sectors of human action, unified by some particular dynamisms of an intersubjective character, such as economy or linguistics. Just as the integration of the diverse dynamisms is made possible by the person's transcendence (that is, that the person by transcending each one of them integrates them), so the integration of the different disciplines which deal with man are made possible only by anthropology. Marxist philosophy of praxis used to integrate the diverse dynamisms on the basis of the fundamental economic dynamism which was assumed to be the basic determinate, the root cause of human action. Since Wojtyła has included the subjective and ethical element in praxis, he is able to see philosophical anthropology as the basis for the integration of the diverse human sciences, a basis which allows them to be critically responsible toward man. Analogously, Wojtyła considers culture to be at the basis of social integration. We cannot help noticing that these notions bear some relation to the way in which John Paul II will later frame the problem of the social doctrine of the Church, as a method based on Christian anthropology, of personalistic integration of the findings of the diverse sciences of man.

51. Naturally this indicates the structure of action as it reveals itself in phenomenological analysis. On this issue Wojtyła develops the distinction between behavior and conduct. Human behavior, which occupies the different behavior schools, relates to externally manifested actions rather than to the way in which they are brought into being. This external manifestation is blind to the difference between what a human being does and the action of the person. It is the latter which shows the true structure and the true significance of actions. The word *conduct,* on the other hand, indicates that which comes about as a result of consciously willed behavior. This expresses the idea that single acts are oriented toward an end and that it is possible through the analysis of conduct to arrive at a perception of the structure of action and of the efficacy of the person.

167

KAROL WOJTYŁA

Intersubjectivity through Participation[52]

Our analysis will not be complete if we do not take into consideration the fact that the action can be performed (and usually is performed) together with another person. Here it is not a question of a circumstance which is extrinsically added to the action, but of a dimension which essentially belongs to it. Of course, Wojtyła does not offer us a sociological dissertation, but he develops the communitarian or social dimension which is immanent in the human act as such. This choice depends on the field of research and also on the fact that it is by beginning from the act of the person, and his structure, that we can understand the social dynamic, and not vice versa. If we were to begin from social conditioning we would run the risk of flying over that irreducible kernel of the human being, the transcendence of the person, which is the key to understanding human action. This error is common not only to Marxism but to all the forms of sociological determinism which attempt to explain the person's action through the set of social relationships in which the person finds himself. But one should not fall into the opposite error, of picturing the intersubjective dimension as indifferent to action or even as something that can be added from outside.

The problem can be formulated in this way: What is the significance of acting with others, from the point of view of the personalistic value of the action? The bearing of this question is above all anthropological and not ethical. There is a personalistic value of the action which precedes every ethical value which is connected with it. The ethical value depends on the objective relationship of the action with the good in conformity to a norm. Here conformity or deviance in relationship to the norm decides the value of the action. The personalistic value of the action lies in the fact that the action is performed and in it the person realizes himself according to the structure which is proper to him. Just as being precedes action, so the value of the person is more fundamental than the value of the action. For this reason every judgment on the moral value of an act must begin by ascertaining the existence of the action, that is, its ascription to the efficacy of the person. The distinction between the ethical value and the personalistic value of the action, and the primacy given to the personalistic one, implies

52. For Husserl, the problem of intersubjectivity is exclusively cognitive. The sense in which Wojtyła speaks of intersubjectivity through participation is neither exclusively nor even principally cognitive.

168

a different emphasis from the traditional treatise "De Actibus Humanis" (On Human Acts).

In a certain tradition the action is seen only as a means which enables the person to take a position in the objective ethical order; much less importance is given to the fact that the action has a value simply as belonging to man. This way of looking at action is unavoidable if willing is understood as a metaphysical faculty and is not analyzed within the context of the diverse dynamisms which enter into the composition of the person's act. Such a perspective is linked to the propensity in this tradition toward an excessive use of the concept of nature, partly to explain those dynamisms which go beyond the order of nature and have a personalistic character. This philosophy speaks of the rational and social nature of man along these lines. While this way of speaking emphasizes the unity of everything which is, it risks obscuring the uniqueness of some decisive fields of experience, and the specific way in which they function.

But the expression "social nature" indicates the experience, with which we are dealing, of acting together with others. Within this experience the word "participation" is used by Wojtyła to indicate the way in which, in common acting, the person protects the personalistic value of his own acting and participates together in the realization of common action and its outcomes.

Participation (the act of participating and the potentiality which it presupposes) therefore manifests itself, along with transcendence and integration, as one of the fundamental characteristics of the acting person. Without it, man would not be able to act in relation with other men, and therefore this relation would be for him nothing but a conditioning, instead of being an occasion for the realization of his freedom. Of course, acting with others implies some conditioning which can go so far as dissolving the person into the mass and, in so doing, depriving the action of any personalistic value. But this happens precisely to the extent to which acting with others is not realized through participation but by prescinding from it. Participation is therefore the condition through which man can remain free and at the same time experience himself as such in relationship with other men and in social life. Participation allows him to avoid either treating the other as an object, or being treated in that way by him, when they are doing something together. The idea of participation also has a normative significance. It realizes a form of social conviviality and cooperation in which the person is respected and is enabled to experience every act of the collectivity as his own. This happens when the choices of the collectivity are directed toward a common good and are made through the responsible involvement of all citizens. This in its turn implies the acknowledgment of a common destiny and a common vocation and therefore of a particular cultural tie between those who must make decisions together. It also presupposes an anthropology in which man realizes himself through the other man and not by separating himself from him and assumes, therefore, that the community forms a constitutive dimension of personal self-realization.

At the heart of every human community lies the fact that man becomes aware of the value of his own person and engages himself in the task of realizing that value only through the recognition that another person gives such a value. If it is true that every man has the task of his own spiritual generation it is also true that man performs such a task only through the other, carrying in himself the person of the other and being carried by him. Running counter to this idea of participation are two views which, by limiting or excluding participation, deny it both at the theoretical and at the practical level. These are individualism and objective totalism.

Individualism contraposes the good of the individual to that of all other individuals. The other is regarded as limiting the activity and the rights of the subject. Existence with others is therefore a necessity to which one must adapt oneself by reducing its negative effects to a minimum. On this view, the person does not realize itself by acting with others. It is concerned more with separating and defending itself as much as possible from the community.

The opposite of individualism is totalism. Both share the same presupposition, which is that the good of the individual is extraneous to the common good. Totalism, however, wants to realize the common good against the various individual goods through the use of coercion. While individualism wants to protect the individual against the community, totalism wants to defend the common good against individuals. In both cases the person is understood as incapable of participation; one cannot, therefore, consider the possibility of the integration of the individual good into the common good. Above all, totalism ignores the personalistic value of the action, which presupposes its freedom. It is so concerned to realize a determinate set of objective values that it ignores the way in which they are realized.

Some commentators on Wojtyła identify individualism as he defines it with capitalism and totalism with totalitarian, especially socialist, systems.[53] Although there is partial truth in this identification, it would be a mistake to restrict the sphere of application of Wojtyła's notions to these examples. We are not dealing exclusively with social systems here but also and especially with human attitudes. Perhaps it is not wrong to see in Wojtyła's concept of objective totalism a polemic against a certain kind of essentialism and theological objectivism which for a long time censored the problem of freedom. On the other hand, many cultural positions are definitely individualistic while, at the same time, understanding themselves as anti-capitalistic. One can think of the emblematic motto of the Marxist existentialism of Jean-Paul Sartre, "Hell is other people."[54]

Against individualism and totalism, Wojtyła holds that individual and community mutually imply one another. Community is the place of acting with others and, in a certain way, the subject of the common action. But only in a certain way because, for Wojtyła, who follows St. Thomas in this, the true subject of action is always the person and the community is only a quasi-subject, a subject by analogy and in a derivative way. The kinds of community in which people participate are different. Some communities are essentially concerned with the being of man. Others are oriented toward action. In this context Wojtyła uses the distinction, traditional in German sociology and also used by Scheler, between society and community.[55] But neither society nor community — neither a community of being nor a community of action — is identified with participation. From this point of view what is decisive is neither the fact of objectively collaborating in a common action nor the importance of the common good in whose realization one takes part, but the way in which one participates in this realization.

The one adequate basis of every communal action and of every community is the common good. The common good of a community of acting

53. Cf. Williams, *The Mind of John Paul II*, p. 212. Equally off target is the criticism which Williams makes of Wojtyła a few pages later, that he considers all voluntary associations egotistical. Williams refers to the comments which Wojtyła has made in passing about the individualistic deviations of some voluntary associations. Despite these defects, Williams's book is a mine of valuable information and intelligent observations.

54. For the parallel between Sartre and Wojtyła see, for example, Marian Jaworski, "Sartre, l'uomo e Papa Wojtyła," in *CESO-Documentation* 143 (1979) (original text in *Weiz*, February/March 1979).

55. It seems to me that one need not give to this the decisive importance which Williams does: his argument for Wojtyła's dependence on Scheler on this point is invalid. Cf. *The Mind of John Paul II*, pp. 212ff.

persons can only be the realization of their persons through their actions, and this requires not only that the action be oriented to the good but also that it be an action proper to the person. For this reason there is no common good without participation, and this is the only personalistic way to perform a collective action. In this sense the common good founds every authentic human community. A properly human community exists inasmuch as it is unified by a common good, objectively true and subjectively lived as such by its members. The diverse communities are then identified by the diverse common goods to which they tend. Natural communities are particularly important: family, nation, religious community. For these are communities of being as well as communities of action. In these communities each member naturally counts on being able to participate by choosing together with others and counts on the fact that in their common choices the community takes account of the requirements of his personal realization.[56] In an authentic human community, according to Wojtyła, the one who participates is open to sacrificing his own particular good to the common good, not because he considers the common good superior to the particular one but because the self-realization of the value of one's own person, which is achieved through sacrifice, is greater and more worthy than what would be gained by achieving one's own particular interest against the common good. This by no means implies a "spiritual selfishness" according to which the end of the action would not be the good in itself but the spiritual advantage of the person. Rather, it simply recalls the principle through which the realization of the person coincides with the ordered realization of the values which enter into its sphere of perception and action.

There are in every human community habits of behavior toward the common good which define the human climate of that community. We will call them attitudes. Some of them are authentic and allow the realization of the person through participation. Others are inauthentic because they hinder or impede such a realization.

Those attitudes are authentic which respect the personalistic value of the action and therefore the dynamic subordination of the action to the truth. They are solidarity and opposition.[57] Inauthentic attitudes are conformism and disengagement. Conformism can be understood as a corrup-

56. One does not have the automatic right to participate in a voluntary community in the way a child does in a family or a citizen does in a nation.

57. It is therefore incomprehensible that Williams claims that Wojtyła has no understanding of the value of loyal opposition.

tion of solidarity, whereas disengagement can be understood as a corruption of opposition.

Solidarity is the openness to playing one's part within a community by aiming at the realization of the common good proper to that community. Human beings intentionally reach out toward the common end, and this allows them to realize their tasks in the best way. This also implies the awareness and the respect for the role of fathers and their specific responsibilities. The awareness of the common good, which must be realized through the contribution of all, makes the "person in solidarity" open to more than his own part, to go beyond his specific duty if this is necessary to achieve the end. By so doing the "person in solidarity" pursues his own self-realization in the service of the common end and in being a conscious part of the common action. This definition of solidarity takes us in the opposite direction from the bureaucratization of the world which preoccupied Max Weber; his descriptions of it are echoed by Bruno Rizzi, among others. For Weber, modern society attributes to each man a particular task which must then be consciously performed for itself. But modern society does not ask for any identification with any collective end, nor service which goes beyond the execution of a compartmentalized task.

The model of this way of understanding the world and life is given by the bureaucrat who accomplishes the job which is proper to him but who is not interested in the collective end to which work is directed and feels no responsibility for the final outcome of collective action. On the contrary, solidarity implies an advertent responsibility for the common end and also for the good or the evil which this end brings about in the world through its realization.

The other authentic attitude is that of opposition. The one who does not identify himself with the end of the collaborative effort, or with the form chosen for its realization, dissents, without giving up his own participation in the community. In natural community the ultimate end of the community is inherently positive (family, nation, Church). The dissent can be about the modality of its realization, that is, the various intermediate ends which should serve the self-realization of the community and of the person within it. Solidarity and opposition are not antagonistic to each other because if one cares about the ultimate end one can loyally dissent about the choice of means. If the possibility of opposition were taken away, then the transcendence of the person in action — that is to say, his particular and personal assumption of responsibility toward the collective end — could not manifest itself. In order for responsibility to emerge it is necessary that the person be given the possibility of consenting or dissenting. Dialogue leads the opposition back into solidarity, and allows it to evaluate its motives and to see in it a creative collaboration with the legitimate definition of the ends and of the means of social life.

Of the nonauthentic attitudes, the most serious is conformism. It is a specific form of submission to the existing situation with which one cannot consent according to one's own conscience, but which one does not have the courage to oppose. The kernel of conformism is the renunciation of participation which covers itself up with a passive acceptance of what happens in one's own community. The person renounces being the subject of social action, to become only the object; that is, he gives up having a stake in social relationships and seeking self-realization in them. The person retreats from the community into himself while submitting himself in a servile way to all external relationships. This generates social uniformity but not true unity. Whereas the social body is ostensibly unanimous, no one in reality is truly interested in the common good and the opposition is not manifested only because there is no openness to risk particular interests for the true common good.[58]

The other nonauthentic attitude is disengagement. In it the individual is disinterested in the end of the community. Disengagement is actually a constitutive element of conformism, but while in conformism the individual pretends to accept the dominant formulation of social ends, in disengagement he openly proclaims himself an outsider.

Disengagement can have a certain personalistic value when it constitutes a statement against a situation of social oppression which makes participation completely impossible. Nevertheless it can never be considered an authentic attitude. It is like conformism, with which it can merge into "conformist disengagement," in which one conforms oneself to a dominant mentality which encourages disinterest, mistrust, and sterile criticism while avoiding the responsibility of elaborating alternatives.

Participation can be considered in relation to two complementary systems of reference, one of which hinges on the concepts of membership in a community and the other on that of the neighbor. The concept of membership of a community sets the person in relationship with the diverse communities to which he belongs. The concept of neighbor is wider and more general; it puts the person in the framework of that fundamental and

---

58. This criticism of conformism is consonant with that of the dissidents of Eastern Europe. See, for example, Vaclav Havel's "The Power of the Powerless," in *Living in Truth.*

primary community which is humanity itself. For this reason, among the true systems of reference the primary one is that which turns on the notion of the neighbor. The deepest root of participation is not the capacity to take part in this or that particular community but the capacity to share, as man, the humanity of other human beings.

"The capacity of sharing the very humanity of every man is the intimate kernel of each participation and the condition of the personalistic value of each acting and existing together with others."[59]

The system of reference which hinges on the notion of *the neighbor* is prior to, and sustains, the one which hinges on the notion of *membership of a community*. All particular communities of existence and action arise on the basis of the common humanity, and from this origin the more or less binding duties which correspond to this also derive. These communities make some men stand out as neighbors, and because of this, far from being meaningless for the wider human community, they are a pedagogical and organic introduction to it. There is a kind of transcendence of being a neighbor in relationship to being a member of a community, and we find indeed the recognition of the human at the bottom of every truly authentic community.

This is what the Christian commandment of love emphasizes. Wojtyła analyzes it not so much in terms of its ethical value as in terms of its anthropological meaning. It directly opposes the contemporary experience of alienation.[60] This arises from the fact that the rules of human participation in one or more particular community (for instance, community of work) are planned without bearing in mind the transcendence of the human as such in relationship to the rules of a determinate sphere of activity. In the performance of his own particular role, man empties himself of his own humanity and alienates himself from it. This interpretation is

---

59. *Osoba i Czyn*, p. 322. The sense of this paragraph is found in *The Acting Person*, p. 271.

60. Wojtyła, "Participation or Alienation," in *Analecta Husserliana*, vol. 6, "The Self and the Other" (Dordrecht: Reidel, 1977). Wojtyła goes more deeply into the theme of participation in his essay "Osoba: Podmiot I wspolnota," in *Roczniki Filozoficzne* 24 (1976), pp. 5-39. This is translated into German with the title "Person: Subjekt und Gemeinschaft" in a collection called *Der Streit um den Menschen. Personaler Anspruch des Sittlichen* (Kevelaer, 1979), pp. 11-68. The same book contains two other essays of great interest for the understanding of the cultural atmosphere in which Wojtyła's thought came to fruition. These are Andrej Stroszek's "Der Ort der Person in der Struktur des Sittlichen" (ibid., pp. 71-110), and Tadeusz Styczen's "Ueber die Frage einer unabhängigen Ethik" (ibid., pp. 111-75).

opposed to those which derive alienation simply from the means of production and the exchange of commodities. Means of production, technique, and forms of cooperation in work are ultimately human products. The alienation of man in relationship to the other man is therefore the root of the conditioning which in its turn confirms and reinforces it. By estranging oneself from one's neighbor, man estranges himself from the terrain of his participation with the other — that humanity which is common to him and to his neighbor.

The answer to alienation must be sought first of all at the level of culture by giving priority to the reference to common humanity over the reference to all diverse communities which under different headings claim human loyalty for themselves (family, class, nation, state). In this way the conflicts and the contradictions which arise among different communities can be settled in a human way, understood in the horizon of a wider unity. The foundation of participation in action is the point of arrival of *The Acting Person*. The new anthropology leads through philosophy of praxis and culminates in a new foundation of political duty and social community. Wojtyła will return to these themes many more times, both in different academic articles and perhaps especially in his poetic works, which show how the person becomes what he is in relationship with an other. Here the fundamental theme which *The Acting Person* attempts to work out theoretically returns: how we can consider the role of collective praxis and the constitutive, mutual belonging of man in the process of self-realization without dissolving the individual in the mass, in the social class, or even in the nation, pictured not as a community of persons but as hypostatized subjects in history? The transcendence of the person in relationship to consciousness of action and the concept of participation allows one to claim the freedom of the individual at the heart of the problem of praxis, by involving *the human modality of its development*.

6. Wojtyła and the Council

As we have already had occasion to note, the Second Vatican Council is at the center of Wojtyła's entire philosophical work. Consecrated bishop on July 4, 1958, he participated in the Council as capitular administrator of the diocese of Cracow, of which he would later become archbishop. *The Acting Person,* the book which crowns and concludes Wojtyła's philosophical activity, was probably conceived in its essential lines during the Council, as an attempt to give a philosophical account of the conception of man presupposed in the conciliar documents.

It will help us to understand this connection if we look closely both at Wojtyła's participation in the Council and at the particular interpretation which he gave to it. Before going into detail about these two elements, it seems opportune to sketch what Wojtyła sees as the nucleus of the conciliar event, thereby creating a hypothesis about the connection between that extraordinary spiritual experience and the fundamental thesis of *The Acting Person.*[1]

1. This task is facilitated by the fact that Wojtyła in many ways kept the faithful of the diocese of Cracow and all the Polish faithful updated about the development of the works of the Council, allowing them to experience the main conciliar events together with him from the inside. His speeches on the Vatican radio, his articles for *Tygodnik Powszechny,* and his other articles in the Polish Catholic press at the time of the Council are evidence of this. Cf. "Przemówienie radiowe" (discourse given on Vatican Radio on 25 November 1963), in *Tygodnik Powszechny* 17 (1964); "List z Soboru do duchowieństwa I wiernych," in *Tygodnik Powszechny* 18 (1964); "O Soborze," in *Tyogodnik Powszechny* 18 (1964); "Problematyka drugiej Sesij II Soboru Watykańskiego. Z kazańks.

The Philosophical Significance of the Council

The heart of the conciliar event is the *acknowledgment of freedom of conscience* as a natural and inalienable right of the human person. This acknowledgment is accompanied by an open confession of the fact that in the past, although the Church has always maintained that no one can be forced to believe, Churchmen often did not live up to this theory and tried, directly or indirectly, to obtain assent to the faith through coercion. This affirmation, contained in the most explicit and complete way in the "Declaration on Religious Liberty," also represents the fundamental cornerstone of the "Pastoral Constitution on the Church in the Modern World" and has an important influence on the "Dogmatic Constitution on the Church" and on all the other conciliar documents.

The "Declaration on Religious Liberty"[2] poses a problem to Catholic philosophy and theology which appears difficult to solve, whether one remains within traditional categories or chooses to abandon them in favor of thinking more typical of the modern philosophy of consciousness. Faith provides us with the certainty that Jesus Christ, dead and risen again for human salvation, is truly the Lord of the universe and of history. There is no higher moral duty than to follow Him by adhering to the Church which He has founded. Moreover, faith and reason together convince the Christian of the existence of an objectively true moral order, to which one must conform his actions in order for them to be good. The violation of this order constitutes an objective evil. Moreover, anyone who consents to the accomplishment of evil, when he could possibly prevent it, himself becomes an accomplice. It seems therefore that a Christian should use all the instruments at his disposal to prevent violation of the moral order. If, then, a Christian has authority and power over other men in any respect, it seems that he is obliged in conscience to use his authority to prevent them from doing evil.

---

metropolity po powrocie z obrad Soboru," *Notificationes e Curia Cracoviensi* 7 (1964), pp. 145ff.; "Kościoł w świecie współczesnym," in *Tyognik Powszechny* 18 (1964); "Lud Boży," in *Przewodnik Katolicki* 54 (1964), p. 65; "Idea Ludu Bożego i świetści Kośioła a posłannictwo świeckich," in *Ateneum Kapłanskie* (1965), vol. 68, pp. 307ff.; "Milenum a Sobór. List do Redakcij," in *Tygodnik Powszechny* 19; "Sobór od wewnatrz. List do Redackcij," *Tygodnik Powszechny* 19; "Logika wewnetrza Vaticanum II. Z problematyki homiletycznej," in *Biblioteka Kaznodziejska*, vol. 77 (1966), pp. 257ff.

2. Cf. Wojtyła, "Przemówienie radiowe . . . Naświetlenie deklaracij o wolności religijnej" (discourse given on Vatican Radio on 20 October 1965), in *Notificationes e Curia Cracoviensi* 11 (1965), pp. 269ff.

This view, which approximates that which was for a long time considered traditional, does not exactly give a negative answer to the claim of freedom of conscience. Rather, it fails to understand properly the meaning of this question. Indeed, is not conscience obliged to obey the truth? How, therefore, is it possible to maintain that it must be free to follow error? Does the claim of freedom of conscience not imply at least an agnostic position with respect to truth? Did not the large majority of those who upheld tolerance and freedom of conscience from a secular point of view do so because they held that in spiritual matters men could not have any certain knowledge of truth, and for this reason every different opinion deserved equal respect? But can an authentic believer allow his faith to be treated as a mere opinion?

As is evident, the arguments from a traditional point of view against the acknowledgment of freedom of conscience as a natural right are neither few nor of small importance. From this starting point, it is possible to go only as far as the acknowledgment that Catholics can renounce imposing their faith and their conception of moral order to avoid a greater evil, such as the breakdown of civil peace, the outbreak of civil war, spilling of innocent blood, etc. In principle, therefore, the acknowledgment of freedom of conscience by the state seems to be an evil. In fact, historically, this can sometimes or even often be the lesser evil. In any case, the possibility of considering freedom of conscience a natural right and a good to be promoted and encouraged by the Church is out of the question.

The position that we have illustrated above is supported by the couplet truth/error and consequently opposes the right of truth to the illegitimacy of error.

The opposite position has its starting point instead in the conviction, also incontrovertible, that man can be obliged in conscience only by what conscience itself acknowledges as true and just, and every attempt to impose a position by force is destined to fail and to produce only hypocrisy and disaffection instead of an honest search for truth. Conscience is the most intimate sanctuary of the human person. The relationship with the Absolute is decided within it. It is not possible to violate this sanctuary without damaging in a radical and profound way the dignity of the person. The fundamental concepts on which the argumentation of this second position is based are those of *conscience* and *person*.

At this point, it seems that there is an irremediable disagreement between the right of truth to be always and in every way acknowledged and the right of the person to make his choice freely, without being subjected to an external imposition from other men or from a public authority. This is the same as the disagreement between individualism and objective totalism which Wojtyła discussed in *The Acting Person*. One viewpoint recognizes only the right of the person and not of the community (nor that of the truth); the other sacrifices the right of conscience to an objective common good.

Current public opinion is convinced that the world ought to choose between the renunciation of the idea of truth (accompanied by a complete domination of subjective opinion) and the imposition of objective truth (or an opinion considered to be objective truth) by authoritarian means. From a political point of view, Western political systems are usually associated with the renunciation of the idea of truth, considered altogether perhaps ungenerously as democracies without values, while the totalitarian regimes are usually associated with the imposition of truth by force, and further differentiated according to the kind of truth they want to impose.

It is evident that for the Christian conscience, as well as for a fully human point of view, it is impossible either to choose for truth against conscience or to choose for conscience against truth. This consideration brings us to an impasse from which we can escape only if we can show that the entire problematic has been grounded in an erroneous way, and that the unacceptable necessity of sacrificing either conscience or truth depends on this error. It is evident at this point that the question of freedom of conscience is not at all a limited or special question, even one endowed with a very high importance. What is at stake here is the whole relationship between Christianity and modernity and between the philosophy of being and the philosophy of consciousness.

The Acting Person reformulates the problem of the relation between conscience and truth as Vatican II requires. In his work, Wojtyła shows how conscience is subordinated to the will, which is in turn oriented — through self-knowledge — to the truth. This entire process is in turn reflected in consciousness, which entails that the search for and the possession of truth are not simply part of an intellectual enterprise, but an adventure which man lives with his whole being. Consequently, the truth enters the very interiority of the process through which the person determines himself and achieves a human act, that is, an act which engages the person as such. In this way, the duty of the person to seek the truth and to conform himself to the known truth, by subordinating his own passions to it, arises from his own interiority. By introducing the structure of self-knowledge into the formation of the person — showing the essentially reflexive function of consciousness — Wojtyła breaks the vicious circle of the philosophies of consciousness which recognize no truth outside of consciousness and, consequently, no duty for consciousness to conform itself to an objective truth outside of it.

On the other hand, it is precisely in order to direct himself toward truth in the way which is proper to him that the person needs to be free, unbound by any external pressure. Indeed, a true human act is constituted neither by conformity to external violence nor by obedience to individual passions which are not oriented to the truth and not judged by self-knowledge. One might ask whether this analysis does not run the risk of disengaging persons from the truth. In other words, is there not a risk of giving primacy to a subjective authenticity which belongs to the emotional component? Is there not the danger that the person will forego mastering his own immediate impressions and fail to direct himself toward the objective truth?

Wojtyła's answer to these questions would be decisively negative. The freedom of man is never, as we have already seen, a pure *arbitrium indifferentiae,* liberty of indifference, as in certain philosophical traditions. Freedom is always attracted by value, not only in the emotional sphere, but already in some way in the natural, instinctual sphere. Consequently, it is in the nature of man both to direct himself towards the good and to desire that the good toward which he directs himself be an objectively true good. The person is obliged, in the face of his own conscience, to seek the good and to adhere to the known good. The recognition of the liberty of conscience as a fundamental human right and indeed as the most fundamental right of all, far from denying this obligation, secures the conditions for its satisfaction. From the traditionalist point of view, however, another objection would still be possible. By tolerating error of conscience, in every case, we allow an evil and we tolerate a violation of the natural order and the moral order. A perfection which belongs in some way to the world by right is subtracted from it. Wojtyła's observations on the difference between the personalist value and the moral value of action, examined in the preceding chapter, here come to our aid. The fact that the person realizes himself through a free act is more important than the content of the act itself. That a man acts as a man, guided by his intelligence and following the impulse of his will, is more important and of greater value than the objective modification itself which his act introduces into the world. By acting freely, in fact, man inserts himself into the personalist order, which is his proper order. The personalist value of the action precedes the moral value in the sense that only an action of the person can have moral value. Without this presupposition, there are no human actions but only acts of man, deprived of any ethical value. By imposing the observance of the order of nature with force, one excludes the principle of the personalist order and therefore deprives reality of a much higher value than the value which is impaired by the fact that man sometimes makes mistakes in the use of his freedom. The traditionalist doctrine uses an equivocal concept of nature and by this equivocation runs the risk of losing sight of the difference between the personalist order (grounded on the particular spiritual nature of man and therefore on freedom) and the order characteristic of the rest of nature (in which nature in the ontological sense coincides with nature in the phenomenal/naturalistic sense or at least differs from it in a less drastic way than in the case of the person).[3]

Obviously, the personalist order does not lack its own precise rule, and this, among other things, binds man, who is also a physical being belonging to nature, to conform himself to nature's laws and ends in the use of his instinctual and emotional energies. So, for instance, in the exercise of sexuality, man must take into account the natural end of sex, which is procreation. However, that can happen only through a response conscious of the freedom of the person enlightened by reason.[4]

The integration of the philosophy of being and the philosophy of consciousness into a complete anthropology of the person seems to be, in the perspective which we have briefly delineated, the only way to recognize in depth the novelty of the conciliar teaching and at the same time its solid anchorhold in the tradition (which is not the same as traditionalism). Such a rethinking is necessary if one is to avoid the two opposite risks of minimizing the conciliar novelty and of yielding unconditionally to the philosophy of consciousness which impairs the fundamental objectivity and certainty of truth. It is likely that a great number of postconciliar errors can be explained by the fact that, apart from certain luminous examples, this new philosophical reflection was lacking here in the West.

The philosophical originality of the Council was not understood, there-

---

3. This is also Wojtyła's position: "Natura ludzka jako podstawa formacij etycznej," in *Znak* 11 (1959), pp. 693ff. This is now published in *I Fondamenti dell'ordine etico*, in a chapter entitled "La natura umana come fondamento della formazione etica," pp. 129ff.

4. Cf. Wojtyła, "Instynkt, miłość, małżeństwa," in *Tygodnik Powszechny* 8 (1952), and Miłość, a odpowiedzialność," in *Ateneum Kapłańskie* 51 (1959), pp. 163ff.; and, of course, *Love and Responsibility*.

fore, and the postconciliar period was transformed into a fight between integrists and modernists, regulated by a wavering center stretched out in continuous and always vain attempts at compromise. The fact that the Council could not be understood according to the dominant categories in the preceding phases of the history of the Church induced many hastily to discard Thomism and to imagine that Christianity could easily be brought into agreement with any philosophy. Some thought it permissible to elaborate a Christian theology on the basis of any philosophy of modernity, chosen not on the ground of its objective truth but rather on the basis of its presumed "capacity for speaking to the modern world," that is, its more or less ephemeral popularity.

As we have seen, Wojtyła has chosen the opposite path. The Council for him necessitates a patient development of hidden possibilities contained in the *philosophia perennis,* but not sufficiently developed in traditional thought. Such a development is facilitated and nourished by an encounter with modern thought and, in this case in particular, by the dialogue with Scheler and the adoption of the phenomenological method, which is used, however, in a special way, so as to form a new phenomenological philosophy.

The adoption of certain elements of the philosophy of consciousness is always critical; the fundamental conception remains solidly realistic, and the philosophy of consciousness is recognized through an autonomous and deepened treatment of the theme of consciousness within the philosophy of the act of being. In order to use aspects and concepts of Scheler's thought in this perspective, it was necessary for Wojtyła first to deconstruct his thought, to verify the congruity between each of its elements and the Christian view of man, to reformulate and perfect the phenomenological philosophy from the rational point of view so as to render it usable for the end to which we aim. We are not speaking about a "Christian phenomenology," a sweetened version of phenomenology reconciled with Christianity. Wojtyła has engaged in a reform of phenomenology in order to render it closer to its original intention of "going to the things themselves" according to rigorous rules of philosophical thought; it is his conviction that the philosophy most capable of rationally explaining the Christian conception of man must also be the philosophy most rigorously founded from the point of view of reason.

Wojtyła's procedure does not involve a form of deconstruction which uses certain aspects of the thought with which it claims to converse in an arbitrary way, outside of the conceptual connection which constitutes them, reduced to the role of code words. Before proceeding with his integration of Scheler and St. Thomas, Wojtyła endeavors to show that what in Scheler contradicts the Christian view of man also contradicts sound reason and the truth as it is accessible to the phenomenological method. In this way his reformulation of phenomenology presents itself as the only adequate interpretation of the phenomenological method according to its own rational principles and should be discussed, approved, or rejected as such. To interpret the Council is par excellence to do the work of Christian philosophy. But that does not imply an effort only of *aggiornamento* of Christian culture but much more progress in the general self-understanding of man, a step forward in the philosophical consciousness of all humanity.[5] Only in this way is it possible to understand the conciliar overcoming of the opposition between modernity and Christianity. It is not a question of a political compromise which one or the other of the two factions can reconsider in order to reestablish an equilibrium more favorable to itself. It is a matter of a new synthesis in which modern elements and traditional elements are harmoniously fused and the tradition shows itself capable of developing out of itself those aspects which it was criticized for neglecting. The philosophy of consciousness ceases to be thought of as another philosophy which is situated beyond the philosophy of being, and becomes one of the articulations of a more complete and wiser philosophy of being, which is purified of the deviations which had made it a mere philosophy of entity. At the same time, the contrast between modernity and Christianity disappears.

The philosophical idea of modernity presupposed the incapacity of the philosophy of being and of Christianity to do justice to consciousness and to freedom. It is because of a new and irreducible point of departure in the understanding of man that the new age rises up against the old, and the quantitative differences between the two epochs assume a qualitative meaning. But if this opposition is superseded and rigorously shown never to have existed in reality, then from the philosophical point of view the very motivations of the idea of modernity disappear. The belief in an epochal rupture of history coinciding with the modern epoch loses its hold, the notion of "modern man" endowed with radically different characteristics compared to men of other historical epochs proves illusory, and the concept of a modern philosophy qualitatively different from classical philosophy falls, too. On the contrary, the idea of the unity and universality of philosophy and of the history of man who in every epoch is confronted, even if in different forms, with the same fundamental questions, is reconstructed.

---

5. Cf. Wojtyła, "Człowiek est osoba," in *Tygodnik Powszechny* 18 (1964). It is this argument which more directly reflects the fundamental message of the Council.

In the years of the Council, the conviction predominated that the philosophy of the future would be a philosophy of man, capable of starting from existence and formulating the human problem in a way open to religious transcendence.[6] This was especially evident among the theologians whose works had prepared for the Council. It was commonly thought that in the ongoing challenge between atheistic existentialism and religious existentialism the latter would get the better of the former. Beyond the different social and political factors, the postconciliar crisis must be imputed, from the cultural point of view, to the collapse of religious existentialism in the face of atheistic existentialism and the subsequent development of atheistic existentialism into Marxism. Because of this evolution, most of the "progressives" in the sixties were forced to focus on the dialogue with Marxism in order to engage with the contemporary world, often making enormous concessions. Those who reacted to this perspective did so because in one way or another they did not accept the end of the philosophy of existence and therefore the possibility that the crisis of modernity could lead into Christianity. In any case, the acceptance of the confluence of a philosophy of existence with Marxism and the renunciation of a possible Pascalian outcome of the philosophy of existence renders unintelligible the spiritual climate in which the Council developed; it closes, moreover, the means of development of Christian philosophy which the Council tried to open.[7]

6. Cf. Wojtyła, "Sobór a praca teologów" (discourse given on Vatican Radio, 12 February 1965), in *Tygodnik Powszechny* 19 (1965).

7. On the problem of modernity as a philosophical category, H. Gouhier, "Les Philosophes du XVII Siècle devant l'histoire de la philosophie," in *XVII Siècle* 54-55 (1962); Augusto Del Noce, *Il Problema del l'ateismo e la storia della filosofia come problema* (Bologna: Il Mulino, 1964), and *Riforma Cattolica e Filosofia moderna*, vol. 1, *Cartesio*. The fundamental theses of the two major books for the problem we are interested in are anticipated in an essay written in 1954, "Problemi del periodizzamento storico: l'inizio della filosofia moderna," in "La filosofia della storia della filosofia," in *Archivio di Filosofia* (1954), pp. 187-210. See also Marco M. Olivetti, *Riforma Cattolica e Filosofia Moderna nel pensiero di A. Del Noce* (Rome: Isituto di Studi Filosofici, 1968). The rethinking of the category of modernity done by Del Noce has more than some affinities from the point of view of the history of philosophy with the rethinking of the philosophy of consciousness done by Wojtyła in anthropology. The parallelism merits study. Although the following statement could seem daring in the light of the polemics of the 70s, it seems to me that Del Noce had made, with his book on atheism, the most complete effort to formulate a history of culture which can overcome the opposition between modernity and Christianity through the rethinking of the idea of modernity in accordance with the spirit of the Council.

By contrast, Wojtyła himself remains entirely within the atmosphere of the Council, although conscious of the difficulties and of the post-conciliar crisis. *The Acting Person* reforms the philosophy of existence, tying it tightly to the philosophy of being, in a certain sense joining together St. Thomas and Pascal, thereby remedying the philosophical weakness of the philosophy of existence which prevented it, both in its atheistic and in its religious version, from being any thing more than a dramatic sign of the crisis, the contradiction, and the impotence of man in our time.[8] It is precisely the insufficiency of the philosophy of existence which forces Sartre to take shelter in Marxism. But in this way the philosophy of existence is forced to deny all the main motives which inspired it and to commit suicide. Wojtyła, in a manner somewhat parallel to Sartre, proposes the encounter between the philosophy of existence and Thomism on the basis of a reform of Thomism which makes it able to welcome the perspectives of the philosophy of existence without denying itself. As everyone knows, the Sartrian reform of Marxism failed because Sartre tried to harmonize ideal perspectives which are intrinsically incompatible.

What will be the outcome of Wojtyła's effort? It is too soon to say. It can be observed that the philosophy of existence and the philosophy of being are not in principle incompatible. The whole internal development of Thomism (it is enough to mention Gilson, Fabro, De Finance, etc.) is oriented toward the theme of existence. In addition, Wojtyła starts from Thomism and tries to develop in it the virtualities which correspond to the requirements emphasized by the philosophy of existence. It is not a question, therefore, of grafting together heterogeneous positions but of a development which entirely saves classical ontology and develops on its basis a phenomenological analysis of the being of man in the world which, far from contradicting it, integrates it and confers on it an existential meaningfulness. However, all of this occurs without looking for fictitious accommodations but by developing, rather, the phenomenological method with complete rectitude and making such improvements as must be made in accordance with its own principles.

In any case, the development of this philosophy is tied to the historical event from which it draws its origin. The task of the Council, according to Wojtyła, is to make faith an experience of life, to bring about its subjective appropriation, thereby creating a Christian mentality and a Christianity

8. Cf. A. Del Noce, "La filosofia dell'esistenza," in *Il redentore dell'uomo* (Rome, 1979).

which is not abstractly apprehended but existentially lived. The philosophy of *The Acting Person* consciously seeks to assist the development of this task and to provide its theoretical justification.

Wojtyła's Participation in the Council

In a poem probably written during the first session of the Council or immediately afterward Wojtyła has left us a document of his existential experience of living the Council:

> Our feet meet the earth in this place;
> There are many walls, many colonnades. . . .
> However we do not lose ourselves. . . .
> Peter, you are the pavement, and the others
> Can walk upon you (without knowing
> Where they are going). You guide their steps. . . .
> The rock is the pavement of the gigantic temple
> The cross a pasture.[9]

It seems that for Wojtyła, the unity of the Church does not arise from the consolidation of human energies and tensions by a unique authority which is situated above them and acts as their guide. Rather, the unity arises from the fact that "Peter" is the terrain upon which alone men and nations can freely move toward the original end which is proper to each.

Of the very intense activity of Wojtyła at the Council the most interesting part is unfortunately hidden to us — his participation in the collegial discussions of the Polish episcopate on the different documents, in which the young capitular administrator of Cracow had a very important role. We must content ourselves with reconstructing his thought through his interventions in the public discussion. The first of these took place in the discussion of the schema on the Church, October 21, 1963. Wojtyła criticized the structure of the schema which then was proposed for the approbation of the Conciliar Fathers, and he asked that the document deal first with the People of God and its unity and then with the ministerial priesthood and the lay status. This suggestion was then incorporated in the definitive version of "Lumen Gentium," which deals first with the "Mystery

---

9. Andrej Jawien (the pseudonym which Karol Wojtyła used as a poet), "Kościoł (fragm.). Pasterze i żódła. Narodziny wyznawców," in *Znak* 15, pp. 1376-82.

of the Church" and then, in the second chapter, with "The People of God"; the third chapter is then devoted to consideration of the fact that "The Church is Hierarchical." In his observations, Wojtyła underlines the unity which must subsist between the ministerial priesthood and laypeople worldwide, thereby realizing both the transcendence and the immanence of the entire People of God in history.

This transcendence of the People of God should presuppose the transcendence of the Church itself in relation to any society of the natural order and in relation to the secular city. In this way the People of God in the Church forms an image of the very mystery of the Incarnation, because at the same time it remains bound to the humanity in any society and human community and yet transcends humanity. These points have, it seems to me, a great importance, though they are not sufficiently developed in the chapter on the People of God.[10]

It is perhaps not daring to sketch a parallel between the transcendence of the person in relation to action and that of the People of God in relation to humanity. In both cases we deal with an orientation toward truth which transcends the dynamisms proper to sensible and visible existence and nevertheless can be realized only through them, by dominating them in a particular way. The dialogue between God and man is the ontological kernel of human history, which is always immanent in each of its visible manifestations but never lets itself be perceived adequately except in that radical obedience of Christ's humanity to the Father which is prolonged sacramentally in the life of the Church. In this perspective, to follow the language which we have come to know (but which Wojtyła at the time of this intervention had not yet fully elaborated), the task of the ministerial priesthood is to realize the transcendence of the human in relation both to itself and to history while the task of the layman is to realize the integration of history on the basis of faith.

Thus we understand how Wojtyła was able to ask for both a clearer emphasis on the peculiarity of the ministerial priesthood and a greater esteem of the value of the laity, as well as a stronger focus on the unity of the People of God within which all the other differences must be considered. Against the first schema on the Church Wojtyła argues that the laypeople do not have merely a "passive possession of the faith." On the contrary, the specificity of their charism, destined to lead every human action to its own

10. *Acta Synodalia Sacrosancti Concilii Oecumenici* 2 (Vatican City, 1970-1978), p. 155.

truth which is Christ, implies an active and apostolic faith. Therefore to the schema ". . . it is necessary to add that the apostolate is something which springs immediately and subjectively from the faith and the love in the soul of the believer in Christ. In the notion of apostolate, even when it is used for the laity, is included the Christian's consciousness of the personal vocation, which surely differs from the mere passive possession of the faith. For this reason, in the apostolate of the laity there is a certain actualization of the faith united with the responsibility for the supernatural good divinely conferred in the Church to any human person."[11]

These affirmations seem to indicate a will to go beyond the usual "theology of the laity" toward a more comprehensive "theology of the People of God" in which the differences are articulated starting from the unity of the task of Christians in the world. To understand their authentic meaning we need to recall the context in which they were pronounced. The predominant theological doctrine of the time did not attribute to the laity a native capacity for apostolic initiative and, therefore, denied the laity an active role in the presence, diffusion, and growth of the faith in the world. A relatively active role of the laity could be assumed only insofar as it was indirectly made part of the ordained ministry through a particular mandate, conferred on the associations of Catholic Action. With the Council, however, the apostolate becomes an original dimension of the presence of the Christian, and it recognizes the layperson's right and duty, by virtue of baptism and not by a particular mandate, to be an active agent of the apostolate. In relation to the apostolic initiative of the laity the task of the hierarchy is not the one of "sending" or fostering in an authoritarian way, but that of discerning and esteeming what is instilled spontaneously by the direct intervention of the Spirit. In taking this position, Wojtyła demonstrates his trust in the human person. In addition, however, his ideas reflect the pastoral perspective of a bishop who operates within a political context in which traditional associations of the apostolate cannot operate freely and where, therefore, much of the life of the Church must be given over to the responsible initiative of laymen who do not operate on the basis of some particular mandate but in virtue of their personal Christian conviction.

The view that Wojtyła has of the laity is also influenced by his view of the interiority of man. The traditional position, entirely objectivistic, has no context in which to situate the apostolic activity of the layperson because the problem of the interiorization and experience of faith escapes it. But

11. Ibid., p. 156.

the apostolic task proper to laymen develops precisely in this interior life. The activity of the layman's faith finds its being in experience, and his apostolate as a layman consists in the communication of this experience of humanity, the reality which witnesses its origin in the sacrament of the Church. Only in this way can preaching achieve existential evidence.

The same concepts then return in the intervention of Wojtyła on the scheme on the apostolate of the laity, "Apostolicam actuositatem," of 8 October 1964.[12] Wojtyła emphasizes that the manifestation of one's own faith, its communication, and realization of the works which make it concrete in the social life is a true and proper natural right of the person. He also forcefully affirms the duty of bishops to guard against the misuse of this freedom by individuals and groups who, under the banner of an apostolic goal, would serve instead other purposes with a political character and tend to divide the Church. Evidently the Polish bishop has in mind here the organizations of priests for peace supported and protected by the Communist regimes in order to fracture the unity of the episcopate and the Christian people.

Another fundamental theme on which Wojtyła intervenes is, naturally, that of religious freedom. In his intervention of September 15, Wojtyła holds that:

> it is necessary that the nexus between freedom and truth be further underlined in the document. On one side religious freedom is a function of the truth and on the other side it cannot reach its own end without the help of the truth. From it these words of our Lord come, which have such an expressive sound for each man: "Truth will make you free" (John 8: 32). There is no freedom without truth. . . . The relationship between freedom and truth has its utmost importance in ecumenical activity. In fact the end of this activity is nothing else than the liberation of Christianity as a whole from schisms; an ideal that certainly cannot be fully realized if the union is not achieved and perfected in truth. Therefore it is not sufficient that the principle of religious freedom toward the Separated Brethren seem only like a principle of toleration. Toleration in fact does not have so much a positive but rather a negative sense. . . . It is necessary that at the same time the progress of the perception of the truth be considered, because finally nothing but the truth will set us free from different types of separation. [13]

12. *Acta Synodalia* 3/4, pp. 69ff.
13. *Acta Synodalia* 3/2, p. 531.

The discourse on the freedom of conscience is here strictly bound to the one on ecumenicism, because at that time the distinction between the project of the declaration on religious freedom and the decree on ecumenism had not been reached. The principle affirmed, however, has universal value. Toleration has a negative value: error is considered and is permitted in order to avoid a greater evil. Or, worse, different errors are tolerated for lack of confidence in the possibility of achieving the truth. It is necessary instead to give attention to the human effort to reach the truth and to the different attempts which people make to achieve it, and to respect this effort in the dynamism which is proper to it. In the acknowledgment of religious freedom the right of error is not sanctioned but rather that of truth to be sought and achieved. The strict connection with Wojtyła's anthropological view is also evident here: the truth is an objective fact but at the same time a subjective experience, a true perfection of man through his free adherence to objective truth. From the objective point of view, Christian truth is protected whole and uncorrupted in the deposit of faith entrusted to the Catholic Church. From the existential point of view, it is necessary, however, that it become experience. In this respect the Catholic will have to learn much from the Separated Brethren as well as from all men who manifest many truths with an existential weight much greater than Catholics have been able to realize because of their personal and cultural limitations. This recognition permits a dialogue which is respectful and attentive to the truth of the other but that does not imply anything like systematic doubt about one's own faith.

Finally, Wojtyła reaffirms the fact that religious freedom can neither be requested nor conceived as a particular right outside of a complete conception of the human person:

This principle constitutes a fundamental right of the religious man in society which should be observed by everyone with the utmost rigour and especially by those who govern the states. It is necessary . . . to consider the following points: (1.) that in the contemporary world different states exist and that their laws are not in agreement with the divine law, revealed and natural. . . . (2.) that the atheists want to see in every religion nothing else but an alienation of the human spirit from which they desire to set man free with all the means which are available to the State. Devoted to materialism, they teach that this liberation should be brought by scientific progress and above all technical and economical progress. Thus in the particular of religious freedom we should with great decisiveness represent the human person as something that simply cannot be considered as a means in the economy and in society — as if that were his own end. It is necessary that the human person appear in the real sublimity of his rational nature and religion as the height of this nature. Religion in fact consists in the free adhesion of the human mind to God, which is from any point of view personal and conscious: it arises from the desire of truth. . . . Religion by its very nature transcends all which is secular.[14]

The principle of freedom of conscience is the foundation of the principle of the transcendence of the person with respect to the simple world of praxis; indeed, transcendence is incomprehensible except in relation to such liberty. This citation also makes precise Wojtyła's criticism of objectivistic totalism. It does not at first glance coincide with the modern criticism of totalitarianism. We have also seen how authoritarian views of the transcendent kind can commit the sin of objectivistic totalism when they are unable to recognize the value of the person in the action and therefore incapable of recognizing the conditions for the free realization of the person in the search for truth. Undoubtedly, however, the recognition of the objective value of the person marks, in every conception of a transcendent kind, an insuperable limit for objective totalism. It comes to its fulfillment in the totalitarian systems which are not only unable to recognize freedom existentially, but unable to conceive its essence because they deny the possibility that man can rise above the sphere of mere objects. The claim of the freedom of conscience, therefore, has a very particular implication with respect to positive atheism and in particular with respect to the forms of atheism which lay at the foundation of totalitarian regimes. Here it coincides with the affirmation of the transcendent dignity of man with respect to any socio-economic configuration and is in profound agreement with the struggle of every man to affirm himself as someone and not simply as something. By contrast, modern totalitarianism embraces the anti-religious interpretation of the principle of toleration. If, in fact, all opinions can be equally tolerated since none of them is true and if man is not capable of attaining the truth, what we are left with is the will to power alone. In the affirmation of his own power, man will not be bound to any respect due to the other in the name of his capacity for truth.[15] Later on, intervening on the same topic on 22 September 1965, Wojtyła develops and enlarges his thought:

14. Ibid., p. 532. On the same theme see also the message read on Vatican Radio by Wojtyła on 19 October 1964.
15. Cf. on this the thesis of J. Tesar, *Il totalitarismo di massa,* in CSEO, n. 151.

It is not sufficient, on this point, to say "I am free." It is necessary to say rather "I am responsible." This is the doctrine which is based on the living tradition of the Church of the martyrs and confessors. Responsibility is the necessary culmination and fulfillment of freedom. This should be underlined in such a way that our declaration be seen as intimately personalistic in the Christian sense but not as indebted to liberalism and indifferentism. Our public powers should respect with great rigor and great sensitivity religious freedom both in its collective and in its personal dimension. . . .[16]

Wojtyła asks, further, that freedom of conscience be understood not simply as freedom of cult or thought but as freedom of acting according to the known truth, yet within the limits set by a just safeguard of the common good. The idea of responsibility remains, nevertheless, the leading idea in his way of understanding religious freedom. Man is free to exercise his own responsible discernment; his freedom is not, therefore, a freedom of opinion but a freedom in the search for truth. Through the concept of responsibility, freedom and truth are tightly bound together. Freedom is the condition for the exercise of the responsibility of man toward the truth.

The interventions of Wojtyła on "schema 13," which would then become *The Pastoral Constitution on the Church in the Modern World (Gaudium et Spes),* are inspired by the same principles. His first intervention on the topic was on 21 October 1964, and on that occasion Wojtyła spoke in the name of the entire Polish episcopate. His intervention was highly critical of the proposal worked out by the experts. One of his remarks is characteristic of the way he took aim at the tone and style of the document:

In schema 13 we should speak in such a way that the world sees that we are not so much teaching the world in an authoritarian way, but rather we are seeking the just and true solution of the difficult problems of human life together with the world itself. The fact that the truth is already known to us is not in question, but it is a question of the way in which the world will find it for itself and will appropriate it. Whoever is an expert professor of his discipline knows that one can teach also with the so-called "heuristic" method, allowing the student to find the truth as if by himself. This method of teaching is very much suited for our scheme. Such a method, as I have just said, excludes in any case things which show an "ecclesiastical" mentality.[17]

16. *Acta Synodalia* 4/2, p. 12.
17. *Acta Synodalia* 3/5, p. 299.

It is rather necessary to make use of human reason and experience enlightened by faith to show that the Christian position is intrinsically reasonable and suited to dealing with the problems of the man of our time. It is again an invitation to start from experience and to show how the objective truth, both the natural and the revealed divine law, more adequately gives value to the human in man by respecting it completely. In our dialogue with the world as already in the dialogue with the Separated Brethren, the distinction between ontological truth and existential truth prevents the attitude of our mutual inquiries leading to relativism. If we respect the two aspects of truth, then there is no need for the project of "being in search together with other men" to coincide with a lack of certainty and a clear proposal of truth for the other men.

Wojtyła added in his intervention a very long series of detailed remarks elaborated in the collegial work with the Polish episcopate. In November of the same year, probably because of the role he played in the discussion in the assembly, Wojtyła was called to be part of the theological commission in charge of rewriting schema 13. In particular he worked on chapter 4 of part 1, "The Role of the Church in the Modern World." On 2 September Wojtyła intervened again in the assembly on the new version of schema 13 on which he had personally collaborated. His intervention was centered on the section on "The Dignity of the Human Person." He specifically linked the content of schema 13 with the content of the "Declaration on Religious Freedom." Here also the problem of the person, as well as the justification and defense of his particular dignity, is central:

> Since the schema is intended to have above all an intimate pastoral character, then it is good that the principal importance be given to the human person in himself and in community (in social life) as well as in general. In fact all pastoral care presupposes the human person both as a subject . . . and as an object. . . . All pastoral care, every apostolate, both priestly and lay, intends for the human person, because of his integral vocation, to know and concretely express the truth in every relation: with himself, with other persons, and with the world.[18]

The human person is the point on which Church and world converge, and the mission of the Church toward the world consists above all in helping it to attain that integral truth about man. Human reason is essentially directed toward this

18. *Acta Synodalia* 4/2, pp. 660ff.

truth but is unable to reach and master it with adequate certainty by itself because man cannot penetrate adequately the mystery of man without entering also into the mystery of God — to which he is ontologically open — although the divine mystery is inaccessible to man if God himself does not choose to reveal himself and to give occasion for man to encounter him.

We are here at the heart of the theological problem of our time — the question of the relation between the creation of the world and of man and their redemption in Christ, or in a different language, of the connection between the order of nature and the order of grace. Wojtyła's intervention responds to it with his customary clarity and directness.

Wojtyła holds that the schema presupposes the whole work of redemption which was consummated on the Cross and it assumes an intimate relationship of man to this work, a deep bond of dependency on this work:

> But it is not enough to say that the entire work of Creation is taken up in the action of Redemption. We must add that this subsumption is consummated on the Cross. We must, moreover, admit that the divine way to subsume the work of Creation in the world of Redemption through the Cross has somewhat fixed forever the Christian meaning of the "World." We cannot hide the Redemption by underlining only one of its aspects; otherwise we would not explain in the schema either the truth about the World or the pastoral truth.[19]

We see in this passage a very precise position on an entire series of decisive questions, and for this reason it deserves our particular reflection. In the first place, by affirming that the work of Creation is taken up in the work of Redemption and by underlining the strict connection between them, Wojtyła takes a position in favor of the "nouvelle theologie." In other words, he sets himself against the position which distinguishes an order of pure nature, within which man realizes himself as a purely natural being, from an order of grace, which is so gratuitous in relation to the natural structure of man that it becomes superfluous and lacks any existential consistency whatsoever. That doctrine was at that time the position of "Roman theology" and was labelled a "right-wing" position. In the subsequent development of the culture over these last years, it would have been seen as "leftist." The theological position that conceives a secular city complete in itself independently from the work of redemption necessarily

19. Ibid., p. 661.

opens up the road to the absorption of the person within the finalities proper to the species. But the person, in fact, transcends every collectivity and even the human species precisely insofar as he directs himself toward the infinity of God and finds in this orientation his most intimate and deep identity. If we deny this direction of man toward God, then we effectively consent to the possibility of a complete city of man without God. God ceases to be the adequate answer to the existential problem of man. From this point of view, Wojtyła is certainly an innovator and arrays himself with the "progressive" wing of the Council.

Nevertheless, we must remark that the "Roman school" rejected the "nouvelle theologie" because it realized better than its opponent the grave danger of improperly subsuming the work of Creation into the work of Redemption. For if one emphasizes that man as a consequence of being in the order of nature and creation is already directed toward God as his personal end, would it not follow that he has a natural right to revelation, in the same way as every being has a kind of natural right to the realization of the potentiality proper to its own species? And, given that only some have access to the Christian revelation, would we not be forced to admit that in extra-Christian history God equally accomplished his work? Would we not then make the history of salvation coincide with the entire history of humanity and, in so doing, make the growing progress of humanity itself the true salvific fact? What would remain, then, of the traditional doctrine of the unicity of Christ's sacrifice and of the necessity to adhere to the Church, to unite sacramentally with Christ in order to achieve one's own salvation? The risk of falling into a form of immanentist and pantheistic historicism of a Hegelian kind is evident if what is proper to grace is attributed to the nature of man.[20]

There are also some theologians who have maintained that in Christ the entire nature of man has been assumed in God and that, after Christ, there does not exist a human nature but instead a unique human-divine nature which realizes itself in history in such a way that the last times are those in which the new human-divine nature achieves its fulfillment.[21] Such

---

20. The objections to *nouvelle theologie* have been restated recently with conviction and clarity by Giuseppe Cardinal Siri in *Getsemani. Riflessioni sul Movimento Teologico Contemporaneo* (Rome: Fraternita della Santissima Vergine Maria, 1980).

21. These themes, already differently present in the Hegelian and young Hegelian theology from Marheineke to Strauss and Feuerbach and Bauer, were again taken up in the 60s by the theology of the death of God and, above all, by T. J. J. Altizer in *The Gospel of Christian Atheism* (Philadelphia, 1966).

a position is naturally exposed to a materialistic overturning when one logically maintains that it is not possible and it is not thinkable that God would annihilate himself in man, so the Christ event is only a mythical way to affirm that it is man who frees himself in his progressive development from his alienation in the divinity toward his reappropriation of the qualities which initially he had placed in the idea of God.

In the second part of his intervention which we quoted above, Wojtyła reacts against this set of dangers, then only in a potential state. To say that the order of grace and the order of nature (or better and dynamically, the order of Redemption and the order of Creation) meet in the Cross of Christ means to reaffirm the traditional Trinitarian doctrine according to which human nature and divine nature do not mix but are united *in the person of Christ*, and men enter the life of God through the person of Christ by adhering to him.

For us, adherence in the present time happens through our participation in the cross of Christ, that is, in his humiliation. And because of this, the history of the world cannot be represented as a linear process in which man progresses continually toward the Kingdom of God. The Kingdom is already present in the history of man and yet, in a mysterious way, the time from now until the end of history is an occasion for decision for or against God and for or against the truth of man. In this way we understand Wojtyła's remarks alleging that the conciliar text was in danger of being too one-sidedly optimistic by confusing the material progress of humanity with its moral perfection. From that essential point of view, contemporary man faces the identical choice for or against the truth which is proper to man in all historical epochs. The greater power over nature which modern science and technology give to us only increases the responsibility for moral choice. Wojtyła thus crafts an innovative position which is not to be confused with postconciliar progressivism. Creation and Redemption are seen in their dynamic unity; however, they are not blended to the point of losing the sense of the transcendence of God and the gratuity of his self-revelation in Christ. He clarifies his idea with the help of his notion of a personalist order which is different from the nonpersonal order of nature, a concept comparable to the classical Thomist doctrine. The person, in order to realize his proper potentialities, depends upon the freedom of the other person and upon his own freedom, and thus a fortiori on the freedom of God. The error of both the traditionalist and the progressive positions lies in not understanding deeply the peculiarities of the personalist order, its dynamic character and the role that freedom has in it. Thus the traditionalist position, no less than the progressive one, cannot think that man is created for God without his having a right over God; they think it implies that God is taken to be an object which man is able to possess on the basis of the effort and the energies which are proper to his simple nature. But in Wojtyła's view the order of nature is a function of the order of grace, and it is reinterpreted starting from the experience of redeemed man and only in this perspective reveals its whole richness. Christ, in fact, comes to bring to man not only eternal life but also the hundredfold in this life, that is, the recovery and the full reorientation of his natural existence. It seems to me that I can show here a strict analogy between the position of Wojtyła and that of those postconciliar theologians, particularly Henri de Lubac and Hans Urs von Balthasar, who have developed similarly the theme of the nature-grace relation and that of the analogy of faith *(analogia fidei)*, by appropriating to Catholic theology some of Karl Barth's fundamental intuitions.[22]

A similar dialectics defines the terms of the Christian dialogue with the world. The Church is not external to the world, precisely because one cannot divide and isolate the work of Creation from the work of Redemption. Yet neither does the Church coincide with the world. She rather situates herself in that point of human history in which God himself comes to encounter the effort of man to transcend his own immanence in nature. This allows her to appreciate every human effort directed toward the good and yet to indicate a fulfillment that human forces alone are neither sufficient to realize nor able fully to understand.

In any case the Church desires to offer to the world every possible service, especially that of truth and morality, and this always according to that transcendence which is proper to her because of the work of redemption. The service of the Church, therefore, is that of eternal salvation, which transcends every immanent end in the world. Clarity and sincerity are necessary for dialogue. Are we not able to say all this in sincerity and with all respect toward the world? In the schema the view of the world as it ought to be prevails over the representation of the world as it is and the view of Christ the Consummator prevails over that of Christ the Redeemer.[23]

22. Hans Urs von Balthasar, *Karl Barth. Darstellung und Deutung seiner Theologie* (Köln, 1951); trans. into English by John Dury as *The Theology of Karl Barth* (New York: Holt, Rinehart & Winston, 1971); H. De Lubac, *Le mystère du surnaturel* (Paris, 1965).
23. *Acta Synodalia* 4/2 p. 661.

The image of Christ the Consummator is situated at the end of time, when everything will become clear and the consonance between every authentic effort of man and Christian salvation becomes evident. It is Christ the Redeemer who belongs to our time, when man's efforts to free himself often rely upon false presuppositions and upon an unwarranted trust in himself. In this time the Church, the people whom God has called and who live in the ethos of Christ, should not only approve the effort of the world but also correct it, clearly indicating what truly and what falsely accords with the human person. Criticism of the world is therefore as essential as the positive attitude toward human effort. The idea of the transcendence of eternal salvation to any worldly end is characteristic of Wojtyła's thought. It is not a question of the simple primacy of eternal salvation but of the fact that the impulse toward it dwells in every human effort, in every authentic goal of man. Indeed salvation transcends and at the same time transforms the impulse and reorients it from within. Again, the analogy of the way in which the person transcends the dynamisms of nature helps us to understand the way in which the Church transcends the history of man even without ever being able to detach herself from it.

This idea of transcendence allows us to understand how Redemption dwells in the history of man, which is centered in the sacrifice of Christ. Although it is always irreducible to this history, it nevertheless guides its dynamism in a secret way, incomprehensible to a purely naturalistic view.

At the Sources of Renewal

As soon as he returned to his diocese at the conclusion of the Council, Wojtyła felt the necessity of paying at least in part the debt contracted with the Spirit for having the chance to participate in that extraordinary human and spiritual adventure.[24] He engaged himself deeply in the implementation of the Council. Of course the pastoral activity of the bishop of Cracow

24. Cf. Wojtyła, *U Podstaw Odnowy Studium o realizacji Vaticanum II* (Polskie Towarzystwo Teologiczne, 1972); Italian trans. by Magdalenea Francszka Kujawska UCJA, *Alle fonti del rinnovamento* (Vatican City: Libreria Editrice Vaticana, 1981); English trans., based on the revised Italian translation: *Sources of Renewal: The Implementation of the Second Vatican Council* (London: Collins and Fount; New York: Harper and Row, 1980).

exceeds the limits of our research, although a historian who would investigate and make clear the terms of it would make a very important contribution to the understanding of Wojtyła's thought. It will here suffice to
mention that his implementation of the Council culminated with the
diocesan synod that he began in 1972 and closed during his visit to Poland
as Pope John Paul II.[25]

The year in which the Synod began, 1972, is also the year of the
publication of *Sources of Renewal,* Wojtyła's book on the Council. The
work is not a commentary on the conciliar texts in the narrow sense;
rather, it reorganizes them in order to facilitate the pastoral implementation of the Council. *Sources of Renewal* was in fact the textbook of the
Synod which gave method and content to the innumerable reflections on
the Council which were formed in those years. The Synod was a systematic
and extensive effort to which all of the members of the believing community, from workers to intellectuals, from priests to laywomen, collaborated with great enthusiasm. A moving witness to that enterprise is
given in *L'arrichimento della fede,* which describes the works of the synod
of the parish of Nowa Huta. (It was edited by Halina Bortnowska, one of
the members of the staff of the Cracow Catholic monthly, *Znak*). Signif-
icantly, the book is subtitled "Elaboration of the Thoughts of Karol Cardinal Wojtyła on Conciliar Renewal."[26]

Wojtyła understood from the beginning that the problem of the Council was eminently cultural and he took care, before starting the concrete
pastoral implementation, to achieve a unitary grasp of the conciliar event
and of the tasks which were the result of it. His book on the Council arises
from this understanding.

25. Among the many writings of Wojtyła devoted to the Synod, cf. "Problem 900
rocznicy św. Stanisław oraz synodu prowincjonalnego (rozważania wtepne)," *Notificationes e Curia metropolitana cracoviensi* (Cracow) 6, pp. 129-35 and "Przemówienie
wygłoszone w czasie otwarcia Duszpasterskiego Synodu Archidiecezji Krakowskiej w
dniu 8-V-1972 r. w. Katedrze Wawelskiej," in *Notificationes e curia metropolitana Cracoviensi* (Cracow) 6, pp. 142-43 and 153-58. Cf. also the closing speech of the synod
pronounced by John Paul II in the afternoon of 8 June 1979 in the cathedral of Wawel
and the speech of Blonie at Cracow on 10 June 1979 for the jubilee of the feast of St.
Stanislaw (which represents the true closing of the synod and also the trip to Poland).
Both these speeches can be read, of course, in the *Osservatore Romano* of the following
day.

The Conciliar Initiation and the Formation of Conscience

The first part of *Sources of Renewal* seeks to clarify the fundamental meaning of the conciliar initiation. This is clearly identified as the necessity for a specific enrichment of faith.[27] The Council had an eminently pastoral goal. It was not the purpose of the Council to add new dogmas to the Christian creed. Nor was its task a political or governmental one. It did not draw political blueprints nor recommend specific solutions of particular concrete problems. Rather the Conciliar Fathers asked themselves the question: What is the meaning of being believing members of the Church today?

> The question "What does it mean to be a believing member of the Church?" is . . . difficult and complex, because it not only presupposes the truths of faith and pure doctrine but also calls for that truth to be situated in the human consciousness and calls for a definition of the attitude, or rather the many attitudes that go to make the individual a believing member of the Church. . . . In the present study . . . we shall *concentrate on the consciousness of Christians and the attitudes they should acquire.*[28]

In short, it is a question of developing the subjective side of faith, a Christian mentality in confronting and judging life and history. If the fundamental question which the worldly ideology seeks to answer is that of "what to do," the question of the Council concerns, rather, "how to be." Moreover, in her dogmatic definitions the Church fixes what one should believe; the Council has instead an eminently pastoral character because it wants to indicate the way in which the patrimony of the faith should be held. The gift of God should be freely acknowledged and become a conscious attitude of man. This reverberation of the objective value in consciousness which modifies it and at the same time modifies the person is

---

26. *L'arricchimento della fede. Elaborazione dei pensieri del Cardinale Karol Wojtyła sul rinnovamento conciliare.* Edited by the Synodal Group of Study of the parish of Mary Queen of the Polish Crown at Nowa Huta; based on *Sources of Renewal.* Introduction by Francesco Ricci; Preface by Halina Bortnowska (1981).

27. That this was the center of the program of Wojtyła was immediately underlined by Bohdan Cywinski's review in "Rzecz o wzbogaceniu wiary," *Znak* 25 (1973), pp. 779-87. See also Adam Kubiś, "U podstaw odnowy (Studium kardynała Karol Wojtyła o realizacji Soboru)," in *Tygodnik Powszechny* 26; Andrzey Polkowski, "Studium o realizacji Vaticanum II," in *Zycie i Myśl* 23 (1973), pp. 130-32; Stanisław Nagy, "Program ocalenia," in *Tygodnik Powszechny* 30 (1976).

28. *Sources of Renewal,* pp. 17-18.

at the center of the Declaration on Religious Freedom but also in all the other documents of the Council. This principle is valid both within the Church and outside of it. The acknowledgment of the truth of dogmatic enunciations is only the beginning of the work of conversion through which they become the form of the person's consciousness. The task the Council poses is therefore the one of passing from a merely objective faith to a fully personal faith. In this consists properly the response of man to the gift of God. It is the question of a kind of answer which is "essentially supernatural . . . and at the same time strictly personal."[29] This response is not part of the order of nature since it requires the supernatural help of grace. However, it is not thinkable except within the personalist order, that is, within that order proper to man insofar as he is human in a particular way which transcends the rest of nature in the direction of God.

The faith, "conceived in a somewhat existential sense, as a state of consciousness and as an attitude on the part of the individual believer"[30] implies an attitude of certainty. However, certainty does not put an end to the human search but rather gives it direction. It is precisely "the ordinary way of the enrichment of faith."[31] The certainty of faith is not certainty of one's own opinion but certainty of the value of that which has been encountered and acknowledged. Such a universal value, however, unfolds and clarifies itself in the confrontation with all the other human experiences, showing its capacity to welcome and give value to everything which is true and human. The attitude of dialogue therefore accompanies (without contradicting but, rather, strictly deriving from) the attitude of certainty.[32] The Christian believes that in the person of Christ God gives human beings the complete answer to the most radical and deepest questions of their very human personal nature. The atheist, the nonbeliever and the non-Christian, can have an experience of humanity richer than that of the Christian and therefore they can live those human questions to a level of consciousness and truth even higher than the one that Christians are able to achieve. From the objective point of view and for the enrichment of their own faith, for the understanding of the very full existential meaning of the Christian answer, Christians have, therefore, much to learn from those who adhere to other religions or from atheists. This does not take away the task that

29. Ibid., p. 23.
30. Ibid., p. 27.
31. Ibid., p. 27.
32. Ibid.

they have of announcing the truth and the objective value which have been communicated to them, not because of their merit but because of the mercy of God. The dialogue, the existential comprehension, situates itself, therefore, in the perspective of the annunciation of salvation. In fact, the believer, "enlightened by the faith, asks himself a question which regards, in different ways, believers and nonbelievers. It is a question, which should not lead him to a kind of indifferentism, but ought rather to make him pause at every circle outside the Church and there encounter every man with full respect due to his human person and human conscience. This respect goes hand in hand with the sense of responsibility to the truth and the duty of every man to seek it sincerely, as we read in the *Declaration on Religious Liberty*."[33] The method of dialogue does not exempt man from the search for truth but offers him companionship along the way toward it.

The dialogue, which in a larger sense is the comparison of the faith with the human experience of life, is the method which the Council proposes both for the growth of faith to maturity and for a Church which no longer understands herself simply as an object but also as an active subject and on the way in history. Through her faith, the Church directs herself immediately toward God and in this way transcends human history. Through the faith in dialogue she directs herself toward other men and incorporates in herself their expectations and hopes. The two dimensions are not independent of each other. A person transcends any single action of his and also their composite whole. But this irreducible transcendence at the same time furnishes the basis for the integration of man. In an analogous way, by virtue of her vertical dimensions the Church transcends human history, but it is precisely through this verticality that she furnishes the basis for the integration of human history, whose unity is provided only in reference to God in Christ, that is, in reference to the Cross in which the vertical and the horizontal poles intersect in a permanent unity. The transcendence of the Church with respect to the history of the world, as we have just said, is strictly bound to the transcendence of the value of the person with respect to the single action in history. The reaffirmation, then, of the particular dignity of man will be one of the first tasks of the Church in history.

"The Church, which in force of her office and of her competence, by no means is confused with the political community . . . is at the same time the sign and the safeguard of the transcendent character of the human

33. Ibid., p. 29.

person."[34] It is on this point that the vertical dimension gives a foundation to the horizontal, even as it respects its autonomy. In this way, also, the Church acknowledges herself wholly dependent upon Christ who is her own Lord. Her foundation is the reality of God, of the Holy Trinity, of the creation, of revelation, and of redemption. She is founded from on high. Without explicitly arguing against ecclesiology and Christology "from below," Wojtyła is unequivocally clear on this point. He is equally clear in his judgment about the epochal rupture with the preceding history of the Church which some thought the Council should represent. The apostolate of the enrichment of faith shunts aside these positions completely:

> ... The post-conciliar integration of the faith is not a mechanical addition, by the magisterium of the Council, to all that was hitherto comprised in the Church's teaching. . . . Integration means . . . an organic cohesion expressing itself simultaneously in the thought and action of the Church as a community of believers. It expresses itself, that is, in such a way that on the one hand we can rediscover and reread the magisterium of the last Council in the whole previous magisterium of the Church, while on the other we can re-discover and re-read the whole preceding magisterium in that of the last Council.[35]

This principle of integration of novelty and tradition, through which the historical identity of the Church and its unity is constituted, is one which leads directly beyond the controversy between integralists and neo-modernists toward the understanding of the new synthesis of the Council.

The first content of the consciousness of the faith proclaimed by the Council is the truth regarding the creation of the world and of man. It is indissolubly bound to the first affirmation of the Creed: "I believe in God the Father Almighty." This knowledge about God, who continuously creates the world and man by keeping them in being, is also the first and main point of contact between human reason and the Christian faith. The knowledge that God exists and that man is for God is what man's inquiry achieves and is also the beginning of the dialogue of God with man. Vatican II, restating the fundamental affirmation of Vatican I, reminds us that "God, principle and end of all things, can be known with certainty by the natural light of human reason from created things."[36]

34. *Pastoral Constitution on the Church in the Modern World (Gaudium et Spes)*, 76.
35. *Sources of Renewal*, p. 40.
36. *Dogmatic Constitution on Revelation (Dei Verbum)*, 6.

An element of revelation is already contained in this initial knowledge of God, which is accessible to human reason insofar as creation itself is the first of the acts by which God reveals himself. "The Council teaches explicitly that God 'provides men with constant evidence of himself in created realities' (CR 3). The term 'evidence' is particularly significant because it indicates the element of revelation in creation itself, which is, as it were, the first and fundamental expression of God, by which he speaks to us and calls for a response of faith."[37]

A series of important consequences springs from the awareness of creation. First, God created the world according to a rational plan, a set of laws which manifest themselves in nature and which are accessible to human reason. God then placed human beings in the world to have dominion over it, and for that he gave them intelligence and the capacity for rationality. By knowing the order of the world and the laws which are proper to every natural reality and every ambit of human activity, man knows God in creation. Because of this possibility the Council shows the utmost respect for the methods and the forms proper to every specialized knowledge, of science and of technology. However, knowing means also to subordinate, to order to an end. Human reason does not limit itself to the knowledge of the mechanisms of functioning of individual aspects of nature but continuously seeks the connection of each of them with man and of man with his end, which is God. Already the awareness of creation, which contains in itself that of the existence of God as Creator, implies not only respect for scientific reason but also respect for philosophical reason which orients the whole process of knowledge to the True, the Good, and the Beautiful.

Hence the two fundamental conciliar affirmations which are integrated in chapter 36 of *Gaudium et Spes*: ". . . It is from the very condition of creaturehood that all things receive their own consistency, truth, and goodness, their proper laws and their order; and man must hold in respect all of that by recognizing the methodological requirements which are proper to each science or art." And again, "If, instead, with the expression 'autonomy of temporal reality' one means that created things do not depend on God and that man can use them in order not to refer them to the creator, then anyone who believes in God sees how false these opinions are." In short, earthly realities are autonomous within the order of creation, which has God in its center, and the order of creation is ordered to revelation and indeed somehow represents its beginning. Secondly, at the center of creation

37. *Sources of Renewal,* p. 47.

stands man, who bears a particular resemblance to God and to whom he is ordered in a particular way. It is by reflecting on his own being in the world and on his own need of salvation that man directs himself toward God in the right way.

The awareness of creation does not exhaust the search for meaning which is proper to man but rather simply orients it and permits the asking of the fundamental questions with clarity.

> "What is man?" the Council asks itself. "What is the meaning of suffering, evil, and death which still exist in spite of the progress mankind has made?" What is the worth of these conquests which are achieved at such a dear price? Man has expressed and continues to express various and contrary opinions about himself, for often either he exalts himself so as to make of himself an absolute rule or he lowers himself, moved by doubt and anxiety to despair. The Church feels these difficulties deeply, and she can give an answer to them which comes from divine revelation, an answer which describes the true condition of man, gives a reason for his miseries, and at the same time helps to recognize his dignity and vocation.[38]

In the statement which we have just quoted at length, the Council brings together both the classical Thomistic and the Pascalian approach to the problem of man. The order of creation is the first and fundamental content of human consciousness. However, it is not a closed order and just to persevere adequately in the awareness of the truth which such an order opens up, man needs the help of a deeper uncovering of his personal mystery. One excludes, thus, even in an extremely positive evaluation of all human progress, the pretense that human beings can adequately regulate their lives from a merely natural point of view, by excluding God and any opening toward transcendence. The progress in the knowledge of the objective mechanisms of nature cannot be considered true human progress if it is not accompanied by a progress in the capacity of ordering to the moral good of man the power thus gained over nature.

In the Christian consciousness creation and redemption are therefore strictly bound together. It is good to start from creation to exclude those positions that, under a Barthian influence, have attempted too one-sidedly to set revelation at the source of Christianity and in so doing have cut the bond between natural human existence and Christian existence. Against

38. *Pastoral Constitution on the Church in the Modern World (Gaudium et Spes)*, 12.

them the Council reaffirms (although it does not name it) the principle of the analogy of being, the *analogia entis*. All of reality is under the sign of God; so also all the religions and philosophies in which men express the feeling and knowledge of their own dependence upon the divine have a positive value as long as they do not attempt to close themselves to their completion and fulfillment in Christ. In this way the road to any pretense of imposing a rupture between Christianity and religion by imposing a nonreligious or post-religious Christianity is barred. On the other hand, the *analogia entis* is rethought in the analogy of faith, the *analogia fidei*. It is in the light of revelation that one understands the mystery of man; through it the creation is understood in its authentic meaning and in a deep penetration of its intimate rationality. This excludes any dualism, any opposition between an earthly city, ordered according to pure nature, and a heavenly city founded on the redemption of Christ.

Revelation is, in fact, one and the same with the work of redemption. God reveals himself by revealing his will of salvation for man. "The Church confesses the truth of a God who saves, and this truth complements that of God as the Creator. Awareness of salvation is, as it were, superimposed on awareness of creation, which it penetrates through and through, and is the true response to the mystery of the most Holy Trinity."[39]

By manifesting his will of salvation for man, God reveals his own personal nature, and by permitting himself to be encountered in Christ, he reveals his communal nature as a Trinity of persons. The revelation of the Trinitarian mystery is not without deep significance for anthropology. It is not, for example, coincidental that Aquinas primarily elaborates the concept of person in order to consider the Holy Trinity and only afterward applies it to man. The Holy Trinity offers to us the model of a community of persons in which each of them lives entirely in the other through his own free donation of himself. In this dynamic lies the deeper resemblance between man and God in the nature of their personal being. This allows us to think a personal relationship between God and man, a kind of relationship in which, without losing one's own personality and human nature, man is admitted to the very interiority of God. This is precisely what happens in faith: man affirms the fundamental truth *about God* and, in a certain sense, *in God* himself. This is where the roots of the communion of the Church lie. It is man's discovery of the root of his being a person which is made possible by his being drawn into the life of God.

39. *Sources of Renwal,* p. 55.

Our Lord Jesus, when he prays to the Father that "all may be one" (John 17:21-22), putting before us vistas inaccessible to human reason, has suggested to us a certain resemblance between the union of divine Persons and the union of the children of God in truth and charity. This resemblance shows that man, who on earth is the only creature that God wanted for his own sake, cannot fully find himself except through genuine self-giving.[40] It is a question, Wojtyła says, of a genuine "metaphysical analogy" between God as a person and the Trinitarian community on one side and the community of believers in charity and truth on the other. Communion is not, therefore, an element which is added externally to the person but is the act which vivifies him from within by letting it discover unity with the other as the revelation of his own most authentic interiority. By thus communicating himself God also provides in revelation the only adequate answer to the mystery and the desire for fulfillment of life which is proper to man. At the same time the participation through Christ in the reciprocal donation of the persons of the Holy Trinity is the source of the energy which permits man to achieve his fulfillment.

This view of man, of course, is incorporated in history, and is therefore deeply dialectical. Redeemed man is also sinful man. All men are saved and called to full communion in Christ, but it is only through history that this call can be understood and received. History remains, therefore, the place of struggle and ambiguity. On one hand, man is unceasingly animated by a strong desire for a liberation that leads him to seek in a thousand different ways a deeper truth of his own existence. On the other hand, this effort clashes continuously with contradictions and injustices, and in the struggle against them it continuously risks deviating from its duty by substituting new injustices for those of the past. So although the Council notes with approval the fact that "individuals . . . and organized groups desire an entirely free life worthy of man which puts in its service all that the world today offers so abundantly,"[41] it also recognizes a darker truth. For it acknowledges that "the imbalances which the contemporary world suffers are connected with the more profound imbalances which are rooted in the heart of man. . . . On the one hand, as a creature he experiences in myriad ways his own limits; on the other hand, he realizes that he is limitless in his aspirations and is called to a superior life. . . ."[42] The effort of man

40. *Pastoral Constitution on the Church in the Modern World (Gaudium et Spes)*, 24.
41. Ibid., 9.
42. Ibid., 10.

toward liberation will always be hindered by this dualism which is within him and ultimately by original sin, until this fracture is healed. In this sense communion with God and with fellow men appears as the radical condition for the liberation of man which also purifies his attempts to build a humanly just city on earth. This communion is instituted by Christ, and so "the consciousness of this restoration of man's value by Christ is an integral element of faith."[43]

The reevaluation of man, that is, the just and definitive manifestation of his true nature, founds a new morality. By being received in the dwelling of the Spirit of Christ, the Christian enters into his ethos. The logos — objective truth of the world since the beginning — thus becomes ethos — subjective dwelling of man — and in this way generates in him a new nature. Through Christ, what used to be external law becomes an intimate demand of the person.

In this way the creativity of the faith in the person and, therefore, his authentic subjectivization become manifest. We noted before an implicit argument against those who separate Christianity from religion; now an implicit argument against those who separate Christianity from morality becomes equally evident. In fact, "the key problem of life as actually lived by Christians is that of the link between faith and morals."[44] Where this connection is not made, the very dynamism of faith, which tends to pervade the whole person, is blocked. In order to be able to give himself and in such a way to discover himself, a man must first possess himself. This dominion over himself which makes possible the gift is the first component of the royalty which is proper to the Christian and exemplified in Christ. This does not happen, however, without moral discipline. Only after having amply developed the awareness of creation, salvation, and redemption does Wojtyła, in the enunciation of the contents of Christian consciousness according to the Council, come to speak about the Church. The considerations about communion that we have already expounded introduce the topic. They show how the approach to the mystery of the Church must necessarily pass through the awareness of creation, of the situation of man in the world, of God's offer of salvation in Christ. The communion founds the belonging of the Christian to Christ and to each other. To it is bound the conception of the Church as *the mystical body of Christ*. The ecumenical Council has also proposed another image of the Church by defining her as

43. *Sources of Renewal,* p. 77.
44. Ibid., p. 99.

the people of God and the people of God on the way in history. It is a question, according to Wojtyła, of two aspects of the Church which cannot be disjoined and which anyway have always the mystery of communion at their center.

If we did not proceed in this way, Wojtyła remarks, or if we were to pass too quickly over the reality of redemption to move to that of the people of God, the second reality would not appear to us in its full and deep significance. If it were so, we would speak of a one-sided "sociologization" of the concept that is in itself charged with an intense theological potential. This richness comes to it from the fact that the "people of God" is contained in the "mystical body of Christ," and, conversely, the "mystical body of Christ" is contained in the "people of God."[45]

The idea of a rupture between creation and redemption also entails an emptying of redemption. It cannot be understood as an initiative of God the creator and therefore is unavoidably reduced to human understanding which is inadequate to it. In this perspective the ontological value which gives foundation to the being of the Church, as being a communion and therefore as being the one body of Christ, gives way to a merely sociological interpretation which sees in the Church only the "people of God." Actually, the expression "people of God" is for the Council simply the deepening and reflection in consciousness, the subjectivization of that objective reality which is the "Mystical Body." Precisely for this reason the basic affirmation that the Church is the "mystical body of Christ" is deprived of existential efficacy if it is not appreciated as the consciousness expressed in the Church as "people of God." Yet the objective content of this consciousness is entirely determined by the affirmation that the Church is the "Mystical Body of Christ."

The call of God is for all of humanity. The content of the faith, indeed, questions every man about the value and the destiny of man. It is a question of recomposing the internal split of man, by enlightening and perfecting his own natural dynamic in Christ. For this reason the faith "throws a new light on all things and makes known the full ideal which God has set for man, thus guiding the mind toward solutions that are fully human."[46] This enlightenment of his nature and his destiny is nevertheless offered by God to man through an historical covenant, in which God first makes himself available to a select few, founding a new people who are united by a unique

45. Ibid., p. 120.
46. *Pastoral Constitution on the Church in the Modern World (Gaudium et Spes)*, 11.

access to the truth of man which is revealed by God himself. Man has an intelligent and free nature which finds expression in his consciousness and, therefore, in his moral acting and in the quest for truth and the good. By his covenant, God welcomes in himself these natural dimensions of existence by transvaluing them. The call to communion with God also reveals the final destiny for which man has been created from the beginning. As we have already mentioned, this communion also establishes a new relationship among men, namely their essential reciprocal belonging. This fundamental communion with every person becomes more visible in history through the communion among those who acknowledge the coming of Christ and are participants in the covenant of the people of God. This covenant, which reaches out to the whole of mankind, subsists in the meantime in the form of a historical people, which at any one time can be a small people apparently lost in the infinite events of the history of mankind. Here the fact that human beings are persons and the fact that they are made to live in community are fulfilled by being brought together. In other words, there is no such thing as *the man* and *the Christian* as separate entities; the Christian is the mysterious fulfillment of man. This affirmation must be carefully considered because it is from misunderstanding this idea that all the postconciliar difficulties derive.

To say that a separation between man and Christian cannot exist does not mean affirming that only Christians are truly men. In the light of our previous explanations concerning objectivity and consciousness, I believe that it is easy to understand that the affirmation that Christ is the Man does not imply at all that Christians are personally better than other men. Many non-Christians can live with greater richness the dimensions of the human which Christ comes to fulfill. However, every human experience of truth is directed toward Christ, and the Word of God is secretly in action in the entire history of the world, both within and outside the visible realm of the presence of the Church.

On the other hand, the affirmation that there is no separation between Christian and human should not be taken to mean that what is human is already Christian in itself, as is claimed in the theory of "anonymous Christianity." The way that God has chosen to introduce man into communion with himself is the person of Christ, and one partakes of this communion through the Church by participating in the life of this new people. To be sure, the "new people" is the invisible Church of the true disciples, but the sign in the world which allows one to orient oneself towards the invisible Church is the visible Church. Here the reality of creation, of redemption, and of salvation are affirmed and the beginning of personal experience which is the *sequela Christi*, the following of Christ. Everything to which God gives rise in the world with a view toward leading man to his fulfillment is ordered to unity with this visible sign, even if such unity in this phase of history can be only imperfect. Hence the requirement that the visible Church maintain vigorous ecumenical and missionary activity.

The Council conceives of humanity as a series of concentric circles. Its kernel is constituted by believers in Christ reunited in the Catholic Church which is instituted by him. There are then Christians not united with the visible Church, those who belong to the great religions of humanity, and lastly those who have "not yet arrived at an explicit knowledge of God, and who, not without grace, strive to lead a good life."[47]

We should not draw from these conciliar texts the impression that nothing external to the Church exists. Objectively, all mankind is called to communion with God in Christ. Subjectively, men, in their freedom, can either adhere to this call or remove themselves from it.

By adhering to it, they approach also, objectively and according to their situation, the message of Jesus guarded by the Church. By not adhering to it, they distance themselves from it. The Church, to which this message has been confided, has the duty to give a judgment, at all times, on the main directions of development of the history of mankind in order to judge it from the point of view of the history of salvation. In particular, in the midst of the human adventure, we find men who even without knowledge of Christianity are interiorly inclined toward it through a just view of man and God; side by side with them, as it were, we also encounter men who have refused the religious view of reality which manifests itself to natural reflection: "But very often, deceived by the Evil One, men have become vain in their reasonings, have exchanged the truth of God for a lie and served the world rather than the Creator (cf. Rom. 1:21, 25). Or else, living and dying in this world without God, they are exposed to ultimate despair."[48] Of course only God can bear judgment on the conscience of men, by knowing their good faith and the real circumstances in which their freedom made its own choices. The Council, however, confirms that man decides by his own freedom concerning his own destiny. It confirms, moreover, that as there are human doctrines directed toward the truth which help human-

47. *Dogmatic Constitution on the Church (Lumen Gentium)*, 16.
48. Ibid.

ity along the path toward its own end, there are also false doctrines which obstruct the way: "Without doubt those who willfully try to drive God from their heart and to avoid all questions about religion, not following the biddings of their conscience, are not free from blame."[49] The condemnation of atheism and religious indifferentism which deny the fundamental human duty to search for truth does not, of course, apply directly to individuals who, insofar as their subjective conscience is concerned, remain confided to the mercy of God.

Thus, in view of these real possibilities the Church accepts the duty of preaching the truth of man against those positions which would want a Church which is "totally other" in relationship to the world, and would limit her to accepting the self-understanding which the different secular ideologies express concerning liberation and human progress. The Church knows that the presence of Christ, which transcends history, is also the basis of the judgment on herself and on her wholeness. Such judgment does not happen simply in an abstract way, through a doctrinal enunciation but concretely, through the presence of Christians in the world, in different nations and in different moments of history. The very articulation of the people of God and the diversity of gifts within it is understood in the function of its missionary presence in the world, which is immanent and at the same time continually transcendent. The Church is nothing else but that part of humanity which already explicitly acknowledges Christ as the one in whom the human transcends itself and, at the same time, acknowledges Christ as the basis of its real integration. The call to both transcendence and integration accounts for the differentiated duties and the interconnections of the hierarchy and laymen, equally necessary to the fulfillment of the universal priesthood of believers which consists precisely in the reconstruction of the relationship with God as the final content of the consciousness of mankind.

This principle, which governs the relationship of the Church to the world, also rules the relationship with the different cultures and with the different national identities. Here Wojtyła doubtless reads the Council in the light of the rich Polish elaboration on the theme of nation, but this is not at all in disagreement with the conciliar attitude which urges us to see in the culture of every human group a set of authentic values, an original path toward the truth of man, which certainly ask to be judged and purified but with equal certitude must be utilized as an indispensable channel for

49. *Pastoral Constitution on the Church in the Modern World (Gaudium et Spes)*, 19.

evangelization and Christian education. In this framework, the Church forms the judgment on modernity, that is, on that particular acceleration of our capacity for mastering nature witnessed over the course of recent centuries. Corresponding to this acceleration is a tendency on the part of man to read history in a dynamic sense as progress and development. "There is a growing conviction," says the Council, "of mankind's ability and duty to strengthen its mastery over nature and of the need to establish a political, social, and economic order at the service of man to assert and develop the dignity proper to individuals and to societies. . . . Man as an individual and as a member of society craves a life that is full, autonomous, and worthy of his nature as a human being; he longs to harness for his own welfare the immense resources of the modern world."[50] The Council is wholly sympathetic to the desire for economic and social development. Man does not have the task of adapting himself to an invariable natural order but of conquering and subordinating nature and, in so doing, to make it more and more apt to serve and to manifest the particular dignity of the person. However, the objective progress of the work of man which in a more and more efficacious manner subdues nature and makes a great abundance of goods available is not yet the true fulfilled progress of man. It is necessary that at the same time the subjective side of work be developed and that the material elements of progress be integrated among them on the basis of a just knowledge of the transcendence of the human person. It is through the consideration of this essential point that we can adequately understand not only how the ideal of development and of the progress of man are congenial to the nature of the gospel, but also how the realization of a more human world also passes in a certain way through the history of salvation.

This new world, in which nature is subdued by man and at the same time man is fully led back to himself, is the object of the deepest aspirations in human history. These motivating ideals, however, are continually challenged by the contradiction of sin and of evil. But God, by revealing himself to man in Christ and by admitting him to communion with himself, restores and thereby brings to fulfillment that dynamism which is proper to human nature. On the one hand, Christian salvation is not extraneous to the becoming of the world and to the unfolding of history. It happens in history, and it is an answer to the fundamental desire of authentic life which impels man through history. On the other hand, Christian salvation

50. Ibid., 9.

is irreducible to any kind of particular historical realization, to any partial concretization. The final end adequate to man is not the realization of a perfect society in the world from the point of view of the organization of the state or society. The adequate end of man is that full experience of his own dignity as a person, a dignity proper to the image of God, which arises from transcending the social dimension which makes of him only a member of the species. Living in dignity is the end to which every just society and every worldly progress aims. It is right that every man have bread, freedom of expression, and the possibility of familial life, because this is part of his dignity. However, dignity is not the sum of these goods. It is possible to live in dignity without having any of them; it is also possible to have them all and nevertheless lack the proper dignity of man. From this point of view, the eschatological goal of the Church, which is holiness, enlightens all the temporal goals of man, while it does not have its source in any of them. Holiness is the fullness of living in dignity, which is accessible in the most unhappy conditions. The Church, the community of the saints, by transcending the world seeks the conditions of her truth. "The plan of salvation sinks its roots into the most real aspirations and purposes of human beings and humanity. . . . Nonetheless, the history of salvation always embraces more than the history of the 'world'."[51] It

> bears witness above all to the constant need for purification of the most human values, of man's aspirations and purposes, in which the history of the world in a sense encounters the history of salvation. The reality of redemption attests the need to find in these values, aspirations, and purposes the divine dimension which is proper to them so that they can become "substance" of the kingdom of God. . . . As a result of all this, the redemption . . . with its profound and eloquent dynamism orients the "world," through the Church, towards its final fulfillment.[52]

It was during the time of the Council that Catholics argued about the merits of Teilhard de Chardin's evolutionism. From one point of view it offered a framework for acknowledging a positive dimension in the history of the world, while from an opposite standpoint it threatened to absorb Christian redemption within the ends of human history as such and, in so doing, re-created a theory similar to one of the varieties of Hegelian-Marxist historicism. Wojtyła not only restates the Catholic doctrine of the transcen-

51. *Sources of Renewal,* p. 176.
52. Ibid., pp. 176-77.

dence of the end of the Church in relation to that of the history of the world but also furnishes an implicit but penetrating critique of the evolutionist position from a philosophical point of view; his critique, moreover, eschews a reactionary separation of the history of the Church from the history of the world and consequent reciprocal irrelevance of these two histories. It is by letting the history of salvation transcend it that the history of the world reaches its own completeness and is able authentically to be integrated into it.

The Formation of Attitudes

The third part of *Sources of Renewal* is devoted to the "formation of attitudes." While, in the first pages of the book, Wojtyła explains the fundamental meaning of the conciliar initiation and, in the second, he elaborates the doctrine of the Council in a form which leads to its appropriation by the conscience, the last section deals with the formation of vital attitudes which correspond to that conscience, which render it sensible and active and therefore capable of promptly intervening in reality. Conscience and attitudes refer to the internal and the external aspect, respectively, of the mode of being of the person. "Faith is expressed in a certain 'attitude.' . . . The essence of faith consists of more than a purely intellectual assent to the truth revealed by God, or a kind of reflection of that truth in man's consciousness. 'Self-abandonment to God' as a response to revelation bears witness also to the fact that faith expresses itself through man's attitude."[53] In a decisive way the subject existentially realizes faith in himself in the formation of attitudes.

In the ongoing postconciliar discussion in Italy, the deepening of the theme of the formation of attitudes was delayed because of the emphasis given to the problem of "cultural mediation," understood as the correct analysis which allows one to pass from the theoretical enunciation to the practical judgment. To be sure, this topic has its importance, but it runs the risk of obscuring the fundamental fact that the passage to the practical judgment is effected by "mediation" more by way of existential attitudes than particular analyses. It also ignores the fact that the task of the Church is not so much to provide analysis of social reality as to form the Christian mentality and the existential attitude which support and motivate any analysis.

53. Ibid., p. 204.

The attitudes in which the faith expresses itself give to it a historical consistency and prevent faith from becoming merely an intellectual exercise, even if, in the totality of the person, the attitudes are concerned with intelligence. The attitude ". . . follows upon cognition and enriched awareness, but is something new and different from these. It involves 'taking up a position' and being ready to act in accordance with it. . . . We have to do with the human expression of the enrichment of faith, as we know from revelation and experience." [54]

The first attitude by which the faith expresses itself is that of mission and witness. It manifests itself in *"accepting God's witness to himself and responding to it with one's own."* [55] Mission is, indeed, simply the communication to others of one's own existential encounter with the Truth. This presupposes that the offer of such an encounter which God continuously makes has been welcomed and has become the basic content of existence. This communication is made believable by the changed life of the one who affirms it. It consists in a change which affects the most diverse and visible aspects of existence. Christian mission reflects a strong disposition to stand out against the dominant mentality, to let oneself be recognized in one's own Christian singularity. While sharing the culture of one's people and its reasonable aspirations, one resists the temptation to camouflage oneself in common opinion.

The fundamental attitude of the Christian, which is that of mission and of witness as existential expressions of the faith, realizes itself in a series of particular attitudes, refractions, and concretizations of mission and witness. Wojtyła analyzes in particular four of these attitudes: participation; human identity and Christian responsibility; the ecumenical attitude; and the apostolic attitude. We will consider each of these in turn.

1. *The attitude of participation* arises from the emergence in the conscience of one's belonging to Christ. By virtue of this belonging, the Christian takes part in Christ's task in the world together with his primacies over the world. The Christian witness unfolds itself therefore in participation in the threefold office of Christ: *priestly, prophetic, and royal.*

The *priestly* dimension expresses itself in the complete abandonment of one's own life to God, in which the interiorization of the fundamental law of existing as a person is fully realized: "if man is the only creature on earth that God has wanted for its own sake, man can fully discover his true

54. Ibid., p. 205.
55. Ibid., p. 208.

self only in a sincere giving of self."[56] Although the care of people of God is entrusted to those in the ministerial priesthood in a special way, it still lies at the heart of the vocation of all Christians. Only on its basis can the task of the "layperson" to recognize the value of worldly realities and to promote their development unfold. Wojtyła underlines the decisive importance of the sacraments and liturgy for the development of this attitude. In the history of the Church, beginning with St. Augustine, the anti-Donatist polemic has led to a dominant emphasis on the efficacy of the sacrament as such, independently of the subjective behavior of the one who administers it. If this is true objectively, then from the subjective point of view, that is, from the point of view of the formation of the right liturgical attitude, the *opus operantis* has a great importance, for it has the capacity of transforming the objectivity of the sacrament into conscience and growth of the conscience. This is the fundamental concern of the liturgical reform desired by the Council.

Acknowledgment of the truth involves responsibility, and this responsibility expresses itself in the *prophetic* dimension of mission. Indeed, in prophecy the known truth enlightens behavior and choices. In such a way, prophecy is the sure affirmation of Christian hope and expresses, so to speak, a certainty in that hope and in its capacity to enlighten the concrete choices of human beings in the world.

Thus the Council exhorts Christians not to hide this hope "in the depths of their hearts, but rather express it through the structure of their secular lives in continual conversion and in wrestling 'against the world rulers of this darkness, against the spiritual forces of iniquity' (Eph. 6:12). *The laity become powerful heralds of the faith in things to be hoped for (cf. Heb. 11:1) if they join unhesitating profession of faith to the life of faith.*"[57]

Prophecy shows how faith enlightens the human condition. This requires a particular and continual attention to the relationship between philosophy (understood as man's attempt to understand his own nature, his own destiny and position in the world) and theology. Prophecy finds its place in the responsibility to the truth which is proper to every man and to all mankind. The Council warns against a direct relationship between theology and the human sciences which would avoid philosophical mediation. "Careful attention should be paid to the bearing of philosophy on the real problems of life, as well as to the questions which engage the minds of the students. The students

---

56. *Pastoral Constitution on the Church in the Modern World (Gaudium et Spes)*, 24.
57. *Dogmatic Constitution on the Church (Lumen Gentium)*, 35.

themselves should be helped to perceive the connection between philosophical arguments and the mysteries of salvation which theology considers in the higher light of faith."[58] Moreover, "the Christian outlook should acquire, as it were, a public, stable and universal influence in the whole process of the promotion of higher culture. The graduates of these institutes should be outstanding in learning, ready to undertake the more responsible duties of society, and to be witnesses in the world to the true faith, in other words, to be mature participants of the *munus propheticum*, the prophetic function."[59]

Prophecy also exercises itself, of course, in relation to history, with its urgent desire for justice and for increasingly human conditions of life. It does not focus one-sidedly on the future, but first of all on the truth about man which is even now available to experience, no matter how much the present historical epoch is fraught with contradictions. This truth gives rise to the judgment on the social evils which must be fought and to the choice of the human way to fight them.

The *royal* office of Christ, finally, consists in reunifying all things under his own power in such a way as to render them fully themselves, conformed to the original plan of creation. Man realizes his participation in such royalty first of all on the moral level, by living fully the value of his own person and, therefore, mastering tendencies that would prevent him from realizing the most essential value through a free gift of himself. Christ is the only king for whom to serve is to reign. By submitting to the truth and by transcending himself in face of truth man indeed finds himself and at the same time makes himself capable of mastering the earth by governing temporal realities according to a just order of values.

The moral aspect of the *munus regale*, the royal function, is prior to and also determines the subsequent aspect, which consists in *"mastering the earth."* He who is not able to master himself in justice cannot master the earth. Accordingly, material progress is subordinated to moral progress. Only by this subordination, which seems to correspond to that which St. Augustine sets between *scientia* and *sapientia*, science and wisdom, can one speak in general of human progress. This despite those who uncritically borrow the notion of progress from naive evolutionism and end up considering any advance in technology and in social organization, apart from responsibility to the essential human values, as unconditionally positive. In any case the consciousness of belonging to Christ and the experience of

58. *Decree on the Training of Priests (Optatam Totius)*, 15.
59. *Declaration on Christian Education (Gravissimum Educationis)*, 10.

him as the renewed measure of the human becomes, for Christians, the criterion by which to relate to temporal realities with respect to their proper structures and, in fact, to enhance their respect for such structures. The faithful must remember that *"in every temporal affair they are to be guided by a Christian conscience."*[60]

This understanding of the royal office of Christ and of the Christian affords a more enlightened assessment of contemporary atheism. For in its most secret origin, it arises from a way of understanding the royalty of man which denies dependence on anything, as unworthy of him.

> Those who profess this kind of atheism maintain that freedom consists in this, that man is an end to himself, and the sole maker, with supreme control, of his own history. They claim that this outlook cannot be reconciled with the assertion of a Lord who is author and end of all things, or that at least it makes such an affirmation altogether unnecessary. The sense of power which modern technical progress begets in man may encourage this outlook.[61]

The reference to the Marxist conviction that man through his praxis transforms reality and also himself, and in so doing converts himself finally into his own creator, is manifest here. Such a position fails to acknowledge, even materially, the finite character of the mastery of nature which technological progress can give to man. At a distance of hardly twenty years from the naive progressive optimism which dominated the sixties, we live in a cultural atmosphere which is already totally different — conscious of the limits of development, of the fact that nonrenewable resources of the earth are close to exhaustion, and that not everything in nature is submitted to our mastery, less still our own life.

From another point of view, one can observe that what escapes atheism is the fact that man is not his own master. His personal intimacy, the fundamental structure of his being a person, and the ethical requirements which follow from it, cannot be conditioned and manipulated beyond very strict limits. There is in this a decisive limit to the Marxist idea that by transforming nature man transforms himself; it fails to recognize that it is not only transformed nature which conditions man but that the very act of working and transforming nature also influence the subject who accomplishes it, making them ethically better or worse, more truly or less fully human.

60. *Dogmatic Constitution on the Church (Lumen Gentium)*, 36.
61. *Pastoral Constitution on the Church in the Modern World (Gaudium et Spes)*, 20.

The Council says here: "When he works, not only does he transform matter and society, but he fulfills himself. He learns, he develops his faculties, and he emerges from and transcends himself. Rightly understood this kind of growth is more precious than any kind of wealth that can be amassed. It is what a man is, rather than what he has, that counts."[62] By ignoring the right relationship between moral *self-mastery* (linked to the self-transcending of the person toward God and the acknowledgment of truth) and mastery of nature, atheism is doomed to see its humanist intentions overturned wherever it is realized in practice.

2. The attitude to human identity consists in the effort to attend fully to one's own humanity, to take seriously the fundamental human aspirations in oneself and in others and always to start honestly from them. Only in such a way can one verify how the affirmation that Christ entirely redeemed the human in man is true. Moreover, human and Christian identity always determines itself in time and space. One is always human in a place, in a determinate nation, and in a determinate moment of history. The Christian attitude to humanity implies the acceptance of being a man of one's own time, in solidarity with other people who live in the same historical conditions. This implies the courage also fully to assume the condition of contemporary man even with its contradictions, which the Council acutely described:

> A transformation of this kind brings with it the serious problems associated with any crisis of growth. Increase in power is not always accompanied by control of that power for the benefit of man. In probing the recesses of his own mind man often seems ever more uncertain of himself: in the gradual and precise unfolding of the laws of social living, he is perplexed by uncertainty about how to plot its course. . . . Small wonder then that many of our contemporaries are prevented by this complex situation from recognizing permanent values and duly applying them to recent discoveries. As a result they hover between hope and anxiety and wonder uneasily about the present course of events. It is a situation that challenges men to respond; they cannot escape.[63]

The fact that the Christian shares the situation of his own time does not entail erasing his own certainties in order to participate in the universal confusion, but rather putting lucidly, in the light of faith, the human

---

62. Ibid., 35.
63. Ibid., 4.

problem of our time. This could be epitomized in the desire and necessity to use the immensely increased power over nature which science and technology render available in order to realize a more humanly worthy life for individuals as well as to forge a community of life in actual solidarity within a given society and among different human societies. The awareness of creation and redemption allows the Christian to acknowledge how these aspirations can be satisfied only by recognizing the primacy of moral values and how the full answer to these questions lies in lived Christian communion. The quest of the individual who seeks his own liberation can be accomplished only in the acknowledgment of the objective value which is the Truth itself.

"Right conscience and the objective moral order correspond to each other and together constitute the dignity of man."[64] Where the ability to master nature makes man lose the capacity for recognizing the moral order and leads him to regard it as a fetter to his freedom rather than as a means to his own realization, the search for community and for dignity will never be successful. Even the capacity for understanding the reality with which one will be able to engage depends on the way in which one poses this fundamental problem. In the first case "the analysis of social reality . . . is not only 'sociological' but 'evangelical', in terms of the categories of that truth concerning man which we derive from the unique source in the Gospel. However, the Christian vision of the truth concerning man, who is called on to live and to work in society, does not lose sight of socioeconomic conditions."[65] The first level of analysis precedes the second and also in a certain sense follows it; in any case, it integrates it in itself. In this way the Christian assumes responsibility for the world and in particular for just conduct of the great process of economic, social, and cultural transformation which characterizes our epoch.

This call to responsibility corresponds to the intimate nature of man in virtue of his intelligence and freedom. The attitude of human identity implies that the Christian cannot seek his own salvation apart from the salvation of all other men, he must not retire from the world and condemn it. He has a duty to feel responsible for the world, so the dignity of the person may be realized in it. The idea of responsibility should be immediately connected to the idea of freedom. In order to be responsible for his own acts man needs first of all to accomplish them in full freedom. Re-

---

64. *Sources of Renewal,* p. 281.
65. Ibid., p. 288.

sponsibility postulates freedom. On the other hand, the principle of responsibility excludes a Promethean and atheistic view of freedom which implies not having to account to anyone for one's own choices and actions. With this important clarification, the choice of the Council for freedom is clear and unequivocal:

> The Council emphasizes that the attitude of responsibility is conditioned by the "integral freedom" of man in society, while experience constantly teaches us that internal and external liberty is essential for the development of a responsible attitude. But we must also note that only mature responsibility conditions freedom of either kind. In other words, only the responsible man derives true profit from inner freedom. There is, moreover, no good reason to limit his external freedom; any such limitation is contrary to social morality and to the fundamental "economy of human values" which is both the purpose and the essential condition of the true development of society.[66]

It is necessary, then, to start by respecting freedom so that the fruit of responsibility can grow; this fruit in its turn deepens and qualifies freedom itself.

The development of the attitude of responsibility happens first of all in the family. Here man acquires that moral personality which makes him feel the need of the other, and leads him to take as his own the other's joy and pain; in the family he learns to live in an ethos, that is, in a spiritual dwelling which is always and undoubtedly both his own and others'. Therefore, in the interest of fostering the growth of an attitude of human responsibility, which gives real human content to freedom, the Church is concerned first of all about the family and reminds all men of its role in sustaining essential human values.

The second milieu in which the attitude of human responsibility is reflected and matures is culture. Here the ethos, learned in the family, opens up until it informs the entire nation and, eventually, all mankind. Modern culture knows many antinomies, but insofar as it is a culture, like every human culture it is intrinsically positive. Every culture, indeed, reflects the aspirations of a civilization, and these are always tied to some essential values: the good, the true, and the beautiful. Within every culture, then, an unceasing struggle for the defense of these values occurs against possible misunderstanding and corruption.

66. Ibid., p. 292.

When man gives himself to the various disciplines of philosophy, history, and mathematical and natural science, and when he cultivates the arts, he can do very much to elevate the human family to a more sublime understanding of truth, goodness, and beauty and to the formation of considered opinions which have universal values. Thus mankind may be more clearly enlightened by that marvellous Wisdom which was with God from all eternity, composing all things with him, rejoicing in the earth, delighting in the sons of men. In this way, the human spirit, being less subjected to material things, can be more easily drawn to the worship and contemplation of the Creator. Moreover, by the impulse of grace, he is disposed to acknowledge the Word of God.[67]

Christianity, then, while it does not coincide with any culture, can enter into alliance with the positive ferment of every culture while it simultaneously fights the corrosive elements of every culture, the negation of the true, of the beautiful, and of the good. In this way, while refusing the integralist identification of Christianity with a particular culture, the Council also resists the uncritical acceptance of every direction of thought and in particular those which accept atheism or which deny in any other way the attraction toward the true, the beautiful, and the good which are the main attributes by which the soul raises itself toward God. The attitude of responsibility implies a readiness to work on behalf of affirming and deepening the truth in the midst of the historical struggle of one's own culture.

The third field in which the attitude of Christian responsibility exercises itself is socio-economic life. Here the Council reasserts that "the fundamental finality of this production is not the mere increase of products nor profit or control but rather the service of man, and indeed the whole man."[68]

Economic activity produces the goods which serve life through the work of man. One must exercise one's own responsibility so that the goods produced be authentic, and above all so that the work which produces them be authentically human.

Human labor which is expended in the production and exchange of goods or in the performance of economic services is superior to the other elements of economic life, for the latter have only the nature of tools. This

67. *Pastoral Constitution on the Church in the Modern World (Gaudium et Spes)*, 57.
68. Ibid., 64.

labor ... comes immediately from the person who, as it were, stamps the things of nature with his seal and subdues them to his will. ... It happens too often ... that the workers are reduced to the level of being slaves of their own work. ... The entire process of productive work, therefore, must be adapted to the needs of the person and of his way of life.[69]

Work is part of that great system of communication and exchange of meanings (in strict relationship with the family) in which human life consists. While the Marxist analysis sees in the socioeconomic system an organization for the exchange of products, the Council invites us to see rather a system of exchange of meanings and values, which lie beneath the system of exchange of goods and of services and determine it at a deeper level. In a certain way it is from this analysis that the fundamental concern which Wojtyła approaches so rigorously in *The Acting Person* takes its start. His conception of the human act can indeed be considered the philosophical development of the view of work enunciated by the Council.

The attitude of responsibility should inform the sphere of politics, too: "In their patriotism and in their fidelity to their civic duties Catholics will feel themselves bound to promote the true common good; they will make the weight of their conviction so influential that as a result civil authority will be justly exercised and the laws will accord with the moral precepts and the common good."[70]

At this stage, the exercise of responsibility is ordered toward the most complete possible realization of the rights of the person insofar as they are understood by human reason and more clearly manifested in the Christian revelation. It excludes any political approach on the part of Catholics who would, for instance, promote a confessional cause such as privileges or special rights for the Church insofar as it is a worldly institution. But neither would it give legitimacy to those Christians in politics who would appeal to the latest fashionable ideology whenever it is a question of defining true progress or recognizing violations of human rights. In Wojtyła's view, the Council, far from discarding the Catholic social ethic, has modernized it and extended and deepened both the criteria and the sphere of its application.

The attitude of responsibility finds itself in its final important field when it takes up the problem of peace and the formation of an authentic

69. Ibid., 67.
70. *Decree on the Apostolate of the Laity (Apostolicam Actuositatem)*, 14.

225

moral unity among all men. The formation of an authentic culture of peace requires in part the adoption of nonviolent methods for the solution of international conflicts. It also demands an engagement against the scandal of hunger whereby some people lack the most basic necessities while others live in abundance. Both the Marxist and the bourgeois science of politics share the common conviction that violence is the midwife of history and that the ultimate foundation of every human community must be force. Our epoch imposes on us the difficult responsibility of giving an ethical foundation to the common life among individuals and among nations because, in the presence of the modern technology of mass destruction, the use of violence can lead to the extinction of human life on earth.

3. *The ecumenical attitude* is a particular modification of the attitude of human identity faced with religious problems and in a particular way with the problems regarding the unity of Christians. The Christian is indeed in solidarity with the religious quest of all mankind; not only does he not isolate himself with the presumption of having already discovered everything; he also makes of his own certainties secure guides for his own further research and for dialogue with others similarly engaged in the search for the truth about God and man. The ineliminable presupposition of such an attitude is the recognition of the freedom of the other, and therefore the greatest respect for religious freedom. "It is therefore fully in accordance with the nature of faith that in religious matters every form of coercion by men should be excluded."[71] Moreover, "the Church . . . faithful to the truth of the Gospel, is following in the path of Christ and the apostles when she recognizes the principle that religious liberty is in keeping with the dignity of man and divine revelation and gives it her support."[72]

Since we have already discussed this topic at length in the first part of this chapter, we can now take many elements for granted. With regard to ecumenical dialogue understood in a strict sense, that is, the relation that pertains among the diverse Christian confessions, it is only necessary to remark how it cannot be conceived as a transaction, a negotiation, or a compromise about the truth. There is an approach to ecumenical dialogue which wants to advance it through reciprocal concessions which, however comprehensible and fair in a disciplinary context, become unacceptable and absurd with regard to the substantive matter of faith. Indeed, the presupposition of every dialogue about truth is the common conviction

---

71. *Declaration on Religious Liberty (Dignitatis Humanae),* 10.
72. Ibid., 12.

that one does not dispose of the truth as though it were one's own property but that, on the contrary, one depends upon it. No matter how great the practical benefits of union among Christians, they do not legitimate behavior which judges a thing of little importance because it becomes a point of division, and orients itself toward the search for formulas of compromise rather than toward a more exact and full formulation of Christian doctrine. It is only by going with depth to the roots, to the fundamental reasons of their own presence in history and of their faith, that the Christian churches can discover what unifies beyond the divisions.

In the face of the multitude of doctrinal difficulties such a method may offer little cause for hope. It is nevertheless the only thing which continuously reminds Christians that the miracle of unity is a gift of the Spirit to be won by prayer, by reciprocal welcoming, and by continuous deepening of the reasons for one's own faith.

4. *The apostolic attitude* is the concretization of the responsibility for the truth insofar as it is lived by the Christian recognizing that it is through the presence of Christ in history and therefore through the Church that the truth can be encountered by men and incorporated in a full and adequate way into their lives. It represents, then, a responsibility for the presence of the Church in the world. This apostolic vocation is proper to the Christian as such, and it is only afterward that one can distinguish the particular ways in which the hierarchy and the laity live out such a responsibility. In any case, even such diverse modalities can be understood only in their reciprocal interaction. One is responsible in a general way as a Christian before being responsible in a particular way as a bishop, or as a religious, or as a layman.

"As regards *the relationship between the apostolate of the laity and that of the hierarchy,* and hence the apostolic attitude, it must be emphasized that *the two complement each other....* These diverse forms of the apostolate have *their unique origin in the Christian vocation* from which they derive and which they are aimed at finally realizing."[73]

We have already noted that this way of posing the problem is not — particularly as regards the apostolate of the laity — completely without consequences, even juridical and organizational ones. The apostolic attitude, if it belongs to the Christian vocation, shapes a specific duty and a specific right in the Church. This contrasts directly with the conceptions, rather widespread before the Council (and, to tell the truth, also afterward),

---

73. *Sources of Renewal,* pp. 333-34.

which tend to make the layperson a passive member of the Church or to maintain that the apostolate of the laity should unfold uniquely within the association of *Catholic Action,* which, in force of a specific mandate, participates in the apostolic mission of the bishop. Actually, the idea of a lay apostolate legitimated by a particular participation in the apostolate of the hierarchy was the way in which the apostolic vocation of the laity was given practical validation within an ecclesiology that generally did not grant the lay vocation its autonomy in the economy of the Church.

On this, the Council is very explicit: "The Church can never be without the lay apostolate; it is something that derives from the layperson's actual vocation as a Christian."[74] Moreover, "from the fact of their union with Christ the head flows the laymen's right and duty to be apostles. Inserted as they are in the Mystical Body of Christ *by baptism and strengthened by the power of the Holy Spirit in confirmation, it is by the Lord himself that they are assigned to the apostolate.*"[75] And finally, "From the reception of these charisms, even the most ordinary ones, *there arises for each of the faithful the right and duty of exercising them in the Church and in the world* for the good of men and the development of the Church."[76]

The apostolate of the laity manifests itself in a particular way in ordering temporal realities around the fundamental value of the human person and in showing in such a way how the faith is the legitimate fulfillment of the human. While the Council does not stop to reassert the autonomy of temporal realities, it confirms that they are, spontaneously and according to nature, in full continuity with sacred realities if they are rightly understood. The specific task of the layperson is precisely that of working for this right understanding. In such a way, temporal realities and sacred realities, distinct from an objective point of view, find their unity in the person who lives them with identical conscience and within the same fundamental attitudes. Moreover, the Council observes:

> The laity, carrying out this mission of the Church, exercise their apostolate therefore in the world as well as in the Church, in the temporal order as well as in the spiritual. These orders are distinct; they are nevertheless so closely linked that God's plan is, in Christ, to take the whole world up again and make of it a new creation, in an initial way here on earth, in

74. *Decree on the Apostolate of the Laity (Apostolicam Actuositatem),* 1.
75. Ibid., 3.
76. Ibid.

full realization at the end of time. The layman, at one and the same time a believer and a citizen of the world, has only a single conscience, a Christian conscience; it is by this that he must be guided continually in both domains.[77]

The exercise of an apostolate through which the Church brings its proper characteristics and qualifying contributions to the temporal sphere without engaging the Church as such in the solution of the contingent social and political questions remains a problematic task. In the certainty with which Wojtyła makes the argument — so controverted in the West — we hear an obvious echo of the historical experience of a Church which has never hesitated to intervene in all the decisive questions of the life of the nation in the name of the kingship of Christ. Yet in this engagement the Church does not exercise power, but clearly and precisely indicates, in contrast to prevailing opinions of the world, the rights of the person, and the fundamental values which give meaning to the life of the nation. As a condition for the realization of such an attitude, Catholics, especially in the West, must disabuse themselves of a cultural inferiority complex that leads them to believe that worldly ideologies provide the truth about man and the rule for behavior in temporal affairs.

Instead, in the position recalled by Wojtyła and expressed by the Council, the central fact of the apostolate of laypeople which arises from the very presence of the Christian in the world — since the Christian vocation is by its nature apostolic — is based essentially on the coherence between life and faith. This fundamental condition marks the very personality of every Christian and not only of the layman. This coherence demands a visible presence which not only helps to realize the fundamental values of the person, but also is clearly penetrated by a spirit of Christian witness:

> It is not sufficient for the Christian people to be present or established in a particular nation, nor sufficient that it should merely exercise the apostolate of good example; it has been established and it is present so that it might by word and deed proclaim Christ to non-Christian fellow countrymen and help them towards a full reception of Christ.[78]

All this can happen only through the ceaseless work of forming an integral mind-set and a global apostolic style of life. Here Wojtyła endorses

---

77. Ibid., 5.
78. *Decree on the Church's Missionary Activity (Ad Gentes)*, 15.

the direction given by Msgr. Cardijn to the *Jeunesse Ouvrière Chrétienne* and the fact that "training for the apostolate must form the whole Christian personality."[79] This requirement of integrality and globality penetrates all that we have discussed concerning diverse attitudes. The ideal Christian is one who continually lives the way of Christ and so reacts to any situation of life in the full light of faith.

The discourse about attitudes is, then, a new way to propose again the ancient discourse on the Christian virtues which are also a habitus, that is, a concept that we might now reasonably translate as an ensemble of attitudes.

The fact the Wojtyła chose as his methodological point of view the self-realization of the Church through the formation of attitudes explains the absence of some themes which have characterized the postconciliar discussion. One of them is the topic of "cultural mediation." It is not difficult to understand the reason. The issue of "cultural mediation" belongs to a class of problems that is objectivistic in its concern; it asks a question such as: "Is Thomistic philosophy still adapted to the spiritual conditions and the cultural problems of the modern world?" Wojtyła does not at all underestimate the importance of such problems; on the contrary, as we have seen, he devotes himself to their solution and in fact has provided constructive and creative work toward a new cultural mediation. However, when it comes to the task of realizing the Council, the solution of such a problem is not fundamentally methodological or pastoral. It is necessary to achieve cultural mediation in concrete attitudes and actions rather than in the discourse on the theme of cultural mediation. When we see the priority of Wojtyła's starting point we realize that an attitude of cultural mediation does not exist. Rigorously speaking, cultural mediation is inserted into the framework of responsibility toward culture, which is in itself creative and which comprehends in itself the moment of mediation as one of the conditions and forms of creativity.

However, the basic task is the formation of the subjective attitudes which flow from the Christian way of thinking. The right attitude in the face of events is to subsume them within the mentality which is formed by the faith rather than putting them on hold, so to speak, while waiting to proceed to the right cultural mediation of the stimuli coming from them. The authentic cultural mediation is always a complex process in which the spontaneous sensibility of the community takes precedence over the anal-

79. *Sources of Renewal,* p. 362.

ysis of the professional intellectual. In other words, the intuitions of the saints and of the artists which shape emotional material with their human attitude provide the professional philosopher or intellectual with insights which they then subject to a rational synthesis.

The Council's aim is the construction of the Christian community, that is, the adequate interiorization of the faith through the freedom and the conscience of man and through a modification of his affective attitudes toward the Church and the world. This conversion of the intelligence and of the will transforms the baptized person from a passive, and in a certain sense inert, member of the Church into an active, responsible, and adult participant. This is the pastoral aim of the Council: it indicates the way in which being a believer today is possible by proposing to all men that salvation for which the world is more than ever in search through the witness of personal faith conjoined to the witness of one's own life.

It is worth recalling, in conclusion, how in the organization of the conciliar material Wojtyła took aim at the problem of the *formation of the conscience* and that of the formation of attitudes which are the active projection of the conscience. The reflection of *The Acting Person* on these themes, which derives from participation in the Council, is likewise mirrored in the organization of the book on the Council, and gives philosophical method and depth to this eminently theological effort.

7. The Poetry of Karol Wojtyła

Wojtyła began his philosophical journey within the pages of literature. It was only later that he came to academic philosophy per se. But his love for literature, which he has carried with him throughout his life and which is a distinctive trait of his personality, has from the outset taken the form of a search for the truth of man. If one sees philosophy and literature as intermingled, that might legitimate a philosophical reading of the poetic works, such as we are equipped to offer. Moreover, as Krzysztof Dybciak has noted in his essay about Karol Wojtyła, the cross-fertilization of literature and philosophy has always been a part of the great tradition of Polish culture.[1] Mickiewicz, Słowacki, Krasinski, and Norwid have not only built beautiful castles of words; they have always tried to express universal truths and to direct us toward them through their poetic creations. Polish philosophers, moreover, typically engaged in the practice of literature or at least of literary or artistic criticism: they have done so from Znaniecki to Witkacy and from Kotarbinski to Kolakowski and Ingarden himself. Within the Polish tradition, the work of art is understood as giving form to the ethos of the nation; and it is by virtue of that ethos that universal value is concretized and made affectively available within it. But literature also represents a rediscovery of the values of the experience of life, following upon the failure of the totalizing systems which had presumed to demonstrate such values.

---

1. Cf. Krzystof Dybciak, *La grande testimonianza* (Bologna: CSEO, 1981). The essay about Wojtyła is "Penso . . . ci· che sento col cuore. Sull'opera letteraria di Karol Wojtyła," pp. 167-86. See especially p. 167.

This particular role of literature in developing a realistic philosophy can be explained from the ineliminable necessity which philosophy has of beginning from experience in order to grasp universal categories. But poetry is the most general and supraindividual form in which the experience of a nation, or of a generation, is expressed.[2] It has an irreplaceable role in elaborating an ethos through which man's nature is brought near fundamental moral truths. This particular cultural function of poetry is made very evident in Wojtyła's work. Of course, Wojtyła clearly distinguishes the task of philosophy from that of poetry, and he loves the techniques of both disciplines. Philosophy contains its own criterion of truth, as does literature. Nonetheless, one could readily show that, from the point of view of their contents, Wojtyła's poetical reflections always accompany philosophic reflection and, on some decisive points, precede it. It is noteworthy, for example, that *Love and Responsibility* was published in the same year as *The Jeweller's Shop*. The latter is a poetic reflection on the identical problem discussed in the former — so much so that the interpretation of the philosophical text is enriched if one reads it alongside the poetic text.[3] Likewise, the fundamental intuition of *The Acting Person* about the personalistic evaluation of action is in some ways anticipated in "The Quarry," a lyric poem which appeared in 1957.[4]

Before going to some of Wojtyła's principal poems, it is important that we sketch the history of Polish poetry in this century. It is against this backdrop that the philosophical significance of his literary work will become evident.

Some Notes on Twentieth-Century Polish Poetry

In this century Polish literature presents a panorama of particular complexity, in which it is not easy to find one's way. For many historical reasons,

2. It is perhaps not outside our scope to note that Plato repeatedly returns in his arguments to the witness of poetry and that art has a similar function in the theories of the German Romantics, particularly in the writings of Schelling and Hölderlin.

3. Both of these works appeared in 1960. "Przed sklepem jubilera. Medytacja o Sakramencie Małżeństwa przechodzaca chwilami w dramat," under the name of Andrez Jawień, in *Znak* 12, pp. 1564-607. The English translation of Wojtyła's poems used in this chapter is Karol Wojtyła, *Collected Poems,* trans. Jerzy Peterkiewicz (London: Hutchinson, 1982).

4. Under the name of Andrej Jawień, "Kamienołom," in *Znak* 9, pp. 559-63; "The Quarry," in *Collected Poems.*

Poland is a sort of crucible or melting pot, the place in which the many different literary tendencies of continental Europe flow together.

One might observe, first of all, that there is a Polish literature which has defended throughout the times of partition its own originality, organizing its defense around the three great poets Mickiewicz, Słowacki and Krasinski. On the other hand, the spiritual history of Poland is still an integral part of that culture of Central Europe which marks the first, decisive appraisal of the conscience of European civilization, and which is still unmatched in radicality. Cracow is, alongside Prague and Vienna, one of the cultural capitals of Central Europe, and participated in the culture of the Austro-Hungarian Empire in the period of its decadence. The study of logic undertaken by the Vienna Circle found an immediate echo in the work of the Warsaw school of logic, just as the linguistic reflections of the Prague circle were promptly echoed among the avant-garde in Cracow.

Part of the territory of Poland is drawn into the sphere of influence of its shared German language, while another part is attracted by Russian culture. Poland is therefore a privileged place for a dialogue between the cultural universe of Central Europe and the different avant-gardes which influence Russian culture, a fact which has special importance in the field of research and of literary criticism. And at the eastern borders of Poland especially occurs an extraordinary cross-section of nationalities; it is impossible to draw neat lines around the different national identities. Many of the greatest Polish poets were born on the fluid borders where Poles are mixed with Lithuanians, and with Ukrainians; they carry in their imagination the traces of this contact with the great agrarian cultures and with profound values which, though known almost chthonically, are not lacking in expressions of great refinement. Finally, before the Nazi holocaust, there existed a great and unique Jewish-Polish culture, which enjoyed an intimate (and insufficiently explored) relationship with the other elements occupying this cultural space between the Tatra mountain and the Baltic Sea, and which stretches into Kiev.

Between the two World Wars, Polish literature, like other Central European literatures, underwent the harsh experience of the dissolution of values — a deep crisis of the presence of man to himself and of the meaning and value of life.[5] Politically, this feeling was tied up with the dissolution

---

5. Some Italian commentators have spoken in a journalistic way of Wojtyła's culture as being primarily a culture in crisis. If one reflects on the way in which Central European culture has, for example in the work of Massimo Cacciari, become an unparalleled

of the Austro-Hungarian monarchy and of the Romanov dynasty. In philosophy, the same state of mind was connected with the crisis of metaphysics and the ascendancy of atheism. With the great exception of Lukacs, in Central Europe the optimistic historicism of Hegel and Marx had never spread, and the replacement of the ancient personal God with a totalizing positive history which realizes truth and good in its own immanent processes had not been fully achieved. The experience of sadness and oppression was too profound, and the memory of heroism and of justice to which history denied any acknowledgment too great for such historical optimism to be able to prevail. Rather, Central European culture (at least in its Polish variant) remained unharmonic, devoted to the destiny of the individual, to which it is difficult for great social forces to do justice. It is possible to draw a line which leads directly from Leibniz and Kant to Wittgenstein's neo-positivism, which was introduced into Poland and developed by Adjukiewicz. The development of the scientific way of thinking destroyed the old philosophy but did not replace it with historicist illusions. People become inured to a cold and meaningless life. Human individuality seems to be threatened. The individual builds himself by making a personal shape out of the great natural and social forces which enter into his constitution. But today all of these energies are planned by the great power mechanisms which seize hold of the individual and ultimately dissolve him, by denying the possibility that he can be created by choosing a personal project in which his freedom is realized.

Witold Gombrowicz's work is particularly imbued with the awareness of this situation, and he was doubtless one of the great masters of the literature of crisis.[6] Such feelings agitated the so-called avant-garde of Vilnius, who reacted against the historic optimism and the linguistic experimentalism of the Cracow circle. From within Vilnius's avant-garde, Czeslaw Milosz's personal journey is exemplary. In his early work Milosz explored the crumbling of certitudes and the loss of the feeling of stability in a world which is facing the terrible and definitive crisis of war. Out of the suffering of the war, however, new certainties were born. In *Swiat-poema*

---

symbolic expression of the crisis of European man, culminating in the dissolution of the individual person, one will not be content with such superficialities.

6. It has been well said by Konstanty Andrej Jeleński, who is probably the greatest of his critics, and an atheist to boot: "Gombrowicz's work contains the reckoning that contemporary thought begins to say: the 'death of man' follows on the 'death of God.'" See his "Dramat i anty-drama," in *Cultura* 9 (1969).

naiwne the naive feeling of essential values which make man human and the world his world, returns. These are values which manifest themselves with indubitable certainty in the experience of those who do not abdicate their own humanity. These, in a certain sense, assert themselves most persuasively in boundary situations. In *Piesn*, the chorus hymns the earth and, with it, the force which stands over against the individual and sweeps it away in the perennial becoming of things and of history. The poem announces the fundamental dogma of earthliness:

> All joy comes from the earth,
>   there is no delight without her,
> man is given to the earth,
>   let him desire no other.
> To which the Woman responds
>   You God, have mercy on me,
> From the earth's greedy mouth deliver me.
>   cleanse me of her untrue songs.

When he is put through the mill of history, man rediscovers the values of his existence and the irrepressible questions of justice and truth which dwell in him. These carry the affirmation that the true and great drama in history and in art is that which develops the consciousness of every man. It is here that the most basic cells and the life of the world lie. Milosz says: "The mystery of love in relationship with man does not consist in belittling oneself, but in the powerful growth of one's own personality, and in the art of discovering in every passer-by an encounter with an equally important personality, but at the same time one who is diverse because he is given his own task, which extends itself toward eternity, and because he is given a path made of trials reserved to him alone."[7]

From one side, therefore, Polish literature experiences the loss of the ontological consistency of existence and the diminution of the depth of being; one is reduced to superficiality and to play acting by the rupture of the classical chain of being. In addition to Gombrowicz, one could mention

---

7. The poem is translated as "The Song," in Czeslaw Milosz: *The Collected Poems* (1931-1987), various translators (London: Penguin Books, 1988). The prose citation is: C. Milosz, "Zejście na ziemje," in *Pion* 1 (1938). It is difficult not to think of the close analogy with Wojtyła's work, which describes all of the grand adventures of the common man (love, work, paternity, and death) and of the tests through which he must pass in order to realize his destiny.

Lesmian and Iwaszkiewicz, who was a satanist. On the other side, where values are no longer guaranteed by a logical a priori metaphysical construction, they were represented as an evidence which did not require any further justification through the eyes of poetic meditation. We have seen the results of this in the works of Milosz; but perhaps it is another poet, a pupil and friend of Milosz, in whose works this rupture is shown most fully. This was Zbigniew Herbert. It is hard to imagine that Herbert could have influenced Wojtyła as much as the great masters of the previous generation who have been already named, since he and Wojtyła were more or less contemporaries. Nonetheless, the parallels between their two poetic contributions is much more significant; it indicates a spiritual atmosphere which relates to all of the more lively elements of Polish culture.

After traditional values have been exhausted, Herbert's point of departure must be the autonomous manifestation of value within experience. Living is listening to life, and therefore being able to hear the emergence of what is valuable in it. It is through fidelity to the perception of value, that is, to the encounters which constitute existence, that man comes to self-awareness and discovers his own dignity. But fidelity to human authenticity asks a very high price of man: that is, his own life. Herbert deprecates every metaphysical or otherwise totalizing system, which pretends to possess the truth.

But he also refuses any concessions to nihilism or to the conviction that reality is absurd and senseless. Herbert values a particular idea containing wisdom, an individual conviction containing truth, a singular virtue which serves the good, but he opposes as utopian the rationalistic and totalitarian vision in which the good of a man is deemed less important than the well-being of the system, in which the ambition to know suffocates or falsifies existential experience, or links it to a prioristic schemes.[8]

The fragmentation of truth offers man two options — either to withdraw from life or to conceive of it as a struggle for the affirmation of truth in which one can at every step lose one's life.[9] Power continually blackmails man to betray truth, and the price of fidelity can be life itself. But that to which one feels unable to deny a fidelity which transcends this life must be

---

8. Dybciak, *La grande testimonianza*, pp. 222-23.

9. To begin with, there is a concentration on single objects and single values, because the meaning of being in general is disintegrating in the crisis of our times. This fragmentation entails that the sense of being is always incomplete, and can only be regained through the different sensibilities of different traditions.

more than an illusion; this ideal must have its own specific form of reality, higher than that to which one's senses testify. Life is a journey which leads from the human to the divine and which travels not through things but through the values which are manifested in human experience and which, above all, pass through the human heart. For this, ". . . we see a reciprocal compenetration: human things take on a seriousness and an importance which reproduces and transforms the divine dramas, and gods are reanimated and become akin to human beings when they reveal personal traits and come into touch with earthly beings."

Christ is the God who, in order to save mankind, has renounced all of the attributes of power, of perfection, and of happiness. He is the object of reflection of much of Herbert's poetry, becoming the "protagonist" not only in the poetic sense typically conferred on this word.[10] There are many analogies here with Wojtyła's reading of sacred history as a "type" and criterion of the interpretation of the history of every human being.

Faithfulness to value is ultimately carried to the encounter with the terrain upon which all values are germinated and to the divine atmosphere which propagates them. There is nostalgia for the God who it is not possible to touch but who nourishes — with his absence or otherness — all experience of truth in the world:

Only in a great silence
can one feel
the pulse of your existence
incessant and evanescent
like a wave of light.
Luring
as all which is not it
renders you homage
touching the body
of your absence.[11]

The approach to Deity is conditioned not by the recognition of a rational order of the world but, on the contrary, by the discovery of ir-

10. Dybciak, *La grande testimonianza*, p. 227.
11. Cited in Dybciak. This naturally recalls Milosz, Hölderlin, and Heidegger. In a world empty of hope and indwelt by absence, the *memory* of their presence is the only thing which allows one to distinguish good from evil. This is a line of thinking little different from that found in the writings of Horkheimer and Adorno.

rationality and evil. This should not be taken literally: the poet discovers a universe of values which have their own coherence and rationality, but this is deeply concealed under the surface of historical events; in every case, it remains entrusted to a fulfillment which art alone is unable to obtain. In a certain way, such poetry reflects a religious vision following upon the failure of Hegelianism and of Marxism, taking Schopenhauer as a point of departure. In Poland between the two Wars, a similar philosophy was consistently elaborated by Marian Zdziechowski, who exerted a great influence on the young poets of the time.[12]

This poetic discovery of value in experience perhaps helps us to understand why a young philosopher like Wojtyła with a strong passion for literature had an immediate feeling for Scheler's philosophy of values. From another side, this literary pre-understanding provokes a particular series of questions to a rediscovered Thomism after the great crises of Central Europe.

Being, the point of departure of philosophy, can no longer be thought of as something in general but must be understood as an original experience in which value is given along with the thing. Only in this way is it possible to construct a philosophical knowledge which rises above the confines of an understanding of pure objects and which recovers the field of knowledge proper to philosophy, combining both the mind of poetry and the mind of science. Contemporary Polish poetry was able to indicate the possibility, after the crisis of traditional and of immanentist metaphysics, of starting afresh on the journey of philosophy from the particular experience of value which is enclosed in the encounter of one person with another — typified by Plato in the *Symposium* as that encounter with Socrates which has in some way remained the basis of Western philosophy. If one begins from this firm recovery of the original experience of being, manifested in encounters, it is possible to reread the traditional metaphysics of being in a way which recovers it and regains and partly transvalues its original meaning.

12. Cf. also the work of Henryk Dembinski, similarly aware of the seriousness of the crisis but closer to French Catholic thinking, especially to that of Mounier. Dembinski collaborated on *Zagary*, the journal of the Vilnius Avantguard, and after many years wrote an essay about C. Milosz, who also belonged to the Vilnius group.

The Water and the Land

The metaphor which recurs most often in Wojtyła's poetry is that of the mirror — the reflection of an image in water, in glass, and also in human eyes. We come on this metaphor in one of the first of his poems, the *Song of the Brightness of Water:*

> Look now into the silver scales in the water
> where the depth trembles
> like the retina of an eye recording an image. . . .[13]

The water mentioned here is that in the well at Sychar (John 4:5). According to the traditional interpretation of the Fathers, this water is a symbol of grace; this is, indeed, how Krzystof Dybciak interprets Wojtyła's metaphor.[14] This interpretation is sound, but perhaps partial. It seems that, for Wojtyła, grace operates through a particular deepening of conscience which brings about an authentic awareness of truth. After the analysis of consciousness which we have given, following the theses of *The Acting Person,* the idea of consciousness as a field in which reality is reflected, and, through that reflection, properly experienced and given subjective meaning, should be familiar to us. Without denying, then, that water is a traditional symbol of grace, one may add that grace operates through a specific deepening of consciousness (or conscience).

Grace and conscience oppose themselves to the pure facticity of things, to their chthonic, indistinct, non-subjectivized way of being. In all of the Slavic tradition the symbol of this primordial force of nature is the earth. It becomes a symbol of irrepressible pagan vitality in Dostoievski's writings; in the Polish tradition it inspires a revolt against Gombrowicz's "form." In *Pandora,* and perhaps in Wierzynski's *Grzmi,* this identification of the poet with the telluric forces attains maximum intensity. In any case it is the same Wierzynski who initiates the transformation of the symbol of the earth, perhaps taking up the allusions of the Polish tradition of the preceding century. Thus in *Ogrodnicy* Wierzynski identifies culture as the earth which

---

13. A. Jawień, "Pieśń o blasku wody," in *Tygodnik Powszechny* 6 (1950); English trans. in Wojtyła, *Collected Poems:* Song of the Brightness of Water: "Looking into the Well at Sichar" (p. 50). A. Jawień was the first pseudonym used by Wojtyła in his literary writings; it is borrowed from a popular Polish work, *Cielo nelle fiamme* by Jan Parandowski. The other pseudonyms taken by Wojtyła were Stanisław Andrej Gruda and Piotr Jasień.

14. Dybciak, *La grande testimonianza,* p. 172.

fructifies with intelligent fecundity for the sake of human life and thus responds to the loving care of man. The symbol of earth is also present in Wojtyła. We find it in "Thinking My Country":

> To you earth, we are descending to increase your measure in all men, earth of our defeats and of our victories; in all hearts you rise as the paschal mystery.

> Earth you will always be part of our time. Across this time, learning new hope, we move towards a new earth.

> And we raise you, earth of old, as the fruit of the love of generations that outgrew hate.[15]

The chthonic forces which bind the successive generations together are presented in the perspective of their transfiguration, in their journey towards an Easter in which love gives a perfect form to the earth, in which all the vital forces are expressed without malfeasance.

In the collection entitled *Easter Vigil, 1966,* the symbol of the earth is closely bound up with that of the tree. The tree spreads its roots in the earth, but its head stretches toward the sky; the roots which are nourished by the earth also assimilate and transform it. The home country is identified with language and culture; it is through these features that the earth is humanized and takes on a subjective meaning. At the roots of culture, at its historical beginning (however coincidentally) and even more at its spiritual beginning, it is the water of baptism which reconciles the earth with man and begins his transfiguration.[16] In "Thinking My Country," the symbols of river, tree, and earth are connected to the Church: "The tree of the knowledge of good and evil grew on the river banks of our land. Together with us it grew over the centuries; it grew into the Church through the roots of our conscience."[17]

History is the time given to man in which to become conscious of the gift of the earth, because the impulses which make up his flesh and blood are expressed in a life ordered toward truth. This is the meaning of life for the individual and for nations as well.

---

15. Stanisław Andrej Gruda, "Myślac ojczyzna," in *Znak* 31 (1979); English trans. in *Collected Poems,* Thinking My Country: "Thinking My Country I Return to the Tree" (p. 156).

16. A. Jawień, "Wigilia Wielkanoczna 1966," in *Znak* 31 (1979); English trans. in *Collected Poems: Easter Vigil 1966* (pp. 131-48).

17. *Thinking My Country:* "Thinking My Country I Return to the Tree" (p. 155).

We have discussed two texts which embrace his most fundamental questions. His is a poetry of consciousness which describes the transfiguration of life. The lesson of phenomenology is visible in the fact that it does not exhort, or damn, or praise. It simply describes. It is a profoundly religious poetry, but it is not Christian apologetics in verse. It simply shows the transformation of hearts, the implacable deepening of authentic personal reality which existence, honestly experienced, imposes. In our time, faith is under attack not so much by militant atheism as by the belief that it is possible to live out a mediocre and decent life without too much effort or very many tensions. By describing the existential situations which mark every human life, Wojtyła shows the drama which inheres in each one of them and which drives human beings out of mediocrity, compelling them to choose between sanctity and the loss of their humanity. Although we may sleepwalk through much of our life, we are sometimes awakened by the objective recognition that life makes implacable inroads upon our conscience. The Cross and the Resurrection are the way through which man achieves his authentic maturity, becoming aware of his own value and his destiny in communion with other men.

The Encounter with the Sacred and the Seriousness of Life

This is the central theme of the collection entitled *Thought — Strange Space*[18] (as also of *Profiles of a Cyrenean*). [19] *Thought — Strange Space* is a kind of phenomenology, not so much in the Husserlian as in the Hegelian sense. It speaks of the purification of conscience: from the confusion and despair of a banal life, one is called to awareness through the encounter with the sacred.

The tone of the first part of this composition is like that of T. S. Eliot's "The Love Song of Alfred J. Prufrock," but the register is deeper and expresses a more tranquil seriousness. The second part shows the encounter with the sacred, symbolized by the battle of Jacob with the angel. It is this encounter which restores to man his presence to himself, and gives him the the vision, within which events are reduced to absurdity and one receives

---

18. A. Jawień, "Myśl jest przestrzenia dziwna," in *Tygodnik Powszechny* 8 (1952). English trans. in *Collected Poems,* pp. 70-77.

19. A. Jawień, "Profile Cyrenejczyka," in *Tygodnik Powszechny* 12 (1958); English trans. in *Collected Poems,* pp. 89-103.

the energies which enable him to place them within the sphere of conscience. Already in the first part, the poet has said:

> You say one always suffers for cardinal change.
> You say, man will awake in the depths of his hardest tasks.
> You are right. How immeasurably right your reason.
> But man suffers most, I think, deprived of his vision.[20]

The theme of work comes to light here, and in a way which is quite distinctive from the development of the same theme in Eliot's poetry. In the latter there is a disgust for the directionless life of the offspring of the comfortable bourgeois. Where work seems to be senseless, and is therefore painful, what one hopes for is *liberation from work*. This liberation from work will come about only through a *vision*.

With Wojtyła, by contrast, one returns to Norwid's ancient idea that work is for the Resurrection. One can perhaps also see here an anticipation of later texts about the subjective dimension of work, that is, about the emergence of culture in the very sphere of work.

In "Jacob," the crisis of man's self-awareness is overcome by an encounter with the sacred. This uproots man from his tranquil belonging to the earth and, at the same time, introduces him to an unexpected dimension of the depths of his own personality:

> That someone — the same one — broke open
> his awareness; in the same way, yet different
> from the way of children, sheep and chattels.
> And He did not crush them or push them down.
> In one whirl of embrace they were all in Him,
>   trembling like petals stirred by anxiety within.[21]

Wojtyła probably came into contact with the theme of the crisis of presence through his wide reading of anthropology in the milieu of Kotlarczyk's Rhapsodic Theater. It is certain that these themes were familiar to Kotlarczyk and were also part of the general culture of Eastern Europe. The encounter with the sacred occupies only brief moments of one's life, but it leaves behind a memory. Thereafter, every moment becomes a memory of

20. *Collected Poems: Thought — Strange Space*: "Sentences snatched from a conversation long ago, now recollected" (p. 71).
21. Ibid., "Jacob" (p. 73).

that encounter, a discernment of the depths which have been revealed and immediately lost. But man, after such an encounter, can no longer forget *to be for truth*. The poem concludes:

> But when reality's weight leans over and collapses
> then it fills with thought and subsides
> into man's deep pit
> which I rarely tread — I wouldn't know how.
> But this I know:
> I can't fall apart any further.
> Both the vision and the Object entire inhabit
> the very same pit. I speak of it seldom,
> always draw a conclusion instead
> about the world's proper weight
> and my own innate
> depth.[22]

The same theme of encounter recurs in the *Profiles of a Cyrenean*. There is, here too, an emphasis on the everydayness of a common life where thought needs to escape from being exhausted by meaningless work:

> Take a thought if you can plant its root
> in the artisans' hands, in the fingers
> of women typing eight hours a day:
> black letters hanging from reddened eyelids.[23]

Thought is an adventure which continually proposes itself to man. The risk of responsibility to the truth disrupts the banality of life, but in the face of it one may experience self-doubt and an obscure feeling of danger. It is the risk of losing oneself in the encounter with the mystery, which is both fascinating and terrible. To this the poet invites us:

> You had better walk with the wave. Walk the wave —
> don't hurt
> your feet.
> In the wave's embrace you never know you are drowning.

---

22. Ibid., "Proper Weight" (p. 76). The theme of "specific weight" recurs in *The Jeweller's Shop*, but this time with the emphasis not on the weight of the world, but on the weight of man.

23. *Profiles of a Cyrenean*: "Before I Could Discern Many Profiles" (pp. 90-91).

And then He comes. He lays his yoke
on your back. You feel it, you tremble, you are awake.[24]

The situation of the man carried in the depths of the sacred, of which the sea is the symbol, is found in almost the same words at the end of Eliot's "Love Song of J. Alfred Prufrock." This is probably not a direct influence; it is likely that the parallelism reflects the fact that both authors drew upon the same symbolism. But it is equally significant that the Anglo-American poet's invitation to enter the sea is made by the sirens and that the awakening, provoked by a human voice, accompanies and causes death. When it is not Christian, the magic of the sacred is deceptive, melting in the face of reality and consuming the lives of its acolytes. The awakening that comes from Christ, by contrast, defies death and is stronger than death.

The collection continues with a series of profiles: the melancholic, the schizophrenic, the blind man, the actor. . . . All the usual human types which one encounters every day bearing the weight of their particular mundanity or their solitude. They are a banal tribe, and yet each person is called, through an encounter, to live the drama which enfolds the meaning of the cosmos and of history. The encounter prompts a dilation of conscience, as it comes to reflect Christ and to be reflected by Him. "Eye to eye with this Man. . . . My petty world: justice squeezed out, rules, regulations. Your world is so big, the eye, the cross-beam and he."[25] When he ceases to measure out justice to others from his position of self-sufficient isolation, man begins to enter the mystery of life. This gives him insight in distinguishing the greatness and the drama at stake in the humble everyday events of which existence is made — love, death, work, paternity, maternity — and through which everyone achieves or betrays his own humanity.

Work

Work is the essential theme of *The Quarry,* but it also occurs in other places. We see it, for example, in *Profiles of a Cyrenean,* in the figures of the car factory worker and the armaments factory worker. The first says:

24. Ibid.
25. Ibid., "Simon of Cyrene" (p. 104). The speaker is Simon of Cyrene, the man who was made to carry the cross. All men, who must learn to choose their own destiny, discover the same thing.

> Smart new models from under my fingers:
> whirring already in distant streets.
> I am not with them at the controls
> on sleek motorways; the policeman's in charge.
> They stole my voice; it's the cars that speak.
> Just be back every day at six in the morning.
> What makes you think that man
> can tip the balance on the scales of the world?[26]

The armaments factory worker echoes:

> I only turn screws, weld together
> parts of destruction,
> never grasping the whole,
> or the human lot.
> I could do otherwise (would parts be left out?)
> contributing then to sanctified toil
> which no one would blot out in action
> or belie in speech.
> Though what I create is not good,
> the world's evil is not of my making.
> But is that enough?[27]

What is expressed here in poetry is the drama of the workers' alienation, of work which is deprived of purpose and of sense. These short verses testify to a deep assimilation of the Marxist theory of alienation, but they express with great conviction a novel reflection which is, at the same time, a self-reflection on the real experience of what work is. Thus the worker in the armaments factory emphasizes not only the human loss of control in the social whole in which he functions, but also the falsification of motives and of the communication surrounding the world constructed by work. Man is expropriated from the meaning of his work and the human experience of a just relation with other men. We see in Wojtyła's writings neither the idealization of labor nor its Promethean exaltation which are typical of socialist realism; nor do we see its spiritualization, such as may be found in Catholic tradition.

In the first place, the poet lets work be itself, and brings to light the

---

26. Ibid., "The Car Factory Worker" (p. 98).
27. Ibid., "The Armaments Factory Worker" (p. 100).

bleeding body and the muscular effort which, like a strong column, support the entire edifice of civilization. Work has a primeval character which constitutes humanity in a primordial way. Nothing is further from Wojtyła's way of thinking than the notion that working with one's mind is somehow above working with one's hands and with bodily effort. Rather, Wojtyła (Jawien) sees how culture flowers from within human work, just as water flows from within the earth and makes it for the first time truly fertile. In this way, the relation assumed by Marxists between work and culture is overturned, but without recourse to idealism. Rather, apart from its technical and practical requirements, work reflects the exigency of human self-affirmation and self-understanding; it is only when this connection is broken that people are alienated from their labor.

The Quarry recalls the death of a fellow worker in an industrial accident. The first part describes the wrestling of man with materials in which his labor consists. In order to overcome the resistance of matter, he must make himself into matter, engaging with matter on its own ground, using his body as an implement for dominance. But work is, at the same time, a fully human experience, the comprehensive act of the whole person through his body:

> Hands are the heart's landscape.
> They split sometimes
> like ravines into which an undefined force rolls.
> The very same hands which man only opens
> when his palms have had their fill of toil.
> Now he sees: because of him alone others can walk in peace.
>
> Hands are a landscape. When they split, the pain of their sores
> surges free as a stream.
> But no thought of pain
> no grandeur in pain alone.
> For his own grandeur he does not know how to name.[28]

Even before this, Jawied had claimed that "The grandeur of work is inside man."[29] Work is born in the intimacy of the heart. Human beings work in order to perpetuate their life on earth, to obtain food and the means of a more comfortable life. It seems that at one level the basis of work is a selfish human instinct which man shares with all the other animals, that is, self-

28. *The Quarry:* "Material" (p. 81).
29. Ibid., p. 80.

preservation. Yet human beings, as they are understood in *Love and Responsibility*, are creatures not only of instinct but also of tendencies. The human form of the instinct for self-preservation passes through a relation with people whom one loves and, in particular, with children. Man works not for himself but for his family. The fact that family and work are related gives work a particular character. This is an intuition which had already been stated by Péguy: "one only works for one's children." In Jawien's writings such a recognition becomes a stage of the process through which human beings become conscious of the meaning of work, and work, in its penetration of conscience, is transfigured: "Children will carry them into the future, singing: 'In our fathers' hearts, work knew no bounds.'"[30] In *Easter Vigil 1966* this figure of work is represented by Miszko, who plants in the soil of Poland a tree whose fruits he will not see.[31]

It is from this complex reality that love and rage arise in human heart. In Jawien's thinking about work, rage is a central category. In work, in the bloody wrestling against earth, man endangers his own life. The energy which the effort of mind and limb bring to domination is an ever present snare, ready to take revenge and to turn against human dominance. Man risks his life, endangering the responsibility which he has toward other men, toward his wife and children. Of course, this generates anxiety before the earth and in the face of men. Man faces the earth in solidarity with other men; labor is always *something shared. Loyalty and honesty* are decisive facts about common work.[32] If one's fellow workers are not honest, the effort is aggravated; if they are not loyal in their efforts they endanger other people's lives. All disloyalty in work is an attempt on the life of man, and it is not possible to work truly without trust. Work is a system of communication which binds men together in ethical relationships. Rage arises because of the resistance of matter and the untrustworthiness of men. Great is the anger of a workman against the lazy fellow who places him in jeopardy, or who unnecessarily makes his work a misery. Even greater is the anger toward an entire social system which is founded on unjust relationships, in which others seize the fruits of one's labors — not incidentally but systematically — and would make the la-

30. Ibid., "Inspiration" (p. 83).
31. *Easter Vigil 1966:* "A Tale of a Wounded Tree." The English translator notes that Mieszko was "the first historical ruler of Poland, who introduced Christianity in 966. 'Easter Vigil' was inspired by Poland's thousand years as a Christian state."
32. J. Tischner, a philospher from Cracow who was an intimate member of Wojtyła's circle and collaborated with him, has written beautifully on this theme. See especially *Etica della solidarieta* (Bologna: CSEO, 1981)

borers' existence more miserable in order to affirm their social dominance. Anger is born when the terrible seriousness of labor is not appreciated. It is in this anger that love is at stake in its definitive form. Work is the martyrdom of man, the place of his suffering and witness. *What is the right place for rage in one's conscience?* Jawien's answer indicates a means of recognizing one's participation in the mystery of the transfiguration of all things. In boundary situations participation in the gift of being becomes a concrete witness. And the boundary situation par excellence is death.

> How splendid these men, no airs, no graces;
> I know you, look into your hearts,
> no pretense stands between us.
> Some hands are for toil, some for the cross.[33]

But what is the meaning of the affirmation "Some hands are for toil, some for the cross"? The hands which belong to the cross are the hands of one who must die. In the following verse, there is the record of the incident in which a fellow worker was killed: there comes a time for everyone to belong to the cross; no one can escape this destiny.

In another sense, the hands which belong to the cross are those of the priest, and in particular of the young man who meditates upon his priesthood. But if one takes these two meanings to a deeper level, do they converge? Does not the priest affirm the same cross and the same mystery of the transfiguration of the world and of love as the ultimate meaning of sorrow and rage which all men find in the moment of death as any man does when he recapitulates the meaning of life and of work? Every death repeats the sacrifice of Christ, as does the Mass. The priest's task is to manifest its meaning in the midst of the carnality and materiality of the world. Only he who enters into this meaning truly possesses the world and lives his own life: this is decided before the cross in every moment and, particularly, in the moment of death:

> There is silence again between heart, stone, and tree.
> Whoever enters Him keeps his own self.
> He who does not
> has no full part in the business of this world
> despite all appearances.[34]

33. *The Quarry:* "Participation" (p. 85).
34. Ibid., p. 86

The final part of this poem describes the death of the worker and asks about its meaning. What is the meaning of the life of the working man, and of that particular symbolic form which is the worker's condition:

> He wasn't alone. His muscles grew into the flesh of the crowd,
> energy as their pulse, as long as they held a hammer,
> as long as his feet felt the ground.
> And a stone smashed his temples
> and cut through his heart's chamber.
> [. . .]
> They laid him down, his back on a sheet of gravel.
> His wife came, worn out with worry; his son returned from school.
> Should his anger now flow into the anger of others?
> It was maturing in him through its own truth and love.
> Should he be used by those who come after,
> deprived of substance, unique and deeply his own?[35]

For both a strict materialist and a dialectical materialist, the body and the spirit will be taken back into the earth: if one includes within this the anger of the proletariat, the meaning of death enters historical memory as a demand for revenge. But this does not do justice to what man really is. Marxism sees the motor of history in the enormous power of negativity which sweeps away all the social and cultural forms in which for the time being history is imprisoned. The future is born out of this destruction of the present order.

For Wojtyła, on the other hand, there is always something positive which comes to maturation in the life of each man; no life is unconcluded, for each one contains its own unrepeatable encounter with truth which must be brought with trepidation and respect to its fulfillment; this is part of the global course of human destiny. The meaning of a life is not to be subsumed into the masses, class, or history, but transcends in its personal depth all of these categories even if it passes through them, and by so doing transfigures their human and psychological content: "But the man has taken with him the world's inner structure, where the greater the anger, the higher the explosion of love."[36]

---

35. Ibid. "(In Memory of a Fellow Worker)" (pp. 87-88). We also see the theme of the meaning of death in Stanislaw Andrej Gruda's "Roswazanie o smierci," in *Znak*, a. 27 (1975). English trans. of Wojtyła's "Meditation on Death," in *Collected Poems*, pp. 157-67.
36. Ibid. "(In Memory of a Fellow Worker)" (p. 88).

Death

Where *The Quarry* ends, a later collection, *Meditation on Death*, begins, taking up the mysterious connection between the meaning of life and the meaning of death.

> . . . we pass from life to death
> such is the experience, and the obviousness therein.

> For passing through death toward life is a mystery.[37]

The desire for eternal life is like an imprint on the human heart. This does not reflect so much the individual's desire for survival, as the intuition that the values which one has vitally experienced and the love which embodies them, and the person which is the place of their manifestation, deserve to last forever. This is the intuition which is most of all present when we meditate upon the death of those who have affected our lives with special profundity. We experience their death as an injustice and by union with it we reach in vain over the abyss of human destiny which condemns everyone to death. But

> If that One unveils the record,
> reads it, tests in on himself, and
> Passes Over,
> only then we touch the traces
> and take the sacrament in which
> He who went remains
> and so, still passing towards death,
> we stay in that space called mystery.[38]

The fact which transforms the matter of the world is Easter. In it, by union with the death of Christ, man reaches beyond the abyss of death in order to retrieve, in complete loss of himself and in his return to earth, the plenitude of his self which in life was only occasionally present to his consciousness but which sustains his existence. To experience death in this way is for the first time genuinely to possess the elements of life, and beyond their apparent randomness and beyond their belonging to earth, because the whole earth is the body which is drawn up for the resurrection.

37. Ibid., *Meditation on Death:* "Mysterium Paschale" (p. 161).
38. Ibid.

In that space — the world's fullest dimension
You are
and therefore both I
and my slow fall to the grave
have meaning:
my passage unto death;
the decay turning me to dust of unrepeatable atoms
is a particle of Your Pasch.[39]

Love and Family

In the journey of man, during which rage is transformed into love, love has a decisive importance. The encounter with the woman and the generation of children fosters awareness of the meaning of work, and gives it an adequate, or genuinely human, motivation. It is no accident that the greatest of Wojtyła's poetic works, *The Jeweller's Shop,* is a meditation on love. In this work, the thought is harmonically expressed in simple and quiet rhythms, so polished that its depth is an occasion not of difficulty but of perpetual wonder. The problem which the text poses to a facile understanding is the same as that which life offers; one moves easily from meditation on the text to meditation on the enigma of one's own destiny — its drama ánd its mysterious profundity.

In the first of the *Cyrenean Profiles,* Jawien shows a melancholic man bathing in his own misery, refusing to live life to the full. Often in life we seal ourselves off in this way; dreading unhappiness we hold ourselves back from the drama of life and sink into neurosis, which is only apparently a self-contented mediocrity. But human beings are not made to be mediocre. In direct continuation of the tradition of the Theater of Word, Jawien sets himself the task in *The Jeweller's Shop* of bringing the reader before the pain of his life so that he can experience it existentially and, by living it out, find the material of existence transformed, illuminated by the manifestation of authentic meaning.

The Jeweller's Shop presents three couples, each faced with the decision of how to shape their life together. Teresa and Andrew will have only a short time: Andrew is destined to die in war. Stefan and Anna have the gift of long lives, but this creates indifference and rancor between them. Chris-

39. Ibid., *Meditation on Death:* "Hope Reaching beyond the Limit" (p. 165)

topher (Andrew and Teresa's son) will marry Monica (the daughter of Stefan and Anna): their union will carry all of the weight, the uncertainty, and the torment which are born out of the family history. They will also be the bearers of a hope of redemption for all that evil; they carry the love which their parents did not succeed in expressing and which, in the case of Stefan and Anna, has been corrupted into silent animosity. In Christopher and Monica is the hope of ransom for all.

The acute psychological insight with which Wojtyła describes the formation of the relationships and the breakdown of marriage, as well as the continuing presence of parents within their children, is impressive. As part of his friendly participation in his apostolate among young people, Wojtyła had doubtless followed the formation of many young families. But from the analysis of *Love and Responsibility* and of *The Acting Person* we have seen that Wojtyła was also able to draw knowledgeably upon a rich psychological culture — in which some psychoanalytic elements are assimilated (despite explicit cautiousness about Freudianism). He also had access to the great Polish psychologist, A. Kepinski, author of a genial existential restatement of modern psychology,[40] whose influence on the Cracovian philosophers deserves study.

In Andrew's first monologue, Jawien describes with great accuracy the process of falling in love. There is initial attraction, followed by the fastening of attention when the thought of this woman silently accompanies all of one's thoughts, and then transformation into a companionship which lifts the man out of his existential solitude and allows him to picture the bridge which will join his own unfathomable personal depth with that of the other. The other becomes like the road toward his own destiny, which allows his own true self to emerge and to become self-aware. In the encounter with the other, the experience of love liberates the man, releasing what was implicit and unknown to him and manifesting it to all. Whoever does not live this encounter dies without coming out of himself, that is, without his original grandeur ever having the power to manifest and so to realize itself.[41]

This experience involves a great deal more than physical attraction,

---

40. J. Tischner has written some fascinating pages about this in *Il pensiero ed i valori* (Bologna: CSEO, 1979).

41. The theme of the encounter is beautiful and profoundly consonant with the construction which we find in the writings of Stanislaw Grygiel, another member of the Cracovian circle, as in *L'uomo visto dalla Vistola* (Bologna: CSEO, 1978). See also Grygiel's *La voce nel deserto* (Bologna: CSEO, 1981).

which depends upon the physical presence of the other. Mere attraction lacks constancy; it is fickle, always ready to yield to a new or stronger physical appeal. We have seen that, according to the thesis of *Love and Responsibility*, love requires dialogue with the truth of the other and not a preoccupation with appearance. The dialogue goes beyond emotion and encounters that mysterious aspect of existence which we call destiny. In *The Jeweller's Shop* these elements are introduced through the theme of "calls."

Teresa, who has for some time loved Andrew without having been noticed or loved by him, hears a call during a trip to the mountains in which her friend is visibly interested in another girl. Everyone hears it and responds, thinking perhaps that someone is lost, but their own shouts go unanswered. This is perhaps, for Theresa, a symbol of Andrew's lack of interest in her. But it is also a premonition of the sorrow which life holds in store for her: in life, rarely is love spared a trial. At this point in the development of the poetic narrative, we are introduced to the symbol of a shop window. The glass represents conscience and reflects the unity of man and woman — the growth of the one into the other in a reciprocal mirroring which is also a reciprocal gestation, and which culminates in the mutual regeneration of each person's world from the conscience of the other. The mirror becomes the objective conscience which reflects this maturation.

The first window which we come upon is that of a shoe shop. Matrimony is, in one sense, an economical and worldly event. One has to equip a house, prepare for a life together, and even buy shoes. In this there is already a stage of particular profundity, which emerges slowly and with precision in this reflection of Teresa:

> I wasn't thinking then about signals any more.
> And I wasn't really thinking about Andrew.
> I was looking for high-heeled shoes.
> There were many sports shoes,
> many comfortable walking shoes,
> but I was really straining my eyes
> for high heeled shoes.
> Andrew is so much taller than I
> that I have to add a little to my height
> — and so I was thinking about Andrew,
> about Andrew and about myself.
> I was now constantly thinking about us two;

he must surely think like this too —
so he must rejoice at my thought.[42]

We might read these verses bearing in mind the *prayer of the heart*, which has been woven into Orthodox tradition and which close contact with the Ukraine makes less foreign to Poland than to Western Europe. *The prayer of the heart*, which emerged in the theology of Simeon the New Theologian and St. Gregory Palamas, is in a certain way a response to the question: How is it possible to pray without ceasing? The prayer is united with one's breathing, and one's conscience recognizes that the breath of life is the first form of prayer.[43] This theme is developed in the Greek tradition in a rather ascetic and monastic sense. It seems to me that Jawien may be creating here a this-worldly and secular version of such a prayer. The idea of the husband or of the wife accompanies all thinking; but this thinking expresses the acceptance of destiny and of the mystery which dwells within it. Love for the woman, or for the man, becomes a fundamental reality which accompanies all of life, the authentic prayer of the heart in all circumstances of life for those who are not monks.

From the first, such a prayer is a gift which one does not even notice. In the beloved's danger, in her suffering and in her death, in her distance and in her betrayal, this prayer, if one can persevere with it, may come to coincide with a cross to be borne in one's life. This is what Andrew and Teresa and Stefan and Anna will have to learn. But first it is necessary that what emerges in conscience be consciously willed and assumed as destiny. For this Andrew and Teresa will move from the glass of the shoe shop to that of the jeweller, which sells wedding rings.

Andrew speaks of the glass of the shop as "a lens absorbing its object. We were not only reflected but absorbed."[44] And Teresa comments: "The window absorbed my person at various moments and in different situations — first as I was standing, then kneeling by Andrew, when we were exchanging the rings. . . . I am also convinced that our reflections in that mirror have remained forever, and cannot be extracted or removed. A little while

---

42. Karol Wojtyła, *The Jeweller's Shop: A Meditation on the Sacrament of Matrimony, Passing on Occasion into a Drama*, trans. Boleslaw Taborski (London: Hutchinson, 1980; San Francisco: Ignatius, 1992), p. 32.

43. Cf. I. Hauscherr, *La mèthode d'oraison hésychaste* (Rome: Orientalia Christiana, 1927); Thomás Spidlik, *La doctrine spirituelle de Théofane le Reclus. Le coeur et l'esprit* (Rome: Orientalia Christiana, 1965), pp. 239ff.

44. *The Jeweller's Shop*, p. 42.

later we concluded that we had been present in the mirror from the beginning — at any rate, much sooner than the moment we stopped in front of
the jeweller's shop."[45]

How should we interpret the symbols of the mirror and of the jeweller?
We have already said that for Wojtyła mirroring typically indicates conscience
and, additionally, grace. The jeweller's shop points to the sacrament of
marriage and that particular empowerment of conscience, enabled by grace,
which affords stability and conclusiveness without changing the fundamental
dynamism of his nature. Faith is the ring which seals the faithfulness of the
spouses, their acceptance of an unknown destiny in which they will grow
through the other and in this way discover themselves. The faith is also the
faith of the Church, in which each one accepts his *own* destiny, and through
dependence on the other is dependent on the design of God conceived before
the world was created. As Jawien sees it, the Church, which the shop represents, does not intervene in people's lives to overrule them. It is an implacable
reflection of the objective truth of conscience, resisting falsehood and offering
a force with which to face destiny. (An analogous conception of the Church
appears, for example, in Zanussi's film *The Contract,* which also describes the
sacrament of marriage; there too the Church — and through her, the priest
— limits herself *to telling the truth* and to restoring to men the feeling of their
responsibility.) How can we live this responsibility?

> Love — love pulsating in brows,
> in man becomes thought
> and will:
> the will of Teresa being Andrew
> the will of Andrew being Teresa
>
> . . . .
> How can it be done, Teresa
> for you to stay in Andrew forever?
> How can it be done, Andrew
> for you to stay in Teresa forever?
> Since man will not endure in man
> and man will not suffice.[46]

This question concludes the first part of the drama, reflecting the first phase
of human love.

45. Ibid.
46. Ibid., p. 41.

The second part of the drama presents the story of Stefan and Anna, a couple whose love is consummated but not fulfilled. From the beginning one sees in it the incapacity of the woman to make stable the gift of self, through having to live it daily in an unexalted reality. And one sees also the inclination of the man to take this love for granted, not recognizing that love must be continually renewed, beyond the fulfillment of all of the diverse duties of matrimony, because the value of the person is always beyond that of everything one can do. In this context Anna makes the decision to sell her wedding ring. Is it not only a useless piece of precious metal? At one time signifying the tension-charged value of the love of two persons, this piece of metal had an enormous importance, a concrete reality in which is condensed the whole emotional content of two lives. Now, Anna thinks, nothing remains of this. But she is wrong. Matrimony is not an occasional union of two states of mind. It is the reality of persons who meet and are transformed; this transformation remains when the emotions which accompanied its origin have disappeared. Emotion will have to be reconquered in an infinitely purified form at the end. It is significant that the decision to sell the wedding ring comes from an incapacity to forgive. We are never told what it is that Anna refuses to forgive Stefan; perhaps it is not a specific sin or fault but only his human limitations, the fact that it is not "enough to be man." The Jeweller recalls this truth: after weighing the ring, he says:

> "This ring does not weigh anything,
> the needle does not move from zero
> and I cannot make it show
> even a milligram.
> Your husband must be alive —
> in which case neither of your rings, taken separately,
> will weigh anything — only both together will register.
> My jeweller's scales have this peculiarity
> that they weigh not the metal
> but man's entire being and fate."[47]

It is clear that the Jeweller's words reflect the reform which Wojtyła undertook of the Schelerian theory of values. Values cannot be reduced to emotion. They persist at a deeper level, which is that of conscience, even if

---

47. Ibid., p. 52.

awareness barely registers them or even denies them. It is then above all that faithfulness is necessary. At this point Anna encounters Adam.

> He said, "Anna" (so he did mention my name),
> "how very like me you are"
> — you, and Stefan too,
> you are both like me.
> And my name is Adam.[48]

As his name indicates, Adam is man. As such, he has experienced with honesty the vicissitudes of life from the beginning and he knows the truth. Adam stands in sin, and he is also its origin. He therefore knows the truth of sin and is not deceived by any ideology. Moreover, he is aware of the truth of hope, which God has given to men despite sin. Because of this, Adam speaks to Anna of the Bridegroom, and recounts the parable of the foolish and the wise virgins; this lifts the veil from her mind, so to speak, so that she can recognize the foolish and the wise virgins in people who pass by in the street.

> I also asked that woman,
> "Why do you wish to sell your ring here?
> What do you want to break with this gesture — your life?
> Does one not sell one's life now and again?
> Does one not break one's entire life
> with every gesture?
> But what of it? The thing is not to go away,
> and wander for days, months, even years —
> the thing is to return and in the old place
> to find oneself. Life is an adventure,
> and at the same time it has its logic
> and consistency —
> that is why one must not leave thought
> and imagination on their own!"
> "With what is thought to remain, then?" Anna asked.
> It is to remain with truth, of course.[49]

One of the most difficult truths to accept, but also the most decisive, is that everyone has only one life. It is this triviality which all those who deny an

---

48. Ibid., p. 54.
49. Ibid., p. 55.

objective moral law seize upon, choosing therefore to regulate their liberty according to the situation, spending their only life accumulating the greatest possible store of things. A certain religious ethic fights against this conception of life without managing to overcome it, by affirming that there is a second life and that it is necessary to give up this one in favor of that. Jawien, on the other hand, finds the affirmation that every person has only one life to be entirely sound. But the metaphor of the consumer, packing into life as many emotions and sensations as possible, appears to him to be a poor one with which to depict the life of man. Life resembles rather *a work of art,* a vast sculpture hidden in the marble from which one has to draw it out. It is necessary that one's life be linear and simple. It is necessary to be faithful throughout all difficulties to the figure which demands to emerge, without deviating from it or becoming distracted by the accumulation of useless ornaments. Such commitment requires that one does not lose sight of the essential form.

When two lives meet in the sacrament, they remain marked by their mutual promise. There is not an extra space in life in which one can carry out another competing responsibility. It is necessary to persevere also in sorrow, so that the common salvation for which one married may be fulfilled. It is precisely against this that Anna kicks:

> Is not love a matter of the senses and of a climate
> which unites and makes two people walk
> in the sphere of their feeling? — this is the whole truth.
> Adam, however, did not fully agree with this.
> Love is, according to him, a synthesis of two people's existence
> which converges, as it were, at a certain point,
> and makes them into one.[50]

Anna is fascinated by the idea of the Bridegroom. In him is concentrated her aspiration for a boundless perfection, which, in the first place, redresses Stefan's limitations. For it is certain that the Bridegroom will be different from Stefan. He could, in effect, be any man or all men, because he is different from Stefan, and Anna is ready to give herself to any man whatsoever. But Adam calls a halt to this:

> I want to, I think I want to very much. I think I had already put my hand
> in the door handle. I only had to press it. Suddenly I felt a man's hand on
> mine. I looked up. Adam was standing above me. I saw his face, which was

---

50. Ibid., p. 56.

tired: it betrayed emotion. Adam looked me straight in the eyes. He did not say anything. His hand was just lying on mine. Then he said "No."[51]

And Adam, in his turn, comments,

> The divergence between what lies on the surface and the mystery of love constitutes precisely the source of the drama. . . . The surface of love has its current — swift, flickering, changeable. A kaleidoscope of waves and situations full of attraction. This current is so stunning that it carries people away — men and women. They get absorbed by the thought that they have absorbed the whole secret of love, but, for a while, thinking they have reached the limits of existence and wrested all of its secrets from it so that nothing remains. . . . Love is not an adventure. It has the taste of the whole man. It has his weight. And the weight of his whole fate. It cannot be a single moment. Man's eternity passes through it. That is why it is to be found in the dimensions of God, because only He is eternity.[52]

To touch in love the irreducible ontological core of another person means to encounter the highest possible value. Although this value can be betrayed by everyday life, the meaning of one's own life entails remaining faithful. In this faithfulness one becomes aware of the faithfulness of God; he perceives that he can expect to be awaited. Through a curious paradox it was at the beginning of love, thinking about the husband that used to nourish the prayer of the heart, sustaining every moment of the day the memory of the presence of the highest value; this meaning became, through human love, the criterion by which one judged all things — even the type of shoes to be bought. Now, in a sadder phase of the maturity of life, it is faithfulness to the Bridegroom which sustains one in commitment to the person to whom her own life is joined. Now it is necessary that the prayer becomes conscious, so that one sees in the other's face the face of Christ. This is the test to which Anna is put when, finally, the Bridegroom which Adam has announced comes. The Bridegroom has Stefan's face.

> It seemed to me I clearly saw Stefan's face. . . .
> I have seen the face I hate, and the face I ought to love.
> Why do you expose me to such a test? And Adam says:
> In the Bridegroom's face each of us finds a similarity to the face of

---

51. Ibid., pp. 61-62.
52. Ibid., pp. 57, 60.

those with whom love has entangled us on this side of life, of existence. They are all in him.[53]

The task of life is, in a certain sense, to allow the figure of the other to grow in oneself until the face of Christ emerges in it. This task is accomplished through human limitations and in the acceptance of the cross which those limits bring with them. The recognition of the Bridegroom is, in effect, the condition of the relation between the man and the woman remaining in truth; at the same time, it is the fulfillment of truth in which love is incorporated, in an unmistakable and personal way, in the mystery of the infinite love of God for man. In this vast conception, matrimony is an ascesis, a journey of man to God *(Itinerarium Hominis in Deum)*, the ordinary road through which one may enter into the divine reality, to be assimilated to it through a continual prayer, a perpetual recollection of God.

The Mystery of Paternity and of Maternity

In the final part of *The Jeweller's Shop* the study of human love becomes a meditation on paternity. Monica and Christopher are, respectively, the children of Stefan and Anna, and of Andrew and Teresa. They carry in them the marks of their parents' human limitations. In the case of Andrew and Teresa that limitation does not involve the progressive decay of a relationship toward mutual estrangement but rather the separation caused by Andrew's death in war. Both children bear in themselves the wounds of their fathers; in carrying them, they create a new unity of the families from which they come — rekindling in their parents the anxiety surrounding the meaning of their union. One has here a distinct impression of concordance between Wojtyła's poetic text and the modern analytic psychology which speaks about the marriage bond and the relation between parents and children.

This spiritual constellation is expressed in the strongest way in a monologue spoken by Teresa, the wife of Andrew, who addresses her husband who has died but who continues to be present to her spirit:

This evening I could not help realizing, Andrew,
how heavily we all weigh upon their fate.

---

53. Ibid., pp. 65-66.

Take Monica's heritage: the rift of that love
is so deeply embedded in her that her own love
stems from a rift too. Christopher tries to heal it.
In him your love for me has endured, but also your absence
— the fear of love for someone absent. But this is no fault of ours.
We have become for them a threshold which they cannot cross without
     effort,
to reach their new homes — the homes of their own souls.[54]

The wounded love of Stefan and Anna is bound up in the lives of their children. Now they must render an account of the responsibility which they took in generating them. In order to give a reason for this responsibility they are obliged not to resign at the failure of their own love but to take it up in their hand — because if their union is stabilized in their children, it must have a human profundity and a value which their disagreements have obscured.

Christopher carries in himself the trauma of his father's death. Although he is aware of the presence of his father *in his mother,* and this stabilizes his image of masculinity, he does not have before him the image of a human fullness shared in the life of a couple.[55] Because of this, he is burdened by fear and with a felt need to give love as a consolation and a reparation to heal the life of a damaged woman. The life of Monica is in some ways similar to that of Teresa:

I am my mother's child and find her in you too.
I do not remember my father, so I don't know what a man ought to be.
I am beginning my life anew. I lack ready models.
Father remained in mother, when he fell somewhere at the front,
and did not visit me any more, was not with me day by day.
Mother implanted the idea of Father in me — thus I grew up,
thinking more often than you imagine about her woman's fate,
about her loneliness full of the absent man,

---

54. Ibid., p. 78.

55. The importance of the image of the father in the mother for the formation of the children is also emphasized by psychoanalysis. A specific study of this theme in the work of Wojtyła, placing it in its psychological context, would be very interesting. On the question of direct influence it is important to observe that the Cracovian milieu was saturated with Central European cultural ideas which flowed together in the field of psychology. One might think of Wojtyła's work in terms of a meditative restatement of the original themes of Freudianism in the light of Polish personalist psychology.

whom I embody with my presence. . . .
But I don't want this fate for you.[56]

Monica's situation is a precise symmetrical counterpart to Christopher's. She has known her father and lived with him, and she has known affection. But she has not known *the figure of the father in the mother*. She has not therefore really known him as a father and has not been brought up to her full maturity as a woman, which is ultimately the capacity to generate the image of the man within her self and, together with that image, the son which will nourish himself from her in order to grow.

Monica says:

Your father went away and died, and yet the union remained
— you were its spokesman, the love passed to you.
My parents live like two strangers,
the union one dreams of does not exist,
where one person wants to accept, and to give, life for two.
. . . Is human love at all
capable of enduring through man's whole existence?[57]

In order to fill the emptiness which that has created in Monica's life Christopher must bring about a reconciliation between the father and the mother. It is only through his forgiveness and living in her that they will be saved and recalled to the lost truth of their love. Monica is as estranged from them as they are from each other, and she repeats their error: she cannot give credit to the destiny which has united them. She does not see the profundity of this destiny over and above the ordinary banality of life and for this reason she condemns them without appeal. She must come to acknowledge humbly the unfathomable mystery of their lives and to renounce a judgment that has hitherto lacked mercy. Only in this way will she be able to enter with truth into Christopher's love.

At a certain point, Christopher says:

It was strange, dearest Mother, the story of my love
for Monica — whom I had to win over for herself,
and also for her parents . . .
people have their depths, not only the masks on their faces.

56. *The Jeweller's Shop*, p. 74.
57. Ibid., p. 75.

Monica, what do you know about your mother's depths,
and your father's — Stefan's?

For Stefan and Monica, as also for Teresa, the children's marriage is an occasion to rethink their lives. Anna recalls her meeting with Adam. She has not accepted everything which he has said to her, but has understood enough to leave the road which led to the definitive breakup of the family. The family has survived, but the estrangement remains. Anna has not managed to accept the fact that the Bridegroom has for her the face of Stefan but carries this revelation in her heart. Without understanding how such a miracle can be realized, she nevertheless has enough conviction to persevere.

Adam takes part in the marriage. Together with the Jeweller, he is the story's true conscience, one who knows what is in the heart of man. Whereas the Jeweller, in priestly fashion, pronounces the truth in the moment of the sacrament, Adam represents a companionship of the truth throughout life. He also expresses that attitude which, in his book about the Council, Wojtyła called the human identity. The Christian vision of life emerges within the human effort to live with dignity the fundamental affections and values of the human condition.

Perhaps because they are the children of an atheist society, Christopher and Monica do not understand most of the Jeweller's words. But they don't escape Adam's companionship, they don't escape his call to living in truth in accordance with the "regal gift" (munus regale), which consists in the capacity to experience all things at their deepest and most profound level without violating them. From this point of view Adam is the symbol of Christ, the "new Adam," just as much as of the "old Adam." He also represents the Church, especially in its this-worldly and laical aspect, which accompanies, and herself lives through, the passage from the old to the new Adam. Adam, who knows the original sin of man, speaks the truth in order to stop men deceiving themselves and "getting lost in the labyrinth of their thoughts." The loss of the meaning of human love, and all other evils, has its origin in an original transgression against the mystery of man and against the dependence of that mystery upon the God who creates it. Adam's final words recall this:

> The cause lies in the past. The error resides simply there. The thing is that love carries people away like an absolute, although it lacks absolute dimensions. But, acting under an illusion, they do not try to connect that love with the Love that has such a dimension. They do not even feel the

need, blinded as they are not so much by the force of their own emotion as by lack of humility. They lack humility toward what love must be in its true essence. The more aware they are of it, the smaller the danger. Otherwise the danger is great: love will not stand the pressure of reality.[58]

This is the lesson of *The Jeweller's Shop:* to love truly, to generate and to be generated as a person, it is necessary to incorporate one's own human love into the infinite love of God, transcending the sphere of emotions and sensibility and turning toward the core of the person, where one's relationship with God makes him what he is. This calls for an encounter with the Incarnation. But it also allows one to enter into the Trinitarian reality, into the eternal process within which the Father generates the Son out of himself and all of the Persons subsist fully in the other, without residue. The human experience of marriage is the beginning of the comprehension of the mystery of the Trinity, and it is the existential lesson which renders it comprehensible to human beings. Entering into this mystery through Christ, man is helped to be fully a person and to live the entire depth of his humanity.

Wojtyła turned to the theme of paternity again some time after *The Jeweller's Shop.* In *Reflections on Fatherhood*[59] he sets out a monologue of Adam, perhaps originally intended for the first part of a drama.

Adam meditates upon himself, upon his own identity. He is the common denominator of all men: but what does it mean to say this? Does he represent the gray and anonymous mass in which every personal originality is confused and lost, or the most intimate essence which makes man human? Adam's destiny is staked on this choice, and with his, that of mankind. The original sin of Adam is said to have been wanting to be as God, but his aspirations were based upon a deformed and partial vision of who God is. Adam wanted to imitate God in his aspect of power. It is evident, in this consideration of the figure of Adam, that he is brought up against the Promethean atheism of Marxism, with its conception of praxis as a transforming activity through which man dominates nature. Humanity has had some successes in doing this, but in the end it has not been enough. Such initiatives are only distractions from comprehending what the true heart of God consists in, what God is.

But here are Adam's words to God:

58. Ibid., p. 88.
59. "Rozwazania o ojcostwie," in *Znak* 16 (1964). English trans. in *Collected Plays and Writings on Theatre*, trans. with an introduction by Boleslaw Taborski (Berkeley: University of California, 1987), pp. 365-68.

"If, having formed me out of clay, You had said, Clay, go on forming, I would have formed many a thing. You know best the staggering temperatures of kilns where clay is baked — You for whom the entire computation of atoms is the simplest intuition, not a compilation of figures and formulas. I would surely pluck out many more things from Your intelligence and implant them in my world — calling It is I, it is I, that is true — that would be Yours, anyway. . . . For what am I? . . . I, who am transient all the time.

"Did you have to touch my thought with Your birth giving and my will with the love that fulfills itself because I cannot give birth in this way. That is why You were disappointed in me in this way."[60]

By appropriating the secrets of nature man creates the illusion that he has made himself as powerful as God. But man's essential dependence on God does not so much pass through his dependence upon nature (as a certain type of traditional metaphysics argues), as through his being a person who structurally exists inasmuch as he is generated bodily and spiritually by another person. The power of God which man cannot in fact imitate is paternity. Whenever man loves and regards another person with authentic affection he is not in flight from the experience of his own radical insufficiency. About this, true love cannot fool itself:

"After a long time I came to understand that You do not want me to be a father if I am not also a son. The son is wholly Yours; You always think 'mine' about him. And You utter this word with absolute justification, with credibility. Without such credibility the word 'mine' is a risk; love is a risk too. Why did You inflict on me the love that in me must be a risk?"[61]

Man flees from the risk of love. In order to overcome his reluctance, God took the risk upon himself, through the Son. He has left the perfect experience of love which binds the persons of the Trinity in order to seek the love of man and to suffer its refusal. In this way he has known solitude. In this "Your Son wanted to enter it. He wanted to because He loves. Loneliness opposes love. On the borderline of loneliness, love usually becomes suffering. Your Son suffered."[62] God accepts suffering in order to conquer man through love and to gain the assent of his freedom. To accept this love means to recognize that one is a child. One is a child because he is a creature. But more than that, a child because constituted and reconsti-

60. Ibid., p. 366.
61. Ibid., p. 367.
62. Ibid., p. 101.

tuted through a new spiritual generation. Christ gathers all men in himself and makes them live and grow in himself just as the Bridegroom lives and grows in the Bride to his definitive maturity. In this way men are incorporated into the life of God and become part of him, through the person of Christ. "To gather in himself the irradiation of paternity does not only mean 'becoming a father' — more than that, it means 'becoming a child' (becoming a son)."[63]

The fundamental question with which man is set is whether to accept or reject the fact that it is being a son which allows one to be a father. We have seen that this is the question set for Monica and Christopher in the moment of their marriage. At a deeper level, however, it is the question for all human beings. From this point of view, atheism may be understood as the rejection of being a son, which implies also a radical incomprehension of the mystery of paternity. Nothing refutes atheism more effectively than the demonstration that man does not dominate the earth as absolutely as modern atheism pretends it does. Our power is not absolute; even in the final instance of transforming created things, we are incapable of creating, of drawing them out of nothing.

But even more important is the fact that atheism is born from a response to the essential alienation of man. It is possible for human beings to reconstitute a sense of identity only by grasping the meaning of the paternity of God and, with it, of all human fatherhood.[64] It is in the experience of love for the other, whoever the other may be, that man discovers a true way of being a son of God and the fundamental rule of his being a person. Seen in this way Wojtyła's philosophy can be understood as personalist — not only because it recognizes the value of the human person but also because his essential point of departure is the analysis of the experiences of persons, and of their existential life.

The language of poetry offers essential assistance to a hermeneutic of existence which grasps simultaneously universal value and the irrepeatable uniqueness of the event. It is for this reason that we justify attributing an essentially philosophical importance to Wojtyła's poetry. The examination of these poetic works has, in other words, permitted us better to grasp the lived connection between human experience and faith and between philosophy and Revelation. The Revelation is also a revelation of the real human

63. Ibid.
64. For a recent Italian work on this theme, see Testori-Giussani, *Il senso dell nascita* (Rizzoli, 1979).

depth, and it is through the deepening of the experience of human paternity and of being male and female that man is introduced to the paternity and the Trinity of God.[65]

---

65. How far this theme of paternity and maternity is central to Wojtyła's reflection, and in particular to the poetic ascesis which rises above emotion to ontology, can be seen from the fact that he dedicated his first poetic work to it: "Matka," in *Tygodnik Powszechny* 6 (1950); English trans.: "Mother," in *Collected Poems,* pp. 59-67. The significance of maternity is relived through the figure of Mary, just as that of paternity is relived through that of Adam.

8. Conclusion: A Dialogue with Contemporary Philosophies

Now that we have analyzed Wojtyła's thought in its historical development, we must, finally, attempt to formulate a tentative interpretative synthesis. In order to do so, we will explore the connection between Wojtyła's thought and that of three central schools in contemporary philosophical thought in which, in different ways, he has found conversation partners. The choices are quite clear: in Poland in the years between 1950 and 1960 there were certain evident philosophical positions with which Wojtyła would naturally have had to dialogue. We will speak therefore of his relation with phenomenology; with existentialism, particularly that of the early Sartre; and finally, with Marxism.

With respect to phenomenology, the question is how far Wojtyła can be considered a phenomenologist and what kind of phenomenology his philosophy is. The question of existentialism is more complex. The influence of existentialism in Poland is anything but negligible, both as an autonomous philosophical position and as a correction to Marxism: it is able to free Marxism from its original mechanist basis by giving it a spiritual element. It is clearly a philosophy which attempts to begin from man and his own experience of life, and it pursues this objective by using the phenomenological method. It is therefore very interesting to see how two programs of philosophy as similar as those of Sartre and Wojtyła come to two completely opposite conclusions.

Finally, the confrontation with Marxism concerns the nature of things.

Of course, in the Poland in which Wojtyła pursued his philosophical work, an open critical confrontation with Marxism was not possible; one cannot, in fact, find in Wojtyła's work any direct reference to Marx. Nonetheless, an attentive examination shows that the problem of a philosophy of praxis is anything but foreign to him: it is, at least in my interpretation, the explanatory key to his work. His is a philosophy of praxis which is richer and makes more sense than the Marxist theory; it solves the unresolved problem of Marxism, namely the relation between culture and praxis, as well as demonstrating how a philosophy of praxis must be thought out not in opposition but in relation to the philosophy of being and as its articulation (if one wishes to keep sight of the way in which human experience takes effect in the world).

Wojtyła and Phenomenology

If one is to understand the relation between Wojtyła and phenomenology, one must give a clear explanation of the history, the terminology, and the concepts of phenomenology. What does Wojtyła mean by the word "phenomenology"? We will put the question in this way rather than asking simply "What is phenomenology?" The reason for formulating my question in this restricted way is the fact that it might not be possible to answer it if it were formulated in the more radical sense. There are many different interpretations of what phenomenology is, some of which are antithetical to one another, and it would not be easy to reduce these to a single common denominator.[1]

If we study the textbooks of the history of philosophy, we will be told that phenomenology is a school of philosophy founded by Edmund Husserl at the beginning of this century. The difficulties begin when, having accepted this external and purely historical definition, one attempts to move

1. Gerd Brand observes: "In the middle of the century after the first work of Husserl we find ourselves in a very particular situation, definable through two aspects: from one side Husserl's thought has been very fruitful and influential; from another side, most of those who know of Husserl have wondered what phenomenology really is. How can we explain this? There are two reasons for it: first, that the greater part of the work which Husserl published in his lifetime was purely programmatic; and second, that the thematic reflection on phenomenology which he continuously attempted to practice has not been completely successful, as Husserl himself admitted. . . ." Cited in Carlo Sini, *La fenomenologia* (Milan: Garzanti, 1965), p. 8.

on to an internal and conceptual definition. It is not only that, within the successive developments of this movement, we find a variety of positions and of interpretations, but also that the work of Husserl himself, which is phenomenology's grounding theory, presents a complicated series of stages, full of twists, turns, and (real or apparent) contradictions. Those who enter into Husserl's thought receive the impression of moving through a work in progress, of entering a conceptual laboratory which is constantly throwing up new discoveries in a process which gropes forward, formulating new hypotheses which will themselves be discarded and replaced with others which are wider and more comprehensive. It is not easy to find one's way in such a labyrinth.

This is not to say that the system is without its own inner coherence, but the coherence is not that of a philosophy which has been thought out in a single way without variation from the beginning until the end of a thinker's life. Quite the contrary. And historical developments put phenomenology under the compulsion continually to rethink its own foundations, returning to the basis of the method in order to discover new horizons of meaning within it, and in order to modify the angle of the phenomenological reflection which it had initially undertaken. Husserl himself opened a way which he himself was not able to follow, and which others have taken instead. Yet, having pursued a direction which was deserted by the Master, and assuming that they had definitively separated themselves from him, they found him again by taking a turn which his own thinking had not foreseen.

For these reasons, then, I will not begin by discussing phenomenology in general, but will restrict myself in the first place to the phenomenology with which our author was connected. We are dealing with the early Husserl, the Husserl of the *Logical Investigations*.[2] I know that Wojtyła was not ignorant of the later works of the founder of phenomenology, and that he does not regard them lightly. Moreover, it is not difficult to discover in his writings this or that Husserlian idea. In such instances, however, while his own thinking may be prompted by a Husserlian text, and while the intellectual proximity between them might be considerable, he retains his in-

---

2. Edmund Husserl, *Logische Untersuchungen* (Halle, 1901-1902). This, as we have seen, is the beginning of phenomenology. The only relevant work which Husserl had published before this was his habilitation thesis on the concept of numbers and the volume on the *Philosophy of Arithmetic*, which he would later severely criticize.

dependence of judgment. Among Husserl's texts, his meditations in *The Crisis of European Sciences,*[3] in which he developed the concepts centered upon the idea of the "life-world," are particularly important. Although these aspects of Husserl's philosophy had great significance for Wojtyła, the influence of the *Logical Investigations* is of a different order. The latter sets out the essential elements of the phenomenological method which Wojtyła will utilize in his own thinking.

The value and the significance which one can assign to Wojtyła's use of the rest of Husserl's work depend upon the importance which one attributes to the *Logical Investigations* within Husserl's work as a whole, as the source by which one judges whether an interpretation of his later developments is well grounded. But this represents a lengthy detour which it is not for us to enter upon and which would take us away from our specific objectives. Such a study, which could engage a thoroughgoing comparison between the integral development of Husserl's thought and of Wojtyła's philosophy, would be interesting.

If we stay near the Husserl of the *Logical Investigations,* in the area of phenomenology within which Wojtyła was to design a personal path, we will find the greatest of the disciples of the founder of phenomenology in the first phase of his thought: Max Scheler.

One must also consider alongside Scheler the great Polish philosopher Roman Ingarden, who taught for many years at the Jagellonian University in Cracow. From a biographical perspective, Scheler and Ingarden had one thing in common: both of them clearly distinguished the path of their own philosophical research from that which Husserl followed in the period after the *Logical Investigations,* inasmuch as this moved toward a pure philosophy of consciousness which ultimately becomes a new form of transcendental idealism.

Having delimited in this way the central areas of contact between the school of phenomenology and Wojtyła's thought, we are able further to specify the question with which we began. From the perspective which we have described, what does phenomenology look like? We would say that it largely appears as a *return to the object,* as against the subjectivism of modern philosophy. We have observed that it takes the form not so much of a complete philosophy, as of a *method of philosophical understanding.* For modern philosophy, however tendentially, knowledge is a pure event

3. *The Crisis of European Sciences and Transcendental Phenomenology,* trans. David Carr (Evanston: Northwestern University Press, 1970).

within consciousness. It begins by distinguishing primary qualities and secondary qualities within bodies; here we have a first unconscious reduction, because objects are taken to be simply like extended bodies. The primary quality par excellence is extension, which alone can be recognized as having an authentic extramental reality. Secondary qualities are the other bodily qualities, such as color, smell, and so on; they are not measurable and cannot be brought within the framework of geometry. Secondary qualities are imputed to subjective perception: they are not found in the body but constitute, rather, a modification of the sense organs which happens on occasion to perceive bodies.

Kant radicalized this position: for him, also, the primary qualities, extension and temporal succession, are a priori faculties and not properties of objects. Objects are removed from the sphere of knowledge and replaced by facts, that is, by modifications of the faculty of perception. Brentano was perhaps the first to observe that the modification of the perceptive faculty goes together with a reaching out toward an object: it enters into a tension with a real element which stands outside itself. Moreover, it is not only perception which reaches out toward objects. Conceptual thought does so as well, for it moves from isolated perceptions to seeing the complete form of the object, and is thus even more radically referred to things outside of cognition. Even if we claim that the object of conceptual understanding is the construct of the subject, we must still recognize that it is constructed as external to the subject, and as subsistent in itself.

The discovery of intentionality, then, which stands as the ground of phenomenology in the *Logical Investigations* is the discovery of the reaching out of consciousness toward objects.[4] On the other hand, knowing does not consist in the subject's pure and intentional reaching out toward an object; knowing something is always also a self-giving of the object within the subject's reaching. This is why phenomenology wanted to be a return to the things themselves. Phenomenology did not restrict itself to analyzing an empty cognitive faculty but also included the analysis of the experience which is precisely the givenness of objects within the cognitive faculty. This givenness of the object is the form of the object, as it is experienced in the cognitive act. It produces a picture of the act of knowledge which is relatively similar to that assumed in Aristotelian and Thomistic metaphysics of knowledge. The form of the object occupies the cognitive faculty and in such a way makes knowledge possible.

4. See especially the Fifth *Logical Investigation.*

Nonetheless, the difference between the "intentional" form and the form as understood in the Aristotelian and Thomistic sense is not a minor one, and this precludes us from identifying them. The "intentional" form connotes not a real object but the object as it is constructed in the subject's intentional reaching out. It is not possible to give a definitive judgment as to the real ontological constitution of the object.[5] Reality is a predication which the subject attributes to an object which is constructed in one determinate way. Aristotle's and St. Thomas's form, on the other hand, is an essential attribute of the object itself, through which it is made present to thought. Therefore, according to St. Thomas, it is through the form that one knows the essence of things.

Despite this limitation, phenomenology also tries to go beyond formalism, but given that the intentional form is not the substantial form of the thing, it is unable to go further than the pure self-giving of the thing in consciousness. It cannot enter into the relations of causality which hold between objects. This is an element to which we will have to return and which is significant because of the degree to which Wojtyła makes use of phenomenology. But before we develop this point in detail, we must briefly recall the importance of Max Scheler for phenomenology.

Drawing on phenomenology as a method of investigating human moral experience, Scheler discovered that we never come into contact with cognitively pure intentional forms; rather, the perception of objects is bound to the perception of a specific value. Experience is thus not only of pure forms but also of values. This discovery of value made phenomenology into an investigative method which could be applied to human interiority. On this base, Scheler constructed an entire ethical system.

Wojtyła's first engagement with phenomenology came about through his examination of the possibility of constructing a Christian ethics on the basis of Scheler's work. The examination led to a substantially negative conclusion, in part because of a specific vice of Scheler's system, and in part because of a particular limitation inherent in all phenomenology.

Scheler's weakness is that he takes his anti-Kantian polemic too far (forgetting that phenomenology owes a consistent philosophical debt to Kant). He understands the moral conscience in such an emotionalized way that its role is reduced to practically nothing. Conscience, therefore, simply registers the person's experience of value without motivating him to act.

5. From this point of view it is necessary to emphasize that Wojtyła was careful to adhere to a realistic understanding of phenomenology.

But Kant had rightly understood the value of the experience of duty, the experience of active responsibility which the person comes to feel through his own choices. In his rejection of Kant, Scheler closed the way which leads to the recognition of personal responsibility through one's own choice and to the configuration of the person's moral obligation toward objective moral values.

But as Wojtyła also concluded, phenomenology as a whole, as a descriptive method which refers to the givenness of intentional objects of consciousness, fails to enter into the causal relations of behaviors and cannot understand the interventions made by persons in their moral choices from the inside. A nonemotionalist phenomenology can describe the phenomenon of moral choice and in this way pose the problem of the active efficacy of the person: in order adequately to confront and work out this problem, however, the instruments which we need cannot come from the phenomenological method. Here, Kant's philosophy proves helpful. According to Kant, moral conscience and a feeling of duty offer the only point of transition from which the phenomenal can move into the noumenal, enabling one to enter into the interior of that particular thing in itself which is the subject. Here we find that it is the person as subject who is the cause of action and who to that extent is responsible. But the correction of the phenomenological method cannot stop at Kant's philosophy, if one does not want to fall into the quicksand of formalism. In a Kantian perspective, the efficacy of the person is resolved in the empty formula of duty. The person does not enter into a real, cognitive relation with things in themselves in a way which would create conformity between one's own action and the objective values which are contained in it. It is necessary to acknowledge this before going beyond Kant's philosophy and recovering the idea of *induction*,[6] which permits an objective knowledge of reality.

Here St. Thomas's ontology of the person comes to our aid. It alone is capable of adequately explaining the phenomenon of choice and the moral conscience. In this perspective (influenced by Edith Stein) the recovery of ontology is the achievement of a movement which begins from experience

---

6. For St. Thomas, induction enables one to ascend from the particular to the universal. The concept of induction has undergone much criticism from modern philosophy of science; nonetheless, as it is used by Wojtyła it simply implies the giving to the subject's act of consciousness the form of the object and the possibility of ascending through discussion from the particular to the universal. The problem of the way in which this ascent to the universal takes place remains beyond the scope of our present inquiry.

understood in a phenomenological sense and which tries to take to its furthest conclusion the desire to make contact with the things themselves, which is the starting motor of the phenomenological project.

Such a recovery of ontology does not reject, but rather deepens, the task to which modernity is called, that is, to begin from the human, rather than from being or from any abstract categories.

An authentic beginning from the human naturally does not forget that the person is himself a being, and therefore a creature. Thus the notion of being enters into the composition of the notion of the person, but the existential perspective leads one to begin from the person rather than from the category of being, although it is a simpler category. In other words, one guards against the transformation of Thomism into a closed and earthly philosophy by keeping in view the perspective of a philosophy of the person open to the infinitude of God.

An ontology permits one to grasp values not only as they are given to us, but as they are in themselves. In an ethical perspective this is an important turning away from a purely phenomenological attitude. Nonetheless, it would be wrong simply to infer from this that ontology is superior to phenomenology or even to adduce that phenomenology is useless. That would be to disregard the fact that the ontology which one seeks to recover is conditioned by the mode of its recovery. Phenomenology adds to our understanding an unprecedented perception of the way in which objective values are given in the experience of the person and penetrate our conscience:[7] it gives an entirely new perspective on a Thomistic ontology of the person. This knowledge of the mode in which the experience of value is given has eminent pedagogical significance. Moreover, this is not the only significance of phenomenology for a new ethical philosophy. For a more complete appreciation of the bearing which phenomenology has on moral philosophy we must briefly lay aside the methodological issues which we have been pursuing in order to consider at least one other aspect of Scheler's philosophy which has had a deep influence upon Wojtyła's own reflections.

We are dealing with the person, which is the fundamental reality both from the ontological and the ethical point of view. Objective values are concretely realized in the person inasmuch as they are realized by his free will. Only in this way are they truly welcomed into his interiority, where

7. See E. Lévinas, "Note sul pensiero filsofico del Cardinale Wojtyła," in "Strummento Internazionale per un lavoro teologico," *Communio* 54 (November/December 1980), pp. 99ff., esp. p. 102.

they can shape it. Phenomenological description helps us to grasp this element with a new liveliness, and to shield it against any pretense that one can impose an objective truth upon a conscience which does not freely assent to it. In most cases, this means that it is impossible to impose on the person an objective truth in which he does not see a radical clarification of his authentic emotional experience. The ontological proposition can demonstrate its truth only insofar as it can reconstruct the intentional experience of values more coherently and more profoundly, appreciating every authentic experience, and, at the same time, showing that it is able to assign them to their appropriate position within the whole of the person's life.

I have explained the way in which Wojtyła reintroduced this induction. But we must perhaps ask what form the induction which is regained through the phenomenological method takes. If we look to Stanislaw Grygiel's philosophical work, considering it as, in a sense, an ideal extension of Wojtyła's theoretical enterprise, we might say that this view of induction retraces the path to its origin, which is the Socratic concept.[8] It is the result of the encounter of a person with an object, within which the object is drawn into the interior of the subject, into his culture, concretely to grow there. This concept has no desire to be transformed into a technical knowledge, which reduces the things one knows to plastic material upon which one can act. That type of wisdom, which we do not wish to deny, belongs to other faculties of the human soul.

The knowledge of objective truth happens, rather, within the experience of love, which is the welcoming of the other and of reality as a gift. By developing the inside of reality within eros (which is part of the hope of redemption and of absolute truth) one becomes capable of transcending the intentionality toward objective value. Such overcoming, with the human search, always remains partial and provisional. In every case, it implicates the whole person, his freedom no less than his intelligence. Only the one who loves the good with an intransigent and impassioned trust is able to know the truth. It is because of this that such encounters, through which

8. See the analysis of Gyge's ring in S. Grygiel, "L'uscita dall caverna e la salita al monte Moria (Saggio su cultura e civiltà)," in S. Grygiel, *L'uomo visto dalla Vistola*. See also his *La voce nel deserto* (Bologna: CSEO, 1982). On Grygiel see the pertinent assessment of Francesco Mercadante, in "L'Euroecumenismo del Papa slavo," in Francesco Grisi (ed.), *Papa Wojtyła una certezza* (Rome, 1980), p. 77, and that of J. Seifert, "Karol Cardinal Wojtyła (Pope John Paul II) as Philosopher and the Cracow/Lublin School of Philosophy," in *Aletheia*, vol. 2 (1981), pp. 192-93. It is through Mercadante that Seifert discovers in Grygiel a dimension reminiscent of Gabriel Marcel.

human nature is introduced to truth, remain within human limits. And it is because of this that philosophy is structurally directed toward the hope of a definite encounter in which the truth gives itself with an infinite openness.[9]

Wojtyła and Existentialism

Jean-Paul Sartre's thought can be considered a radicalization of the existential significance of the Cartesian *cogito,* conceived and described as the fundamental experience of man in the world. In this perspective, Sartre's early work acquires a particular importance.[10] It was in the phase of Sartre's thought which began with his discovery of Husserl's philosophy and which culminated in *Being and Nothingness* that atheist existentialism found its most rigorous statement. In its later stages Sartre's thought yielded to Marxism. Such a yielding may perhaps appear as a confirmation of the fact that atheist existentialism in its pure form is — precisely from an existential perspective — unsustainable and unlivable. It is this which necessitated its giving way to another position (in this case, Marxism), which understands itself as the critical and humanizing moment.

The unsustainability of atheist existentialism in its pure state led many people in the '50s, before the *Critique of Dialectical Reason,* to believe that sooner or later atheist existentialism would inevitably yield to religious existentialism. Such a development, some thought, would consitute the definitive healing of the separation between Catholicism and modern culture. This hypothesis may appear rather abstract in the light of subsequent developments, but it was not, in the circumstances, unreasonable.

From one perspective, Sartre's existentialism is a *reductio ad absurdum* of the pretense of modern subjectivity to be founded upon itself, by denying its originary dependence upon the Other and upon Being. From another point of view, the phenomenologically concrete aspect of Sartre's thought

9. This is the strand of continuity between philosophical inquiry and the recovery of the religious sense of life as something given which comes about in revelation and a personal relation with God. In this way, the process of the formation of intellectual evidence is made to include a quasi-Pascalian moral element which preserves it against any temptation to reduce the process to a merely intellectual movement. The true, like the good, can only be grasped by encountering it. See Plato, *Phaedo,* 63.

10. See E. De Dominicis, "Il primo Sartre ed il problema dell'intersoggettività," in *Hermeneutica* 1 (1982), pp. 241ff.

indicates that it is impossible not to detect the unbearable anguish of an existing which, from the moment in which it is founded upon itself alone, discovers that it is thrown into a hostile and foreign world, within which it is impossible to establish relations of sympathy or mutual belonging. Immanent within the radical formulation of atheist existentialist is a moment of disharmony and even of nihilism; Sartre's atheism has a negative character which recalls the thought of Schopenhauer rather than that of Marx, and this very element, as in the famous historical precedent of libertine thought, calls for a reconciliation with the faith through the Pascalian path of a search which begins from the insuperable contradictions of the human condition.[11]

All of this makes it plausible that religious existentialism is superior to the atheist variety. Religious existentialism, in the very depth of the abandonment of man in the world, discovers hope and the possibility of a mutual belonging in the love of one person for another and of human beings for the world. This breaks the circle of solipsism in which man otherwise appears to be enclosed and opens his interiority to the world of life, which is always a world shared with others.[12] Yet this was not the choice which Sartre made toward the end of 1950. The atheism which appeared to be a constitutive element of his conception of freedom made it seem preferable to yield to Marxism rather than to religion, so he created a theoretical alliance between existentialism and Marxism. Such an alliance explains, in large part, the history of European culture in the last twenty years.

Marxism had, before this, remained on the fringes of high European culture: its new contemporaneity is inexplicable apart from this alliance with existentialism, which allowed it to present itself as the heir of modernity on the point of its greatest depth and its deepest problems. On the other hand, the existentialist crisis is reduced by Marxism *from a crisis of human beings in general to a crisis of the bourgeois individual,* and expresses in its superstructure the mortal sickness of an historical epoch which has come to its end. As a result, Marxism appropriates the inheritance of high bourgeois

11. It is above all Groethuysen who has shown the negative character of atheist libertarianism, its inability to found a human community and thus its necessary weakness in the face of a religious position which — from the same perspective — is able to respond to the need to say what human life means.

12. It seems to me that this is the position taken by Gabriel Marcel, as he has recently been interpreted in a good book by Enrico Piscione, *Antropologia ed apologetica in Gabriel Marcel,* with an introduction by Armando Rigobello (1980).

culture[13] without actually conceding any of its fundamental philosophical positions. It regards existentialism as a sign of the crisis, which one must take account of in the formulation of a revolutionary strategy for the West, but which actually only expresses the problem of the petty-bourgeois subject which has not adapted to mass society. In the new post-revolutionary society, the postulates and the questions of existentialism will not be satisfied, but rather will lose their significance with the discovery of a type of human being who will rise above existential problems, and with the emergence of an "active man of the masses,"[14] who will in an immediate way live a collective identity which goes beyond the problematic of the subject of modern bourgeois philosophy and especially of its radical and anarchical versions.

Existentialism offered Marxism the possibility of thinking out the problems within culture and human philosophy to which it would otherwise have remained an outsider. Nonetheless, these problems had to be rigorously subordinated to that of the dialectic of the economic structure and of class struggle. Where it evades this subordination (which allows us to speak of an organic instrumentalization of the bourgeois intellectual by the Marxist intellectual), Marxism itself runs the risk which faces existentialism, of absorbing into itself the anarchistic and nihilistic elements which constitute the unresolved problem of atheist existentialism.

The way in which culture moved in the 1960s and '70s shows the development, and also the failures, of this cultural ambition.

In one part of the new culture which was born of the confluence of existentialism and Marxism, Marxism assumed an existential character and thus turned into a direct expression of contemporary neuroses, including the irrationalism which goes with them. The fact that some who had imbibed this existentialized Marxism became terrorists speaks more eloquently than any argument.

On the other hand, where the subordination of the activist moment to the structuralist aspect was maintained,[15] Marxism lost the ability to remain

---

13. This becomes the project of Western Marxism in the 1930s, with the work of Korsch and Lukacs, which is not typically recognized as the beginning of dialogue between Marxism and existentialism.

14. The expression comes from Gramsci, but it is a good indication of the transformation that, in every coherent Marxist perspective, human nature itself undergoes in the course of revolutionary change. It follows that the earlier philosophies (including that of the revolutionaries) are incommensurable with the new post-revolutionary condition, except insofar as it is anticipated within the working classes.

15. As Louis Althusser has attempted to do.

in contact with a society *which had become radically aware of the crisis of man.* In general the cultural and social evolution of these recent years shows that the crisis cannot be understood simply as a crisis of bourgeois man or of the petty-bourgeois intelligentsia, but must be understood as a *crisis of conscience within man as such.*

The subordination of existentialism to Marxism, and, correlatively, of the crisis of human self-consciousness and of culture to the crisis of the capitalist socioeconomic structure, is contradicted by a situation in which the crisis of work may be presented, once and for all, as *the crisis of the meaning and the ethical content of work.*[16] In the 1960s, the existential angst arising from the awareness of one's own thrownness in the world, that is, of the lack of valid reference and adequate reason in relation to action, was the property of only a relatively restricted group of intellectuals; Marxism relativized even further this unhappy consciousness, opposing to it a *working-class consciousness,* compact and self-confident, secure in its own value and in its historical destiny. The *existential* problem was thus subordinated to the *social and political problem.*

Later, however, the awareness of the crisis of culture has spread through all of the social spheres: even the class which Marxists see as the supreme value, which stands at the basis of the structure of reason (the context of work) and which is therefore self-explanatory, asks for an higher legitimization. It is precisely because it is no longer possible to subordinate the existential crisis to that of social economics that one must, rather, beyond the original manifestation of the philosophy of existence, deepen the crisis of ethics and the metaphysical crisis of man. This situation is found in a surprisingly homogeneous way in all European countries. At this point, it has become inevitable that a new division should arise between existentialism and Marxism, which will naturally restate the original terms of the philosophical questions of existentialism. It is not by chance that many of the dissidents and the underground intellectuals who have rediscovered phenomenology have developed along these lines religious existentialisms of various hues. Unsurprisingly, Poland (together with Czechoslovakia) has been in the forefront of this development, partly because of the influence of such great philosophical personalities as Roman Ingarden and Jan Patocka.

---

16. J. Tischner has written beautiful pages on this theme, in *Etica della Solidarietà* (Bologna: CSEO, 1982). Tischner's considerations are connected to contemporary events in Poland, but his reflections have a more universal import and touch directly upon the crisis of work in the West.

In any case, the same spiritual situation which has today brought about the division between Marxism and atheist existentialism compels us to ask whether it is possible to reconcile Catholicism and an existentialist philosophy. We cannot here, of course, provide more than a token summary of the situation. One element appears indubitable: the dialogue of Catholicism with the philosophy of existence must necessarily pass through a fresh consideration of the problem posed by Pascal.[17]

Pascal grasped with tremendous profundity the dissonance within modern consciousness. He exhibited it as a disclosure of the necessity of salvation, which for such a consciousness is essential, despite its efforts to appear self-sufficient. Pascal's thought commences from the ground of modern consciousness, although it can trespass, so to speak, beyond it. It is necessary, here, to separate Pascal from his Jansenist theology and from his philosophical irrationalism. Pascal did not deny the truth of the philosophy of being but rather firmly emphasized that *there is sufficient obscurity in the world to enable one to disregard the truth if one does not love the truth enough.* The legitimate exercise of philosophy therefore necessitates a preliminary purification of the heart: we must love the good in order to know the true.[18] It is precisely this preoccupation with the purification of the heart which led Wojtyła to his dialogue with Scheler. The traditional position really tends to see acts of the will as merely confirming the judgment of the mind. It does not grasp the importance of the way in which judgments and their conditions are subjectivized and lived within the conscience.

In Wojtyła's thought, despite the structure and the dynamisms of understanding and self-understanding which allow one to analyze the person metaphysically, the main effort is focused on conscience and its relation with the truth, which is mediated through knowledge. For that reason one aspect of his philosophy bears the mark of a union of Pascal with St. Thomas Aquinas.

Pascal's questioning of consciousness shows the necessity of transcending it: but this transcending is not voluntarist or fideist but rather philosophical and contains a phenomenological analysis of the person in his acts and the metaphysical substrate which sustains them.

17. On the centrality of the "Pascalian problem" for the history of modern philosophy, see the chapter dedicated to Pascal in A. Del Noce, *Il problema dell'ateismo,* 2nd ed. (Bologna: Il Mulino, 1970).

18. Cf. *Pensées,* ed. Brunschvicg, nos. 242, 543.

It is here that Wojtyła's problematic intersects with that of the early Sartre, before the later development of the French philosopher carried him into Marxism and to a dead end. Sartre's philosophy in fact appears as the ultimate destination and the logical conclusion of the modern philosophy of consciousness, which prepares its own overturning or at least its qualitative transformation.

The theme with which one must begin, in engaging the relationship between the thought of Sartre and that of Wojtyła, is intersubjectivity, or, better, the subject's recognition of the "I" of the other.[19]

In Sartre's philosophy the novelty of phenomenology is incorporated within an interpretation of the Cartesian *cogito* which is centered on consciousness. The "I" apprehends through the consciousness which accompanies its acts. It has been rightly observed that the "I think therefore I am" is not a syllogism which produces a consciousness; rather, it indicates an act of self-perception on the part of a consciousness which apprehends and intuits itself. If this is interpreted existentially, it follows that one knows oneself in an internal mirror, and that one has no way of seeing oneself from the outside. The act with which man perceives himself as a subject digs an unpassable ditch between himself and material reality, between the I and everything which comes to be classified as "not-I." The modalities of apprehending one's *self* and of apprehending the *other* are entirely different. The *res extensa* comes to be considered only as an instrument or a means which the subject uses to affirm himself, a limit which (as in Fichte) must be overcome.

The subject inevitably becomes the center of reality and confers sense and value upon objects on the basis of the only experience which appears to endowed with value and sense, that of the subject's own existing and living. Such a subject could never see its own true objective form and thereby recognize his own freedom, the freedom to perceive a value and to choose it, and to acknowledge a binding superior norm which derives from a human essence which precedes self-experience in the present moment.

Inasmuch as man is free, he will be considered a being in which existence precedes essence. It is through his own free decision — supposedly from the standpoint of thought — that man gives himself an essence, assigns himself a task, and confers a value on his own life and on the entire world of objects, which would otherwise be entirely gratuitous and prey to absurdity.

19. See Marian Jaworski, "Sartre, l'uomo e Papa Wojtyła," in CSEO Documentazione 145 (the original article is in *Wiez* 2/3 [February/March, 1979]).

Even if Sartre has a vivid sense of corporality and does everything he can to avoid this consequence, it follows, strictly speaking, that one's own body is part of the world of objects from which the subject separates himself. In any case, the world of objects includes the "I" of the other. The "I" of the other discloses the Achilles' heel of Sartrian subjectivity, which sees itself as the center of the world and attempts to recreate the world from within (if only in an axiological sense).

Sartrean consciousness always exists in the overcoming of the object: but before someone else's gaze, it finds that it is an object, dominated by that gaze. The existence of the other reminds us that "I" myself am a thing, an object for the other. The mere fact of the existence of a plurality of self-consciousnesses entails a battle to death between them, like that which Hegel described in the *Phenomenology of Spirit*. Only by reducing the other to a thing can I maintain my privileged position as the axiological center of reality; otherwise the freedom of the other reduces me to a thing, the alien. Sartre's view differs from that expressed in the *Phenomenology of Spirit* in that here, the battle between the two equal and diverse absolute freedoms can know no reconciliation. In this way there is an important similarity between Sartre's dialectic and that of Pascal: both express the tragedy of an existence without illusions, which cannot be resolved on a higher synthesis. Hence the meaning of Sartre's famous phrase "hell is other people." The alienating force of the other's regard turns subjectivity to stone. Sartre rigorously rejects Kant's solution of the problem, the law as a rational regulation which allows for the compresence of freedoms. This concept of the law presupposes the possibility of a *"suum cuique tribuere,"* but it entails that subjectivity would be bound to a determinate setting, would not be able freely to invent its own essence, and would have to renounce making the whole as its own. In a Sartrian perspective, freedom is absolute or it is nothing.

Further, when Sartre sought to construct non-antagonistic rapport between men (this was the path which led him into Marxism), he had no other option than to provide a theory of a "genuine group."[20] He leaped

---

20. Cf. J.-P. Sartre, *Critique de la raison dialectique: Tome I Théorie des ensembles pratiques* (Paris: Gallimard, 1960), and *Critique de la Raison Dialectique: Tome II L'intelligibilité de l'histoire* (Paris: Gallimard, 1985). Both have been translated into English: *Critique of Dialectical Reason*, vol. 1: *Theory of Practical Ensembles*, English trans. Alan Sheridan Smith (London: New Left Books, 1976), and *Critique of Dialectical Reason*, vol. 2: *The Intelligibility of History*, trans. Quintin Hoare (London: Verso Books, 1991). For commentary, see Armando Rigobello, *L'impegno ontologico. Prospettive attuali in Francia e riflessi sulla filosofia italiana* (Roma, 1977), pp. 38ff.

beyond individual subjectivity and landed in a collective subjectivity construed as a battle against a common enemy, the unifying force of which is hatred rather than love or, at best, a love which is born from a common hatred. In the "genuine group" the subject experiences the emotions of the other in himself; he does not experience the other as alien to himself.[21] Nonetheless, the "genuine group" is a provisional and unstable reality which breaks into but does not cancel out the original and fundamental estrangement between man and man, his peculiar solitude within the world. In any case, it excludes the recognition of the right of the other, of the foundation of the right in respect for the other as other. It may be possible, in this context, to ask to what extent love, as Sartre understood it, is a way of expressing contempt and hatred for the people closest to one (in accordance with Nietzsche's classical definition). Or to ask to what extent, for example, his idea of "the negro" reflects European cultural stereotypes rather than an authentic encounter with African experience.

This issue is closely connected to Sartre's atheism. For the claim that there is irreconcilable antagonism between the "I" and the other implies that the "I" is not able to recognize its dependence upon an other in his very being. The solution given to the problem of intersubjectivity necessarily implies a hostile relation between the "I" and the Other par excellence which is God. This atheism has a postulative and axiological character: it is not so much a negation of the existence of God as of the compatibility between a positive relation with God and the sovereign freedom of the subject.

From this angle, atheism is a specific consequence of the Sartrian understanding of intersubjectivity. From another point of view one could also claim that it is precisely the presupposition of dogmatic atheism which compels Sartre's theory of intersubjectivity to isolate each subject within its own shell. The recognition of the possibility of a positive relation between the "I" and the other, together with the immanent limit to every empirical human relationship between the "I" and the other, necessarily implies the postulation of a relation with an absolute Other capable of completely revealing the value of every person, and therefore capable of

---

21. It is difficult to deny that this presents a parallel with Scheler's thesis about sympathy, which is precisely the point at which Wojtyła moves away from him, that is, on the theme of the possibility of living the interior emotion of the other. Cf. Scheler's *Nature and Form of Sympathy,* ch. 2, "The Classification of the Phenomenon of Fellow Feeling."

furnishing the horizon within which the encounter with the other is the authentic location of the manifestation of the value of the person. God appears, then, as in Scheler's writings, as the place within which one can recognize the reciprocity of persons and as the condition which founds such a recognition (Person of persons). Atheism, taken as a presupposition, sets up a barrier against understanding the relation of the "I" with the other as a welcoming: this condemns atheist existence to an axiological solipsism which has as its result, precisely, something which is as intellectually coherent as it is humanly unlivable, and which therefore represents a self-refutation through a *reductio ad absurdum* of its own way of thinking.

The human limitations which mingle together in human relationships, welcoming together with mutual betrayal and mutual alienation, become, for this position, insurmountable. One thereby nullifies every experience of truth and of love which comes about in particular experiences. One also denies the possibility of forgiveness, which is the fundamental condition of all authentic recognition between human persons.

These ideas highlight the distinctiveness of Wojtyła's position. Wojtyła (and other authors of the "Cracow school" who have followed him such as Marian Jaworski)[22] actually turns toward the connection between the recognition of the other and of God as an absolute Thou. Wojtyła explicitly discusses the problem of intersubjective relations between human persons. The renunciation of the prejudices of atheism is, for him, the fundamental condition of correctly setting out the problem of intersubjectivity since these prejudices hamper the adequate comprehension of the data of experience.

In the formulation of the Cartesian cogito, this appears to be not so much a cognitive deduction of being from thought as an act of self-intuition on the part of consciousness. The knowledge of the self as a being in the world is founded on this act of self-intuition on the part of consciousness. The structure of self-knowledge and of self-consciousness thereby risk appearing to be inextricably confused with one another, and it becomes impossible for the structure of self-knowledge to be autonomous with respect to self-consciousness. While the classical conception did not manage to create such autonomy, and retained the specific function of consciousness in relation to knowledge, modern thought, in the moment in which it discovered and valued consciousness, concealed the way which leads to

---

22. Cf. "Człowiek a Bóg. Zagnadnienie relacij znaczenoiwej pomiedzy osoba ludzka i Bogiem a problem ateizmu," in *Logos i Ethos* (Cracow, 1971).

the recognition of the specific function of self-knowledge and of the knowledge of man in general. In modern thought human access to knowledge depends entirely on self-consciousness, inasmuch as there is no knowledge of men which does not coincide with self-consciousness.

At the basis of the "cogito" there lies a systematic doubt which consciousness poses in relation to man's knowledge of reality and of himself. This doubt has, of course, a profound philosophical significance. That which is and that which manifests itself to the cognitive structure is not yet for this reason for the subject, standing in a living relation with the subject.

That which is known must still be experienced, subjectivized, existentialized, interiorized by consciousness. The world is for me inasmuch as I live it within my consciousness and I include it in my act of self-perception: in this way it becomes my life-world. The necessary condition of this is radical: the placing of the simple being there of things within parentheses, so that that particular structure of consciousness, which conditions the human way of understanding the world, surfaces.

Naturally, the problem which immediately arises for the philosophy of consciousness is when to remove the parentheses from knowledge and self-knowledge, so that consciousness does not remain empty and contentless.

It is here that the ambiguity and the limit of the "cogito" come to light. The interpretation which is usually given, which bases knowledge on self-consciousness, reduces the objectivity of known objects to the pure succession of states of consciousness. This leads to an absolute primacy of subjective consciousness and, at worst, to the subject's refusal to recognize as real, founded, and autonomous, anything which is external to consciousness.

One side of this position leads toward anarchism, because it ultimately sees freedom as an arbitrary and subjective volition which follows its own feelings without submitting to moral laws.

Paradoxically, the same position can also lead to totalitarianism. Since it is taken to be impossible to find an adequate basis for the communication between subjects, and thereby to explain the dimension of sociality and of history, a kind of social macrosubjectivity is postulated, within which the individual is nullified. The separation between the "I" and the other is overcome by intellectual *force majeure*. The true subject is turned into a collectivity, whether it be the state, class, or humanity, by contrast with which the empirical subject is reduced to the phenomenal manifestation of collective subjectivity.

Individualism and totalism are the two sides around which modern consciousness, eternally restless, necessarily turns and turns again. It is not the case that Sartre has explored both sides of this horizon. The problem is not only epistemological but, above all, axiological. What is really decisive is the process through which man recognizes objective value and either adequates himself to it by respecting it, or tries to confer value on things and on other people and, by so doing, enters into a structural contradiction with all other subjects.

The reform of the relation between the structure of self-consciousness and the structure of self-knowledge, which Wojtyła draws out in the first part of *The Acting Person,* therefore stands in a direct and close relation with the problem of participation, with which the final part of the book deals. By means of his own specific explanation of the concepts of *knowledge, self-knowledge,* and *consciousness* Wojtyła proposes a *reinterpretation of the Cartesian "cogito."* The moment of consciousness and the decisive function of the process of subjectivization are now recognized. At the same time the functions of knowledge and of self-knowledge are not denied, and he does not found knowledge on consciousness. Consciousness does not know anything but rather subjectivizes, opening out and bringing to light what has been known to the interior of the subject. To the objective value which knowledge recognizes, consciousness adds the participation of the person. This is done in a such way that there can be an objective judgment on states of consciousness and that a knowledge of man is made possible which is not simply the self-reflection of consciousness but also an external observation of the life and the history of oneself and all other men. Moreover, the structure of self-knowledge and the knowledge of man allows one to recognize, over and above the states of consciousness which deal with the "I" and the other, *subjectivity in the metaphysical sense of the "I" and the other.* Beginning from such a recognition, he is also able to explain the problem of intersubjectivity in a completely different way. The perception of the "I" and that of the "we" occupy consciousness alternately, and this is correctly reflected in Sartre's consideration of the incommunicability of subjectivity and of its extreme opposite, the "genuine group." The "I" perceives itself first in its isolation, then in its relationship with the other, and finally in its recognizing itself in the relationship with the other. The logical contradiction between the two states of consciousness does not take away the fact that both are presented as authentic and they are — according to Sartre — bound together.

But here the analysis of the states of consciousness, although it is conducted with a phenomenological method, is no longer sufficient, and it is necessary to take up a metaphysical analysis, with an inductive method. This reveals the unique complexity of the human subject which, simultaneously, exists in itself, and takes cognizance of its own existence through its relation with the other. In this way of looking at it, the "we" is treated after the analysis of the I-Thou relationship and is interpreted in the light of it.[23]

To understand that the person is the subject of his action signifies that he exists in himself prior to his action.

Metaphysically, the subject precedes his actions and the free choices which he makes. Inasmuch as he is a being in the world, man has a nature and a normative essence to which he has to conform; one certainly cannot say that his free decisions create his essence, as atheist existentialism does. In the same way one could never say that the "I" exists through the relation with the other which constitutes the "we."

The "I" precedes the "we," as it precedes the social relations in which it finds itself engaged. Both an individualist existentialism and an existentialism which allies itself with Marxism and which emphasizes the idea of the constitution of subjectivity through social relations[24] are contradicted by the recognition of the "I" as the subject of actions. Both are contradicted by the knowledge of the I as an object, which comes after the *knowledge of man and self-knowledge.*

It remains true, however (and here Wojtyła breaks fresh ground within the neo-Thomistic tradition), that the *"I" becomes aware of itself through its relation with the other.* This awareness is not something added on extrinsically, because the human mode of knowing and being implies a reflection on the data which is known in consciousness if it is to be humanly lived. It is above all Stanislaw Grygiel, of those philosophers whom we have considered as disciples of Wojtyła, who has insisted upon the fundamental importance of the encounter of the "I" with the other.[25] It is in welcoming the other and in being welcomed by him that the "I" becomes aware of itself and in a way begins to be fully human. The distinction between consciousness and knowledge and the recognition of the metaphysical sub-

23. On this point, and for the important conceptions which are developed out of the themes of *The Acting Person*, see "Osoba: Podmiot i Wspólnota," in *Roczniki Filozoficzne*, vol. 24 (1974), pp. 5ff.
24. According to the sixth of Marx's *Theses on Feuerbach.*
25. Cf. Grygiel, *L'uomo visto dalla Vistola*, pp. 17ff.

jectivity of the "I" also explains how one can encounter the other without losing oneself in him, without becoming a thing or turning the other into a thing. The meeting of the "I" and the other is circumscribed by a law which prescribes that each one realizes itself through the free gift of oneself to the other, and that such a gift implies reciprocity and mutual respect. In fact, one can only will the good of the other inasmuch as one wills his realization as a person; this rules out letting oneself be used as a means by the other. There thus comes about the idea of a just relation between persons — not a legalistic relation but a relation of giving: this is Wojtyła's conception of the personalistic norm. If the encounter with the other is the place in which the person becomes aware of himself and experiences himself, then the only just attitude toward the other is love, that is to say, the opening to encounter. Sartre's conception of the other's regard as "nullifying" is replaced by a hypothesis of a relation with the other which is the one true way in which the subject can entirely fulfill himself, yet which does not claim that the "I" exists only in relationship to others, having no independence or original presence to himself. The fundamental problem is this: *how is it possible for the "I" to be an object for the other without being alienated from itself?* In other words: how is it possible for the person to become an object of the other's action without being violated and objectivized?[26]

Wojtyła responds to this question with the theory of love which is the center of his personalist philosophy. When an action is motivated by a common good and created by a benevolent love, it does not negate but affirms the person of the other. It is only in such a relation that the person is genuinely and primarily affirmed. The experience of love as the realization of freedom in the reciprocal gift of oneself replies to Sartre's idea that the "I" is incommunicable. This is a kind of servitude which is the most complete realization of freedom, and it consists in the gift of self out of genuine love.[27]

26. This is the central problem of *Love and Responsibility*.
27. The genesis of this theme, which develops the belief that "to serve God is to reign," may lie in Wojtyła's reflection on the act placing Poland in the service of the Virgin, an act which was conceived and many times repeated by the Polish bishops under the guidance of Cardinal Wyszynski. This is a dominant theme in the Polish church — from consecration to the Immaculate Heart of Mary on 8 September 1946 and an act of total servitude to the Mother of God to the act of consecration to the Madonna pronounced by John Paul II at Jasna Gora on 4 June 1979. It is part of the Polish character to conceive of such actions not only as devotional (forming the con-

Such is the foundation of the "I-Thou" relation, which can be a relationship of reciprocal alienation and manipulation, but which, far more, can be relation of love. It also creates a different way into the "we" from that proposed by Sartre. Understood in the right way, the "we" is created by a common good which is shared by many persons and effects mutual belonging; this belonging goes beyond the one which binds two persons, taking on a wider social dimension.

Whereas in Sartre's thought one passes without mediation from the isolation of the individual into the "genuine group," in Wojtyła's thinking a series of successive mediations beginning from the pairing of man and woman (which is the best existential training in the I-Thou relation) leads to the family as the basic form of the "we," and culminates in the nation and in humanity as a whole, moving through a sequence of successive engagements governed by the logic of the love of the neighbor, This love is the opposite of that *ressentiment* which does not forgive the other's limitations and which, in fact, affirms itself by opposing those limitations. The possibility of a fuller realization of the self through communion with the other and of reciprocal giving allows one to sketch an alternative to the Hegelian master-slave dialectic, in which each affirms himself by humiliating the other. The significance of this alternative becomes obvious when one considers how this Hegelian dialectic has furnished the presuppositions and the methodology of most of contemporary social science. In particular, it opens a way toward a fundamental critique of Marxism, engaging with the basic idea upon which the theory is constructed.

The master-slave dialectic lies at the basis of the Marxist theory of alienation and is the fundamental point of dialogue and confluence between atheist existentialism and Marxism. Wojtyła's approach creates an alternative theory of alienation to those of Marxism and of atheist existentialism. Alienation is seen as the result of the *loss of one person's participation in another.*

The overcoming of this dialectic is not important only for the realization of a social order which is just from an objective point of view but also for the way in which such an order is brought into being. For human beings, justice can only be an order which comes about through the assent of one's

---

science of the nation) but as a stimulus to profound philosophical reflection on the relation between liberty and love. Cf. the discourse at Jasna Gora and the act of consecration in *Jan Pawel II na Ziemi Polskiej* (Vatican City: Vatican Library Editions, 1979), pp. 65ff. Cf. also the chapter "Serve God and Reign" in the encyclical *Redemptor Hominis.*

freedom and with the conscious participation of the person. By participating in the realization of a common good, recognized as such, the person takes others to be objects in their normal actions and is willing, also, to be taken as the object of their actions, without being reduced to a pure object but in a manner which realizes his dignity and freedom.

For Sartre, man is a being who gives himself his essence, and in this consists his freedom; for Wojtyła human beings realize their interior freedom by internalizing in consciousness the truth and the good which are offered to their knowledge. Human destiny is achieved neither by a pure and conscious authenticity which is not turned toward objective truth, nor by obedience to an objective norm without the authentic participation of the conscience. The way of participation appears as an alternative both to an individualism which considers that the other cannot be recognized without denying one's self, and to a totalizing system which abandons the subjectivity of the individual to the collective. Through this twofold negation the ideal of the *communio personarum* (the communion of persons) is affirmed; the realization of oneself by participating in the humanity of the other and through communion with him.

Toward a New Philosophy of Praxis

Direct references to Marxism are rare in Wojtyła's work. Some of his earlier comments, which are scarce, have more to do with the Polish regime's anti-religious campaign, and with the positivistic culture within which it came about, than with Marx's writings.[28] The reasons for this apparent lack of attention to Marxism could probably be explained in two ways. First, no anti-Marxist polemic would have been tolerated by the state. The whole free culture of Poland had to adapt itself to an oblique confrontation, since open criticism was off limits.

Second, there are many indications that, for Wojtyła, victory in the great struggle in his country would depend less upon a refutation of the positions of adversaries than upon the ability to deal in a convincing way with the question of what human beings are. An authentic overcoming of Marxism would consist in a renewed Christian philosophy which could

28. I am thinking of the polemic against "scientific ethics" contained in the *Elementarz etyczny*, and above all the "Problem etyki naukowej," in *Tygodnik Powszechny* 2 (1957). Translation in *Educazione all'amore*, 3rd ed. (Rome: Logos, 1978), pp. 27ff.

fully and adequately explain the idea of praxis to which Marx pointed, but which he was not able to describe in a human way.

The Acting Person, in offering a reformulation of the Cartesian *cogito*, simultaneously provides a *restatement of the philosophy of praxis*. We have already touched upon the way later essays, such as "Osoba: Podmiot i Wspolnota," throw light on the intention of *The Acting Person*. The meaning of Wojtyła's confrontation with Marxism can be illuminated by reference to a conference paper which he gave at the Catholic University of the Sacred Heart in Milan on 18 March 1977: "The Problem of Developing Culture through Human 'Praxis.'"[29] It would be difficult to exaggerate the significance of this brief paper (it is only a few pages long) as an index to Wojtyła's thought. Its importance for our discussion may be gauged from the fact that it has provided the key to the interpretation of Wojtyła's philosophical work which we have offered throughout this book. In this paper, he confronts Marxism directly, not in the Soviet scholastic "DiaMat" but from the fountainhead of all Western interpretation of Marx, that is, the *Theses on Feuerbach*, read as a manifesto of the philosophy of praxis.[30]

It is important to emphasize this point because some interpreters have tended to consider Wojtyła's approach to Marxism as a narrowly Eastern view of bureaucratic socialism. Our approach shows, rather, that our author understood the philosophical importance of Marxism, including Western Marxism, very well.

It is generally known that Soviet Marxism consists in a naive metaphysical naturalism which a philosopher could easily dispatch, formulated by Engels in the last part of his life, and then taken up as the dogmatic inheritance of Russian Marxism — first by Plekhanov, and then by Lenin. Western Marxism, rather than basing itself upon a materialistic naturalism and upon a problematic conception of the dialectical evolution of matter, was to found itself on the thesis that man creates himself through his own work. This idea of the self-creation of man through praxis constitutes the authentic core of Marx's thought and permits him to be presented as one who has both inherited and actualized the Promethean dream dormant within the whole of modern thought.

Wojtyła begins from this interpretation of Marx's thought, and opposes it without disregard for what is true in it. The problem of Western Marxism is not only philosophical but also political. The socialist revolution could

29. In *Rivista di filosofia neoscolastica* 69, pp. 513ff.
30. Ibid., pp. 516ff.

not present itself as authentic unless it became worldwide; yet the Russian revolution did not succeed in becoming so. In 1920, the Red Army, western bound, hoping to help the German revolutionaries who had risen up after the fall of the Hohenzollern Empire, was held back and defeated just in front of Warsaw by the Polish army under General Pilsudski. The event is significant not only as military history but, far more, as part of the philosophical history of our century. The Polish workers and countrymen, instead of joining the soldiers of the Soviet revolution, rushed together under the national flag and gained the victory which, after more than a century, allowed Poland to be reborn as a nation. Just outside the Russian border, the Soviet revolution came up against the national idea and was not able to defeat it. It was precisely this which stopped it from imposing itself as a worldwide revolution. The person who best understood the significance of these events was Stalin. The Georgian dictator was the first to understand that the revolution would be saved only by becoming national in its turn, subordinating the interest of an ever more unlikely world revolution to that of the power politics of the Russian state.

But it is also from the turning point of the battle of Warsaw that there emerged in the West a new type of Marxism (precisely, Western Marxism) which would overcome the resistance of the national idea and give the Marxist revolution a worldwide dimension. People began to look for a formula which would enable the communist revolution to triumph upon the "highest point" of the capitalist system. One should place the interpretation of Marxism as a *philosophy of praxis* in this framework. The national idea, which the coarse Marxism of the Soviets could not overcome, is above all cultural. The West refused to be conquered by Russia out of the conviction of its own irrenounceable cultural superiority which vernacular Soviet Marxism refused to recognize and did not understand.

Subsequently, Marxist philosophy refines itself in order to become able to understand culture. Culture, according to this reformulation, ought not to be considered a mere superstructure which will infallibly follow upon a revolutionary process which has its own motor within the dynamics of the structures. Marxism ought to be modified to understand the way in which culture, the so-called superstructure, reacts on the so-called structure and changes it. The problem of democracy and of the possibility of Marxism rising to dominance in a democratic state is structurally tied to the problem of culture. Cultural hegemony alone can create that consensus which will lead toward a pacific triumph of the revolution. On the other hand, the inability to think about culture hinders and destroys the revolutionary process within

Soviet society. The working class and the agrarian population, for whose unification there is no political and cultural strategy, are held together by force alone and by the most repressive state apparatus in the world. The revolt at Kronstadt, and that of the Ukrainian peasants of Machno, show that, from the beginning of the 1920s, the power of the Soviets was only an ideological facade for the power of the party over the Soviets and the mass of the population. The cultural insufficiency of Russian Marxism would impede it from dealing with the problem of democracy.

In a certain sense all Marxist research on the October Revolution is dominated by the preoccupation with giving a Marxist analysis of a culture which would have been able to sustain the revolutionary process which was forestalled after 1917. The fruit of this new phase of the revolution was supposed to able to conquer the "highest point" of the capitalist system and the democratization of the countries of "real socialism." In Italy Gramsci sought to elaborate the strategy for revolution in the West in his *Prison Notebooks*. Korsch and Lukacs made analogous attempts to do this in Germany.

So long as the discussion remains within Marxism, it is difficult to take the attempt to think about culture very far beyond Engels's obvious assertion that the superstructure somehow reacts to the activity of the conditioned structure. It is difficult to do much with such an assertion.

There are only two possibilities. One might argue that culture conditions the economic base as much as the economy conditions cultures, and then the distinction between the base and the superstructure loses its meaning, so that one turns a materialist conception into a Hegelian, Idealistic conception. Or, on the other hand, one might make the case that the economic base exercises an influence which is *ultimately decisive*, and then the concessions on the terrain of the autonomy of culture are merely tactical. The first of the two positions is typical of that Hegelian-Marxism which goes from Marx back to Hegel. The Hegelian affirmation of the primacy of Spirit as the final cause of the history of the world does not have to be understood in a hastily teleological way. The actual fact that the diverse spheres of human action mutually influence one another without it being possible to attribute to one of them an ultimately determining role leads Hegel to hypostatize the notion of the Spirit as the general direction of historical events. The second position fails to detach Marxism from positivism, which is falsified by all of the significant developments of contemporary history and of modern epistemology. In both cases the discovery of the *philosophy of praxis* and of the centrality of human work within history remains infertile. In the one case praxis is ultimately reabsorbed into a vague conception of the progressive evolution of humanity through work. In the other it is imprisoned in a restricted vision of the dialectic between the forces of production and the relations of production.

These failures are rooted in the fundamentally erroneous way in which Marx has conceived and defined praxis. *Marx considers praxis from within the same forgetfulness of the "subjectum" which inheres in the Cartesian "cogito" and precisely because of this he dissolves the subjectivity of the concrete man into praxis.*

The sixth of the theses on Feuerbach states: "Feuerbach resolves the religious essence into the human essence. But the human essence is an abstraction inherent in each single individual. In its reality it is the ensemble of social relations."[31] If one posits a human essence which precedes the action of man, one will necessarily be led toward a metaphysical analysis of this essence, and on a metaphysical plane the weakness of Feuerbachian materialism is all too apparent. So, rather than placing the essence of man in a metaphysical element, we place it in a social element; we consider the consciousness of man as an effect of his work through which he continually produces and reproduces his material existence, and our attention will turn toward the level of actual economics and sociology. It is in this way that Marx achieved the departure from philosophy which is an essential feature of his thought. We have here not so much an alternative response to the fundamental problems of philosophy as a *radical change of horizon:* this, in a sense, renders the language of Marxism incommensurable with that of traditional philosophy.

The last point of contact which remains is the philosophical justification of the departure from philosophy, which is exactly what Marx offers in the Theses on Feuerbach.[32] It is just because of this that much of the dialogue, for example, between Catholicism and Marxism, takes place on the basis of a misunderstanding and a real inability to communicate. On the other hand, however, on the ground of the philosophy of praxis — the philosophical justification of the death of philosophy — a dialogue should be opened, for it is susceptible of real progress.

31. In the analysis of the Theses on Feuerbach which follows, I am indebted to the magisterial interpretation of Augusto Del Noce. Cf. A. Del Noce, "I: Lezioni sul marxismo," in *I caratteri generali del pensiero politico contemporaneo* (Milan: Giuffrè, 1972), pp. 167ff.

32. This is the interpretation of Del Noce in *Il Problema dell'ateismo,* against that of Althusser in *Pour Marx* (Paris: Maspero, 1965).

If we think of the person as an effect of praxis, then we would have to turn our attention away from the problems which consciousness asks about itself, about its destiny, and about the meaning of its being in the world. Such problems will be the effects of the determinate configurations of human praxis, destined to be exhausted once the context of his social activity is transformed.

Once having lost the reality of the individual subject, one foregoes also the fundamental and ineliminable religious questions, which flow from man's questioning of his finite individuality.

The transformation of praxis, which is the true motor of history, is expressed much better in collective subjectivity than individual subjectivity, which in its turn is traversed by the contradictions of praxis which would impose its revolutionary reversal. Just as in traditional philosophy of consciousness the subject is lost in thought, so in the philosophy of praxis the concrete human subject is lost in social work.

It is also evident that it is not possible on this basis to reclaim the autonomy of culture by reference to the material development of praxis. Man creates himself through his effort to dominate nature and to mediate the organic exchange of his material existence. In this context, work is understood as an instrument with which to subdue the resistance of nature and to make nature the prime matter of human freedom.

Here we have that real overcoming of objectivity at which existentialism aimed. It is achieved in a spiritual way because it is not able to comprehend the collective character of this process. The environment, changed by human work, in its turn reacts on the subject, and changes it. This is the principal claim of the third of the Theses on Feuerbach: "The materialist doctrine that men are products of circumstances and upbringing, and that, therefore, changed men are products of different circumstances, and changed upbringings forgets that it is man who changes circumstances, and that it is essential to educate the educator himself. . . . The coincidence of the changing of circumstances and of human activity can be conceived and rationally understood only as revolutionary praxis."[33] In other words, the traditional materialist doctrine has not gone to the bottom of the fact that human praxis, conditioned by circumstances, in its turn has transformed them and by transforming them continuously regenerates human subjectivity, for this is the product of circumstances. We thus have the idea that work transforms the

---

33. Marx, *Thesis on Feuerbach III*, p. 144. Cf. A. Del Noce, "I: Lezioni sul Marxismo," in *I caratteri generali del pensiero politico contemporaneo*, pp. 129ff.

surroundings, and the surroundings in their turn transform man. Man makes himself through praxis, but this making oneself is nonetheless indirect: it passes retroactively through the subject as the effect of his action upon his surroundings.[34] It necessarily follows that what is really important is to achieve control of material surroundings and of social relationships. The efficacy of work in the transformation of nature becomes the single criteria with which man views his history and his progress.

It is difficult to deny that this position, like its equivalents in the philosophy of consciousness, has a certain fascination. In a particular way the introduction of the concept of praxis and the study of the concrete configuration of human praxis allow for a picture of human history as the history of human work; this is more dramatic, rich, and articulate than the traditional view. One need not be surprised that Catholics have often lost the cultural debate with Marxism on the theme of the *interpretation of contemporary history,* or that Marxists had become the leaders of the Workers' Movements: this has come about largely because they have succeeded in *thinking about human work* and *the self-creation of man through work.*

It is no less evident that the insufficiency of this notion of praxis is at the root of the totalitarian character which Marxism has assumed in practice, as also of the bloody and violent way in which it has pursued its achievement in history. The radical negation of the metaphysical subjectivity of man is the reason that within Marxism it is impossible to speak of "human rights." Moreover, human rights are seen as the reactionary defense of the "old man" who seeks his individual self-realization and refuses to be dissolved in the collective flow of history.[35] The one-sided attention to the transformation of our surroundings implies that any price in terms of human value and of the individual's suffering is acceptable in order to achieve that revolutionary change of objective structures which will in the future bring about a completely new humanity.

Such criticisms, which represent traditional moves in attacks upon Marxism, and which usually checkmate it, fail to eliminate a certain attractiveness: that appeal relates to the fact that, even if in a distorted way, Marx has placed a real truth in a light which escapes "natural law" positions. These positions can offer an ethical judgment of history in a theoretical way, but they do not enter efficaciously into the structural

34. This is also the theme of the whole of the first section of Marx and Engels's *German Ideology.*

35. Cf. K. Marx, *The Jewish Question.*

mechanisms which heavily condition human social and political action. On one side we have a *philosophy of praxis* which is not able to provide an ethical judgment about the evil which is affirmed and sometimes even triumphs in history, because in this philosophy of praxis ethical values must depend upon the evolution of historical struggles and alter with the results. On the other side we have an ethic which judges but by judging reveals its impotence, since it never achieves a concrete judgment in the particular historical and social struggles of the world. The problem which Wojtyła faced can therefore be stated in this way: Can we appropriate the moment of praxis to a philosophy of good and of being, by radically reformulating it?

We find ourselves, and it is important to say so explicitly right away, on a completely different line from earlier Western attempts to reform Marxism. These attempted to transcend Marxism but at the same time to maintain the Marxist negation of metaphysics. By a variety of complex paths, these different supersessions of Marxism led to nihilism. Wojtyła attempts to appropriate the philosophy of praxis to metaphysics by developing those potentialities not yet made explicit by the philosophy of being and, in so doing, to grasp that authentically human element of novelty which is seen by the philosophy of praxis.

The problem can also be put in this way: How can one think about praxis without renouncing the fundamental principle of the existence of a subject *(subiectum)* or metaphysical substratum *(hypokeimenon)* of man, which underlies any historical change, dictates, with its specific conformation, the fundamental lines of any possible modification, and furnishes the criterion upon which one can make an ethical judgment on them?[36] It goes without saying that by posing the question in such a way one implicitly takes a stand against those positions which, beginning from the declaration that Christianity is not a philosophy, assume that any philosophy whatsoever can be compatible with Christianity, and which imply that Christianity has nothing to do with the philosophical controversy about what it means to be a human being.

---

36. There is an interesting intellectual parallel between the criticism which has recently been made of Marxism by Lucio Colletti (applying to Marx the criticisms which Trendelenburg made against Hegel) and that of Wojtyła. In both cases it is the question of the removal of the metaphysical substratum. Cf. Lucio Colletti, *Tramonto dell'ideologia* (Bari: Laterza, 1980, pp. 87ff. See also Trendelenburg, *Logische Untersuchungen* (Hildesheim, 1964). In all of these cases, the resemblance can be explained by their common reference to Aristotle.

For Wojtyła, on the other hand, the category of the "person" must be fundamental in the controversy over the "humanum," in which Christianity, also, must take part.[37] The center of his argument on this point is the conception of human action which he takes over from St. Thomas. According to Wojtyła:

> human doing, that is, the act, is simultaneously transitive . . . and non-transitive. It is transitive inasmuch as it goes beyond the subject, seeking an expression or an effect in the external world and objectivizes itself in some product. It is non-transitive inasmuch as it "remains in the subject," by determining its quality and value, and establishes an essentially human becoming *(fieri)*. Before this conception of the act, man, by acting, not only accomplishes some action but in some way realizes himself and becomes himself.[38]

In comparison with this conception of the act (and thus of praxis), the Marxist picture can be seen to be limited. For here only one of the two effects of action is emphasized, that is, the transitive aspect, the transforming praxis of nature. For Wojtyła, however, the act always has an immediate effect in the man who carries it out, and it is through this that human truth is realized or negated. Having eliminated the metaphysical aspect of the subject *(suppositum humanum),* Marx does not have a sufficient grip upon this fundamental effect of action, that is, its moral significance.

This implies the centrality of the scholastic saying, "operation follows being" *(operari sequitur esse):*

> Work . . . is possible to the extent that man already exists. The priority of man, as the essential subject of human action, is metaphysical priority, and is bound to the idea of praxis, in the sense that it decides about it. The absurdity of the opposite position becomes clear when one considers that it would then have to be an indeterminate praxis which defines and determines subjects. Nor, further, is it possible to think an a priori praxis, as if from this quasi-absolute praxis would emerge, in the path of world evolution, categories, particular forms of the operation, which would determine its agents. Our thesis is that human doing (praxis) permits one to consider the agent in a more complete way. . . .[39]

37. K. Wojtyła, "Il Problema del Costituirsi della cultura attraverso la 'praxis' umana," p. 515.
38. Ibid., p. 516.
39. Ibid.

If Wojtyła is deeply rooted within the Thomistic tradition, his conception is also innovative. One can actually say that man ontologically pre-exists his action but that he realizes himself in it, and that the praxis, which uniquely takes place in work, is given as the place for the realization of the humanity *(humanum)* in man. One can see that this is a break with a certain tradition (Aristotelian, if not Thomistic), which ranks theory higher than praxis, the intellectual activity of comprehension higher than doing. From another angle, what is brought to the center of attention is an acting which, always and indissolubly, is immanent within ethical decision. At the same time man modifies his external surroundings through his work, adapting them to his needs, and modifies himself.

During the last century, Western tradition has given an absolutely privileged position to the objective aspect of work, the mastery of nature. It has forgotten that work is also — and in a fundamental way — a web of connections between men and a process through which persons realize themselves. If we wish fully to grasp the richness of human praxis, we must consider not only the way in which the objective effect of the praxis (a domesticated nature and a transformed environment) reacts upon him by changing him, but also the way in which praxis directly changes the man who brings it into being, either by making him more authentically human or by causing him to lose his humanity. This new way of looking at the matter strongly affects the way in which we look at economic and political praxis. In the case of economic practice there is a glimmering within many phenomena (found most of all in mature capitalist countries) which shows a growing demand for *quality of work* and *self-realization through work.*

Especially, but not only, in those societies in which the stimulation of material need is not felt with drastic immediacy, people ask for work not only to guarantee their material survival but also to be personally fulfilling. This has clearly not been considered within the traditional philosophy of praxis, but can be considered within a philosophy of praxis which knows and appreciates *the subjective side of work.* Wojtyła's friend, Jozef Tischner, has provided an important contribution to this perspective as an accompaniment to his philosophical reflection upon the events in Poland; he elaborates an ethic of work and of solidarity which begins from the desire for an honest and true relation between men and with the nature of their work.[40]

If one looks at political praxis, it is necessary to emphasize that Wojtyła's

40. J. Tischner, *Etica della solidarietà; Etica del lavoro.*

position allows one to draw the problem of political ethics into political praxis. The way in which the objective of transformation is achieved is reflected in those who gain it and in the outcome of their work, because the new social relationships are still human relationships. It has become common to emphasize the method of persuasion and dialogue, of common human growth. The repudiation of the notion of violence as the *midwife of history* arises from the awareness that no *new man* can come from a praxis that is morally dehumanizing for those who carry it out.

One could perhaps say (although this is only one interpretation) that this revision of the philosophy of praxis enters finally into the heart of the analytic instrument which Marx used to examine society. For Marx, human work creates values, but work itself does not, properly speaking, have a value. According to the author of *Das Kapital,* every commodity has a *use value* and an *exchange value.* The *use value* is the capacity to respond to a specific human need. The exchange value is the rule of the exchange of commodities; it is measured in the last instance by the content of objectivized work in each commodity. Work is a good which has an exchange value (the salaries and the quantities of goods necessary to the survival and the reproduction of the worker); it does not, however, have a use value. In the first chapter of *Das Kapital,* the use value of work is identified with its capacity to produce exchange value. By making the worker work longer than the time objectivized in his salary, the capitalist entrepreneur obtains a surplus-labor and a surplus-value. In this way Marx specified the contradiction between proletariat and capital in purely quantitative terms. His analysis of alienation would ultimately be based on this conception of labor. Wojtyła, conversely, allows one properly to understand the use value of work, the specifically human need for self-realization to which the the act of working responds, and allows one to explain the problem of the *alienation of work* in a more expansive and more liberating way. If one begins from the Marxist conception, for example, it is equally difficult to analyze the alienation of work which occurs in socialist societies. Alienation is understood in connection with the problem of the ownership of the means of production, which in such a society would be collectivized. The way in which Wojtyła sets out the issue allows one to think about alienation in connection with the effective organization of labor, with the way in which this offers the possibility of a complete realization of man through genuine and morally valid relations between persons which are founded upon participation: without such an effective organization of labor, human realization is stifled or eliminated.

It remains true, even from Wojtyła's perspective, that there is a unique relation between work and culture. Culture is not a secondary epiphenomenon of work but its emergent meaning, inasmuch as the person realizes himself in work. The person, who ontologically precedes his act, realizes himself through it and existentially becomes himself through praxis. This self-realization is not an arbitrary shaping of oneself but a giving of a full realization to the ontological potential, which is present from the beginning, through a free gift which is inscribed within his existence. In this way of looking at it, culture is not an abstract wisdom which is distinct from the human struggle for life, but the proper attitude through which man engages in reality in a relation of openness and of reciprocal giving toward both other human beings and nature. Culture is the capacity to love, respect, and make use of all things, each according to its proper dignity. In this perspective, things are not merely neutral "primal material" to be transformed by human action. The way in which man is related to them has a profound ethical content, implying at every turn the discovery of unique values, and a consonance between man and things, even though such a recognition must often be brought about through a struggle against untamed nature. The attitude of respect for nature, the capacity to feel wonder before it, and to recognize that it is charged with values is the opposite of a brutal exploitation of natural resources, or pollution of the environment. The destruction of the natural human context of existence is the fruit of Promethean arrogance which assumes man is empowered to transform nature for its own project; it involves an attempt to escape the recognition of human limits and a denial, therefore, of the fact that man is first of all a creature.[41] As a creature, man must assume a nontyrannical government of the world: he must simultaneously use it and hold it in respect.

On this theme, Wojtyła cites the words of Norwid:

the beautiful is such to make work fascinating
the work, in order to resurrect.[42]

In one way, our author's whole idea of work can be considered as a commentary on what Norwid has said poetically. Man's relation with nature, which arises from his transforming actions, cannot be separated from

41. Because of this truth, there is a different interpretation of the figure of Prometheus, which is bound to this understanding of human work. Cf. Norwid's *Promethidion*.

42. C. K. Norwid, *Promethidion*, Dialogue I: cited in "Il Problema del costituirsi della cultura attraverso la 'praxis' humana," p. 519.

a contemplative moment. Contemplation actually rests at the center of work. The thing with which man comes into increasingly intimate contact through working reveals the values of which it is full — practical values but also intrinsically aesthetic values. The thing constantly regenerates wonder in the human heart: an analogous wonder is generated by human relationships, which continually deepen through work.[43]

When man treats other men and nature in this way, "then we can say that such an acting, or such a working contains in itself *a specific irradiation of humanity*, thanks to which the work of culture is inscribed within the work of nature. There is thereby disclosed the roots of the union of man with nature and simultaneously there is revealed the place of the encounter of man with the Creator in his perennial plan, in which man has become part thanks to his intelligence and wisdom. 'Nature' and the 'world' lie in wait for this human activity, namely, the irradiation of humanity through praxis."[44]

While it brings about man's existential fulfillment, work historically realizes the reconciliation of man with nature and reveals the vocation of nature to be for man. Because of sin, this reconciliation, which reveals God's original plan for man, is not without pain and hardship. It nonetheless shows the correspondence which God originally intended between the external and the internal world.

In this sense human practice always has, to the eye which can see it, an aesthetic moment, and it is this aesthetic moment which makes it fully human.

> Through human praxis a culture is formed, if and insofar as man does not become a slave of his action, of his work, but achieves an admiration for reality . . . inasmuch, that is, as he finds in it a strong sense of the "cosmos" and the order of the world in its micro-cosmic and macro-cosmic dimensions. . . . Fascination, admiration, contemplation, constitute the essential basis out of which culture is made through human praxis.[45]

The transformation of material reality, which is a result of the objective side of human work, has at the same time an echo in the subjective side of

43. Cf. also Wojtyła, "Teoria e Prassi nella filosofia della persona umana," in *Sapienza* 29, pp. 377-84.

44. Wojtyła, "Il problema del costituirsi della 'cultura' attraverso la 'praxis' umana," p. 520.

45. Ibid., p. 521.

work. The world will have a kinship with the agent who created it through his work. If it is true that culture comes about through praxis, it is equally true that culture has a constitutive effect upon praxis and that this bears in itself the characteristics of culture and of the ultimate human goals which it brings into being.[46]

Culture embodies that aspect of human praxis on account of which it is a continual struggle against death. Men must die, just as all animals do. *But men know that they will die.* The thought of the end throws a shadow over all of man's life and casts it into question. Under sentence of death, man protects his life through working. This is a very fragile defense, destined to crumble. Work produces things which are consumed; it cannot prevent the final outcome that human life itself will be consumed. That which is not consumed in time is above all the intransitive aspect of work, through which man becomes what he is. In human culture as preserved the results of that struggle with death which men in the flow of the generations have conducted within themselves.

This testimony says that in man there is that which is eternally valid, even if the individual men who have produced it are dead. Everyone who lives experiences values which have a universal character and which will perpetuate them after they are gone. The work and the historical action of man speak of a "care" which extends beyond his physical existence, and even beyond his generation: "The imprints which remain in human culture are not only in themselves in opposition to death insofar as they always live and inspire new generation, but they also imply immortality, and even more than this, they appear as *a witness to the personal immortality of man*, which is based on that in him which is 'intransitive.' Culture becomes a perennial experience and witness, which one encounters as a response to all existential pessimism about man."[47] This is a sign of transcendence.

Envoi

The text which we have analyzed reproduces a conference paper given on 18 March 1977. A little more than a year later, on 16 October 1978, the philosopher Karol Wojtyła was elected to the episcopal chair of St. Peter in Rome and became, under the name of John Paul II, Supreme Pontiff of the

46. The teleology of the human subject is reflected in nature through his work.
47. "Il problema del costituirsi della cultura attraverso la 'praxis' umana," p. 524.

Catholic Church. Our reconstruction of his philosophical thought must break off here. The criteria and the hermeneutical methods of philosophical thought differ from those which can be used to interpret the Pope's teaching, which have as their immediate antecedents not the thinking of the philosopher Wojtyła, but the acts of his predecessors and the entire Magisterium of the Church in its historical development.

Naturally, the individual personality of the man who is elevated to the Chair of Peter, as well as his cultural formation, are not erased by the choice of the Cardinals in the Holy Spirit. These personal factors enter into the composition of the unique event of grace which every Pontificate is in itself. It is not, for example, illegitimate to ask to what degree the notions of work — in a subjective and in an objective sense — used in the encyclical *Laborem exercens* indicate Wojtyła's personal philosophical reflection on the theme of work and of praxis. In what sense is the personal philosophical thinking of Karol Wojtyła reflected in the teaching of John Paul II? But such hermeneutical reflections, although useful, will not prove adequate in themselves, and this is the reason I have narrowly restricted my exposition to the thinking which preceded his election to the Papacy. Although some discourses of John Paul II have been cited, this has been only for the purpose of drawing together and situating certain elements of the historical and cultural context within which the principal argument of my research has been placed.

Finally, it is legitimate to ask in what direction Wojtyła's philosophical thought can be taken. I do not think I am wrong in saying that his late works were developing toward a philosophy of praxis capable of inspiring a new social theory which could bring about the convergence of the bearing of the different human sciences toward an adequate vision of man.[48] Such a social theory, in many ways coincident with a reappraisal of the social teaching of the Church, would be able to respond to the pressing need for critical thinking capable of helping the natural and human sciences to be authentically responsible, in their exercise and their results, to human life.

Wojtyła's work, in any case, remains in many ways incomplete. It indicates paths, delineates hypotheses for research, begins a deep investigation, and shows new horizons. It thereby requires to be taken forward. The purpose of this book is essentially to invite the reader both to grasp the meaning of a new philosophy of man and to participate in the work of its construction.

48. Cf., among other things, K. Wojtyła, "Alienation or Participation," in "The Self and the Other," vol. 6 of the *Analecta Husserliana* (Dordrecht: Reidel, 1977), pp. 61ff.

Translators' Afterword

Buttiglione on Wojtyła's Philosophy of Freedom and an Update on Fifteen Years of Studies of Wojtyła's Thought

This book was published in Italian in 1982 and promptly sparked off a series of debates and seminars on Karol Wojtyła's thought. A French and a Spanish translation appeared two years later. In 1994 Rocco Buttiglione was asked to write an introduction for the third Polish edition of *The Acting Person* (1969, 1985, 1994). This edition is particularly important because it was published in a new climate of press freedom, after the collapse of Communist dictatorship in Poland. That Rocco Buttiglione was asked to write the introduction for this edition indicates the prominence of his understanding of Karol Wojtyła's thought; if one reads this introduction to *The Acting Person* (translated for this volume in the Appendix), one can see why he was selected for this arduous task. In this Afterword we offer the English-speaking reader a few keys to this book (Part I) and a succinct survey-update on the studies which appeared in between the publication of the Italian edition *(Il Pensiero di Karol Wojtyła)* and Eerdmans' English translation (Part II).

I. A Philosophy of Freedom:
Buttiglione on the "Philosopher Pope"

Perhaps even more than most other philosophical tribes, phenomenologists use a highly specialized jargon. Wojtyła's philosophical language, especially in *The Acting Person*, seems to participate in this "family idiom," complicated by the fact that Wojtyła is a Thomist who learned this dialect after his basic Thomistic training at the Dominicans' Pontifical University in Rome. His terminology, accordingly, appears as complex as his philosophical plan. Overly pious Catholics may blame the translators for the difficulties in Wojtyła's texts. But while conceding that there are problems with translations ("translators are traitors," as they say in Italian) as well as acknowledging specific difficulties with Anna-Teresa Tymieniecka's phenomenologizing translation of *The Acting Person*, the fault does not reside entirely on their side. Actually, as someone said, even Germans find it easier to read Heidegger and Kant in English than in German. This may well be true for Polish readers of Wojtyła's works. Wojtyła's style is not just obscure; it is almost cryptic and, above all, it implies familiarity with two philosophical traditions which are not accustomed to communicate so freely with one another. Kenneth Schmitz, author of an excellent English monograph on Karol Wojtyła, candidly admits:

> I first came to appreciate the philosophical reputation of Karol Wojtyła during a visit in Poland in 1978. When the English edition of *Osoba i Czyn* appeared a year or so later under the title *The Acting Person*, I picked it up with some expectancy. . . . Despite many years of professional philosophy, including the study of Thomism and phenomenology, I could not — in my admittedly casual perusal — make out the lines of the argument or reach a conclusion as to the value of the results. I could not quite decide what the author was up to.[1]

We ought to notice that Kenneth Schmitz is no casual reader. He is a professional who reads and digests Hegel, and has been doing so for half a century. His admission is therefore even more telling, and raises the problem of how we should approach and understand Professor Wojtyła, the philosopher. Such an effort is worthwhile because, in spite of the obscurity of his writing, one realizes that he is saying something worth understanding.

1. K. Schmitz, *At the Center of the Human Drama* (Washington, D.C.: Catholic University of America Press, 1991), p. 58.

Yet, we may further wonder, if he had not become a Cardinal and a Pope, would anyone have cared to read Wojtyła? Conversely, we might wonder whether he might not have become one of the major philosophical minds of this century if all of these ecclesiastical honors and duties had not been thrust upon him. Becoming Pope is not the best way to acquire fame as a thinker; it is more common, and generally easier, to achieve a (sometimes justified) philosophical respectability by getting into trouble with Popes and other powerless authorities. Being a Cardinal or a Pope does not appear to be the best way to secure a philosophical readership. On the one hand, pious nonphilosophical minds read everything as dogma or as a direct attack against dogma; on the other hand, impious philosophical minds are for the most part not too free in regard to anything connected with God, religion, and priests. Buttiglione, however, does not belong to either category of reader, and this is the first striking point about his book. Philosophy and piety are not in opposition to one another, and in many ways they are not even separable. Piety is no enemy of philosophy. In the words of Vico, "He who is not pious cannot be truly wise."

There is a striking contrast between two postconciliar Popes' relationships to philosophy, which may help us to understand the significance of Buttiglione's book. An *inverse proportionality* subsists in the relationship between Buttiglione and Wojtyła when it is compared with the relationship of Maritain to Montini. Giambattista Montini (Pope Paul VI) was a diligent student of Maritain's philosophy. As a matter of fact, Fr. Montini spent a lot of time personally translating Maritain into Italian. Maritain was the teacher, and Montini, the Pope who guided the Council, the pupil. Later, in acknowledgment of his intellectual debt, the student-Pope would have made professor Maritain a Cardinal if this would have not ruined Maritain's already troubled reputation as a philosopher.[2] With Wojtyła and Buttiglione

2. "Robert M. Hutchins, in his role as president of the University of Chicago, tried three times to give Maritain a chair in the faculty of philosophy. The philosophy department blocked the appointment on each of the three occasions, even when Hutchins finally offered to pay the stipend with nondepartmental funds. In the words of one member of the department, the reason was that "Maritain is a propagandist." Hutchins replied, "All of you are propagandists." On another occasion, he sent an intermediary, probably John Nef, to speak to the head of department, a well-known positivist. The reply for Hutchins was: "Maritain is not a good philosopher." So the go-between asked: "But do you have any good philosophers in the department?" The response came back: "No, but we know how to recognize a good philosopher when we see one." Jude P. Dougherty, *Maritain e il Precipizio. Dall' Antimoderno al Contadino della Garonna* (1996).

we have a perfect inversion of this relationship: the philosopher is the Pope, Buttiglione the student who joins the somewhat restricted group of the Polish school of Wojtyła.[3] Buttiglione says about his encounter with Wojtyła:

> Monsignor Francesco Ricci was extremely active in supporting the Catholic Church and all who were persecuted in communist countries in the 1960s and '70s. He brought them news and books from the West, and at the same time he brought us news about the great culture flourishing underground in communist countries. He created a group of young people who worked with him in the movement *Comunione e Liberazione* to further a cultural relation to the communist countries. Monsignor Ricci was fascinated by the young Bishop of Krakow, a certain Karol Wojtyła, and he translated some of Wojtyła's writings. I was at the time a law school student, but Monsignor Ricci insisted that I should learn Polish and write a book on this fascinating new philosophy — on the one hand, so open to the world and, on the other hand, so deeply centered in Christianity. I resisted for many years. At last I gave up and accepted Monsignor Ricci's counsel. . . . So I happened to become the last "Assistant Professor" of the Wojtyła School.

It is noteworthy that Buttiglione joined the Wojtyła School with a different formation from his Polish colleagues and with a philosophical horizon quite different from Wojtyła's. Buttiglione is not a native speaker of Wojtyła's "language" in many senses. He speaks the language of civil and public philosophy. At the risk of being misunderstood, we can say, in fact, that Buttiglione speaks the language of political philosophy. This is the kind of language which was forbidden to anyone in Poland who did not represent public orthodoxy. Its use by a bishop would have been exceptionally imprudent.[4] The most political chapter of *The Acting Person* is written in such

3. Derek Cross, "A Conversation with Rocco Buttiglione," in *Crisis*, 10.11 (1992), p. 32.

4. "Cardinal Wojtyła had fully appropriated Wyszynski's tactics, which were based on the primate's conviction that in the long run Catholicism in Poland could escape dismemberment in the grip of Communist ideology only by keeping intellectuals, workers and farmers united, by keeping priests out of politics, and by avoiding the dissipation of Catholic strength and solidarity in Poland that would allegedly issue from dialogue with a Marxist theorist of social justice." G. H. Williams, "Karol Wojtyła and Marxism," in P. Ramet (ed.), *Catholicism and Politics in Communist Societies* (Durham, NC: Duke University, 1990), p. 366.

an abstruse way that even the carefully obtuse Communist censorship would never have suspected that it was a really dangerous piece of writing. Leo Strauss writes in *Persecution and the Art of Writing:*

> For the influence of persecution on literature is precisely that it compels all writers who hold heterodox views to develop a peculiar technique of writing, the technique which we have in mind when we speak of writing between the lines.[5]

Writing between the lines has been one of the techniques which passed under the general name of *Ostpolitik* in the recent history of the Church. This technique is not unfamiliar for those who take uninterrupted political freedom for granted. Karol Wojtyła was a seminarian, the most important moment of formation for a Catholic priest, during the Nazi occupation. He spent most of the rest of his life as a thinker, poet, and pastor under a more stable, yet not less repressive, totalitarianism. Could a philosopher speak his mind freely under Hitler, Stalin, Khrushchev, and Brezhnev? While martyrdom remains always a free mind's last witness to truth, there is plenty of room for prudence between conformism and martyrdom. Cardinal Wojtyła did not seem an enthusiast for death; as a general principle, the crown of martyrdom should not be desired as long as it can be avoided.

Wojtyła lived under regimes which regarded philosophizing and writing as among the greatest threats to their existence. Any manifestation of truth was a threat greater than internal sedition and external aggression. The English-speaking world may not be able to appreciate one of its greatest treasures of this century, the freedom from totalitarianism. But, as the Roman historian reminds us, rare are those happy times in which you are free to think what you want and to say what you think. Wojtyła was not so lucky. How is it possible to philosophize in the vicinity of Auschwitz and under the regime of the inventors of the Gulag Archipelago? Can the Polish

---

5. Leo Strauss, *Persecution and the Art of Writing* (Chicago: University of Chicago Press, 1952), p. 24. An example of such language is found in Williams's *The Mind of John Paul II* (see n. 6 below). In July 1976 Cardinal Wojtyła "gave his second academic lecture at the Catholic University of America . . . : 'The Person's Transcendence in the Human Act and the Auto-teleology of Man,' in which he analyzed the drive of the human person to go beyond humanity to reach the Infinite. His host, Dean Jude P. Dougherty of the philosophy faculty, was permitted to announce the address under the more winsome title, 'Use and Abuse of Freedom.'" The Cardinal gave an incomprehensible title which Dougherty translated into political language.

Wojtyła understand Western freedom, especially in the great liberal political tradition of the Anglo-American experience? Buttiglione told Derek Cross:

> . . . years ago I read a book by George Huntston Williams, *The Mind of John Paul II,* a very good book, very informative, but in this book there was a reproach that the Holy Father did not understand the American mind and the principles of the free society.[6]

Although, like Williams, he belongs to the "happy club of the free world," Buttiglione disagrees with him on this point. While hailing from the free and imperfect world and from a different philosophical horizon, Buttiglione understood that Wojtyła's major concern was precisely human freedom. Williams's thesis is thus reversed in Buttiglione's book. The assumption that Wojtyła knows and understands freedom becomes the guiding idea which Buttiglione adopted to understand Wojtyła and make him comprehensible to Western readers. Under totalitarian regimes, people are still able to think freely — if furtively — and also to think about freedom; paradoxically, the risk of mindlessness seems to be greatest under politically free regimes. Here people seem to have a tendency to stop thinking and to take freedom for granted, as if they believed that their blood were too noble to be enslaved. Buttiglione saw that Wojtyła understood freedom, and on this basis he wrote *Il Pensiero di Karol Wojtyła.*

Buttiglione's philosophical formation is substantially different from Wojtyła's. On the one hand, Buttiglione is deeply influenced by the Frankfurt School, in particular by the thought of Max Horkheimer, about which he has written two scholarly monographs.[7] He does not have an "epistemological approach" to philosophy, which seems to be a prerequisite of any academic phenomenology. On the other hand, Buttiglione is a student of a political philosopher, Augusto Del Noce, who was the most cultured and most outspoken Italian enemy of the Communist strategy for the subjugation of Western Europe through an initial "occupation from within" of liberal institutions.[8] For these reasons Buttiglione's language is not

---

6. Cross, "A Conversation with Rocco Buttiglione," p. 28. Buttiglione refers to George Huntston Williams, *The Mind of John Paul II: Origins of His Thought and Action* (New York: Seabury Press, 1981).

7. R. Buttiglione, *La crisi dell'economia marxista. Gli inizi della Scuola di Francoforte* (Rome: Studium, 1979), and idem, *Dialettica e Nostalgia* (Milan: Jaca, 1978).

8. See R. Buttiglione, *Augusto Del Noce. Biografia di un pensiero* (Casale Monferrato: Piemme, 1991), and idem, *Il problema politico dei Cattolici. Dottrina sociale e modernita'*

Wojtyła's, but the far more comprehensible language of public philosophy. He interprets and incorporates Wojtyła into this language. Moreover, Buttiglione was educated as a Westerner. At sixteen he traveled as a tourist all over the United States, enjoying freedom in a foreign country that was a dangerous dream for citizens of the former Eastern bloc in their own countries.

As if there were not already sufficient differences, we could observe that Buttiglione is not even a Thomist. (We could add, to his merit, however, that he is not an anti-Thomist either.) He does not come from the seminarian culture of the Roman Pontifical Universities or from the hypermetaphysical neo-Thomism of the Catholic University of Milan. Apart from never having experienced political totalitarianism and not having been educated in the culture of the Church under siege, Buttiglione says things that a priest cannot or should not say. He is a married man, and his wife is a "liberated woman," herself a licensed Freudian analyst.

In spite of these differences, Buttiglione understands the Polish philosopher and, even more remarkably, makes him understandable. Yet his book is not a vulgarization of Wojtyła's thought. Wojtyła's philosophy appears in Buttiglione's work as a fiery defense of freedom in an age of political tyrannies. Wojtyła's awareness of freedom and of the real possibility of losing it derives from his direct experience. With the exception of some surviving Jews, few Americans share Wojtyła's dubious privilege of having been educated under Hitler and Stalin and having published their philosophical works in the time of Khrushchev and Brezhnev.

Buttiglione's book is a response to Williams's claim that Wojtyła does not understand freedom. If a critique had to be set out, it should have been the contrary one. It appears, after reading Buttiglione, that Wojtyła does not understand anything *but* freedom and its relationship with the truth, which can be presented *freely* only to a person. From the religious to the politica arenal, and from sexual to economic matters, Wojtyła seems to repeat constantly and rather obsessively that we must respect the person's freedom — that is to say, we should value the person's *self-determination* and treat that person as an end in himself. Wojtyła's insistence on self-determination is so radical that, in retrospect, one might ask if Wojtyła overreacted to his experience of political slavery. In social matters, if he takes the side of the unions, it is because he believes passionately in the

---

(Casale Monferrato: Piemme, 1993). Also cf. Augusto Del Noce, *I cattolici e il progressimo*, ed. R. Buttiglione (Rome: Leonardo Editore, 1994).

freedom (dignity) of blue-collar workers. Unions in his mind are not a limitation of the free-enterprise mentality but an extension of the freedom mentality to everyone. Solidarity is therefore not to be seen in opposition to individual freedom, but as the recognition of the truth that freedom belongs to every human subject, even those who in the economic enterprise appear to be on the heteronomous side.[9] "Participation" is the economic regime of maximum freedom: it is the concrete American experience understood in European language.[10] In his much less popular sexual doctrines, if Wojtyła wants everyone's freedom to be absolutely respected, it is because he wants to bring freedom to an area where freedom and dignity do not appear as the most interesting and attractive values. In other words, he wants a person's freedom defended even from those most attractive values which his mentor Max Scheler was never able to resist.[11] From a political point of view he knows that relativism, the dismissal of truth, leads to the primacy of power and political tyranny. We could say that he defends truth in order to save freedom. In other words, it seems that he values freedom more than truth, and is ready to subordinate the rights of truth to freedom, which is the most basic truth of the dignity of the person.[12] The most important truth for him seems to be a person's freedom.

From an "old traditionalist" point of view Wojtyła's attitude toward freedom appears excessive. He seems to be obsessed by freedom, a condition easily acquired by long association with modern philosophers such as Rousseau and Kant. Though he has been accused of other obsessions, our philosopher's real obsession seems to be with freedom. The thesis that Wojtyła does not understand freedom because he is a Polish priest who lived under one of the greatest tyrannies of history overturns into the antithesis: Wojtyła seems to overestimate freedom. He seems to depreciate the rightful and necessary limitations of self-determination, which come from our bodies

9. Cf. R. Buttiglione, *L'uomo e il lavoro* (Bologna: CSEO, 1982 [Spanish, 1984]).

10. The alliance between the principle of freedom and solidarity, where solidarity is understood as an extension of freedom (and dignity) to everyone, is also at the core of the American system. Michael Novak's *The Spirit of Democratic Capitalism* may be understood as overcoming the opposition between the American spirit and Catholicism in economy. It is significant that Novak's interest is in the American experience of unions (*The Guns of Lattimer* [1978]), and even more significant was the prompt translation into Polish of his major work on the economy of freedom by the Solidarity samizdat press. Also cf. Buttiglione, *Il problema politico dei Cattolici*, pp. 215-31.

11. Cf. R. Buttiglione, *L'uomo e la famiglia* (Rome: Dino, 1991) and *La Crisi della Morale* (Roma: Dino, 1991).

12. Cf. R. Buttiglione, *Il problema politico dei Cattolici.*

as well as from our governments. He seems to dismiss the fact that not everyone wants to live authentically (freely) at every moment of his life, and that often this is not a question of will but of possibility. Freedom requires incessant vigilance and struggle. People do not want to be continually conscious of the freedom of their acts and of the personalistic value (freedom) of the one who cooks a hamburger in the restaurant kitchen. But in everyday life the good of the hamburger is more important than a personalistic norm. *Inauthenticity* has its own attractiveness: we do not need to be always awake as conscious philosophers. A moderate and teleological heteronomy is more bearable than a ceaseless responsible autonomy.

However, it is with regard to religious freedom, or freedom of religion or freedom of conscience, that traditionalists may find Wojtyła's understanding to be far too American. The late Archbishop Marcel Léfebvre described in words and pictures the victory of freedom (liberalism) over truth as the defeat of true European and good French traditions by the American way of life. To an integrist mind "religious freedom" triumphed over the last of its opponents with Vatican II. Wojtyła's thesis on religious freedom would therefore be the obsession of a brilliant young philosophical mind which was prematurely exposed to the revolutionary spirit of Vatican II.[13] Indeed, it appears impossible to separate this thinker from the experience of the Council. Wojtyła's apology for religious freedom is performed without mental reservations: it is, when understood, unbearably authentic.

It is with "freedom of religion" that the experience of this century brought Catholic thinkers to question some assumptions about the relationship between truth and freedom, with respect to political power. About two hundred years passed between the most successful declaration of religious freedom in modernity, Jefferson's *Declaration of Independence,* and Vatican II's (and Wojtyła's) defense of religious freedom. One should not, however, rush to the conclusion that it took two centuries for Catholicism to understand what was self-evident to the Founding Fathers. The American Founding Fathers, and Jefferson above all, wanted to keep politics free from religion and free from the absolute truth and absolutism of religion: truths such as those concerning human destiny, the sense of the world, the meaning of the universe and human life. It does not seem that Jefferson had a particularly high regard for Christianity as such. His concern was with the minimal conditions for the prosperity of a republic.

---

13. Buttiglione outlines Wojtyła's thesis in Chapter 6 of this book.

By affirming the truth of religious freedom, his purpose was to set politics free: religious freedom is necessary to secure a regime of common good (republic). But religious freedom is not what the French and Spanish traditionalists had imagined, that is, religious indifference. Religious freedom in the view of the Enlightened Founding Fathers is a political, not a theological thesis: the traditionalist thesis (which equates religious freedom with religious indifference) is theological. In sum, the main concern of the Founding Fathers was political: they were politicians, not theologians. Religious freedom was to them a release from the confrontation of absolutes in politics.

The European experience of totalitarianism in our century, however, gives religious freedom a new meaning, which is immediately understood only by those who have suffered under such regimes. The idea that the doctrine of religious freedom of the Founding Fathers (Jefferson) simply coincides with the doctrine of religious freedom of the Conciliar Fathers (Wojtyła) should be considered with caution. The two doctrines may coincide *materialiter,* as an Aristotelian scholastic would put it, but not *formaliter.* The American and the Polish bishops may both have voted for *Dignitatis Humanae,* but they did so for different reasons.

The Conciliar Fathers (and Wojtyła) want to liberate religion from political power. Political powers should not be allowed to engage with absolutes, with the meaning of life and people's ultimate hopes and fears. This is the business of religion. Totalitarianism demonstrates the danger of letting secular powers assume a theological character: they end up being beyond good and evil, being unaccountable to anything superior. For the Founding Fathers (Jefferson) the welfare of this world was too important for men to kill each other over theological disputes (and this practical wisdom is admirable). For the Conciliar Fathers (Wojtyła), truths about God are too important to be left in the hands of politicians. Truths about the Absolute, about the meaning and destiny of life, are too powerful to be an instrument. Politicians should make use of less important things, like passions and interests. They should not occupy themselves with these truths, at least insofar as they are politicians, and they should not become secular priests. Their business is not to try to offer answers to the meaning of life.

The opposition to the blurring of politics and religion has found American politics in agreement with Catholic theology in this century. President Reagan did not hate Communism any more than Wojtyła did. They both wanted the end of secular theology from different perspectives: the politician wanted to put an end to Marxist theology's taking the place of politics, the priest wanted to put an end to the substitution of Marxist political hopes for theology. These points, though different, are complementary. But there is a respect in which Wojtyła becomes the advocate of the American *politeia* when he vigorously asserts the difference between "freedom *of* religion" and "freedom *from* religion." From a theological point of view, the American political experiment is founded on freedom *of* religion. In this dimension Wojtyła is a better philosopher than Jefferson or Reagan. The disappearance of religion is the ultimate victory of totalitarianism, a victory which is more powerful than a military conquest because it subjugates a nation from within.

Where nothing is religious or sacred, there everything is religious. Where the spiritual authority disappears, the secular authority will gladly occupy the empty place. When all is relative, then nothing is really relative; nothing is less important than something else. When absolute truths, even moral and religious absolutes, are lost, then even a hierarchy of relative values is relative. Relativism consumes itself; where there are no absolutes, nothing can be said to be "better than," not even the good of the majority against a scratch on a tyrant's finger. Someone needs to be the guardian of absolute truth, in order to save relative values and the importance of their relativity, so that the relative needs of the most powerful members of society do not become absolute by virtue of their power, but are still kept in their apparent and real relativeness.

Those who advocate freedom *of* religion want to keep politics away from absolutes. Politicians manipulating absolutes have killed hundred of millions of peoples in this century, and have destroyed the freedom and the dignity of billions, and not just their religious freedom but also their political, economic, sexual, and personal freedoms. For those who "have" a religion these considerations are valid. For those, on the other hand, for whom this world is everything, the priest and the president will necessarily be identical. Atheism leads to totalitarianism, and agnosticism is too weak to counteract this internal necessity. The battle against totalitarianism has ripened a new understanding of those very absolute truths pronounced by wise yet nonreligious men like Jefferson, a meaning beyond the Founding Fathers' understanding. This is the meaning of Wojtyła's antitotalitarian philosophy of freedom developed in the context of the Vatican II declaration *On Human Dignity*. While religion is too powerful to allow politicians to control it, the alternative of lack of religion is an illusion. Political agnosticism, the belief that the politician deals with relative things, is possible only where people kneel to something higher than political power.

317

A worldly relativism (skepticism and agnosticism) can define itself against an absolute, that is, a God. Atheism leads to the absolutization of the relative.

Wojtyła is so obsessed with freedom that he seems preoccupied by the recurrence of totalitarianism. It even seems that his defense of religion is subordinated to human freedom and human dignity. Wojtyła's "liberalism" is not the kind of liberal position which holds that only governmental issues are essential and dismisses social and religious matters as secondary or private concerns. There is an essential distinction between Wojtyła's philosophy of freedom and the so-called "religion of freedom." As Augusto Del Noce writes about our century:

> The "religion of freedom" is overturned into freedom from religion, into freedom from any religion. . . . this secularism does not express a religious sense higher than the one of positive religions. . . . under the fake name of religious peace indifference is imposed as a public duty.[14]

Religious indifference will let ultimate ends be taken over by politics. But this will create an immanent embodiment of the absolute. Wojtyła is a philosopher of freedom who thinks that promoting religion advances freedom and human dignity. Freedom is the vertical transcendence of the person, who overcomes any form of conditioning and constriction. This vertical transcendence is the dimension of religion, and it is the metaphysical foundation of all freedoms or rights of the person. The spirit of freedom and the spirit of religion go together, and democracy (understood as a system of freedoms) must find in religion the moral strength which allows for the love of other people's freedom, that is, human dignity.[15] Irreligion is the ally of tyranny and of totalitarianism. Atheism is essential to Communism (and totalitarianism), but this judgment is convertible: Communism (totalitarianism) is essential to atheism. If Communism is defeated at the level of the economy only, then its defeat is only apparent. The materialistic belief in the economic defeat of communism reasserts the Marxist dogma that the economy is the fundamental structure to which all other human realities must be reduced. If nothing counts except the economy, then the opulent society is the dialectical realization of Marxism. In this society materialism is realized and freedom (vertical transcendence)

---

14. A. Del Noce, *Il suicidio della rivoluzione* (Milan: Rusconi, 1978), p. 47.
15. R. Buttiglione, *Il problema politico dei Cattolici*, pp. 203-14.

must disappear.[16] In other words, where there is God there is freedom. Wojtyła's *existential personalism* takes the philosophy of freedom to the opposite pole to Sartre's existentialism. Sartre maintains that if there is a God there cannot be any freedom; therefore, since it is evident that we are free, there must be no God. Wojtyła contends that if there is a God there is freedom, and the history of this century demonstrates the factual connection between atheism and the maximal oppression of freedom. Wojtyła's anthropology of freedom is as modern as Sartre's. For Sartre, being religious is the opposite of being free; for Wojtyła, just as for Pico della Mirandola, being religious and being free are the one and the same.

II. Summary Outline of the Literature from 1982 to 1997 on Karol Wojtyła's Thought

Since 1982 the number of studies on Wojtyła's thought has greatly increased. While our survey can by no means claim completeness, we have tried to cover most of the scholarly literature on Wojtyła's thought. We have maintained the methodological distinction between Karol Wojtyła's thought and John Paul II's teachings. The hermeneutic principles pertaining to the secondary literature on the writings of a thinker and those on the doctrines of a Pope are very different. The fact that Karol Wojtyła is, as a *suppositum*,

---

16. "There is an idea of technological society which in theory eliminates the discrimination between slaves and masters through the full exploitation of the forces of nature. This society achieves a world in which the work of machines would allow human beings to enjoy the freedom to exercise only those activities which are specifically human. But there is another idea of technological society, characterized, so to speak, by a totalitarianism of technological activity, in such a way that the entire human activity is understood as oriented to transforming nature and to material possession. I would define this latter technological society in the following terms. On the one hand, it is a society which accepts all the negations of Marxism concerning contemplative thought, religion, and metaphysics. It accepts the Marxist reduction of ideas to instruments of production. On the other hand, it rejects all revolutionary-messianic aspects of Marxism, and those religious remains which are still present within the revolutionary idea. Thus this technological society truly represents bourgeoisie spirit in its pure essence, a bourgeoisie spirit which triumphs over its two traditional adversaries: transcendent religion and revolutionary thought." Augusto Del Noce, *L'epoca della secolarizzazione* (Milan: Giuffre', 1970), p. 14. See also F. Botturi, *Desiderio e verita'* (Milan: Massimo, 1985), pp. 64-96.

His Holiness John Paul II, does not give license for methodological confusion: we limit ourselves, therefore, to Professor Wojtyła.

The bibliography is divided into eight parts, which cover the main literature on Wojtyła: (1) public philosophy or philosophy of society; (2) the encounter/opposition between old and new, between medieval philosophy, that is, Thomism, and modern philosophy, particularly phenomenology; (3) Wojtyła and realist phenomenology (especially Scheler); (4) personalism and ethics; (5) postmodern evaluations or critiques of Wojtyła's synthesis of medieval and modern elements; (6) Wojtyła's theology; (7) writings on poetry and theater; (8) bibliographical aids.

1. Public Philosophy

George H. Williams, "Karol Wojtyła and Marxism" (1990),[17] poses the rhetorical question: Why can one find hardly any explicit references to Marxism and Communism in Wojtyła's writings? Williams promptly answers by noting that Wojtyła was a priest living in a Communist country. After providing some biographical data — Williams reminds us that Wojtyła read Kant's entire *Critique of Pure Reason* in the original German when he was in high school — Williams discusses Wojtyła's *Lublin Lectures*. "On reading them, one would scarcely know that they were delivered to students in the faculty of arts and science . . . in a communist country. . . . The name of Karl Marx is not heard, nor even some code name for communism." Wojtyła avoids any reference to Communism or materialism, and focuses his critique on "utilitarianism." Of course, Communists in power understood the term "utilitarianism" as a reference to corrupt Western ways of life, while in Wojtyła's mind it definitely included Marxist materialism. In an article directed to his clergy (1970) Wojtyła again employed "British Utilitarianism" as a reference to Anglo-American and Marxist materialism. Williams notices, further, that Wojtyła avoids the term "totalitarianism," and prefers to use "totalism." In an article of 1976 Wojtyła defends religion from the (Marxist) accusation that it is a form of human alienation. Also, in a lecture given at *The Catholic University* of Milan in 1977, Wojtyła focuses on elaborating a notion of culture which is not reducible to a superstructure of economy.

17. In Pedro Ramet (ed.), *Catholicism and Politics in Communist Societies* (Durham, NC: Duke University Press, 1990), pp. 356-81. A modified version of "Karol Wojtyła and Marxism: His Thought and Action as Professor, Prelate, and Supreme Pontiff," in the Pope John Paul Lecture Series, College of Saint Thomas in St. Paul Minnesota, 1985.

Nicholas Lobkowicz, "Participation and Alienation" (1984),[18] discusses some notions from chapter 7 of *The Acting Person* (intersubjectivity by participation) and two articles by Wojtyła dealing with similar issues. Any lack of participation, which Wojtyła distinguishes from both individualism and totalism, produces alienation. Alienation (which is a well-known Hegelian and Marxian notion) derives for Wojtyła not from an anonymous state of affairs, but from the way in which an action is accomplished, that is, by an attitude toward acting. There are four main differences between Wojtyła's and Marx's notions of alienation. First, while Marx speaks only of work, Wojtyła considers human action in general. As Hannah Arendt points out, Marx limits himself to *poiesis*. Second, Marx follows the Hegelian ontology of relations, and reduces the human substance to a product of its relationships. Wojtyła is Aristotelian and therefore "substantialist," not a "relationist." The *suppositum* has ontological priority over the action. Third, alienation is a defect, a privation of participation (Wojtyła), not a positive quality (Marx). Fourth, for Marx, a person is not responsible for his alienation, and, therefore, since there is no guilt, there cannot be forgiveness. Marx's depersonalized notion of alienation implies a Manichean understanding of human conflicts. Lobkowicz then, in debate with Methol Ferré, warns against the cozy belief that Marxism has been culturally negated: among his reasons for prudence are the contemporary substitution of sociology for philosophy and the fact that the economy seems, also in Western societies, to be the ultimate foundation for every legitimate public argument.

Pierluigi Pollini, "The Problem of Philosophy of Praxis in Marx and Wojtyła" (1983),[19] compares Marx's and Wojtyła's philosophies of action. According to Marx, the flaw in every previous form of materialism is an understanding of man according to passive categories. Marx wants to substitute for this "passivism" a dynamic philosophy of praxis. Man makes himself through working; he is self-creating. Working objectivizes man and subjectivizes nature, and the humanization of nature coincides with the actualization of human finalities. A philosophy of action ought to take the place of passive theories of contemplation. Marx dissolves metaphysical problems, from the origin of the universe to human consciousness, into

18. "Participation et aliénation," in *Karol Wojtyła. Filosofo, Teologo, Poeta* (Vatican City: Libreria Editrice Vaticana, 1984), pp. 247-51.
19. "Il problema della filosofia della prassi in Marx e Wojtyła," in R. Buttiglione (ed.), *La filosofia di Karol Wojtyła* (Bologna: CSEO, 1983), pp. 61-73.

the question of the transformation of the world through praxis. But the unintended outcome is that Marx's original humanistic position becomes radically anti-humanistic, as any materialism and atheism must be in principle: the realization of this theory demonstrated its anti-humanism beyond reasonable doubt. Wojtyła wants to appropriate those elements of the philosophy of praxis which are *de jure* part of an adequate anthropology. Marx cannot recognize the ethical dimension of human praxis due to his utilitarian and economistic views united with his elimination of the human *suppositum*. In contrast, Wojtyła's philosophy of praxis acknowledges an ontological priority of being over acting *(operari sequitur esse)*. The human act has a twofold dimension: it transforms nature but it also transforms the agent who transforms nature. Marx forgets this essentially subjective side of the action: through acting man becomes himself. The defense of the priority of the *acting person* over the product constitutes the essential humanism of Wojtyła's thesis in opposition to Marxist anti-humanism. For Wojtyła "participation" is essential in common human actions since it is the specifically human intersubjective dimension of action. Pollini calls it the *self–other relation*. It is grounded both at the ontological level and at the level of experience and consciousness. Moreover, for Wojtyła there is a profound relationship between work and culture, and the latter takes precedence over economy. Culture is the place in which human spirit dwells and acts, not merely the superstructure of the economy.

Gregory M. A. Gronbacher, "The Personalistic Philosophy of Karol Wojtyła and Catholic Social Thought" (1993),[20] outlines a short but clear summary of Wojtyła's personalism in regard to a social philosophy. First, the starting point of philosophy is personalism. A personal being is defined by two essential characteristics: subjectivity and autonomy. Subjectivity is consciousness, presence to oneself, and autonomy is the volitional aspect of subjectivity. By being capable of action, a person is no static being but an acting person. In the realm of intersubjectivity Wojtyła's personalism offers two opposite categories important in social philosophy: participation and alienation. Participation respects the personalistic norm, whereas alienation does not.

Paolo Boni, "Community and Society in Wojtyła and Tönnies" (1983),[21] deals with the last chapter of Wojtyła's *The Acting Person* (Intersubjectivity by Participation) and compares it with Ferdinand Tönnies, the

---

20. *Social Justice Review,* November 1993, pp. 166-69.
21. "Comunita' e societa' in Wojtyła e Tönnies," in R. Buttiglione (ed.), *La filosofia di Karol Wojtyła* (Bologna: CSEO, 1983), pp. 85-91.

sociologist who influenced Max Weber and Max Scheler, in his major work *Community and Society*. Tönnies opposes community and society in a Manichean way. Wojtyła's analysis of "acting together" integrates these two dimensions of community and society within the notion of common good.

2. Thomism vs. Phenomenology

Jerzy W. Galkowski, "The Place of Thomism in the Anthropology of K. Wojtyła" (1988),[22] says that Wojtyła's philosophy is interpreted in three main ways: (1) Thomistically, (2) phenomenologically, (3) as a synthesis of 1 and 2. Galkowski defends the fundamental Thomistic core of Wojtyła's philosophy. A quotation from a letter from the 27-year-old Wojtyła to Sophia Pozniakowa substantiates Galkowski's words: "I think that there are many things which can be said about Thomistic studies. . . . This entire system is not only something immensely wise, but also something immensely beautiful, which enraptures the mind. In addition, it speaks simplicity. It is readily apparent that thought and depth do not stand in need of many words. One could even say that the deeper something is, the less it will require words." Wojtyła's Thomism is then synthesized with phenomenology. Galkowski notices, however, that Wojtyła's philosophy underwent an evolution in two respects, since he both turned his attention to new subject matter and somewhat modified his philosophical stance. These changes took place "between the poles of the philosophy of being (Thomism) and the philosophy of consciousness (Phenomenology)." First, Wojtyła's notion of experience is not Aristotelian-Thomistic, but one which moves toward phenomenological analysis. However, Wojtyła desires a possible synthesis, not an opposition, of the two poles (being and consciousness). Second, in anthropology Wojtyła uses a double approach. Metaphysically, the person is the subject of existence and activity; phenomenologically, the person is the synthesis of efficacy and subjectivity. The phenomenological description, though it enriches the traditional approach, is unable to overcome the opposition between nature and person. Phenomenology does not reach the deepest ontic level where these dimensions are integrated into the substantial unity of man. In conclusion, Galkowski states that Aristotelianism and Thomism are the point of departure, but not "an inviolable canon for the Author. He does not assume an apologetic and exegetical attitude toward it." To understand Wojtyła one must take the

22. *Angelicum* 65/2 (1988), pp. 181-94.

third interpretation, that is, that his philosophy is a synthesis of a philosophy of being and a philosophy of consciousness.

Philippe Jobert, "Philosopher of Transition from Classical Anthropology to Modern Anthropology" (1984),[23] underlines Wojtyła's intention of merging the philosophy of being with the philosophy of consciousness. This undertaking had been unsuccessfully attempted before, notably by Edith Stein. Jobert insists that Wojtyła is not simply a phenomenologist, but a Thomist who uses phenomenology to show another way to reach the same conclusions. He criticizes the English translation of *The Acting Person* for eliminating or toning down all of its Aristotelian-Thomistic language. "Phenomenology offered to Professor Wojtyła only a method, not a system."

Jude P. Dougherty, "The Thomistic Element in the Social Philosophy of John Paul II" (1986),[24] sees Wojtyła's philosophy of society as characterized by "his highly individualistic style," which he retains in his Papal documents. For Dougherty, Wojtyła is not a Thomist in "the usual sense." Wojtyła is not interested in textual and historical analysis, nor is he interested in commentaries on Aquinas's text, nor is he a Thomist in the way in which Maritain was. Wojtyła created an independent system, using elements from St. Thomas as well as from Scheler, Blondel, Husserl, and Ingarden. Dougherty emphasizes Scheler's influence (and his anti-Thomistic approach to ethics) as well as Blondel's. Dougherty seems to be one of the few to mention Blondel's influence on Wojtyła. Buttiglione writes on this subject: "Blondel's book *L'Action*, which initiates the modernist crisis, is an attempt to think about that subjective and active side of the person which St. Thomas's objective personalism does not develop fully."[25]

Joseph de Finance, "Human Action and Causality" (1984),[26] begins with Wojtyła's notion of efficacy, which hinges on the Thomistic distinction

---

23. "Jean Paul II, Philosophe de la transition de l'anthropologie classique à l'anthropologie moderne," in *Karol Wojtyła. Filosofo, Teologo, Poeta* (Vatican City: Libreria Editrice Vaticana, 1984), pp. 47-52. Jobert, a Benedictine, refers to John Paul II in the title, but the article is about Karol Wojtyła's philosophy. Jobert, with characteristic Benedictine respect for authority, never refers to "Wojtyła," always to "Professor Wojtyła" or "Cardinal Wojtyła."

24. *Proceedings of the American Catholic Philosophical Association* 58 (1986), pp. 156-66.

25. R. Buttiglione, *L'uomo e il lavoro* (Bologna: CSEO, 1982), p. 41.

26. "Action Humaine et Causalité," in *Karol Wojtyła. Filosofo, Teologo, Poeta* (Vatican City: Libreria Editrice Vaticana, 1984), pp. 39-45.

between the *act of man* and the *human act*. While Wojtyła is interested in the anthropological and ethical points, De Finance deals with the metaphysical implications of human action (efficacy).

Adrian J. Reimers, "The Thomistic Personalism of Karol Wojtyła" (1992),[27] defends Wojtyła's personalism as fundamentally Thomistic. Reimers deals with the question of Wojtyła's emphasis on consciousness, a very important issue in modern philosophy, but of minimal importance in St. Thomas's language. Wojtyła, however, as a modern thinker develops this theme of consciousness which is latent in Aquinas. But for Wojtyła consciousness is not a point of departure of philosophical anthropology: ". . . the being of [the] human subject is absolutely prior to his consciousness. Being and not consciousness is foundational." For Wojtyła consciousness is not a faculty of the soul, and it is part of the will, not of the intellect (though Reimers affirms that "the ultimate function of consciousness is cognitive").[28] "The most profound point of philosophical contact between Karol Wojtyła and St. Thomas Aquinas is . . . [in the] insistence that at the root of a thing's behavior and a person's consciousness is the fundamental act of existence."

Georges Kalinowski, "Edith Stein and Karol Wojtyła on the Person" (1984),[29] compares Wojtyła's and Stein's studies on the person. The comparison is suggested by the fact that Thomism and Phenomenology are the main points of reference for both of them. But there is a fundamental difference between them: Stein encounters Thomism after having studied philosophy under Husserl, while Wojtyła encounters phenomenology after having been trained in Thomism. Moreover, whereas Edith Stein's concerns increasingly move from philosophy to theology, Wojtyła travels from theology to philosophy.

Georges Kalinowski, "Reform of Thomism and of Phenomenology in

---

27. In A. Piolanti (ed.), *Atti del IX Congresso tomistico internazionale* (Vatican City: Libreria Editrice Vaticana, 1992), vol. 6, pp. 364-69.

28. "A corollary of this conception [which identifies personhood with consciousness] is that conscience defines morality, that conscience is the power to *choose* or *define* values. The notion that each person's conscience is inviolable becomes transformed to mean that each conscience is sovereign — a law to itself. Jean-Paul Sartre stands as the most dramatic representative of this view. Karol Wojtyła has decisively criticized this conception of the human person." A. Reimers, "Conscience and the Truth about the Good," in *S. Tommaso filosofo. Ricerche in occasione dei due centenari accademici* (Vatican City: Libreria Editrice Vaticana, 1995), p. 221.

29. "Edith Stein et Karol Wojtyła sur la personne," in *Revue Philosophique de Louvain* 82 (1984), pp. 545-61.

Karol Wojtyła according to Rocco Buttiglione" (1986),[30] is critical of both Buttiglione's interpretation of Wojtyła and (from a strict Thomistic point of view) of Wojtyła himself. Kalinowski reproaches Buttiglione's interpretation for using the term "reform" instead of "transformation." He is especially derogatory concerning chapter 5 of this book. For Kalinowski, Wojtyła brings about a transformation, not simply a reform, of both Thomism and Phenomenology. Kalinowski mentions three moments which separate Wojtyła from a simple reform of Thomism, and these are kinds of breaches. First, for Wojtyła, the will is the essential property of the person (self-determination), and only secondarily is it an intellectual appetite (power). While Kalinowski is clearly thinking of the first part of the *Summa Theologiae*, it seems to us that Wojtyła takes the prologue of the second part of the *Summa* as a point of departure. Second, Wojtyła derives spirituality from the transcendence of the person, while Aquinas derives transcendence from spirituality. Third, Kalinowski contests the idea that being a person (spirituality) is a datum of immediate evidence for everyone. But Wojtyła is clearly not a phenomenologist either, says Kalinowski. Wojtyła's critique of Scheler is too extensive for it to be possible to call Wojtyła's philosophical methods Schelerian. Wojtyła is not interested in either the first or the second of Husserl's reductions. In other words, he neither brackets existence to contemplate essences nor is he interested in the idealistic reconstruction of the world beginning from the "I." Kalinowski emphasizes the significance of the influence of Gilson's existential Thomism upon Wojtyła. He considers Wojtyła's thought a clarification and amplification of Aquinas's rational psychology. In conclusion, while Kalinowski praises Buttiglione's book for the wide-ranging view which it gives of all of Wojtyła's works before 1978, he repeats that it is a mistake to present Wojtyła's philosophy as a completed anthropology which merges philosophy of being and philosophy of consciousness.

Georges Kalinowski, "Karol Wojtyła's Thought and the Faculty of Philosophy of the Catholic University of Lublin" (1988),[31] has the twofold intention of criticizing Josef Seifert's article on Wojtyła and the Cracow-

---

30. "La réforme du thomisme et de la phénoménologie chez Karol Wojtyła selon Rocco Buttiglione," in *Archives de Philosophie* 49 (1986), pp. 127-46.

31. "La pensée philosophique de Karol Wojtyła et la faculté de philosophie de l'Université Catholique de Lublin," in *Aletheia* (1988), pp. 198-216. Tadeusz Styczen wrote a response in the same issue of *Aletheia* to Kalinowski's piece: "Reply to Kalinowski: By Way of an Addendum to the Addenda," pp. 217-25.

Lublin School of Philosophy[32] and of defending Wojtyła's Aristotelian Thomistic positions against the phenomenologizing corruptions of his thought. On this second point Kalinowski furnishes a list of major corruptions and omissions of the English text of *The Acting Person* (in comparison with the Polish original) by the editor, A. T. Tymienienka. Among them there is, for instance, the substitution of the term "suppositum" by paraphrases such as "the structural ontological basis" and "the concrete ontological nucleus of man." Kalinowski's charge against Seifert is that he "assembled" a school of philosophy that never existed: the Cracow-Lublin School. T. Styczen, Wojtyła's successor at the chair of Ethics at the Catholic University of Lublin, has replied to this critique that one may in fact speak of such a school. Wojtyła — initially as a professor in Lublin, frequently commuting between Cracow and Lublin before becoming bishop, and later, after becoming a Bishop and Cardinal, hosting regular philosophical meetings in his residence in Cracow (where Ingarden, one of the participants, read the manuscript of *On Responsibility*) — is precisely the connecting factor between Cracow's and Lublin's philosophers.

Andrew N. Woznicki, "Lublinism — A New Version of Thomism" (1986),[33] places Wojtyła in the milieu of the Catholic University of Lublin. Karol Wojtyła is part of a group of five young professors (Jerzy Kalinowski, Stanislaw Kaminski, Miecyslaw Krapiec, Stefan Swiezawski) who, after the tragic experience of the Second World War, realized that the time of purely subjectivist and idealistic philosophy is over. Wojtyła belongs to this genus of Thomism, but his specific contribution is what is called "existential personalism."

Ralph J. Masiello, "A Note on Transcendence in *The Acting Person*" (1982),[34] deals with the dynamic of the good. Masiello makes the point that Wojtyła uses phenomenology to create an anthropology which is not entirely reduced to consciousness. The moment of "self-determination" (not "in-determination") constitutes the transcendence of the person, which Wojtyła calls vertical transcendence. From a Thomist point of view, Wojtyła emphasizes that the good is not in the "order of being" but in the "order of becoming." The good in the case of the "intransitive transcen-

---

32. Seifert's 1981 article is used and quoted by Buttiglione, see p. 73 of this book.

33. *Proceedings of the American Catholic Philosophical Association* 58 (1986), pp. 23-37.

34. "A Note on Transcendence in *The Acting Person*," in *Doctor Communis* 35 (1982), pp. 327-35.

dence," that is, human freedom, is a good in the order of becoming (and in this case, of self-determination). The traditional emphasis on the convertibility of being and goodness runs the risk of concealing the dynamic dimension of the good, which is essential in personal life.

Costantino Esposito, "The Experience of Being Human in Karol Wojtyła's Thought" (1983),[35] deals with Wojtyła's understanding of human being by placing it in the polarity between the notion of "suppositum" (philosophy of being) and the notion of "I" (philosophy of consciousness). Costantino concludes that Wojtyła's philosophy is not a complete synthesis of ontology and phenomenology, but the beginning of a new way of looking at the acting person.

Vincent G. Potter, "Philosophical Correlations among K. Wojtyła, C. S. Peirce, and B. Lonergan" (1993),[36] compares Wojtyła with the American thinker C. S. Peirce and the Canadian Jesuit Bernard Lonergan. The choice of these authors is immediately significant: Wojtyła shares with Lonergan a certain combination of Thomas Aquinas and Kant, which is usually called transcendental Thomism, and he shares with Peirce's pragmatism the primacy given to action in understanding human being. Potter examines these authors under three coordinates: experience, action, and community. These three authors agree in enlarging the notion of experience and on the importance of action (Wojtyła moves from a static to a dynamic Thomism). Finally, on the centrality of community Potter sees what almost amounts to an identity between Peirce's and Wojtyła's conclusions.

Ronald Modras, "The Thomistic Personalism of Pope John Paul II" (1982),[37] examines Wojtyła's philosophical works (in particular his dissertation on Scheler and his articles) with the intention of demonstrating that Wojtyła is no phenomenologist, but an open-minded Thomist. First, Wojtyła's analysis of Scheler's ethics concludes with a negative evaluation of the possibility of using this system as a Christian ethics. For Wojtyła, a Christian ethics must demonstrate three characteristics: objective, practical, and religious. Scheler's ethics, like all ethics of modern philosophies of consciousness, fails to understand human action and efficacy. A Christian ethics must be objective as

35. "L'esperienza dell'essere umano nel pensiero di Karol Wojtyła," in Rocco Buttiglione (ed.), La filosofia di Karol Wojtyła (Bologna: CSEO, 1983), pp. 17-41.

36. In J. M. McDermott, The Thought of John Paul II: A Collection of Essays and Studies (Editrice Pontificia Universita' Gregoriana, 1993), pp. 205-12.

37. "The Thomistic Personalism of John Paul II," in Modern Schoolman 59 (1982), pp. 117-27. Though the title refers to John Paul II, the article is about Wojtyła's philosophy.

well as dynamic, and requires a philosophy of being and becoming analyzed in the traditional concepts of act and potency. Modras then examines Wojtyła's articles, showing the Thomist foundation of his personalism. In conclusion, Modras wonders how and whether a traditional ethics based on natural law can be justified in terms of a personalistic ethics. He concludes, however, that Wojtyła's Thomistic personalism "not only stands in the mainstream of current discussion but represents a creative contribution."

Ronald Modras, "A Man of Contradictions? The Early Writings of Karol Wojtyła" (1987),[38] is written in a polemical fashion, especially when compared with the piece in the *Modern Schoolman* written four years earlier. Here Wojtyła is seen as a medieval nostalgic (or, worse, a "neo-scholastic"), who uses the language of phenomenology and existentialism as a clerical ruse to advertise the faith to unwitting converts. In his ethics Wojtyła emphasizes the concepts of domination, subordination, government, and control. In sexual ethics he is less a neo-scholastic and more a neo-stoic. The appeal to Kant's personalist norm is deceptive because while Kant forbids the use of the person *merely* as a means, Wojtyła skips or forgets the *merely*. From an ecclesiological point of view, Wojtyła does not realize the revolutionary implications of the Council, because he is Polish. Poland has been enslaved for so long that the Poles have forgotten what freedom is. In addition, Wojtyła does not understand that after Vatican II everyone within the People of God is equal. Modras concludes that Wojtyła is not a man of contradictions: "There is an inner logic to his thinking: a medieval model of the human person, sexuality and marriage, and the Church in which hierarchy and subordination serve as the dominant principle."

Wingand Siebel's "Karol Wojtyła's Philosophy and Theology" (1986)[39] is a collection of essays published in an "integrist" Swiss magazine in the early eighties. These essays deal with the mistakes and breaks with the tradition made by Wojtyła (and John Paul II). They belong to the hermeneutic of Vatican II as "a revolution within the Church," a view which Siebel, an "integrist," shares with Ronald Modras, a follower of Hans Küng. The catch phrase which Siebel uses to identify all errors is "new": this is the recurrent adjective. This book is mostly devoted to an analysis of the break

---

38. Ronald Modras, "A Man of Contradictions: The Early Writings of Karol Wojtyła," in H. Küng and L. Swidler (eds.), *The Church in Anguish: Has the Vatican Betrayed Vatican II?* (San Francisco: Harper and Row, 1987), pp. 39-51. (First published in German in 1986.)

39. Wigand Siebel, *Philosophie und Theologie Karol Wojtyłas* (Basel: Saka, 1986).

with the tradition made by the "new" popes who came after Vatican II, but the first chapter analyzes Wojtyła's *Love and Responsibility*. Interestingly, Siebel points out that Wojtyła's major mistake consists in not understanding the "merely" in the Kantian prohibition on using a human being as a means. Curiously, the identical mistake is pointed out, from the opposite end of the spectrum, by Ronald Modras (1986). The primary substantial philosophical objection of the progressivists and the integrists to Wojtyła's philosophy is the same. Siebel notices that the topic of the love of God, which used to be the foundation of any Christian ethics, is absent from Wojtyła's *Love and Responsibility*. Moreover, the egalitarian consequences of Wojtyła's principle of equalization through love are socially destructive. Egalitarianism implies the displacement of the principles of obedience and social order, and therefore it leads to the disappearance of traditional relationships such as father and son, husband and wife, or even doctor and patient. The common error at the basis of *Love and Responsibility* and *The Acting Person* is modern anthropocentrism.[40]

3. Realist Phenomenology

Jean-Luc Marion, "Self-Transcendence of Man as a Sign of Contradiction in the Thought of Karol Wojtyła" (1984),[41] deals with Wojtyła's philosophy from within the phenomenological movement. In a way, Marion looks at Wojtyła from the opposite end of the spectrum as Philippe Jobert. Marion notices Wojtyła's unorthodox approach to phenomenology. He sees that Wojtyła bypasses the basic notions of intentionality (of consciousness) and transcendence (of the world), in order to move to more central structures, that is, the *acting person* and *self-determination*. Is it still legitimate to describe it as phenomenology? There is in Wojtyła's existential phenomenology a contradiction between content and method. The notion of transcendence, which in phenomenology is applied to the known object (Husserl), to the other I (Sartre) or to the *Dasein* (Heidegger), is applied to man himself. Man becomes self-transcendent. This is the notion of a *vertical transcendence,* as opposed to the horizontal transcendence proper

40. On Thomism and Phenomenology see also Massimo Serretti, "Ethics and Philosophical Anthropology: Remarks on Maritain and Wojtyła": "Etica e Antropologia Filosofica. Considerazioni su Maritain e Wojtyła," in *Sapienza* 38 (1985), pp. 15-31.

41. "L'autotranscendance de l'homme signe de contradiction dans la pensée de Karol Wojtyła," in *Karol Wojtyła. Filosofo, Teologo, Poeta* (Vatican City: Libreria Editrice Vaticana, 1984), pp. 53-70.

to phenomenology. The kernel of this vertical transcendence is the person as self-determination, as freedom. This is also what makes the person an absolute individuality and at the same time unknowable as an object. To manifest the "person," however, one has to construct a phenomenology which substitutes action for intentionality. For Wojtyła the *will* is fundamentally self-determination, not intentionality. The truth of the object of knowledge is subordinated to the truth of the object of will. Marion remarks that Wojtyła's transcendence or overcoming of man does not go in a Nietzschean direction: this transcending of man does not aim to produce an *Übermensch,* but culminates in the discovery of the person. In this vertical transcendence, to be sure, the acting person is not beyond good and evil. "The person alone overcomes man. . . . The self-transcendence of man means that the person frees himself by engaging himself and by deciding between good and evil. This freedom judges everything else." This vertical transcendence is a kind of "new beginning" for metaphysics, after its death certificate had lately been issued.

Hans Köchler, "The Phenomenology of Karol Wojtyła: On the Problem of the Phenomenological Foundation of Anthropology" (1982),[42] outlines Wojtyła's position as a realist phenomenology. Wojtyła accepts that the traditional, nonphenomenological point of departure of anthropology objectifies man; his own point of departure is a phenomenological description of experience. While Wojtyła rejects the cosmological point of departure as inadequate in anthropology, he does not limit anthropology to phenomenology, and points to a transphenomenological approach for a complete anthropology. Wojtyła rejects Husserl's idealistic turn, which leads to a subjectivist reification and absolutization of consciousness. In addition, he emphasizes the subconscious as an essential moment of the identity of the subject and the passive, non-intentional function of consciousness.

Josef Seifert, "Truth and Transcendence of the Person in the Philosophical Thought of Karol Wojtyła" (1984),[43] affirms that the most important contribution of Wojtyła to philosophy is "related to the transcendence of the human person." Seifert insists on the realism of Wojtyła's philosophy, claiming that it is as realist as that of Aquinas. This realism is the corner-

---

42. In *Philosophy and Phenomenological Research* 42 (1982), pp. 326-34.

43. In *Karol Wojtyła. Filosofo, Teologo, Poeta* (Vatican City: Libreria Editrice Vaticana, 1994), pp. 93-106. See also Josef Seifert, "Verdad, Libertad y Amor en el Piensamiento Antropologico Etico de Karol Wojtyła," in *Persona y Derecho* 10 (1983), pp. 177-93; "Fenomenologia e Cosciencia," in *Antropologia e Praxis no Pensamento de Joao Paulo II* (Rio De Janeiro, 1984), pp. 69-94.

stone of his approach to ethics and anthropology. Consciousness is by no means a substance, but an accident; it does not exist in itself and it is always a consciousness *of* somebody (belonging to somebody). In ethics, freedom manifests the transcendence of the person over nature. This vertical transcendence does not imply a primacy of indeterminacy: freedom is not *indetermination* toward something, but *self-determination.* This transcendence over nature is not only a negative response to nature: freedom is freedom *from* in order to be freedom *for.* This "for" is the capacity to give the proper response to values (von Hildebrand). This "freedom for" finds its meaning, to paraphrase Hartmann, in receiving and affirming what is freely offered to us, that is to say, what is ours, and yet not ours. The polarity of freedom in the vertical transcendence of the person finds its corresponding component in the polarity of truth. The "will to truth" constitutes human vertical transcendence from within and therefore freedom. Wojtyła's philosophy of authenticity, also called *existential personalism,* differs from other forms of existentialism, such as those of Sartre and Heidegger, in this rooting of freedom in truth. Thus "the philosopher-Pope" is not more fallible because of his existentialism and his attention to the subjective side of moral experience. The goods and the values encountered in the subjective experience ought to receive our *true* and *adequate* response.

Josef Seifert, *Being and Person* (1989),[44] is an original and independent study which finds its place in the development of the synthesis of realist phenomenology with metaphysics. The study has been published in an Italian translation by Rocco Buttiglione, who wrote a long introductory essay to it.[45] Seifert's endeavor goes in the direction of a metaphysical personalism. While he shares with Wojtyła a realistic understanding of phenomenology, he does not partake of Wojtyła's Thomism. The line followed by Seifert goes from Plato to Augustine, then to Anselm, Bonaventure, and Duns Scotus. Chapter 10 of Buttiglione's introductory essay is devoted to Seifert's "encounter with Wojtyła's philosophy."[46] Seifert agrees with Wojtyła that "modern philosophy discovered the theme of action and the theme of consciousness (which is always consciousness in act and consciousness of an action), but it separated them from the theme of being, and, in so doing, it constitutes a philosophy of consciousness and a philos-

---

44. J. Seifert, *Essere e Persona,* trans. Rocco Buttiglione (Milan: Vita e Pensiero, 1989).

45. Ibid., pp. 9-75.

46. Ibid., pp. 34-40.

ophy of praxis in antithesis to a philosophy of being." Seifert, however, attempts a reform of phenomenology which takes phenomenology as philosophy *tout court*. For Seifert, phenomenology is no less than classical philosophy resurrected in modernity. Seifert's position thus goes beyond Wojtyła's intention and thought with respect to phenomenology.

Massimo Serretti, "Self-Consciousness and Self-Knowledge" (1983),[47] says that Wojtyła's philosophy is not a philosophy of consciousness. He does not make consciousness a substance as if it were the subject of every experience. There are two modern reductions of consciousness: on the one hand, we have the epistemological line which goes from Kant to Husserl, and which reduces consciousness to knowledge. This option tends to identify epistemology as philosophy *tout court*. On the other hand, we have a reaction against this epistemologism, of which Heidegger and Sartre are the most notable representatives. Consciousness is not limited to its cognitive capacity, but goes as far as constituting subjectivity. Wojtyła does not belong to either of these reductions. For him, consciousness is a gateway to man's transcendence, and as Ingarden defined it, "it is the surface of contact between soul and body." Consciousness is understood within a more fundamental ontology of the person. Wojtyła adds another necessary dimension to the person: self-knowledge. *Consciousness* cannot constitute the contents of subjective experience without the objectivization of "the I" in *self-knowledge*. Wojtyła distinguishes between self-knowledge and consciousness: consciousness does not have the intentionality of knowledge. Seretti also underlines the fact that Wojtyła gives precedence to the dimension person-act over the dimension person-person: in other words, while Wojtyła's philosophy is not egocentric or egologic, it is not dialogical either. Seretti then makes a comparison between Wojtyła's treatise on consciousness and self-knowledge and one of the most difficult pages of Kant, the transcendental deduction in the *Critique of Pure Reason*. A major difference with Kant consists in the different mediation of consciousness: for Kant consciousness leads to transcendentality, while in Wojtyła it leads to the transcendence of the person (freedom). Serretti introduces two enticing remarks on the nature of consciousness: first, the notion that consciousness arises in the dialectic between desire and obstacles to desire (Hegel, Maine de Biran, Scheler);

47. In R. Buttiglione (ed.), *La filosofia di Karol Wojtyła* (Bologna: CSEO, 1983), pp. 45-59.

second, quoting Dostoevsky, that suffering is at the origin of consciousness, which is the inwardness and awareness of a contradiction.[48]

Jan Galarowicz, "Poland: Non-Scholastic Currents in 20th Century
Catholic Thought" (1990),[49] includes Wojtyła in the non-scholastic cluster
of Polish thinkers, together with Ingarden and Tischner. Wojtyła shares with
Ingarden a realist phenomenology. Wojtyła forges a new kind of phenomenology which he originally connects with a realistic anthropology, or a
personalism. This personalism subsumes and overcomes Aristotle's and
Aquinas's anthropologies, and is a new approach to Christian ethics.

Andrew N. Woznicki, "Revised Thomism: Existential Personalism
Viewed from Phenomenological Perspectives" (1986),[50] deals with three
issues: Scheler and Wojtyła, cosmological versus personalistic anthropology,
and self-determination as the person's defining characteristic. First, concerning Scheler's influence on Wojtyła's philosophy, Wozinski points out
the following elements: the discovery of the experience which fulfills the
concept of "actus humanus," the phenomenological concept of the human
act as the manifestation of the person, the phenomenological identification
of the experience of man and the experience of morality, and a phenomenological anthropology based on values. Wojtyła's critique of Scheler
amounts to the critique of any phenomenological analysis: the lack of the
dynamic principle of the will. Therefore, the person is affirmed as the cause
of the values, not simply as their spectator. Second, Aristotle's definition of
man is cosmological and, therefore, it is inadequate to express the other,
more important, dimension of man: man as a person. Man is irreducible
to the world or to nature. Wojtyła integrates Aristotle's cosmological definition of man with Boethius's personalistic definition. Third, Wozinski
points out the importance of the notion of self-determination: an "ontic
property of the person and his freedom." Self-determination is a sign of

48. Massimo Serretti's *Self-Knowledge and Transcendence: Introduction to Philosophical Anthropology through Husserl, Scheler, Ingarden, Wojtyła* (1984) is an Italian
monograph: *Conoscenza di sé e trascendenza: introduzione alla filosofia dell'uomo attraverso Husserl, Scheler, Ingarden, Wojtyła* (Bologna: Centro Studi Europa Orientale;
Milano: Istituto di Studi per la transizione, 1984).

49. "Polen. Nicht-Scholastische Strömungen in der katholischen Philosophie des
20 Jahrhunderts," in E. Coreth (ed.), *Christliche Philosophie im Katholischen Denken des
19. Und 20. Jahrhunderts* (Cologne: Verlag Styria, 1987-1990), vol. 3, pp. 785-98. Jan
Galarowicz develops this in a Polish monograph with the title *Foundations of Karol
Wojtyła's Philosophical Anthropology* (Poznam, 1989).

50. *Proceedings of the American Catholic Philosophical Association* 58 (1986), pp.
38-49.

transcendence and belongs to the person as such, not simply to the will. Self-determination is not an intentional act, since any intentional act is oriented toward objects, while self-determination is oriented toward the subject.

Peter H. Spader, "The Primacy of the Heart: Scheler's Challenge to Phenomenology" (1985),[51] discusses the cognitive dimension of feelings and emotional states in Scheler, Strasser, and Wojtyła. Spader considers Strasser's and Wojtyła's critiques of what they take to be Scheler's excessive emotionalism. Strasser *(Phenomenology of Feeling)* acknowledges the essential emotional moment but claims that this needs to be integrated by logos, while Wojtyła defends the precedence of the intellect over the emotions, thus asserting that moral choice is a form of intellectual self-determination. Spader defends the primacy of heart in moral matters and the belief that reason is blind to values. In moral choices reason has only a secondary role in comparison to feeling and willing.

John Nota, "Max Scheler and Karol Wojtyła" (1986),[52] appears to deal more with Scheler than with Wojtyła. Nota, however, wants to stress the similarity more than the difference between the two authors. Since Scheler is the "most neglected of all phenomenologists," Nota discusses those elements of his system which have continued to influence Wojtyła's thought and have led him beyond the negative answer which he gave in his dissertation regarding the use of Schelerian ethics as a Christian ethics. In a way, it seems that Nota proceeds to an integration, if not a revision, of the judgment of the 39-year-old Wojtyła, with the 56-year-old Wojtyła acknowledging his philosophical debt to Scheler: "First of all, Max Scheler helped me to discover that specific experience which lies at the basis of the concept of 'actus humanus' and which must be identified there always anew." Both Wojtyła and Scheler have anthropology and ethics as the center of their philosophical thinking. Nota begins with an integral notion of experience: experience is not something that belongs to the senses, it is something that involves the whole of man. For both Scheler and Wojtyła the person is phenomenologically revealed in all the acts which transcend the animal level. Then, there is a correction of the notion of substance (which Scheler maintains) in the direction of dynamism. The substance/person is neither static nor a mere bundle of actions. The sub-

51. *Philosophy Today* 29 (1985), pp. 223-29.
52. *Proceedings of the American Catholic Philosophical Association* 58 (1986), pp. 135-47.

stance/person is not a thing. Also, it would be a kind of physical reduction-ism to consider the person/substance as the mere sum of sameness and change, since the person transcends space and time. This is where Wojtyła's notion of the "acting person" finds its Schelerian roots. Nota suggests also a political metaphor for two opposite and mistaken attitudes in regard to the substance/person: "A person who wants to be solely conservative be-comes a thing, whereas one who tries to be progressive alone loses his identity: it vanishes into thin air." In addition, (a) the person as including the community and the notion of solidarity, (b) the notion of an absolute order of values which comes from a personal order of love, (c) the notion that the person, image of God, is not most of all an *ens cogitans* or an *ens volens*, but an *ens amans*, (d) the acknowledgment of the importance of authority in the formation and correction of conscience, and (e) the im-possibility of self-redemption are all Schelerian elements which also belong to Wojtyła's existential personalism. Nota's conclusion goes beyond Wojtyła's circumscribed question in his 1959 Dissertation on Scheler, and states that Scheler is a Christian thinker.

Robert F. Harvanek, "The Philosophical Foundations of the Thought of John Paul II" (1993),[53] says that to understand *The Acting Person* one should remember that Wojtyła wrote it with Scheler's *Formalism in Ethics and Non-Formal Ethics of Values* on his desk. Harvanek compares Wojtyła's approach to ethics to that of Dietrich von Hildebrand, another Catholic disciple of Scheler. They both try to take Scheler as a point of departure, but von Hildebrand is far clearer than Wojtyła, and also much farther from neo-scholasticism. In addition, von Hildebrand is more consistent from a phenomenological standpoint, while Wojtyła combines phenomenology and metaphysics. Harvanek also calls attention to the similarities between John MacMurray's Gifford Lectures, *The Form of the Personal,* and Wojtyła's *The Acting Person.* According to Harvanek, Wojtyła's philosophy, and in general Lublin Thomism, is too essentialist in ethics (this essentialism is shared with von Hildebrand) as well as too individualistic and subjectivist. But a positive aspect of Wojtyła's philosophy is having moved Catholic thought out of neo-scholasticism into contemporary thought.

---

53. In J. M. McDermott (ed.), *The Thought of John Paul II: A Collection of Essays and Studies* (Editrice Pontificia Universita' Gregoriana, 1993), pp. 1-21. There is a re-sponse to this article by John J. Conley (pp. 23-28 of the same volume) which, after emphasizing the neo-Scholastic influence on Wojtyła's philosophical formation, con-cerns itself more with John Paul II than with Wojtyła's philosophy.

John H. Nota, "Phenomenological Experience in Karol Wojtyła" (1993),[54] makes the points that Wojtyła understands experience as something much larger than simply the senses — and that this experience is simultaneously subjective and objective. Nota points out that Wojtyła himself called attention to the shortcomings of *The Acting Person* in regard to a theory of community.

Joseph Pappin, "Karol Cardinal Wojtyła and Jean-Paul Sartre on the Intentionality of Consciousness" (1984),[55] compares Sartre's and Wojtyła's notions of consciousness. For Sartre, consciousness is intentional; it is always "consciousness of something," and this is the hinge of Sartre's system. Wojtyła does not regard consciousness as intentional. Knowledge is intentional, as is self-knowledge, but consciousness is not. Consciousness is characterized by a lack of staticity, that is, by action. In other words, consciousness is act. Another characteristic of consciousness is reflectivity, and through reflectivity consciousness subjectivizes experiences and knowledge. Wojtyła concurs with Sartre in dismissing the transcendental ego, refusing to take the path of Husserl's second reduction. But Sartre's position on the subject, according to Pappin, is suspended between the consciousness of a world which is by definition a non-I and the impossibility of giving any positive content to the I. Wojtyła affirms the ego, but not, as Sartre would say, as reified, but as an "ego which itself emerges in acting and is revealed through consciousness. Further it experiences itself as an ego through the reflexive function of consciousness."

4. Personalist Ethics and Freedom (Self-Determination)

Ronald D. Lawler, "Experience as the Foundation of Karol Wojtyła's Personalist Ethics" (1986),[56] remarks that "one cannot begin to speak of Wojtyła's ethics without noting his passion for freedom. . . . Wojtyła has lived under totalitarian rule long enough to care deeply for freedom." Lawler sees Wojtyła as a reformer of philosophical and Christian ethics. In the 1960s Thomistic ethics of natural law was perceived to be "physicalist," as it were, subordinating free human activity to mere factuality.

54. In J. M. McDermott (ed.), *The Thought of John Paul II: A Collection of Essays and Studies* (Editrice Pontificia Universita' Gregoriana, 1993), pp. 197-204.
55. *Proceedings of the American Catholic Philosophical Association* 58 (1986), pp. 130-39.
56. *Proceedings of the American Catholic Philosophical Association* 58 (1986), pp. 148-55.

Thomism in general was accused of being legalistic, a prioristic, and detached from existence. Wojtyła faced these criticisms and gave the foundation for a dynamic and phenomenological approach to ethics which begins from the experience of the most perfect being in all nature, the person.

Tadeusz Styczen, "Human Responsibility toward the Self and the Other" (1984),[57] says that the gateway to anthropology, that is to say, the knowledge of oneself, is moral conscience. Styczen's introduction to Wojtyła's thought is clearly neo-Kantian. It would be purely Kantian if Styczen had not begun with Buber's notion of love and responsibility: "love, that is to say, sense of responsibility, rooted in the 'I,' for the 'Thou'" (Buber). The primary experience of the conscience is the experience of "I ought. . . ." This (absolute) command is the self-introduction of moral conscience. It is also the way in which we perceive (adult) responsibility. Conscience is developed in the following four ways: first, conscience is *self-command;* second, conscience is *self-information;* and, finally, conscience is the condition for the possibility of man's self-realization (third) and human participation (fourth). These four moments more or less mirror the four parts of *The Acting Person.* Styczen assumes the Kantian belief that the essential dignity of man is *autonomy.* The experience of "I ought . . ." is not the experience of a slave of conscience, but the experience of obedience to oneself. The experience of the slave is heteronomy, while the experience of the master is autonomy. Every person's dignity requires the acknowledgment of this autonomy, self-mastery, self-possession. If the understanding of the "I ought . . ." sets one free from obeying someone else (slave morality), it does not set one free from submission to duty. This is the first moment of understanding this submission as an acknowledgment of truth. "Truth is the best guardian of freedom . . . since it is the defense of autonomy and self-realization." Self-realization is indissolubly related to the affirmation and realization of "the other I," of other autonomous persons. "Man is 'condemned' to self-realization through the free choice of solidarity with other men." Therefore, man realizes himself when he loves. In conclusion, Styczen grafts a treatment of love onto a fundamentally Kantian analysis; as Derrida has recently reminded us, for Kant, love was "one of the greatest dangers to morality."

57. "Responsabilita' dell'uomo nei confronti di so e dell'altro," in *Karol Wojtyła. Filosofo, Teologo, Poeta* (Vatican City: Libreria Editrice Vaticana, 1984), pp. 107-27.

Tadeusz Styczen, "Vere tu es homo absconditus" (1984),[58] distinguishes with utmost clarity the *natural law* perspective from the *personalistic* approach. A personalist ethics is founded on the "personalist norm": "persona est affirmanda propter seipsam," while the natural law perspective begins with "bonum est faciendum, malum vitandum." The personalist norm is the mother of all other norms, the foundation of all morality.[59]

John Crosby, "Persona est Sui Iuris: Reflections on the Foundations of Karol Wojtyła's Philosophy of the Person" (1984),[60] discusses the medieval axiom *persona est sui iuris,* which Wojtyła quotes in *The Acting Person* in relationship to self-determination and self-possession of the person (ch. 3). Crosby attempts to reconcile the notion of self-possession, which defines personhood, with the notion of creaturehood. In other words, he attempts to limit the meaning of human autonomy, which, were it understood as absolute, would necessarily imply atheism. Crosby points to Wojtyła's critique of Scheler for having disregarded the experience of the "I ought." The subordination of the person to God is mediated by this experience of moral duty. "The experience of recollection [of recovering the center of my being] discloses my creaturehood no less than my personhood." The tension is created here by the notion of person, defined as essentially autonomous, and the notion of creature, by its very nature nonautonomous. A "dependent person" would be, therefore, just as contradictory as a squared circle or iron wood. Crosby brings to focus this central problem in any definition of person which is centered on self-determination. This issue is also at the center of his concern in *The Dialectic of Autonomy and Theonomy in the Human Person.*[61] While Crosby never quotes Wojtyła here, he clearly continues the discussion of the same

58. In *Karol Wojtyła. Filosofo, Teologo, Poeta* (Vatican City: Libreria Editrice Vaticana, 1984), pp. 129-34.

59. See also the Polish afterword to the third Polish edition of *The Acting Person* (1994), pp. 491-526.

60. In *Karol Wojtyła. Filosofo, Teologo, Poeta* (Vatican City: Libreria Editrice Vaticana, 1984), pp. 47-69. Crosby reexamined the issue of autonomy of the person in "The Dialectic of Autonomy and Theonomy in the Human Person," in *Proceedings of the American Catholic Philosophical Association* 64 (1990), pp. 250-58.

61. *Proceedings of the American Catholic Philosophical Association* 64 (1990), pp. 250-58. Crosby, in "The Dialectic of Selfhood and Relationality in the Human Person," in *Proceedings of the American Catholic Philosophical Association* 66 (1992), pp. 181-89, deals with this same issue in a more polemical way, though he substitutes the notion of relation for the notion of heteronomy. There remains, however, the question of defining the person as freedom, that is to say, as self-determination.

issue found in *The Acting Person*. Crosby attempts to demonstrate the necessary unity of autonomy and theonomy, and he actually reverses the assumptions: creaturehood (contingency) is the only condition of possibility of autonomy. This demonstration hinges on the self-destruction of non-divine autonomy when it is understood as absolute; Crosby's *per absurdum* argument seems to follow Dostoyevsky's Kirilov: if there is no God, then I am (part of) God. In other words, he concludes with the paradox that heteronomy is the condition of possibility of autonomy. Buttiglione expresses this notion with a more evangelical paradox, in the words "servire Deo regnare." This is the problem of the possibility of a limited *freedom*, which is a much greater miracle than the simple possibility of a limited *being*. Crosby discusses this issue further in his book *The Selfhood of the Human Person*.[62] In chapter 8 of this book Crosby discusses nine ways to prove the limitedness of a human person's autonomy.

Juan-Miguel Palacios, "Karol Wojtyła and the Problem of Experience in Ethics" (1984),[63] distinguishes between two main kinds of ethical theories: cognitive and noncognitive, the latter of which he denotes as emotivist. Among the cognitive theories he distinguishes between the naturalistic and intuitive varieties. In a way, Wojtyła assumes some elements of all these theories, and shares the understanding, against the classical deductionistic approach to ethics, that *ethical experience* is the point of departure. Against the "Thomistic position," Wojtyła assumes the experience of moral obligation as independent of the question of ultimate finality and the absoluteness of this experience as primary (T. Styczen). He accepts Kant's critique of the "naturalism" of pre-Kantian ethics, but, with Scheler, he affirms the existence of nonnatural qualities which he calls values. But he goes beyond Scheler in accepting the phenomenological evidence of duty. Palacios defines an ethical explanation as the overcoming of the separation between facts and values, and he concludes with a comparison between Wojtyła's notion of experience of morality and Platonic innatism.

Andrzej Poltawski, "The Epistemological Basis of Karol Wojtyła's Philosophy" (1984),[64] says that it is essential to follow Wojtyła's distinction

---

62. (Washington, DC: Catholic University of America Press, 1996).

63. "Karol Wojtyła et le problème de l'expérience in éthique," in *Karol Wojtyła. Filosofo, Teologo, Poeta* (Vatican City: Libreria Editrice Vaticana, 1984), pp. 71-78.

64. *Proceedings of the American Catholic Philosophical Association* 60 (1988), pp. 79-91.

between a cosmological approach to the anthropological problem (Aristotle's *animal rationale*) and a personalistic approach to the same (irreducible personal element). While this may appear a new issue, it has been a kind of constant in Western thought, often in dialectical polarity such as that between Aristotle and Plato or Thomism and Augustinianism. Poltawski connects Wojtyła's analysis of efficacy (i.e., of being the authors of our actions) with the moral and anthropological issue of responsibility. On this point Roman Ingarden's influence on Wojtyła is considerable. Adequate anthropology implies ethics. While the cosmological approach to morality misses the decisive issue of the subjective experience of values, a merely axiological phenomenology (a phenomenology of values without norms) forgoes the dynamicity of morality. A world of values without good and evil is a static world: "the normative aspect of morality is a necessary consequence of the dynamic structure of man." Poltawski remarks on a peculiar Kantianism (one that, we might add, would very much surprise Kant himself) of Wojtyła: if the truth about God is love — a love which is the cause of the existence of the world — then the way to the *things in themselves* can only be through morality.

Andrzej Poltawski, "Freedom and Dignity in the Work of Karol Wojtyła" (1988),[65] reflects on the sentence that man is a person, that is to say, man is conscious, responsible, free. Poltawski, however, seems to reduce anthropology to personalism, and to make of freedom (and truth) the essence of man. In passing, Poltawski makes an interesting remark on a central concept of *The Acting Person:* "agency" is a better translation than "efficacy" to express the free causality and self-causality (self-determination) of the person. "Agency" does not necessarily imply the success of an action, while "efficacy" seems to do so.

Christof Cirotzki-Christ, *Man and His Acting in Karol Wojtyła's Philosophy* (1986),[66] is a three-chapter monograph. The first chapter deals with the subjectivity of the person and is divided into three sections: passive subjectivity, authorship, and transcendence. The second chapter deals with the existential position of the person and is divided into two sections: a comparison between Wojtyła's and Scheler's views on man, and the personalistic dimension of work. The third chapter deals with the normativity of personal being. It has two sections, one of which discusses the person

65. *Aletheia* (1988), pp. 235-41.
66. Christof Cirotzki-Christ, *Der Mensch und sein Handeln in der Philosophie Karol Wojtyłas* (Essen: Verlag Die Balue Eule), 1986.

as norm of the acting subject and the other the epistemological aspects of the normativity of the person. "The characteristic feature of ethics is normativity. This characteristic distinguishes ethics from the theories of morals or sciences of morals, which are only descriptive." Wojtyła states a strong co-dependence between ethics and anthropology, up to the point that one can define ethics as *normative anthropology*. Both disciplines deal with the same subject-matter, the person, but they treat the person from two different perspectives: "as a *sui generis* being (anthropology) and as value and norm of a person's actions (ethics)."

Andrew N. Woznicki, "The Christian Humanism and Adequate Personalism of Karol Wojtyła" (1985),[67] begins by defending Christianity from the charge that it is an anti-humanism. Humanism is defined by the notion of human dignity, both in the pre-Christian idea of man's superiority over nature and in the Christian idea of God becoming man and the subsequent human elevation to divine life. Wojtyła's thought is a Christian humanism which overcomes naturalistic humanism through the notion of the person, developing into an existential humanism. Human life is described as personal life, and the person is much more than simply an individuation of a universal nature. Two polarities define Wojtyła's humanism: truth-freedom and existence-love. Wojtyła's existential personalism reforms Christian ethics. Wozinski sets an opposition between what he calls the two main attitudes in moral theology: the teleological and the normative (Wojtyła). Wozinski identifies the normative attitude with the value-approach (though Scheler lacked the experience and normativity of duty and, following Kant, he argues that the teleological approach leads to utilitarianism.

Andrzej Szostek, "Karol Wojtyła's View of the Human Person in the Light of the Experience of Morality" (1986),[68] says that Wojtyła is convinced that both man and morality can be known through experience. But his notion of experience must be distinguished both from that found in extreme empiricism and from that of rationalism. The characteristics of this reformed notion of experience are immediacy, an active role for the mind, objectivity, being subjected to (Aristotelian) induction and reduction, and being both external and internal. The experience of moral-

67. In J. Ratzinger and others, *Faith, Philosophy and Theology*, Pope John Paul Lecture Series (St. Paul: College of St. Thomas, 1985), pp. 36-41. Reprinted in Andrew N. Woznicki, *The Dignity of Man as a Person* (San Francisco: Society of Christ Publications, 1987).

68. *Proceedings of the American Catholic Philosophical Association* 58 (1986), pp. 50-64.

ity leads Wojtyła to a theory of morality, that is to say, to a metaethics. The cornerstones of this metaethics are: first, the dignity of the person is the fundamental norm; second, moral values refer directly to the act and indirectly to its author; third, choosing a moral value is self-determination; fourth, normativity: choosing the good and wanting to be good are duties founded in the being of a person or on being a person. Scheler's failure consists in not perceiving the connection between moral value and human action. Wojtyła's metaethics finds its ground in the dignity of the person, which transcends the entire universe. This truth about one's own person and about other persons (and the will to affirm this truth) makes an act as an "actus personae" possible. Obligations brought forth by this truth are indeed obligations to one's self. Fidelity to this truth signifies autonomy, while disloyalty to it implies heteronomy. From autonomy, then, Wojtyła moves to love. Love is the only true attitude toward a person's value. In social philosophy, this true attitude is called participation, and its opposite alienation.

Andrzej Wójtowicz's *Person and Transcendence: Karol Wojtyła's Anthropology of Faith and Church* (1993)[69] is a monograph in Polish divided into ten chapters. The first five chapters deal with Christian anthropology. Chapter 6 deals with Wojtyła and Scheler's anthropology, and chapter 7 is about the philosophy of the person. Questions ranging from ecclesiology to philosophy of culture and sociology are the matter of the last three chapters. According to Wójtowicz, Wojtyła is a radical personalist who puts personal experience before reason. From a sociological point of view, Wojtyła's critique of individualism and totalism comes at the end of a culture based on a mistaken anthropology (which lacks the personal and transcendent dimensions of man). The contemporary crisis is not a crisis of faith, but a crisis of culture.

Kenneth L. Schmitz's *At the Center of the Human Drama: The Philosophical Anthropology of Karol Wojtyła/Pope John Paul II* (1993)[70] is a succinct introduction to the whole range of Wojtyła's writings, from the dramatic and philosophical writings of Karol Wojtyła (chs. 1-3) to the documents of John Paul II (4-5), composed in such a way that it is approachable for beginners in Lublin-style philosophical anthropology and also of interest to trained philosophers. The first chapter describes the plays which Wojtyła wrote for the Theatre of the Word, focusing on *Job, Our*

---

69. Andrzej Wójtowicz, *Osoba i Transcendencja. Karola Wojtyly antropologia wiary i Kosciola* (Wroclaw [Vratislava], 1993). English summary, pp. 219-20.

70. (Washington, DC: Catholic University Press, 1993).

God's Brother, The Jeweller's Shop, and *The Radiation of Fatherhood: A Mystery.* Schmitz emphasizes the "interiority" of the plays, which aim not to be dramas of action or of psychological realism, but to show a group of emblematic characters at a moment of symbolic spiritual transition. Thus, *The Radiation of Fatherhood* is about Adam's exploration of his self-chosen loneliness, which he can only overcome by fathering a child and by understanding that action in the context of the Trinitarian Fatherhood of God. Adam says, "After a long time I came to understand that you do not want me to become a father unless I become a child." Chapter 2 discusses how Wojtyła's Lublin Lectures of 1954-1957 answer the question: "Why Be Moral?" The importance of beginning from this question is that it indicates why, for Wojtyła, ethics requires an anthropology grounded in a metaphysics of being. An ethical act is the act of a free being, and human beings are called to be moral because freedom is at the center of their nature as persons. To be moral is thus, in the traditional terminology, to actualize and perfect one's being as a human person. Chapter 2 emphasizes the Thomistic character of Wojtyła's thought in the 1950s. Chapter 3 gives a clear overview of *The Acting Person.* The key concept of the book, according to Schmitz, is "reflexive self-consciousness," in which one knows oneself both as subject and as object, and in which one is aware of "the drama of good and evil enacted on the interior stage of the human person by and among his actions." Schmitz argues that Wojtyła differs from the main line of phenomenology in defining consciousness in terms of "agency" rather than intentionality: that is, again, to be human is to be morally self-determining and governing. Conscience is thus the ability to be "true" to the goods apparent in a practical situation.

Andrew N. Woznicki's *The Dignity of Man as a Person* (1987)[71] is a collection of essays, some of which have been examined already in our bibliographical essay. There are two more essays worthy of mention in this book: "On the Concept of Catholic Education" [72] and "The Role of Christian Culture."[73]

Ismael Quiles, *Philosophy of the Person According Karol Wojtyła: A Comparative Study with the Anthropology of Interiority* (1987),[74] discovers that

71. Andrew N. Woznicki, *The Dignity of Man as a Person* (San Francisco: Society of Christ Publications, 1987).

72. Ibid., pp. 47-68.

73. Ibid., pp. 69-88.

74. *Filosofia de la persona segun Karol Wojtyła: estudio comparado con la antropologia in-sistencial* (Buenos Aires: Ediciones Depalma, 1987).

344

Wojtyła's philosophy of *The Acting Person* is not much different from his own philosophical path, which he calls an anthropology of interiority. The study is a comparison of Quiles himself with Wojtyła. It is articulated in two parts: ontology of the person and self-realization of the person through action. In the appendix Quiles compares the Western notion of the person (Wojtyła expresses the centrality of the notion of the person in this tradition) with the Oriental metaphysical denial of the person.

5. Postmodern Criticisms

Józef Tischner, "The Methodological Aspect of *The Acting Person*" (1983),[75] briefly praises the book and then concentrates on criticizing it. Tischner finds the notion of participation to be one of its essential points, which allows Wojtyła to overcome isolationism and individualism. Moreover, he finds that the keystone of this work is the following identification: "The person is the Good." Then Tischner claims that Wojtyła's synthesis has structural deficiencies which cannot be eliminated by merely adding a few stories. According to Tischner, Wojtyła does not acknowledge the irreversible decline of Thomistic Christianity. For Wojtyła and for the Thomist tradition the person *is*, while for Scheler, Husserl, and Heidegger the person *becomes*. This dimension of temporality, absolutely essential to any human question, is absent in Wojtyła. Moreover, Wojtyła uses metaphysical notions (act, potency, person) completely foreign to the phenomenological method. Phenomenology brackets the question of existence, and it limits itself to essences and qualities. Wojtyła (who shares this overcoming of pure phenomenological descriptions with Heidegger) wants to move to the question of being (of existence). But for Tischner the Augustinian, not the Thomistic, anthropological tradition is congenial to phenomenological methods. Moreover, Tischner doubts that "act" is the privileged gateway to the person. Tischner — who looks at the anthropological question from the point of view of post-modern philosophy — notices that the idea of man as *rational animal* is in crisis. In short, traditional rationalism is under attack by a more peculiar and more recent form of rationalism. Tischner seems to point to an anti-rationalist tradition (to which even Aquinas may belong) which finds the source of an "act" in something more fundamental than the act itself. Tischner considers *The Acting Person*'s attempt to synthesize

75. "L'aspetto metodologico di Persona e Atto," in R. Buttiglione (ed.), *La filosofia di Karol Wojtyła* (Bologna: CSEO, 1983), pp. 101-6.

"philosophy of being" with "philosophy of consciousness" as unacceptable from the standpoint of both Thomism and phenomenology. *The Acting Person* is for Tischner a dated work: it represents a concluded moment of Christian philosophy in its stage of debate with the contemporary world. What is still alive, according to Tischner, is the inspiration of this work.

Nevio Genghini, "Wojtyła's Metacritique of the Kantian Notion of Freedom" (1983),[76] focuses on the notion of metacritique. A metacritique is a critique which radically modifies the intellectual coordinates within which an object is discussed. Marxism, but also Freudianism, are examples of this metacritique of the notion of human freedom. These attitudes are less interested in the nobility of appearances, and want to put their noses in the "back shop" of life. They want to look beyond the claim of absoluteness of human consciousness and of the Kantian notion of freedom as autonomy. Schopenhauer is the first to notice that "the real motivations of their actions are unknown to those who act morally according to Kantian precepts." Morality does not assumes anything from anthropology, according to Kant: morality, on the other hand, commands a priori laws in the name of rationality. This is Wojtyła's metacritique, according to Genghini, who follows Ricoeur's critique of the Cartesian *cogito*, "we are more than what we are aware of." Wojtyła does not assume the absolute consciousness as his point of departure, but begins with an integral anthropology and with a strong anti-idealistic attitude. In addition, Wojtyła reforms the Freudian notion of sublimation, by reinterpreting it within an anthropology which intends to integrate, not ignore or repress, every aspect of human life, including those which seem to be least noble or rational.

Stanislaw Grygiel, "The Hermeneutic of Action and the New Model of Consciousness" (1983),[77] remarks that *The Acting Person* belongs to the decosmologization of philosophy achieved through the anthropological shift. Grygiel's article is divided into three parts. In the first part he deals with a "hermeneutic reading" of Wojtyła's thought. For Grygiel an "act" can and should be understood as a "symbol" of the person. An act speaks at two levels, just as a symbol does. At a first level it speaks of itself, but at a second level it points to the person. The second part deals with conscience and self-knowledge, in relationship to selves and others. Self-knowledge is

---

76. "La metacritica del concetto kantiano di libertà in Karol Wojtyła," in R. Buttiglione (ed.), *La filosofia di Karol Wojtyła* (Bologna: CSEO, 1983), pp. 75-84.

77. "L'ermeneutica dell'azione ed il nuovo modello di coscienza," in R. Buttiglione (ed.), *La filosofia di Karol Wojtyła* (Bologna: CSEO, 1983), pp. 107-20.

different from any other knowledge because its object is not general: it is the concrete and unique "I." Consciousness, on the other hand, is not intentional. In conscience therefore there is no split between subject and object. An object subsists in consciousness in a nonobjective-cognitive way, but, very importantly, consciousness does not constitute the object. "There are three types of acts: acts of knowledge, acts of self-knowledge, and acts of consciousness: the first and the second have a cognitive-intentional structure, the third does not." Grygiel questions the relationship which Wojtyła posits between consciousness and self-knowledge which seems to lead to an infinite mirroring of the lived experience between consciousness and self-knowledge, a kind of infinite regress of the lived experiences. Grygiel suggests, as a possible way out, an attribution of some intentionality to consciousness. Thirdly, Grygiel questions the point of departure of the distinction between nature and person, as the distinction between "involuntary" (what happens in man) and "voluntary" ("I will" and man's actions). If the person is defined by the voluntary, and man is defined by "I will" and not by "something happens in me," what is the relationship of "the involuntary" to being human? It seems that Grygiel criticizes the excessive Kantianism of Wojtyła, or, even better, what followers of the Angelic Doctor such as Maritain used to call "angelism."

6. Theology

Andrew N. Woznicki, "Ecumenical Consciousness according to Karol Wojtyła" (1984),[78] says that Wojtyła took an interest in the ecumenical movement as soon as he was elected Bishop in Cracow. Cardinal Wojtyła writes about the Polish tradition of respect for freedom: "Poland was never the stage for religious wars." Poland "was a place for the co-living, co-existing, and co-operation of Christians of various denominations and churches." Woznicki reminds us of the Polish historical background in religious toleration. "While the rest of Europe lived by the principle of *cuius regio, eius religio,* Sigmundus II Augustus (1520-1572) announced in the Polish Diet: 'I am your king, but I am not king of your conscience.'" Earlier, in regard to the council of Constance, the Polish delegate Paul Vladimir Wlodkowicz protested against using force to convert people: "It

---

78. *Center Journal* 3/2 (1984), pp. 111-25. The same essay, with some embellishments, is published in A. Woznicki, *The Dignity of Man as a Person* (San Francisco: Society of Christ Publications, 1987), pp. 89-112.

is not permitted to convert pagans to Christianity by the sword and violence, because this would hurt our neighbor. It is not allowed to seek good ends by doing evil." Cardinal Wojtyła follows Vatican II's *Unitatis Redintegratio* and *Nostra Aetate*, and states that Christianity is a matter of conversion, which is based on truth and freedom and realized by faith, hope, and prayer.

Angelo Scola, "Karol Wojtyła's Speeches to the Second Vatican Ecumenical Council: Exposition and Theological Interpretation" (1984),[79] says that Wojtyła gave twenty-two speeches to the Council and his activity was so intense and determinant that, while his election in 1978 was a surprise for the general public, it was no surprise to those who had taken part in Vatican II. The 39-year-old bishop writes in preparation for the Council: "Christian personalism constitutes the foundation of the whole ethical doctrine which, since the Gospel, has been always taught by the Catholic Church." Scola specifies three main areas of Wojtyła's concerns. First, ecclesiology: the Church's ministry is "servitium salutis aeternae." Second, after the modern "anthropological shift" there is the necessity of an integral and adequate anthropology, that is to say, of an integral personalism. The point of departure of ethics is the dignity of the person. Within this ethical horizon there takes place a dialectic between freedom and truth. Here Wojtyła makes his decisive contribution to the understanding of religious freedom, "the novelty" of the Second Vatican Council. Religion is the highest expression of the rational creature, the completion and not the alienation of his rationality, and the relationship with the supreme truth necessarily requires freedom. Third, the presence of the Church in the world is the presence and continuation of Christ's redemption, which, while it is already accomplished forever, still leaves space for the "novum" of history. Within this *novum* there is also an urgent necessity (1964) of presenting Christianity as authentic, especially to young people.

Gerald A. McCool, "The Theology of John Paul II" (1993),[80] deals with *Faith according to Saint John of the Cross, Sources of Renewal,* and *Sign of Contradiction.* McCool notices an evolution between the early Wojtyła theologizing as a Thomist in writing his dissertation on St. John of the Cross,

---

79. "Gli interventi di Karol Wojtyła al Concilio Ecumenico Vaticano II. Esposizione ed interpretazione teologica," in *Karol Wojtyła. Filosofo, Teologo, Poeta* (Vatican City: Libreria Editrice Vaticana, 1984), pp. 289-306.

80. In J. M. McDermott (ed.), *The Thought of John Paul II: A Collection of Essays and Studies* (Editrice Pontificia Universita' Gregoriana, 1993), pp. 29-53.

and his later Thomism after the Council. "Using the language of his later Thomism, we might say that the theology of his first dissertation was built upon a metaphysics of universal 'nature' rather than upon a metaphysics of the conscious concrete person." McCool also notices some similarities with Rahner and Lonergan.

7. Poetry and Theater

Jan Blonski, "Poetry and Meditation" (1984),[81] says that, in authorizing the publication of his poems forty years later, our author wrote apologetically: "Poetry is a great noble woman who requires total devotion to herself; I am afraid of not having been completely honest to her." Blonski remarks that poetry reveals aspects of existence which are otherwise unknown. Wojtyła's poetry is inherently religious; it is poetry of the religious experience and especially of the experience of conversion. The "poet of conversion" attempts to bring together, beyond language, the element of human work and the element of divine grace.

Stanislaw Grygiel, "That Piece of Land . . . (A Reflection on 'Thinking of the Motherland' and on 'Stanislaw')" (1984),[82] reflects on the ethos of a nation. The best way to enslave a nation is to set it free from its ethos, as was attempted under Communism. By not being indebted to anything, a people can be obligated to everything. The common good of the ethos of a nation is propriety of generations, and it constitutes the nation's identity. This common good is higher than the distinction between the powerful and the powerless. Outside this common good and this identity there is no freedom. Freedom is a constant struggle, not a possession. It is a gift which must be conquered over and over again; it is not a state: it is a way of looking at the same things with new and opened eyes (Plotinus), or it is the condition of being awake (Plato). Then, on this topic of freedom, Grygiel draws an important distinction between types of human relationships: the *slave-master* relationship and the *father-son* relationship. There cannot be freedom in the first relationship: sons can fall but slaves cannot, because those who are asleep (not free) cannot fall.

---

81. "Poesie et méditation," in *Karol Wojtyła. Filosofo, Teologo, Poeta* (Vatican City: Libreria Editrice Vaticana, 1984), pp. 325-31.

82. "Quel Pezzo di Terra . . . (Una Riflessione su 'Pensando la Patria' e 'Stanislaw')," in *Karol Wojtyła. Filosofo, Teologo, Poeta* (Vatican City: Libreria Editrice Vaticana, 1984), pp. 333-44.

349

Jozef Tischner, "Irradiation of Creative Reciprocity" (1984),[83] reflects on Wojtyła's "Radiation of Fatherhood." By producing offspring, parents not only produce their children, but they create themselves as parents. It is a reciprocal creation. In this we also see one of the key themes of Augustinian thought: in order to understand man, one has to see him in God, and in order to approach the mystery of God, we have to see it through man. This is a circular hermeneutic which moves between God as Trinity and man. Wojtyła's "Radiation of Fatherhood" is an archetypal drama. One of the most powerful moments is the dialogue between Adam, the stepfather, and Monique, the adopted daughter. In spite of his corruption, "man is better than he seems; he is also better than how he seems to himself."

Giovanni Testori, "On a Line of the Character 'Theresa' in the 'Jeweller's Shop'" (1984),[84] reflects on the line in the *Jeweller's Shop*: "There is no hope without fear, and no fear without hope." Apart from the poetic musicality of this verse in the original language, Testori reflects on the meaning of human fragility. Testori deals with despair, which, together with fear, constitutes an opposite of hope. Even despair, which is not reducible to psychology, is grace, an unmerited act of love toward us. Then, Testori remarks, hope and fear are not really opposite since they belong to each other. They are complementary, not antithetical.

Andrzej Maria Marczewski, "Man in the Face of Fundamental Questions (My Encounters with Karol Wojtyła's Dramaturgy)" (1983),[85] deals with the phenomenon of a dramaturgist-Pope. The fame and success of Wojtyła's dramas cannot be reduced to author's name because of their intrinsic value. Marczewski describes the *Jeweller's Shop* and *Our God's Brother*.

8. Bibliographical Aids and Ph.D. Theses

John M. Grondelski, "Sources for the Study of Karol Wojtyła's Thought" (1993),[86] is the Appendix to Kenneth Schmitz's book and of great value to English readers.

83. "Irradiazione delle reciprocità creatrice," in *Karol Wojtyła. Filosofo, Teologo, Poeta* (Vatican City: Libreria Editrice Vaticana, 1984), pp. 307-12.

84. "Giovanni Paolo II e la disperazione dell'uomo. A proposito di una battuta del personaggio di Teresa nella 'Bottega dell'orefice,'" in *Karol Wojtyła. Filosofo, Teologo, Poeta* (Vatican City: Libreria Editrice Vaticana, 1984), pp. 353-58.

85. In *Dialectic and Humanism: The Polish Philosophical Quarterly* 10 (1983), pp. 111-18.

86. (Washington, D.C.: Catholic University Press, 1993), pp. 147-63.

The following Ph.D. theses, set out here in chronological order, deal specifically with the thought of Karol Wojtyła:

Stephen John Heaney, "The Concept of the Unity of the Person in the Thought of Karol Wojtyła" (Marquette University, 1988).

Gonzalo Beneytez-Beneytez-Barroso, "La libertad en el pensamiento de Karol Wojtyła" (University of Navarre, 1990).

Jerzy Pokerek, "La Normatività della cosciena morale nel personalismo di Karol Wojtyła" (Gregorian University [Rome], 1991).

Tadeusz Rostorowski, "Il Problema Gnoseologico nell' opera 'Persona et Atto' di K. Wojtyła" (Gregorian University [Rome], 1991).

Antonio Quiros Herruzo, "El Sustrato Personal de Habito en Eduacion" (University of Navarre, 1993).

Maria Jose Franzuet Casas, "Persona, Accion Y Libertad en Karol Wojtyła" (University of Navarre, 1996).

Janusz Gzik, "Analisis Antropologico-Moral del Amor en Los Escritos de Karolj Wojtyła (Hacia el Amor Conyugal)" (University of Navarre, 1996).

Appendix

Rocco Buttiglione's Introduction to the Third Polish Edition of K. Wojtyła's *The Acting Person*, Lublin, 1994

Notes on Ways of Reading *The Acting Person*

1. Preliminary Remarks

Works of philosophy also have a destiny. On the one hand, they attempt to express a truth which is beyond time, which is eternally valid apart from the perennial variations of historical circumstances and cultural fashions. On the other hand, philosophical works are always rooted in a time and in a historical circumstance, in a cultural and national specificity, and even in a personal biography. The authentic philosophical work is neither the repetition of an abstract philosophical truth grasped outside of time nor the expression of an individual and arbitrary view of the world. It is rather a witness to truth within a concrete human situation, which embodies truth in that situation and makes it existentially concrete.

For this reason a philosopher's work is both absolutely simple and extremely complex, and philosophy is both essentially one, just as truth is one, and infinitely multiform, like the human minds which think about this truth.

The book which I have the honor to introduce is not exempt from this destiny of philosophy. On the one hand, it can be read purely theoretically, and, on the other hand, it roots its universal truth within a European and a Polish specificity and rediscovers this truth through and within this specificity. Our introduction will therefore have a theoretical and a historical part.

Lastly, a book is made to be read and to influence the thought and the action of those who read it. The history of its influence and the practical results to which it leads must also be examined if we want to understand it thoroughly. But this is a very delicate subject.

The Acting Person is a rigorously philosophical book, which does not yield to the "devotionalism" typical of too many Catholic philosophers. Yet, if one wants to understand the fullness of its meaning, one cannot forget that it is a work of a man of faith, a Cardinal of the Church of Christ.

It is completely justifiable to read an ecclesial intention and the seeds of a theology in the background of the book. This is particularly clear if we compare *The Acting Person* with its author's many rich sermons as well as with his other works such as *Sources of Renewal*[1] and *Sign of Contradiction*.[2]

Our problem becomes even more complex if we consider that this philosopher and man of faith would after a few years become St. Peter's successor in Rome and the first Slavic Pope in the history of the Church. It is undoubtedly wrong to seek out a mechanical continuity between the work of the philosopher Karol Wojtyła and the teachings of John Paul II. The Pope's words ought to be understood within the context of the Magisterium of the Church and in continuity with his predecessors. Moreover, the Magisterium expresses the doctrine of the Catholic Church and requires the assent of faith, at least the assent of the faithful. The work of a philosopher (even the work of a philosopher who has become Pope) always remains exposed to the rational critique of believers and non-believers, and its authority derives only from the sharpness of its insights and the strength of its argument. But the Holy Spirit works in the Church through the matter offered by the men whom He uses. For these reasons His decision to use

---

1. First published in Polish as *Upodstaw odnowy. Studium o realizacji Vaticanum II* (Cracow: Pol. Tow. Teologiczne, 1974).

2. *Sign of Contradiction*, translated by Mary Smith (London: G. Chapman, 1979).

this man, a philosopher, a Pole, Cardinal of Cracow in difficult times, and the author of *The Acting Person,* is perhaps not without meaning.

This book can also offer an important aid for the understanding of the great encyclicals and, in general, for the understanding of the historical significance of this Pontificate.

Our introduction is set out in three parts: in the first we will offer some keys for a theoretical comprehension of this work, in the second we will deal with its historical significance, and in the third we will see how such a significance influences the present and how can it help in the common striving toward the truth in the beginning of a "new age" in the history of "Poland and of the World."

"But" — one could contend — "in doing so do we respect the nature of the book and the intention of the author, or do we impose a method and a criterion of interpretation which are foreign to the book and its author?" It seems to me that such a criterion, which places itself between eternal truth and history, is suggested by the work itself.

One of the most important theoretical points of this work is the distinction between "knowledge" and "consciousness."[3]

According to the Classical tradition, "knowledge" is a receptive faculty, and receives the given. "Consciousness" is rather the faculty which either interiorizes the given or rejects such an interiorization, and by doing these things constitutes the inward world of a person. We move constantly within an external world of reality (and of the eternal truth) and an interior world of our affective interests, which is properly noncognitive but is nonetheless somewhat re-cognitive by creating a context of force, color, and emotional intensity. By influencing our practical action in the external world, the interior world acquires objective consistency (though, in a sense, it possesses it from the beginning inasmuch as the *way in which* we see things exists just as the *way in which* things objectively exist — these two modalities do not have the same ontological consistency) and is the origin of a culture and a society. For this reason, a philosopher's work always simultaneously relates to a state of consciousness and an objective knowledge and attempts to order a "life world" according to an objective truth. In other words, it tries to give back to the objective truth an existential clarity within a specific "life-world." It is therefore in *The Acting Person* itself that we find the methodological categories according to which we attempt to read it and to introduce it.

3. Cf. *The Acting Person,* ch. 1, par. 3: "Consciousness and Self-Knowledge."

2. The Theoretical Structure of the Book

The object which this book asks about is man's action, or man as he is manifested and becomes understandable through action. So it is not a work about ethics, at least explicitly, though it has important consequences for ethics. It is, to be precise, a work of anthropology.

In regard to the methods, the author turns to two great sources. On the one hand, he positions himself within the great tradition of Thomist realism, which he studied intensely in the Dominican and Roman version of Father Garrigou-Lagrange and in the tradition, which is closer to Gilson, which was worked out in Poland by Zwiazawski, and originally developed at the University of Lublin and which, in a sense, culminates in the works of Father Krapiec. On the other hand, he reworks the phenomenological philosophy which he approached through studying Scheler's work[4] and which was present in the noncommunist culture of Cracow because of the influence of Roman Ingarden. Wojtyła has not been a student of Ingarden and his personal relationship with this great phenomenologist became closer after the basic philosophical stance of our Author was already formed.[5] We cannot affirm, therefore, that Wojtyła's phenomenological method is Ingarden's realist phenomenology, even if an indirect influence cannot be excluded and some similarities, especially with Ingarden's *On Responsibility*,[6] are definitely impressive. However, it seems to me that Ingarden's point of departure is phenomenology, and, radically following Husserl's motto "back to the things themselves," attempts to lead it back into realism. To implement this program Ingarden must defeat the transcendental interpretation of phenomenology, according to which the things themselves, to which one ought to go back, are the immediate givens of consciousness. But this is not Wojtyła's concern. Wojtyła is interested in phenomenology precisely inasmuch as it offers a method for the description of the givens of consciousness, that is, of those things immediately experienced and lived within consciousness. What consciousness immediately experiences and lives, however, is not the whole reality; it is not even, in general, the real in its objectivity. We can *know* many things which are not

4. *Ocena mozliwoci zbudowania etyki chrześcijańskiej przy założeniach systemu Maksa Schelera* (Lublin: Tow. Nauk. KUL, 1959).

5. Cf. T. Styczen, "O metodzie antropologii filzoficznej. Na marginesie Osoby i Czynu K. Wojtyła oraz ksiazeczki o człowieku R. Ingardena," in *Rocz. Filoz.* 21, pp. 105-14.

6. R. Ingarden, *Man and Value*, trans. A. Szylewicz (Washington, D.C.: Catholic University Press, 1983).

immediately given in consciousness. Such things can be communicated to us through the experience of other people, or through a purely objective knowledge of the fundamental structure of being and of the world.[7] This is the level at which we generally find Thomist metaphysics and the anthropology based on this metaphysics.

Such objective metaphysics and anthropology retain all of their value for our author. It is not a question of reconstructing them on a phenomenological basis. This is, in my opinion, the difference between Wojtyła's thought and the realist phenomenology of Ingarden, Hildebrand, and Seifert. For Wojtyła, it is not a question of demonstrating phenomenologically that man is a person, but seeing with the aid of phenomenology *in which way man is a person,* in which way the metaphysical structures proper to his being are reflected in his consciousness.

Thomist metaphysical anthropology is therefore like a great fundamental hypothesis, which is to be verified through the phenomenological analysis which, on the other hand, guides this analysis and allows for a greater depth.

An analogy with medical science can help us to understand this point better. There are many organs and functions of the human body which are immediately given to our consciousness. For example, we all know that we have two arms and two hands. There are other organs and functions which are not given to consciousness with the same immediacy, but they can manifest themselves in consciousness in particular circumstances and we can learn from those who found themselves in these particular circumstances. While we are not conscious of our liver or our spleen, those who have had these organs abnormally swollen are painfully aware of their existence, and we can learn from them both the existence of such organs and the behaviors which allow us to become (painfully) aware of their existence. It would be irrational to deny such an existence, and it would be equally irrational to ruin one's liver or spleen through disorderly behavior before accepting the fact of their existence and to convince oneself of the need to protect them adequately. There is something here which we know, in a sense, at second hand, through signs; notwithstanding the lack of immediate awareness, we can be equally certain. Lastly, there are organs of the body which we know in another way: they are immediately given either to our or to an other's consciousness. They are manifest when we open and dissect a cadaver and examine its composition. The enormous contribution

7. *The Acting Person,* Intro., par. 2.

of anatomy to the medical sciences is indisputable, together with that of biology and physics. The knowledge proper to these sciences is not derived from any "consciousness of the body," yet they allow us to know the body much better and to unify in a more adequate way our "consciousness of the body" by unifying phenomena whose connection would otherwise escape us, and which, instead, in the light of the abstract knowledge of the internal structure of the body and its laws, become for us signs of this or that modification of the internal states of our organism.

Metaphysics is to phenomenology what the knowledge of the internal structure of the body is to the lived consciousness of the body. Wojtyła is able, through his philosophical method, to enlarge the horizon of the philosophy of being and fully to acknowledge the right of philosophy of consciousness without blurring distinctions and generating an equivocal syncretism.

There exist, of course, points of connection between phenomenological analysis and metaphysical knowledge, and our author devotes particular attention to them. They are those realities which surface in consciousness and yet which are not fully comprehensible if we confine ourselves only to what is immediately given to consciousness. In *Love and Responsibility* Wojtyła offered a "metaphysical analysis of shame,"[8] which shows how the phenomenologically evident phenomenon of shame presents all the characters of a sign or of an indication, which hints at something else which is not immediately given together with the simple experience of shame and yet which must necessarily be included in order to make such an experience comprehensible. This something else is the transcendent value of the human person, which must be protected against the danger that a too intense perception of sexual values blinds one to the more hidden but more substantial value of the person as such.

At the center of *The Acting Person* there is a phenomenological focus upon another decisive point of contact between phenomenology and metaphysics, which shows the necessity of pursuing and fulfilling the phenomenological description through a metaphysical understanding. This is the case of the experience of "I can but I am not forced to do it" in which the efficacy of the person manifests itself.[9] The Thomist theory of the will offers an explanation of the internal structure of the person which explains the immediately given experience of "I can but I am not forced to do it." I am

8. *Love and Responsibility*, pt. 3, ch. 2.
9. *The Acting Person*, pt. 1, ch. 2, par. 8.

inclined to action by the passions which are present in my state of consciousness; but this inclination is not a determination. How is this possible? It is necessary to admit than man has the potential to take a stand in the face of the objective truth, in the face of objective good and objective evil.

It is precisely obedience to truth which liberates us from the determinism of the passions. The discovery of the operativity of the person, of his efficacy and responsibility for his own actions, appears to us as a phenomenological verification of the metaphysics of potency and act in the particular form which it assumes in the human "suppositum." The person is not just the stage on which perception of values happens but the active subject of just such perceptions; he can choose among them by following the guide of the knowledge of truth. It is for this reason that "to serve God is to reign." The sovereignty of the person is expressed in the decision for truth and in the imposition of the law of truth on one's own passions. Of course, a person always acts within a situation, and he is profoundly conditioned by this situation. He is also able to transcend such a conditioning in order to obey the truth. Transcendence of the person and obedience to truth are the two sides of a single dynamic reality which is the free action of the person.

Through free action a person actualizes himself; he fulfills his destiny and becomes a person in a higher degree. This by no means implies — as Scheler feared — a species of spiritual egoism or pharisaism, as if the end of the action is one's own perfection. Rather, the person acknowledges himself as responsible for the good, and the first good which is given to him and for which he is objectively responsible is his own self-realization in the truth.[10]

So far we have quickly run through the first two parts of the work (besides it very important Introduction on man's experience) dealing respectively with "Knowledge and Efficacy" and "Transcendence and Person in Act." Through phenomenological analysis we have emphasized the existence of an "irreducible kernel"[11] of the person which is easily understandable and interpretable through the classical notion of "subjectum."

In other words, we have joined together the Thomist and the Schelerian notions of person, in a way that the person "according to Scheler" is understood as the manifestation at the level of consciousness of the metaphysi-

10. Ibid., pt. 2, ch. 4.
11. Cf. K. Wojtyła, "Subjectivity and the Irreducible in Man," in *Analecta Husserliana,* vol. 7 (1978), pp. 107-14.

cal dynamisms proper to the person "according to St. Thomas." In synthesis, we can say that the person is understood here as subject and substantial being.

This philosophical operation makes available a wealth of contents about personal integration and participation which appear in the third and fourth parts, respectively.

If we look at our author's two great mentors, St. Thomas and Scheler, we must note that St. Thomas predominates until the end of the second part. So far, we have shown that Scheler's point of view can and should be joined to Thomas's, how Thomism corrects Scheler on some essential points, and how, all things considered, Thomism prevails over Scheler's phenomenology. But this defense of Thomas does not imply a rejection of phenomenology but rather its being reformed and applied in a different way.

But one might ask what phenomenology adds to Thomism, beyond a certain linguistic liveliness about existential matters.[12] This question receives an articulate and extremely important answer precisely in parts III and IV of this book.[13] Here it is shown how the transcendence of the person is and should be the basis for the integration of the person. The diverse and partial passions which vitalize the interior human world cannot be integrated in a consistent and unitary whole without transcending them in the direction of truth. On the other hand, it is impossible to transcend these passions without, at the same time, integrating them. The first affirmation indicates the insuperable limit of any "ethics of feelings," be it a Humean or a Schelerian ethics. The second indicates the limit of any "ethics of duty" and of any moralism. As Aristotle said in the *Politics*, a human being can only command the passions and feelings politically, not despotically, that is to say, by realizing at the same time and in an ordered way their proper finalities. The physiological and psychological dynamisms, upon which the "states of mind" (present in consciousness) are based, are naturally, though blindly, oriented toward the objective good.

Reason, therefore, does not have the task of violating the passions, but rather of illuminating and guiding them. They have (against any Manicheism) their own content of value. Hume, and all of his philosophical

12. Among others, M. A. Krapiec asks this question. Cf. "Ksiazka kardinała monografia osoby jako podmiotu moralnosci," in *Analecta Cracoviensia*, vol. 5/6 (1975), pp. 57-61.

13. This answer is critically developed in Wojtyła, "Osoba: podmiot i wspólnota," in *Rocz. Filoz.*, vol. 24, pp. 50ff.

successors, give to reason only an instrumental role in ethics (they are at the beginning of that conception of instrumental reason against which the School of Frankfurt will direct its critique). Wojtyła, on the other hand, underlines its directive role.[14] Yet in contrast to Kant, who denies any moral value to feeling in order to put the totality of the moral action in the "you ought," our author attributes to reason the role of discerning among moral feelings, of unifying them, and of guiding moral feelings toward the truth. Consequently, the *way in which* conscience experiences the world is not indifferent to the moral judgment and the moral action. It is not an obstacle to eliminate in order to reach the sphere of pure morality, but rather the matter of such action which the truth known by reason ought to embody, and give its form. The "state of subjectivity" poses an objective consistency too, and the rational judgment must take it into account. Here one sees the extraordinary contribution which phenomenology can offer in order to allow a concrete comprehension of the moral experience and to unify the "subjective experience" with the "objective truth." The "subjective experience" cannot be, in itself, false or wrong. It does not show, however, all the truth and cannot have the last say about action.

It is, rather, the judgment of moral conscience which bonds the objective truth, the object of knowledge, with the subjective situation which is reflected in consciousness.

In the light of what we have been saying, the importance of education and of culture for ethics emerges very distinctly. Reason cannot command obedience to the truth externally or prescriptively. It must, rather, enter into to the construction of the affective processes of the person, in the construction of the emotional archetypes and of the "great and profound sentiments."[15] Even if in exceptional situations a human being may be forced to choose the objective truth against his subjective feeling, the ideal of moral education is rather action according to a feeling informed by reason. In the life of a nation, literature, music, and art have precisely the task of forming the social archetypes, of determining the modes in which the great values will be interiorized and lived. Without such interiorization objective truth remains weak and deficient. Man, instead of vigorously channeling all of his energy toward realizing himself, would be engaged in an endless struggle against himself in order to restrain his rebellious passions.

14. Cf. Wojtyła, "O kierowniczej lubsłużbnej roli rozumu w etyce. Na tle poglandów Tomasza z Akwinu, Hume'a i Kanta," in *Rocz. Filoz,* vol. 6, pp. 13-31.

15. *The Acting Person,* pt. 3, ch. 6, par. 8.

Wojtyła's way of proceeding clearly individuates the dimension of the psyche, as an autonomous dimension, connected both with the body and the spirit. This dimension is animated by special mechanisms which mediate between the body and the spirit and which must be studied in their specificity.

This idea is in line with a theory well known to St. Thomas, to Aristotle, and to Plato. But it also represents an important novelty in relation to the Cartesian dualism of mind and body, often absorbed in other non-Cartesian philosophical traditions.

Besides, the clear individuation of the sphere of the psyche allows us to place the psychological disciplines in the right ambience. Of course, they are connected with ethics, but they have a specific formal object which is the study of the psyche and, as a practical purpose, the treatment of emotional disturbances, that is to say, of those distortions which can occur, without the person's responsibility, in the ways in which he interiorizes reality.

The Acting Person offers a clarification of similar importance in regard to the social sciences and their relationship to philosophy. Social sciences have always had the inclination to dissolve the individual in the network of the relationships and conditionings within which the human person finds himself, and which are, on the other hand, the result of historical development. By so doing they have emphasized, perhaps in an unprecedented way, the social character of the human person. Phenomenology, especially that of Scheler and Schulz, greatly contributed to this.

But this leads to the loss of the substantial dimension of the human person, to the loss of the awareness of the fact that the individual is responsible for choices which, in a certain sense, transcend the entire human community and that, in order to make such choices, he has the right to an inviolable sphere of autonomy in respect of the social whole. In the chapter on "Participation" Wojtyła shows the twofold dimension of the person. On the one hand, the person is an irreducible subject, who cannot be understood merely as the sum of his emotional states, brought about by internal and external conditioning. The lived experience of efficacy and responsibility forces us to admit that the person has a substance, which activates itself in emotional states but which also transcends them in relation to the truth. In this sense the person is not, first of all, relation but substance. "Persona est sui juris et altero incommunicabilis" is an old adage which refers to this notion. Wojtyła will deepen this theme in an important later essay called "The Person as Subject and as Community."

But phenomenological analysis exhibits with evidence how the person is not *only* substance (*subiectum*) but also relation. One could say that Wojtyła indirectly appropriates an important truth of Hegelianism. The way in which we perceive ourselves and the concrete historical form of our personality are decisively influenced by social relationships with other human beings. A human being fully discovers himself only in the engagement with another human being. Besides, the discovery of oneself, the self-consciousness, is not an accessory but an integral element of human self-realization. The form of the relationship with the other deeply enters into the success and the failure of man in the realization of the task of fulfilling his own human essence, which is by nature dynamic.

In *Love and Responsibility*, Wojtyła had studied the way in which this characteristic of the person is manifested in sexual and conjugal love.[16] The same anthropological principle underscores *The Acting Person*, where the analysis is directed toward the sphere of human work as well as of civil and political society. The experience of "acting together with others" is at the center of this reflection.

In "acting together with others" the efficacy of the person and his responsibility for the action are realized differently from the case of the action of an isolated individual. This depends on the fact that another human being may be the means or instrument of the action and on the fact that the subject of the action is a collective subject. May another man be the means or instrument of an action? Does one lose sight, in this instrumental relationship, of the special dignity of the human person, toward whom the only objectively adequate response is love? The other can be the instrument of an action — so argues Wojtyła — only if he is at the same time the subject of the action: that is, if through the action he is enabled to realize his personal end. A common action, therefore, can be good only if the men who act share a common purpose, if their relationship is that of a community or a company positively oriented toward the ultimate destiny of man. Participation is the force which continuously generates this community or company. A man can share his own interiority with another man, can agree with him on a common action, can participate in a shared responsibility.

---

16. In order to understand the thought of our author on this topic more precisely it is also essential to study his poetry. See, for example, his "Przed sklepem jubilera. Meditacja o Sakramencie Małżeństwa prechodazca chwilami w dramat," in *Znak* 1/12, pp. 1564-1607.

Wojtyła carefully examines the different attitudes which characterize human relationships. Concurring in a common purpose, being a loyal part of the same community, our author notices, does not imply losing one's own subjectivity in the collective, does not even exclude the possibility of deep disagreements concerning the way in which the common good of a community ought to be realized. A loyal opposition against the decision made by a majority or at least by the legitimate authority of a certain community is a way of participating in the realization of the common good. On the other hand, authority ought to be able to accept and to respect a loyal opposition, and this is one of the things which distinguishes free political regimes from totalitarian ones. But loyal opposition must be clearly distinguished from lack of interest in the common good and from sabotage.

Many of the ideas expressed in the chapter on "Participation" in *The Acting Person* have become popular in recent Polish history under the name of "solidarity." One can say that solidarity is the attitude of responsible care for the common good which constitutes the human community, or, in other words, the social form of love understood as the sole adequate attitude toward the person. It is obvious that the word "love" does not have any emotional or sentimental meaning, but an entirely objective connotation: it is the response to the value of the person of the other and the decision to cooperate in his realization. Such a decision, insofar as it is an objective decision, does not exclude but rather implies an opposition to the intentions of the other, where these were objectively unjust or mistaken.

3. The Historical Collocation of The Acting Person

The structure of this book is eminently, rigorously, and even, I would say, scrupulously philosophical. But there is no doubt that, in the author's mind, philosophy has a noble task, that of being the "handmaid of theology" or an introduction to the message of faith. To go directly to the core of the question, we can ask where we can find the archetype and the model of an act which is fully human; an act in which, in a moment of time, man finds himself unconditionally surrendering to the truth, even to the point of sacrificing himself for it. Paul's words about Christ, who made himself obedient to death and death on the cross for us, are the horizon of the entire book. If the essential structure of the human act requires obedience to the truth and the love of the other as a person, everyday experience shows that man by himself is incapable both of such a love and such a life in truth without a help which comes from heaven and which, in the language of Christian theology, is called grace. By proclaiming Maximilian Kolbe "the patron of our difficult century" John Paul II will show in the act of the martyr (in the speech of Oswiecim-Brzezinka, which is peerless as an introduction to his pontificate) both the fulfillment of the human and the presence of grace.[17]

Philosophical anthropology naturally becomes theological anthropology.[18] Christ is Man: by encountering Him the possibility of becoming truly oneself is open to every man. God, by revealing Himself in Christ, revealed at the same time the truth about man.

This truth is, in a sense, contained in the notion of "person": the person is the most noble being in created nature, and at the same time a person is made for communion with other men and with God. We are here at the center of the programmatic encyclical *Redemptor Hominis,* and also at the core of the Christian gospel.

Because of the eminent dignity of every man, especially of the poor and of the sinner, there exists a justice which goes beyond the simple exchange of equal values. In consideration of this justice, there is human duty to come to the help of other men, over and above the fact that they are accountable to one another. There exists a "right to mercy" which, without erasing all the diverse social obligations, offers the horizon in which these obligations must be interpreted and understood. This is, in a sense, the central theme of *Dives in Misericordia.*

Finally, in *Laborem Exercens,* many of the anthropological insights which we have found in the chapter on "Participation" in *The Acting Person* are confirmed. Work is not only dealing with things but an act which is accomplished together with other people. In such an act a person can never be considered exclusively as a means. While dealing with the material objects of his own work, a person must transcend them and grow as a person in his own action. Moreover, because of its social character, work produces not only things but also human relationships. In these relationships a person is either alienated or finds himself. A person has the right to participate freely in the formation of these human relationships.

17. Cf. S. Dziwisz, J. Kowalczyk, and T. Rakoczy (eds.), *Jan Paweł II na Ziemai polskiej* (Vatican City: Libreria Editrice Vaticana, 1979), pp. 204ff.
18. Cf. S. Nagy, "Karol Wojtyła Teolog," in W. Gramatowski and Z. Wilinska, *Karol Wojtyła w swietle publikacji/ Karol Wojtyła negli scritti* (Vatican City: Libreria Editrice Vaticana, 1980), pp. 34-43.

Of course, the same principle is valid in the wider sphere of social and political relationships.

In each of these three great encyclicals, the notion of person is at the intersection of the relationship between man and God. While this concept possesses a fundamental philosophical dimension, it has been developed historically by Christian theology as a means of understanding the relationship of Jesus with the Father and of the Persons of the Trinity with each other. Here we see how two can become one in obedience to truth and love.

The same notion of person makes it thinkable how the human person can enter into the internal life of God Himself, who is a Communion of Persons. Person and communion are two sides of the same reality, and Christian revelation was decisive in moving philosophy to begin to think of man as a person.

We have briefly seen how some fundamental traits of Wojtyła's thought can help us better to understand John Paul II's Magisterium. If we are to understand *The Acting Person* more deeply, it is now necessary to step back and to enter into the mind and spirit of our author at the time in which he was writing this book. Comparison with *Sources of Renewal* can help us with this. In considering the unity of these two works, one is led to say that *The Acting Person* attempts to face the challenge of a Catholic philosophy *after the Second Vatican Council*. It well known what a profound influence this event, in which Wojtyła was a leading protagonist, had on the young bishop of Cracow.[19] The fundamental theme of the Council is the relationship between Catholicism and modernity. By eliminating the two easy routes of integrist rejection of modernity on the one hand, and, on the other, the absorption of the "modern" as a positive axiological category and an insurmountable horizon of thought, the Council chose the difficult path of "non-modernist dialogue."[20]

In the philosophical sphere modernity begins with the theme of consciousness and freedom. Modern philosophy is characterized essentially as a philosophy of consciousness and of freedom. Generally speaking, Catholic thought opposes it to a philosophy of being and of objective truth. Etienne Gilson has well shown that, at the level of a philosophy's choice of a point of departure and thus of its fundamental theoretical

19. Cf. Chapter Six of this book.
20. We borrow this expression from A. Del Noce, *L'epoca della secolarizzazione* (Milan: Giuffrè, 1970), pp. 108ff.

structure, there is no possible mediation or compromise. Either one begins from being and understands reason as initially receptive, as the place in which the subject enters into an intimate connection with being, or one begins with systematic doubt and with internal states of consciousness, and never gets back to being; one can at best arrive at an internal state of subjective certainty.[21]

If one sets the problem this way, then Wojtyła's philosophy is certainly completely realist. This is the core of his Thomism. But Wojtyła is concerned with another problem: How can one think about consciousness and freedom, which are the two great discoveries of modern philosophy, without renouncing a philosophy of being but, rather, through the extension and development of its latent virtualities? Not only do we know but we also appropriate from the inside what we have known, and only through this reliving from the inside are we able to know in a fully and adequately human way. While in metaphysical knowing reason is rightly passive and acknowledges a state of affairs independent of itself, in the reliving of consciousness the subject is active and builds his interior world. It is not sufficient, for instance, to know in an abstract way that there is a God and that we ought to do the good and to avoid the evil. This knowledge becomes efficacious for life when a subject builds his interior world according to it and develops an attitude which corresponds to it.[22] He *ought to* do it by respecting the knowledge acquired through the cognitive faculty, and yet he can also elude or betray it. The interior world of the subject, on the other hand, because of the dynamic structure of the person which is oriented to acting together with others, is objectified in actions, traditions, social structures, and cultures.[23]

We live in a world which is both created by God and made by people, who embody in their social constructions, in a more or less adequate way, the initial gift of being. The different philosophies of consciousness have the decisive merit of making us aware of this peculiar characteristic of the human world, yet some forms of realism have excluded it in order to focus on the objective metaphysical consistency of being and its primacy. They were wrong to do so.

21. Cf. E. Gilson, *Réalisme thomiste et critique de la connaissance* (Paris: Vrin, 1947).

22. Cf. Wojtyła, *Sources of Renewal*, pt. 3.

23. Cf. Wojtyła, "Il problema del costituirsi della cultura attraverso la 'praxis,'" in *Rivista di folosofia neoscolastica* 69, pp. 513-24.

Authentic realism cannot limit itself to the defense of objectivity. The subject, his emotional dynamisms, the results of his actions, are as real in the world as purely objective eternal truths. Moreover, the destiny of values is to be embodied and lived in human life. Making the distinction between a faculty of objective knowing and a faculty of subjective interiorization allows for a grafting of the discovery of subjectivity into the trunk of philosophy of being. This might almost be called (though our author does not deal directly with this issue) an Augustinian interpretation of the Cartesian cogito. In this perspective the problem is not how to pass from the consciousness of the Ego to the being of the world, but rather the way in which one can obtain the state of subjective certainty about what is objectively given.

I would like to make a comparison between the end of philosophy of modernity in Horkheimer's and Adorno's *Dialectic of Enlightenment*[24] and Wojtyła' *The Acting Person*. In the *Dialectic of Enlightenment* the philosophy of consciousness and of freedom reaches the awareness that, in separating itself from objective being, it ends by destroying itself, because freedom itself — consciousness and human dignity and rights — must be radically relativized and lose the status of values and objective truths. In *The Acting Person* the legacy of the philosophy of consciousness is welcomed and receives objective consistency because it is organically rejoined with the philosophy of being. This occurs through an extension of the "philosophia perennis" which corresponds in an exemplary way to the motto "vetera novis augere." It is my opinion that in this way the fundamental weakness of Catholic thought in this century, which consists in its poverty at the level of historical interpretation and of the methodology of social sciences, is overcome. By acknowledging the ontic autonomy of the process of formation of the historical world, *The Acting Person* opens the way to a realist interpretation of them. Man truly makes his own world (and the acknowledgment of this fact is a fundamental condition for understanding what man is), but he makes it on the basis of a primary gift of being by God and in continuous dialogue with divine Providence. This is a rigorous reelaboration of the conciliar doctrine of the "autonomy of earthly realities," yet this theme was already present, in the Italian tradition, in Giambattista Vico. Vico does not belong to Wojtyła's direct philosophical horizon, but this makes their agreements even more impor-

---

24. T. Adorno and M. Horkheimer, *The Dialectic of Enlightenment*, trans. John Cummings (London: Verso, 1979).

tant.[25] In conclusion: consciousness and freedom have the task of making the interiorization of truth and self-giving in love possible.

If they systematically evade this task (that is to say, if they absolutize themselves and reject the link between themselves and truth and love) they annihilate themselves. The plan of organically grafting the philosophy of consciousness into the foundation of the philosophy of being is not without consequences for the philosophy of being itself. Some of these consequences make a difference in metaphysics. If we thematize the personal being carefully, as *The Acting Person* does, it becomes almost necessary to acknowledge an important difference of value even at the ontological level between the being of the person and all other forms of being. Being speaks and reveals its mystery in the person more than in any nonpersonal being. Wojtyła did not develop this idea organically, which appears to be a necessary consequence of his thought. Seifert's work *Being and Person*, which originates from deep reflection on the thought of our author, shows that this way is open and can lead to extremely engaging results.[26]

Other consequences of the approach of *The Acting Person* pertain more to social and political philosophy. They are already directly verifiable in the text of this work, as well as in several later articles by Wojtyła, and their echoes can perhaps be discerned in several Papal pronouncements.

The notion of the "common good" is traditionally a hinge of classical social thought, and we find this notion in *The Acting Person*, in the chapter entitled "Integration." Every action performed in common with others implies that the objective good of each one of the participants in relation to the action has to be taken into consideration. Only in this way is it possible to insure that no one is instrumentalized through the action. This concern for the objective common good, however, does not say much about different political regimes. An "enlightened absolutism" can sometimes accomplish the objective common good better than a democracy; moreover, if energetically guided and directed, authoritarian regimes are often more efficient than democratic ones, at least in the short run. These accurate observations explain why Catholic political thought has been often suspicious of democracy. But if, following *The Acting Person*, we introduce the dimension of subjectivity

25. A history of Vico's studies in Poland would be interesting and has, as far as I know, never been done. Several elements suggest that, if there is no direct influence, there is at least a parallelism in the development of Italian philosophy and the development of Polish literary culture.

26. Cf. Josef Seifert, *Essere e Persona* (Milan: Vita e Pensiero, 1989).

and of consciousness, the field of our concern is greatly extended. In order for an action performed together with others to be just, it is not sufficient for it to protect and to accomplish the objective good of all the participants. Beyond this, it is necessary that the participants take part in it in a fully human way, engaging their intelligence and will in it. A social action without participation cannot be just even if, hypothetically, it would realize the objective good of a particular social group. Of course, such a social group would, through this action, attain certain more or less important objective advantages, but it would not be constituted and grow as a human community. If one looks at the teaching of John Paul II about the political order, one sees that it is characterized by the defense of freedom and human rights. Of course, the Church remains indifferent in relation to the specific political forms which each national community adopts. But it cannot regard a political regime without participation or without democracy as just, inasmuch as democracy is understood to imply respect for human rights and popular participation.[27] This is a significant innovation and extension of the sociopolitical doctrine of Catholicism. For the first time, not only the content of the action of government is relevant (the fact that it realizes the common good of society) but so too is the way in which this is accomplished. The common good of a *human* community cannot be accomplished with a method which disregards freedom and the responsibility of the person. The condemnation of totalitarianism follows from these premises, as does the critique of any species of authoritarianism (although the positive role of authority itself is upheld). The Catholic acceptance of democracy becomes more convinced and open-armed, and this also, of course, implies the more precise delimitation of the positive sense of democracy, which is chosen over against the negative and relativistic meaning of democracy. To be sure, the right of being guided politically, in a participatory way, does not originate at all from an uncertainty about the truth and, therefore, from a leveling of all opinions as if they shared equal value. It originates, rather, from a specific dignity of the human person, who, to perceive the common action as his own and to grow through it, needs to be guided in a reasonable way by an authority which gives reasons for its actions and which solicits the assent of those subordinated to itself.

Another consequence of the approach proposed by *The Acting Person* can be drawn in the very delicate and particularly heated field of moral philosophy and theology.

27. Cf. John Paul II, *Centesimus Annus*, ch. 5.

In recent years a "new moral theology" has been embraced, which energetically underlines the decisive role of conscience in the moral field, and consequently comes into conflict with a certain objectivism in traditional moral theology.

The new moral theology argues that, in order for a norm to be valid, it must be proposed by conscience. A norm which is not posed by conscience cannot bind a conscience. From this principle it is easy to derive an absolute moral relativism: I am the only authority on what is good or evil for myself, and no one is entitled to judge the decision of my conscience. This emphasis on the rights of the conscience is generally linked with an equal emphasis on the social and historical conditioning of the action. An action always takes place in a materially and culturally determinate context. It is within this context that what the subject considers as good and evil is constituted. The judgment of conscience, therefore, becomes the last court of appeal not only because of the objective dignity of conscience, but also because no one can judge situations except the one who is immersed in them and is affected by their conditioning. The necessary result is that there cannot be a norm which binds in an absolute and unconditional way. Ethics does not have the task of indicating what is good and what is evil, but only that of attempting a general interpretation of the situation in which the action takes place, by individuating general norms. But such norms are always variable, and they can never claim absolute value (permitting no exceptions) in every concrete situation.

The supporters of the "old moral theology" accuse the "new moral theology" of relativism and sociologism, while proponents of the "new moral theology" accuse its predecessor of abstractness, legalism, and pharisaism.

What does *The Acting Person* tell us about how to deal with this conflict?

It seems to me that the fundamental distinction between knowledge and conscience (consciousness) allows for an understanding and an authentication of the truth of both the old and new moral theology.

The old moral theology is right in stating that reason (and therefore moral conscience, which is *based on the norm* of reason) can transcend the given historical situation, know the truth, and orient its own behavior to it. This capacity of cognitive transcendence characterizes the human faculty of "knowing," and excludes sociologistic and historicist relativism.

But the new moral theology is also right in claiming that the passage from the knowledge of the abstract norm to action is neither easy nor mechanical. *Knowing* the norm is not sufficient; *acknowledging* the norm is necessary. In other words, it is necessary that the norm not only be known as true in abstract and general terms: it must be known as true for me in the concrete and particular. The energy of the person is available to actualize the norm inasmuch as the norm is defined in the conscience and is subjectified. The sovereignty of conscience consists precisely in this: conscience transforms norms into a norm of my action, imposes the norm in the sphere of action proper to the person, and formulates the pertinent norm. Of course, this activity is creative of norms, but of subjective norms on the basis of an objective norm which it derives from the cognitive faculty.[28]

Continuing these reflections provoked by the reading of *The Acting Person,* we are rapidly compelled to move to an authentic phenomenology of the moral norm which is the essential precondition of discerning the numerous and complex problems which come with the pole of normativity in ethics. Wojtyła himself worked intensely on this issue between 1972 and 1974. In those years he was planning to write, together with his friend and close collaborator T. Styczen, an ethical sequel to *The Acting Person,* largely devoted to the treatment of the problem of normativity in ethics. Unfortunately, the project was never finished. However, during the time I have been writing this introduction, I have received through the courtesy of my friend A. Szostek the notes for the first draft of that book, written by Wojtyła in preparation for the discussion with Styczen, as part of the activities of the Chair of Ethics of the Catholic University of Lublin. These notes were later published by Szostek under the title *Clwirek w polu odpowwiedzielnosci,* on the occasion of the International Congress of Central European Theologians, which took place in Lublin, 11-15 August 1991.[29]

4. The Acting Person *and the Pontificate of John Paul II*

We have said that this book can offer important help for the understanding of the pontificate of John Paul II, granted, however, that the book must first be interpreted in the general context of the Magisterium of the Church. We have also mentioned some of the themes of the Pope's great encyclicals which can be identified in the pages of his main philosophical work. Finally, we have shown how *The Acting Person* is, in a primary way, a reflection on the Second Vatican Council and on the reconciliation of the Church with the idea of

28. Cf. Rocco Buttiglione, *La crisi della morale* (Rome: Dino, 1991).
29. For a critical confrontation with "the new moral theology" from this point of view see A. Szostek, *Natura, Rozum, Wolność* (Lublin: Redakcja Wydawnictw KUL, 1989).

freedom. Such a reconciliation is founded on the essential dignity of every human person. It does not by any means imply a yielding of Catholicism to relativism. John Paul II could repeat the words of his predecessor, Pius IX, who refused to accept the errors of modern times. But the rejection of the errors of modern times does not mean that we should not correct the one-sidedness of the exposition of sound doctrine, which furnished the occasion for the rise of these errors. A new and deeper examination of the essence of human freedom is necessary, which will show, on the one hand, that human freedom is inviolable and, on the other hand, that this freedom, from its intrinsic nature, ought to submit itself to truth. This issue is of central importance in order to understand both Karol Wojtyła's pontificate and Vatican II and the contemporary crisis of the Church. A human act which will not acknowledge truth and which will not welcome truth in love, is a failed act. It is not, properly speaking, a free act. Being free is not doing whatever one thinks and pleases, but mastering and possessing oneself in a way which makes it possible to perceive the attractiveness of truth, and giving oneself to correspond to it.[30] A relativistic notion of human freedom, such as the notion in several fields of moral philosophy and theology, does not perceive an essential factual given: freedom determines itself only by facing the truth, in the presence of truth. Augustine had already seen clearly this role of the light of truth (veritatis lumen or veritatis splendor) for human freedom. The light of truth is not extrinsic to the act of freedom but intrinsically constitutive of it, to the point that an act is not authentically free without it. This is precisely what distinguishes human freedom from either an arbitrary subjectivism or the spontaneity of animal instincts. Precisely in virtue of its obedience to truth, human freedom presupposes the mastery of merely instinctual reactions. A man who is not master of himself is the slave of his own passions.

On the other hand, the great freedom which is expressed in the gift of oneself in love is not possible if the minor freedom is denied, that is to say, the freedom of saying no, of rejecting such an act. A gift presupposes that the subject can give his life and that this life is not taken against his will. Respect for subjective freedom is therefore an unrenounceable condition if one's destiny, or end, is to be realized.[31]

30. Cf T. Styczen, "Responsibilità dell'uomo nei confronti di sè e dell'altro," in *Karol Wojtyła. Filosofo, Teologo, Poeta* (Vatican City: Libreria, Editrice Vaticana, 1984), pp. 107-28.
31. J. Crosby, "Persona est sui juris: Reflections on the Foundations of Karol Wojtyła's Philosophy of the Person," ibid., pp. 25-38.

Today there are "traditionalists" who do not see this truth and carry on insisting on the objective rights of freedom and of God's rights, as if they could be achieved along a path which would not go through the freedom of the individual person. Many "progressivists," on the other hand, carry on insisting on freedom and human rights as if freedom could be achieved in a way other than through self-giving in love and the acknowledgment of truth.

The Acting Person guides us into the synthesis of these two points of view. Freedom and truth are dynamically tied together; they require one another. An abstract truth which does not become the form of life of the person through a free act of his will (or is imposed from outside) does not save anyone. Nor could an abstract freedom which withdraws and isolates itself, refusing to grow into love, and which opposes itself to truth, achieve its end: it becomes the slave of the passions and of circumstances, that is to say, of those who have the power and the means to condition and manipulate it.

In the face of human freedom God chose only two means in order to communicate His love. Wojtyła speaks of these in his poem "Stanislaw," the symbolic meaning of which could be taken as a program not only of the pontificate but also the priesthood of Karol Wojtyła.[32]

The first means is the word. Against a society that does not want that truth to be spoken, which does not want to be bothered in its conscience by the message of truth, preferring to live in illusions, the task of the priest is to announce truth. Such a witness cannot be silenced by the slanderous pretense that it violates the freedom of the person to whom the announcement is directed: it uses the word, not force, to call forth the following of its sign. Yet even words can sometimes be unbearable, especially if they revive dimensions of conscience which had been thought permanently buried. When Socrates' voice of warning resounded in the Agora people could not help but listen but did not want to hear.[33] Likewise, after many centuries, the voice of Stanislaw of Szczepanow. Such a voice must be silenced. The most efficacious way to convince someone to be silent is to threaten him with death. Before such a threat every voice is struck dumb. Does a truth exist for which it is worth giving one's life? Or, to put the question in the terms of "Stanislaw," do we need the second means — the means of blood? Truth, after all, does not seem to need our witness; it remains true whether we affirm or deny it, while we have only one life.

32. Wojtyła, "Stanislaw," in *Collected Poems*, pp. 177-82.
33. C. K. Norwid, "Cos ty Atenom zrobił, Socratesie."

God is not the one who needs the witness of the martyr. It is the martyr himself who needs this witness, so he may not betray what he has encountered and which has transformed his identity and his existence.[34] Even more, it is the murderer who needs this witness, so that his conscience may be disturbed by those very words which he needs to silence. The silence of the martyr would serve to convince the murderer that there is no truth beyond money, lust, and power, and that the internal voice awakened in him by the martyr is only an illusion or a fraud.

The martyr loves the world which wants to murder him, and his witness comes from this love. But what is this love for? Is it not unadulterated folly to give one's own life for murderers? But Stanislaw, the martyr, is not the first to have loved those people who wanted to murder him. God is their first lover, and He has given His Son. Now the same God gives Stanislaw.

Earlier on, we said that God does not need Stanislaw's witness, but now we need to correct ourselves: God needs Stanislaw's witness to convert Stanislaw's murderers, whom God loves, and Stanislaw, through God's love, loves with the same love. For this reason, when the word fails, when it is not listened to, the martyr faces the last and decisive wager: "If the word did not convert you, the blood will.[35] By persevering in his witness until bloodshed the martyr shows that he belongs to a strength capable of challenging the nothingness of death, and confirms the truth of his message with an extreme witness for the conversion of the sinner.

In the poem "Stanislaw" quite an unusual conception of divine omnipotence comes to light. God's omnipotence does not reside in the fact that he has the power to send those who contradict and disobey him to hell. Such an omnipotence is a trivial omnipotence for the Christian God. The Christian God does not want to be obeyed out of fear. He wants to be loved. For this reason he does not want to be forced upon the subjects by a state power which is capable of eliminating the resistance of its opponents. In order to be loved God is forced to take human freedom seriously, and must abdicate coercion. The Omnipotent must become a beggar, and, in a sense, give up omnipotence in order to respect freedom. And yet does God really give up his omnipotence? To be sure, He abandons the omnipotence of force, but not the omnipotence of truth and love. The cross, the witness of truth up to death, is the manifestation of another omnipotence. A man

34. T. Styczen's *Wolność w prawdzie* (Rome: Fundacja Jana Pawła II/ Polski Institut Kultury Chrzescianskiej, 1988).
35. "Stanislaw," p. 181.

perceived the greatness of God's love and offered his whole self to correspond to this love. He has accomplished fully the human act, the act of acknowledging truth in love. This man is at the same time the Son of God. The Cross is the manifestation of this omnipotence of love which entices men's freedom by giving a sign of this love.[36] This sign is repeated in the lives of saints and martyrs. Its eloquence is infinite, but human freedom is infinite too. This is the dialogue of salvation which is spoken in history until the end of time. On one hand, there is theological error in stating that God's welcoming of human freedom implies his welcoming with equanimity and indifference any content which man chooses to give to his freedom. On the other hand, there is theological error in claiming that God wants to impose His Law through coercive means. God wants the law to be received by freedom through love. This is the bewildering challenge to which divine omnipotence exposes itself. The true content of the Council is the understanding of this challenge, which is inseparable from the acknowledgment of the value of human freedom. This is also the aim of *The Acting Person*, whose philosophical content is illuminated by the poetic reflection "Stanislaw."

It is not without profound symbolic meaning that Wojtyła, author of the poem "Stanislaw," has been the first Pope after many centuries to corroborate his witness to the faith with blood. The attempt against the life of the Pope in Vatican Square in 1981, though it has not been yet fully clarified in its roots, definitely originated from hatred for the Christian faith. Once martyrdom was almost the common destiny, the norm rather than the exception, for St. Peter's successors. This tradition has been rejuvenated. A Church which gives up imposition insists with even more conviction — up to bloodshed — on the right to propose her announcement at the center of the life of the city, in the public square, in the agora. This, not the capitulation to relativism, is the meaning of the acknowledgment of freedom of conscience in religious matters. This profound persuasion allowed John Paul II to assume the spiritual guidance, in a sense, of the resistance to Communist totalitarianism. In spite of the contemporary penetration of many relativist currents of thought in Central and Eastern Europe, we must remember that the struggle against Communism has not been engaged under the banner of relativism, but in the name of firm convictions about the dignity and value of the human person. Under the banner of relativism one does not fight, but compromises.

36. Wojtyła, "Rozwazania o oicostwie," in *Znak* 16, pp. 610-13.

Vaclav Havel has brilliantly shown that Communism, in its last phases, defended itself not as doctrine of truth, but as a *de facto* situation guarded by force, which, in any case, was not worth challenging since, if there is no truth, there is also no reason why one would want to risk his life for it.[37] The rebellion against Communism has been a witness to a truth about man and about freedom. It has been a witness which, by its very nature, was a plea to conscience, also to the conscience of the oppressor, and in virtue of this was able to overcome a situation completely blocked from the point of view of *Realpolitik*. The role of the Catholic Church in this process has been decisive. Yet the Church would not have been able to play this role without the Second Vatican Council and its decisive clarification of the theme of freedom. It is the "conciliar" Church that commits herself to fight for human rights rather than protecting her own rights through retreating into compromise with the status quo of the regime. It is the "conciliar" Church that sees in the affirmation of the dignity of a single human being and of his freedom one of the essential contents of Christian revelation. This is also the attitude which allows for an overcoming of the old separation from a secular independent culture and the beginning of a dialogue which leads to moral unity of the nation, molded in common opposition to totalitarianism, which leads to the collapse of the Communist tyrannies.[38]

It would, of course, be excessive to consider these epochal events among the effects of *The Acting Person*. Yet these are results of the shift made by the Council and which *The Acting Person* attempts to thematize. We might say that these are the effects of the Council reinterpreted and relived in the history of Poland and of other countries struggling with the totalitarian oppression of Communism. This is exactly the experience, both theoretical and existential, which one can see through a careful reading of our book.

This might, of course, be thought reason enough hastily to dismiss it, since, for all of its historical importance, it belongs to the past, a past which now is overtaken by more contemporary issues. On this view, *The Acting Person* would be a monument of the cultural struggle against Communism and of the way in which the Council has been interpreted in this struggle, but it would be without contemporary relevance after the defeat of Communism and the establishment of a new cultural milieu. No doubt it would

---

37. Cf. V. Havel, *The Power of the Powerless: Citizens against the State in Central-Eastern Europe* (London: Hutchinson, 1985).

38. George Weigel makes some interesting remarks on this subject in *The Final Revolution* (New York: Oxford University Press, 1992), pp. 70ff.

remain a moving document of a backward culture, one which would of necessity be bypassed in the realignment of Poland and the other ex-Communist countries with the broader culture of the continent, which is permeated by relativism.

We face here another fundamental problem for Europe's culture and history. We could express it in this way: Where was Europe in the years of Communism? According to one hypothesis the history of European culture continued unabated in the Western countries, while for those under the Communist regimes time was simply lost. Today those coming out from under oppressive tyrannies must hurry to catch up with their more advanced and luckier neighbors, not bearing, through the experience which they have undergone, any contribution of an essential value for the self-consciousness of Europe. But let us consider an alternative hypothesis, that what happened in Eastern Europe conveys a decisive meaning for the self-consciousness of the whole of Europe, which it must reflect upon in order to find itself.

At the time of the collapse of Communism the market economies of the Western extremity of Europe seemed to enjoy an enviable state of health, at least if seen from Warsaw or Cracow. However, the view is different from Bonn, or Paris, or Rome. Western democracy is evidently undergoing a crisis. Corruption is a more powerful enemy than Communism, and it threatens to destroy democracy. A democracy which is ruled by relativistic ethical conceptions no longer has a definite criterion by which to distinguish good from evil, right from wrong. Consequently the dominant elite does not share a community of values with the people, though it is in the name and in virtue of this community that they can make laws. Every organized social group raises its voice to enforce the recognition of its own interests, and even to obtain special privileges. A weak and nonauthoritative political class always ends up by yielding to pressure, at least to the pressure of the strongest. This, instead of appeasing discontent (since everyone is convinced of being at a relative disadvantage in comparison with luckier ones who obtained more), drives the state budget to financial disaster, since it cannot satisfy every social claim. For a little while the problem is resolved through state debts. Giving something to everyone by taking nothing from anyone is possible only by shifting the cost, in the form of debts, on to the next generations. But sooner or later the time comes when debts have to be repaid, and then the crisis of the state and of politics comes about. This is not the crisis of capitalism which Marx foresaw. It is rather the crisis of democracy, which comes about under two different aegises: on the one

hand, there is what has been called the "revolution of increasing expectations," according to which every social group expects more and more advantages from the state budget without paying for them; on the other hand,
there is "the fiscal crisis of the state," which is increasingly insolvent. Putting
off payment by stretching public debt and shifting the cost to the next
generation is no solution. Again: sooner or later one must repay his debt,
and this brings about the crisis of the state.

The first root of this crisis is the lack of a precise reference to a system
of values which allow one to discriminate legitimate from illegitimate
claims, and therefore reasonable motivation to say yes and no to them.[39]
In addition, the crisis of modern democracies has other and less noble
causes. It is not only the case that the political class lacks the precise criteria
to discriminate among the claims of organized social groups. The political
class has an unavoidable inclination to redistribute economic and social
power to itself. The uncertainty about the system of values and the inclination of the elite to promote their own particular interests go side by side.
On these issues a relativist view of democracy shows all of its limitations.
It must swing between two extremes: a politics of redistribution of wealth
with no criterion, on one hand, and, on the other, an extreme individualism
which opposes any redistribution and attempts to drain not only the welfare
state but also the sphere of politics of any content.

In facing these problems, one is also able to see the importance of *The
Acting Person* for Western societies. They need to be reminded of the constitutive nexus which exists between freedom and truth, especially freedom
and truth about the human person. This is a core problem of Western
democracies, which increasingly show the lack of a criterion of judgment.

Another theme of *The Acting Person*, which is central in this context,
is contained in the last chapter of this work. It is the theme of participation
and acting together with others. When the encyclical *Centesimus Annus*
came out, an eminent American economist whom I met at a meeting of
Kaltenbrunner Gesellschaft told me that it seemed that the Pope had read
and deeply reflected on the writings of L. Von Mises[40] or I. Kirzner,[41] who
are among the most significant writers on modern economic science. While
at that moment this seemed to me a bizarre hypothesis, and even today I

39. John Paul II, *Centesimus Annus.*
40. L. Von Mises, *Human Action* (Chicago: Regnery, 1966).
41. I. M. Kirzner, *Competition and Entrepreneurship* (Chicago: University of Chicago Press, 1973).

retain the conviction that these authors, like economic studies in general, are rather foreign to the culture of this Pope, more attentive reflection convinced me that there is, in fact, a certain relevant parallel. The methodological individualism of the most advanced currents of contemporary economic thought reduces any economic phenomenon to the agent who is engaged in it, that is to say, to the man who chooses and decides through his own action the reality around him. Against the uncritical hypostatization of social action into independent forces and mechanisms, a methodological individualism systematically takes us back to man and human intentionality as the fundamental means through which to understand social realities. Undoubtedly this constitutes a similarity to Wojtyła's approach in *The Acting Person*. In this line, therefore, a comparative reading of L. von Mises' *Human Action* with *The Acting Person* would be very engaging. But there is a tremendously important difference. For Wojtyła, the human person is at the same time individual subject and human community. Community, as a dimension of the subject's action, and thus as a reality which emerges from the action, and not as a totalist superimposition upon the human action, is the fundamental theme of the last chapter of *The Acting Person*. Acting together with others is a fundamental dimension of acting. Its comprehension allows us to assimilate the methodological lesson of Austrian individualism without, at the same time, renouncing the comprehension of the role and the value of the political sphere, and also of the rights and duties of the state in regard to political intervention in the economy. In the process of writing new constitutions and of the transition from collectivist economies to a market economy, the path which *The Acting Person* indicates is worthy of attention. This is the line which acknowledges the rights of the market but also the existence of spheres of action which go beyond the market and which are based on the specific nature of "acting together with others." Another dimension in which Wojtyła corrects the individualistic approach is the ethical dimension of the person; ethics arises from the encounter with the value of the person, a value which cannot but be acknowledged. Human action always has to take into account the truth about the good. Such truth about the good is not a prison which limits the action, but a guide to it. The good that is at stake is the value of the person. Just as the acting together with others founds the autonomy of the political sphere, so the reference to the objective value of the human person founds the autonomy of the ethical discourse and therefore frames the economical acting as a decisive but not exhaustive part of the whole. This is needed not only in the countries which are reconstructing their economies in the aftermath of communism but also in the Western democracies which search for a balance between market logic and state intervention. Moreover, *The Acting Person* indicates an alternative to the notion of social actions which condemns man to alienation in a society in which functioning requires the expulsion of any trace of subjectivity and therefore also of the meaning of life.[42]

The first part of the pontificate of Karol Wojtyła has been devoted, though not by his own choice but by an inscrutable providential design, to the pacific overcoming of the Yalta world order and of Communist systems. Perhaps the fundamental concern of the second part of his pontificate will be the reform of the capitalist system and struggle against Western alienation. It is not an easy task; indeed, it is an almost impossible one. Many will raise their voices with righteous indignation: "One cannot change the course of history." But is this not precisely what they would have said if one had told them in 1945, or in 1956, or again in 1978 about the end of Communism?

42. Wojtyła, "Participation or Alienation," in *Analecta Husserliana*, vol. 6, pp. 61-73.

Index

Abramowski, 71
Ache, 71
Adamczyk, Stanislaw, 38
Adjukiewicz, 235
Adorno, Theodore, 10-11, 52, 367
Anselm, Saint, 78
Aquinas, Saint Thomas, 5, 46, 48, 64,
    66, 72-82, 84, 89, 91, 96, 106, 110,
    129, 133, 163-64, 171, 183, 186, 207,
    274, 275, 282, 300, 359, 361
Aristotle, 64, 66, 80, 119, 274, 359, 361
Augustine, Saint, 4, 59, 75, 78, 97, 218,
    219
Averroës, 50

Barth, Karl, 198
Baruzi, 45-46
Baziak, Msgr., 39
Becker, Oskar, 55
Bednarski, Feliks, 38
Benedicta of the Cross, 54
Bloch, Ernst, 50
Blondel, Jacques-François, 125
Blonski, Jan, 349
Bochenski, Prof., 30
Boethius, Ancius Manlius Severinus, 80,
    88
Bonhoeffer, Dietrich, 14

Boni, Paolo, 322-23
Bortnowska, Halina, 200
Brentano, Franz, 119, 273
Bruno, Giordano, 50

Cardijn, Msgr., 230
Ciappi, Mario, 34
Cirotzki-Christ, Christof, 341-42
Conrad-Martius, Hedwig, 55
Crosby, John, 339-40
Cross, Derek, 312

Debowska, Kristina, 23
de Finance, Joseph, 324-25
de Furstenberg, Massimiliano, 34
Del Noce, Augusto, 185n.7, 312, 318
de Lubac, Henri, 198
Descartes, René, 87, 120
Dostoievski, Fyodor, 240
Dougherty, Jude P., 324
Dybciak, Krzystof, 232, 240
Dybowski, M., 71

Eliot, T. S., 242, 243, 245
Engels, Friedrich, 295
Esposito, Costantino, 328

Feuerbach, Ludwig Andreas, 89, 296

INDEX

Fink, Eugen, 119
Freud, Sigmund, 139, 160, 165

Galarowicz, Jan, 334
Galkowski, Jerzy W., 323-24
Gandhi, Mohandas, 115
Garrigou-Lagrange, Reginald, 34, 35, 44, 45, 47, 355
Genghini, Nevio, 346
Gilson, Etienne, 34, 75, 355, 365-66
Gombrowicz, Witold, 235, 240
Gramsci, Antonio, 295
Gregory XVI, 20
Gronbacher, Gregory M. A., 322
Grygiel, Stanislaw, 1, 41, 277, 289, 346-47, 349

Hartmann, Nikolai, 55
Harvanek, Robert F., 336
Havel, Vaclav, 376
Hegel, G. W. F., 4, 5, 50, 86, 87, 89, 235, 284, 295
Heidegger, Martin, 55
Herbert, Zbigniew, 237-38
Hildebrand, Joseph, 356
Hitler, Adolf, 22
Horkheimer, Max, 312, 367
Hume, David, 359-60
Husserl, Edmund, 54-55, 150n.38, 270-72, 355

Ingarden, Roman, 36, 37, 44, 54, 55, 232, 272, 281, 355, 356
Iwaszkiewicz, 237

Janski, Bogdan, 20
Jaworski, Marian, 41, 286
Jefferson, Thomas, 315-16, 317
Jobert, Philippe, 324
John of the Cross, Saint, 34, 45-53, 67

Kajsiewicz, Hieronim, 20
Kakorowska, Emilia, 18
Kalinowski, Georges, 325-27
Kalinowski, Jerzy, 36, 38
Kamiński, Stanisław, 38

Kant, Immanuel, 55, 62-72, 92-93, 110, 118, 136, 235, 273, 274-75, 284, 314, 360
Kepinski, A., 253
Kirzner, I., 378
Klosaka, Kazimierz, 31
Köchler, Hans, 331
Kolakowski, 33, 232
Kolbe, Maximilian M., Saint, 9, 11-14, 15, 364
Korsch, 295
Kotarbinski, 232
Kotlarczyk, Mieczyslaw, 21-22, 243
Krapiec, Mieszysław A., 38, 40, 355
Krasinski, Zygmunt, 18, 24, 232, 234
Krolikiewicz, Halina, 23
Kurdziałek, Marian, 38
Kwiatowski, Tadeusz, 23
Kydrynsky, Julius, 23

Labourdette, 45, 46
Lawler, Ronald D., 337-38
Leibniz, Gottfried Wilhelm, 139, 147, 235
Lenin, Vladimir, 293
Leo XIII, 81
Lesmian, Boleslaw, 237
Lobkowicz, Nicholas, 321
Lubicz-Milosz, 26
Lukacs, György, 235, 295
Léfebvre, Marcel, 315

Marczewski, Andrzej Maria, 350
Marion, Jean-Luc, 330-31
Maritain, Jacques, 8n.9, 34, 36-37, 309
Marx, Karl, 5, 50, 85, 86, 89, 120, 121, 149, 235, 270, 279, 292, 293, 295, 296, 298, 302
Masiello, Ralph J., 327-28
Maurras, Charles, 49
Mazarski, Jan, 28
Mazzini, Giuseppe, 7
McCool, Gerald A., 348-49
Michalowska, Danuta, 23
Michotte, 71
Mickiewicz, Adam, 18, 20, 232, 234

Mielczarska, W., 71
Milosz, Czeslaw, 235-36
Modras, Ronald, 328-29
Montini, Giambattista, 309

Nietzsche, Friedrich Wilhelm, 22
Norwid, Cyprian, 18, 25-26, 232, 243, 303
Nota, John, 335-36, 337

Palacios, Juan-Miguel, 340
Palamas, Gregory, Saint, 255
Pappin, Joseph, 337
Pascal, Blaise, 61, 74, 112, 186, 282, 284
Patocka, Jan, 281
Paul VI, 309
Philippe, Pierre-Paul, 34
Piasecki, Boleslaw, 32
Pico della Mirandola, Giovanni, 319
Pollini, Pierluigi, 321-22
Poltawski, Andrzej, 340-41
Pilsudski, Józef Klemens, 30, 294
Pius IX, 20, 372
Piwowarczyk, Jan, 31, 32
Plato, 239, 361
Plekhanov, Georgy Valentinovich, 293
Potter, Vincent G., 328

Quiles, Ismael, 344-45

Reagan, Ronald, 316, 317
Reimers, Adrian J., 325
Reutt, J., 71
Ricci, Francesco, 310
Rizzi, Bruno, 173
Rousseau, Jean-Jacques, 314

Sapieha, Adam, 29-30
Sapieha, Adam Stephan, 16, 28, 29-31, 36
Sapieha, Leone, 29
Sartre, Jean-Paul, 33, 171, 186, 269, 278, 283-85, 288, 290, 291, 292, 319
Scheler, Max, 36, 48, 54-63, 68-70, 71, 72, 77, 78-79, 81, 82, 84, 91, 92, 93, 99, 103, 108, 110, 117, 118, 133, 136,
142, 143, 145, 146, 154, 163, 171, 183, 272, 274-75, 276, 282, 286, 314, 355, 358, 359, 361
Schmitz, Kenneth, 308
Schopenhauer, Arthur, 139, 279
Schmitz, Kenneth L., 343-44
Schulz, 361
Scola, Angelo, 348
Seifert, Josef, 87n.3, 331-33, 356, 368
Semenenko, Piotr, 20
Serretti, Massimo, 333-34
Siebel, Wingand, 329-30
Simeon the New Theologian, 255
Slawinska, Irena, 31
Słowacki, Juliusz, 18, 20, 232, 234
Spader, Peter H., 335
Spencer, Herbert, 10
Spinoza, Baruch, 5, 87
Stalin, Joseph, 294
Stanislas, Saint, 9
Stein, Edith, 54, 275
Stomma, Stanislaw, 32
Strauss, Leo, 311
Styczen, Tadeusz, 38, 41, 338-39, 371
Swiezawski, Stefan, 31, 36, 38
Szostek, A., 342-43, 371

Teilhard de Chardin, Pierre, 215
Teresa of Avila, Saint, 45
Testori, Giovanni, 350
Tischner, Jozef, 17, 41, 301, 345-46, 350
Towianski, Andrej, 25
Turowicz, Jerzy, 31
Tymieniecka, Anna-Teresa, 37, 41, 118
Tyranowski, Jan, 23, 28-29, 45

Vico, Giambattista, 367
von Balthasar, Hans Urs, 198
von Hofmannsthal, 22
Von Mises, L., 378-79

Wais, Kazimierz, 31
Weber, Max, 151, 173
Wicher, 36
Wierzynski, Kazimierz, 240

INDEX

Williams, George Huntston, 24, 126, 312, 320
Witkacy, 232
Wittgenstein, Ludwig Josef Johan, 84-85, 235
Wójtowicz, Andrzej, 343
Woznicki, Andrew N., 327, 334-35, 342, 344, 347-48

Wyspianski, Stanislaw, 18
Wyszynski, Stefan, 15, 16

Zdziechowski, Marian, 239
Zegadlowicz, Emil, 18
Zgorzelski, Czeslaw, 31
Zwiazawski, 355